Heidegger and the Thinking of Place

Heidegger and the Thinking of Place

Explorations in the Topology of Being

Jeff Malpas

The MIT Press
Cambridge, Massachusetts
London, England

For information about special quantity discounts, please email special_sales@ mitpress.mit.edu

This book was set in Stone Sans and Stone Serif by Toppan Best-set Premedia Limited. Printed and bound in the United States of America.

Library of Congress Cataloging-in-Publication Data

Malpas, Jeff.

Heidegger and the thinking of place : explorations in the topology of being / Jeff Malpas.
    p. cm.
Includes bibliographical references (p.   ) and index.
ISBN 978-0-262-01684-1 (hardcover : alk. paper)
1. Heidegger, Martin, 1889–1976. 2. Place (Philosophy). I. Title.
B3279.H49M2719   2012
193—dc23
                                                        2011021053

10 9 8 7 6 5 4 3 2 1

We shall not cease from exploration / And the end of all our exploring / Will be to arrive where we started / And know the place for the first time.
—T. S. Eliot, *Four Quartets* ("Little Gidding")

Contents

Epilogue: Beginning in Wonder   251

Acknowledgments

I would like to thank Philip Laughlin and the team at the MIT Press for their support in bringing this project to fruition. Thanks are also due to the Australian Research Council for providing the fellowship that enabled this work to be completed, as well as the Alexander von Humboldt Foundation for their continuing support over a decade or more.

There are many friends and colleagues who have contributed in various ways to the ideas set out here, but I would particularly like to thank Bernardo Ainbinder, Andrew Benjamin, Miguel de Bestegui, Andrew Brennan, Chan-Fai Cheung, Steve Crowell, Stuart Elden, Ingo Farin, Hans-Helmuth Gander, Laurence Hemming, Norelle Lickiss, Linn Miller, Dermot Moran, James Phillips, Edward Relph, Glenda Satne, Ligia Saramago, David Seamon, Lucy Tatman, Lubica Ucnik, Jin Xiping, Julian Young, and Günter Zöller. I am also grateful for the continuing support of the School of Philosophy at the University of Tasmania, and especially the help of Irene Sawford, as well as Bronwyn Peters and Sally Laing.

I would like to thank the original publishers for allowing me to make use of the following material:

"The Place of Topology: Responding to Crowell, Bestegui, and Young," *International Journal of Philosophical Studies* 19 (2011): 305–325 (chapter 3); and "Heidegger in Benjamin's City," *Journal of Architecture*, 12 (2007): 489–499 (chapter 11)—both with kind permission of the publisher, Taylor & Francis Ltd., http://www.informaworld.com.

"From the Transcendental to the Topological: Heidegger on Ground, Unity, and Limit," in *From Kant to Davidson: Philosophy and the Idea of the Transcendental*, ed. Jeff Malpas (London: Routledge, 2002) (chapter 4); "Objectivity and Self-Disclosedness: The Phenomenological Working of Art," in *Art and Phenomenology*, ed. Joseph Parry (London: Routledge, 2010) (chapter 12); "Death and the Unity of a Life," in *Death and Philosophy*, ed. J. E.

Malpas and Robert C. Solomon (London: Routledge, 1998) (chapter 12); and "Beginning in Wonder," in *Philosophical Romanticism*, ed. Nikolas Kompridis (London: Routledge, 2006) (epilogue)—all with kind permission of Routledge and the Taylor & Francis Group.

"Nihilism and the Thinking of Place," in *The Movement of Nihilism*, Laurence Paul Hemming and Bogdan Costea (London: Continuum, 2010) (chapter 5), with kind permission of the Continuum International Publishing Group.

"Heidegger, Space, and World," in *Heidegger and Cognitive Science*, ed. Julian Kiverstein and Michael Wheeler (London: Palgrave-Macmillan, 2010) (chapter 6), with kind permission of Palgrave Macmillan.

"Heidegger, Geography, and Politics," *Journal of the Philosophy of History* 2 (2008): 185–213 (chapter 7); and "Philosophy's Nostalgia," in *Philosophy's Moods: The Affective Grounds of Thinking*, ed. Hagi Kenaan and Ilit Ferber (Dordrecht: Springer, 2011) (chapter 8)—both with kind permission of Springer Verlag.

"Locating Interpretation: The Topography of Understanding in Heidegger and Davidson," *Philosophical Topics* 27 (1999): 129–148 (chapter 10) (©1999 University of Arkansas, http://www.uapress.com), with kind permission of the University of Arkansas Press.

Last, but by no means least, I would like to acknowledge, and express my thanks for, the continuing love and support of my wife, Margaret, without which neither these essays, nor much else besides, would have been possible.

Introduction: The Thinking of Place

Accordingly, we may suggest that the day will come when we will not shun the question whether the opening, the free open, may not be that within which alone pure space and ecstatic time and everything present and absent in them have the place which gathers and protects everything.

—Martin Heidegger, "The End of Philosophy and the Task of Thinking," in *On Time and Being*

The idea of place—of *topos*—runs through the thinking of Martin Heidegger almost from the very start. Although not always directly thematized—sometimes apparently obscured, displaced even, by other concepts—and expressed through many different terms (*Ort, Ortschaft, Stätte, Gegend, Dasein, Lichtung, Ereignis*),[1] it is impossible to think with Heidegger unless one attunes oneself to Heidegger's own attunement to place. This is something not only to be observed in Heidegger's attachment to the famous hut at Todtnauberg;[2] it is also found, more significantly, in his constant deployment of topological terms and images, and in the situated, "placed," character of his thought, and of its key themes and motifs.[3]

Heidegger's work exemplifies the practice of what might be thought of as "philosophical topology," yet Heidegger must also be counted as one of the principal founders of such a mode of place-oriented thinking.[4] The aim of this volume is to contribute to both the topological understanding of Heidegger and the continuing articulation and elaboration of topology as philosophically conceived. In this respect, the essays aim to supplement and expand the analysis of Heideggerian topology already begun in my *Heidegger's Topology*,[5] but they can equally be seen as contributing to my own project of philosophical topography as first set out in my earlier volume *Place and Experience*.[6] The essays collected here (essays that span a decade or more of writing) thus focus on the idea of place, first, as it appears in Heidegger's thinking as it arises in a number of ways and in relation to a range of issues, and, second, as it can be seen to provide the focus for a distinctive mode of philosophical thinking that encompasses, but is not restricted to, the Heideggerian.

In this respect, the focus on place that appears here, while certainly finding a fruitful setting in Heidegger's work, does not derive from a Heideggerian perspective alone. It is not that, taking Heidegger as a starting point, the idea of place as philosophically significant comes into view, but rather, beginning with the idea of place as philosophically significant, one comes to a different reading, and perhaps a different appreciation, of the thinker from Messkirch, as well as of a number of other key figures—most notably perhaps, Kant, Aristotle, Gadamer, and Davidson, but also Benjamin, for instance, and, although they make but the briefest of appearances here, Arendt and Camus. The idea that place should be philosophically so significant in this way—that it might actually be central to philosophy as such (and that it is so is the underlying claim throughout much of my work as well, I would argue, of Heidegger's)—is to some extent a claim defended and elaborated upon, in various ways, throughout the essays contained here, but it is perhaps worth saying a little more by way of such a defense or elaboration from the very start. What underpins my conviction concerning the philosophical centrality of place, not only in Heidegger, but also more generally, is something that involves both a philosophical idea as well as a matter of personal experience or personal "phenomenology." I will say a little about the personal element that is at issue here, but first let me address the philosophical.

One of the features of place is the way in which it establishes relations of inside and outside—relations that are directly tied to the essential connection between place and boundary or limit.[7] To be located is to be within, to be somehow enclosed, but in a way that at the same time opens up, that makes possible. Already this indicates some of the directions in which any thinking of place must move—toward ideas of opening and closing, of concealing and revealing, of focus and horizon, of finitude and "transcendence," of limit and possibility, of mutual relationality and coconstitution. It is not surprising, therefore, to find such an important focus on "being-in," essentially a focus on place and placedness, within Heidegger's analysis in *Being and Time* (notably in §12)—although it is also a problematic focus within the structure of the early work in that Heidegger struggles to find a way of understanding the topological structure that is at issue here.[8] If we are to take the primary datum for philosophy to be our own being-in-the-world (a datum that is not first given in terms of an encounter with consciousness, with sense data, or with any other such "derivative" notion, but rather first presents itself precisely as an encounter in which self, other, and world are given together as a single unitary phenomenon), then where philosophical inquiry must begin is indeed with place or placedness, since this is fundamentally what is already at issue in the phenomenon of being-in-the-world. Although Aristotle's mode of thinking operates within a very different vocabulary and frame, his own emphasis on the importance of *topos* in the *Physics* captures something of this priority of place, particularly given his analysis of *topos* as precisely a mode of "being-in." Unfortunately, but perhaps not surprisingly, the primacy of place that appears here has been too often overlooked in philosophy—partly because it is so ubiquitous as to seem "commonplace" or even trivial, and partly because place remains so resistant to the forms of more "technical" analysis to which philosophers so often tend. Heidegger is perhaps unusual in this respect, in that his own thought seems already to begin with a recognition, even if not well worked out or articulated, of the primacy that must be accorded to place. The development of his thinking is a gradual working out of what this involves and of how it must be understood, and so also a gradual making explicit of the fundamental role of topology. Not only the analysis of being-in-the-world as worked out in *Being and Time* (and with it the understanding of originary temporality), but also the idea of the clearing (*Lichtung*) that is the happening of truth, the *Ereignis*, and the happening of the Fourfold all turn out to represent successively developed attempts at the articulation of the *topos* that itself lies at the very heart of the question of being.

The personal experience or phenomenology that is also at work in my thinking on this matter may be said to derive from a childhood lived between Australia, New Zealand, and the United Kingdom (at a time when travel between these places was still by sea, and so necessarily involved encounters with many other places besides just these), from a traveling lifestyle that was operative even when my family was in a more settled location (a result of the fairground work in which we were often involved), and also from the strong sense of place that is such an important element in the New Zealand culture (both Pakeha and Maori) in which I mostly grew up, and that is equally powerful, if not even more so, in Tasmania, where I now live. The experience of place, and the significance of a sense of place, has never seemed to me simply a matter of sentiment or feeling, but to be something much deeper and more profound—so that it should be unsurprising to find it clearly and powerfully evident in so many different forms of human expression and experience—and to be indicative of exactly the sort of philosophical or ontological primacy of place that emerges from philosophical reflection.

The understanding of place that is evident here is thus one that implies a changed conception of both our usual ways of thinking about philosophy, about ourselves, and about our own experience of involvement in the world. The ubiquity of topological or topographical ideas and images, the sense of place that is such a common feature of human experience, can now be seen to be not mere psychological or social artifacts (or just as products of an evolutionary history), but rather to arise from a more fundamental *ontological* structure (albeit one that is not to be found *beneath* the surfaces of things so much as in the very iridescence of surface itself— surface, like boundary, and also, I would argue, like the concepts of unity and ground, being itself an essentially topological concept). The structure at issue here is the structure of place, of *topos*, a structure that encompasses the being of individual places, of individual human lives, and of much more besides (the being of all that Heidegger includes in the term *Seiendes*). It is also a structure that resists any reductive analysis, being constituted through an essential mutuality of relation at every level, and that is unitary even while it also contains an essential multiplicity. The aim of this volume, as with much of my work elsewhere, is the exploration of this *topos*. It is an exploration that can never be complete, but always and only proceeds through the following of particular pathways that follow particular directions and move through particular landscapes. Recognizing the topological character of such thinking gives an added significance to Heidegger's insistence on his own thinking (and genuine thinking as such) as always "on the way." Moreover, because the project undertaken here is indeed a form of topological exploration, a series of philosophical peregrinations, it assumes a willingness on the part of the reader to participate in that exploration, and in the peregrinations that make it up. This is not to say that it requires an uncritical acceptance of the particular paths that are taken—far from it—but it does require some degree of willingness to walk along those paths, and to participate in the conversation that ensues. For this reason, too, one might say that the approach adopted in these essays tends not to be a polemical one. Although some disagreements are noted here (perhaps most often with certain pragmatic readings of Heidegger), the aim is more to work from within a certain place, rather than give too much attention to taking issue with other places, or other paths.[9]

The volume presented here is divided into three main sections, together with this introduction and also an epilogue. Part I deals with the ideas of *topos* and topology as they figure in Heidegger's thinking in general (although these chapters also address particular issues that arise out of responses to my topological reading as developed elsewhere); Part II concerns particular concepts and problems in Heidegger's work as these arise within a topological frame; in the case of Part III, the focus broadens out to consider the way Heideggerian topology plays out in relation to a more diverse set of topics, and in ways that go beyond a specifically Heideggerian frame. Although almost all of these essays have been published previously, they have appeared in quite diverse places, and in ways that have not always drawn attention to the underlying themes that connect them. The aim in bringing them together in here is not only to integrate them more directly with the work undertaken in *Heidegger's Topology*, but also to enable them to be more closely integrated with one another. To this end also, almost all of the essays have been revised, sometimes quite significantly, and where necessary, updated. Nevertheless, given the different directions in which each of these essays move, they do not constitute, and are not intended to constitute, a single seamlessly woven narrative. Instead, they take up different aspects of what may well be seen as a single story, but as with all such perspectival accounts, the story is presented in different as well as sometimes overlapping ways. The aim in revising the essays has been to ensure a greater degree of integration than was true of the works in their original publication (although all are underpinned, even in their original form, by much the same key ideas), but there are undoubtedly some points throughout the volume in which the varying provenance of these essays is evident—I can only hope that where such particular ambiguities or inconsistencies do remain, they are not so serious as to constitute a significant barrier to genuine engagement.

The essay that makes up the first chapter, "The *Topos* of Thinking," takes up the question as to what topology means in Heidegger's work, the way in which such topology brings a particular mode of philosophizing with it, and how this relates to the way in philosophy must itself be understood. The essay originally arose out of an invitation to speak at the Bariloche Colloquium in Argentina. The focus of the essay is perhaps the broadest of any of the essays contained here, aiming to give consideration to the idea of thinking as it stands in relation to place and the implications of such a relation. Chapter 2, "The Turning to/of Place," examines Heidegger's later thinking in relation to the earlier, arguing that a topological reading of Heidegger inevitably leads us, against a widespread countertendency, to a greater estimation of and focus on the later works. The essay provides something of an overview of (and so also an introduction to) my reading of Heidegger, and of the role of place in his thinking. Chapter 3, "The Place of Topology," addresses specific responses to *Heidegger's Topology* from Steven Crowell, Julian Young, Miguel de Beistegui, and Edward Relph. Those responses raise questions about the understanding of place, both in relation to Heidegger's thinking, and to philosophy and our contemporary situation. Although the discussion engages with various objections and criticisms, the aim is less to give voice to disagreement, than to find constructive ways of advancing the conversation of which the discussion presented here is only a partial reflection.

The concept of place stands in an essential relation to a number of other concepts that also play important roles in Heidegger's work and in Western philosophical thinking more generally—concepts of ground, limit, unity, position, organism, space, time, and world. The four chapters that make up Part II of this volume explore these concepts along with a range of connected issues, particularly those of nihilism, subjectivism, and the transcendental. Compared to the broad perspective adopted in Part I, Part II is thus much more closely focused. Chapter 4, "Ground, Unity, and Limit," examines the relations between the three concepts named in its title, together with Heidegger's rethinking of the transcendental in light of the topological. All three of these concepts are central to the thinking of place, each of them appearing throughout the discussions in other chapters. It is only fitting, therefore, that they should be given more concentrated attention here. Chapter 5, "Nihilism, Place, and 'Position,'" not only looks at the way in which the thinking of place is connected with Heidegger's thinking of nihilism, but also with the central role of the concept of "position" (the Greek *thesis*) in that thinking, and its connection with "subjectivism." In chapter 6, "Place, Space, and World," I return to some of the issues already sketched in chapter 2, but with an eye to the way in which the development of a topological orientation in Heidegger's work is connected with his rethinking of concepts of space (and time) and world. The discussion focuses particularly on Heidegger's 1929 lectures published as *The Fundamental Concepts of Metaphysics*, but it also deals with aspects of Kant's treatment of space and time, as well as with Jakob von Uexküll's concept of *Umwelt*. Of all the essays contained here, this has perhaps a slightly more polemical air to it than any of the others, in that it is partly directed against the pragmatist reading of Heidegger associated with the work of Hubert Dreyfus— although even here any polemic is very much in the background (and mostly confined to the notes). Von Uexküll appears again in the final essay of Part II, chapter 7, "Geography, Biology, and Politics." Here the issue of subjectivism (a theme that arises, if slightly differently, in each of the chapters that make up Part II) comes more directly to the fore, but in a way that is connected to what Julian Young calls "the problem of place"—the supposedly regressive and conservative character of place-oriented thinking.

Part III brings together essays across a much broader range of themes than in either Parts I or II, while the focus is also less directly on Heidegger. The essay that begins Part II, chapter 8, "Philosophy's Nostalgia," examines a mood or disposition, the nostalgic, that has often been taken to be characteristic of Heidegger's thinking in general, and to be indicative of the problematic character of that thinking. Here, however, the nostalgic is understood in a more positive light, and as directly tied to the topological. The essay thus attempts to address an issue once put to me by Karsten Harries: if one is to make *topos* central to the reading of Heidegger, then one must also be prepared to offer a defense, or perhaps a reappropriation, of the idea of nostalgia. Chapter 9, "Death and the End of Life," sets out an argument for what might be thought of as a topological approach to the understanding of human life, emphasizing the placed character of such a life, as well as its necessary delimitation by death. As originally developed, the essay took two forms: one was explicit in presenting an account of death in relation to life from within a broadly Heideggerian framework; the other developed the same argument, but held back from any explicit reference to Heidegger until the very end (the latter version being that which appeared in print). The version of the essay that appears here is to some extent a revised amalgamation of the two earlier forms of the essay. In chapter 10, "Topology, Triangulation, and Truth," Heideggerian topology is juxtaposed in relation to Davidsonian triangulation, focusing particularly on their respective treatments of truth, with the aim of showing the convergence of both Heidegger and Davidson (as well as Gadamer) in the direction of a similarly topological or topographical orientation. If Heidegger's thought is often taken to be nostalgic, then it is often also seen as essentially provincial in character—a provincialism often contrasted with the cosmopolitanism of a thinker such as Walter Benjamin. Chapter 11, "Heidegger in Benjamin's City," contests this opposition through an examination of the way each thinker takes up ideas of place and image. In chapter 12, "The Working of Art," the reader is returned to a specific Heideggerian text, but the treatment of that text aims at placing Heidegger's account within a much broader context, emphasizing the way in which it enables a view of the artwork as itself placed in its very materiality.

"Beginning in Wonder" is the final essay in the volume, functioning as an epilogue to the collection as a whole. Inasmuch as it is the final essay, "Beginning in Wonder" attempts to delineate a certain end that is also an origin. Exploring the ancient tradition that places the beginning of philosophy in wonder, the essay explores the character of wonder in a way that leads, inevitably perhaps, back to *topos*. In beginning in wonder, philosophy is also seen to have its beginning in place and in the experience of place. Since philosophy is determined by its beginning, so this essay also sets out a conception of the philosophical that can be read back into all of the essays that come before it. Not only does this involve a conception of philosophy as topological, but also of topology, and philosophy, as consisting essentially in the attempt to respond thoughtfully to the wondrous as well as to retain a sense of such wonder—and in so doing to retain a genuine sense of the ever-present questionability of being. The place that appears in this final essay—the place of philosophy, of wonder, of questionability—is also, of course, the same place with which the volume begins: it is the very *topos* of thinking. It is also the *topos* from within which the explorations in the topology of being that are attempted here find their direction and their ground.

Finally, one might well ask to what extent this volume, and the essays it contains, are to be viewed as contributions to contemporary Heidegger scholarship—and if not, then how are the essays themselves to be placed within contemporary philosophy? I have to admit, as I have said elsewhere, that there is a deep ambivalence in my own attitude on this matter. Although I would argue that my approach to Heidegger's thought is well grounded in both the letter and spirit of his thinking, I am more interested in the questions that are addressed through the encounter with his thought than with mere scholarly exegesis, and the same applies to my engagement with other thinkers such as Davidson, Kant, or Gadamer—in this respect, the essays should perhaps be seen as first and foremost contributions to the project of philosophical topology (or topography), and secondarily as contributions to the study of Heidegger—or the other thinkers on whose work these essays touch. Yet I also find it difficult to separate off my own approach from that of Heidegger, or of other thinkers with whom I am closely engaged. Thus, although I am sometimes critical of aspects of Heidegger's thought, there is also a sense in which it seems to me that the points of convergence outweigh any divergence, and it is the points of convergence that are my main interest.

Like Gadamer, in particular, I take the task of thinking to be a dialogic one—it lives only in the medium of conversation as that is granted through the engagement with text or speech. When one is genuinely involved in conversation—in a conversation in which one is, as Gadamer says, genuinely caught up—one cannot readily separate out one's own contribution from that of one's conversational partners. Should one expect, in a genuinely philosophical dialogue, to be able any more readily to separate off one's own contribution, one's own reading, one's own position, from the thinkers in relation to whom that dialogue is sustained? That one may find it difficult to do so should be taken not as a failure of self-discipline or self-critique, but rather as an indication of the genuine attempt at thinking that is undertaken. This is not to say, of course, that the thinking that is attempted may not fail in some other way, and it will certainly not be immune to criticism, but it should be deserving of some respect. I hope that the essays contained here, no matter their other shortcomings, will be viewed in such a light. These essays are indeed "explorations," and although they aim to be explorations that are successful in illuminating a certain place, no exploration can hope to be definitive, nor can it ever bring such exploring to an end—or, at least, the end to which it may bring us can only ever be the start of another beginning.

I Topological Thinking

1 The *Topos* of Thinking

We may venture the step back out of philosophy into the thinking of Being as soon as we have grown familiar with the provenance of thinking.
—Martin Heidegger, "The Thinker as Poet," in *Poetry, Language, Thought*

If Heidegger's thinking is, as he himself says, a "topology of being" (*Topologie des Seyns*)[1]—a saying of the place of being—then what is the place that appears here? What is the place of being, and in what place does this thinking take place? These questions direct our attention not only to the role of *topos* or place as that which is the object of Heidegger's thinking, and so as that toward which it is directed, but to the very *topos* or place within which Heidegger's thinking emerges, and the character of that thinking as itself determined by *topos*, as emerging out of it, and as returning to it.[2] As such, these questions move us within the domain of a form of "metaphilosophy" that looks to uncover the essential framework within which Heidegger's thinking takes place.

Understood as topological, Heidegger's thinking can be said to be concerned with place in at least three ways: (i) with place as the proper *focus* of thinking, and so as that which it is concerned to think and to speak, to address and to articulate; (ii) as that which is the proper *horizon* of thinking, that holds thinking within it, that bounds it, and that thereby allows thinking to appear as thinking; and (iii) as that which is the proper *origin* of thinking, out of which thinking emerges, and from which it gains its direction as well as its sustenance.[3] In exploring these three ways in which *topos* appears in Heidegger's thinking, it is important to note that they are not sharply distinct from one another, but instead reflect different aspects of what is a single, unitary *topos*—a place that encompasses focus, horizon, and origin, and that always appears as containing within it an essential indeterminacy and multiplicity.

It is only appropriate that the exploration of the place of thinking should begin where thinking itself begins, and so take as its starting point the placed origin of thinking. Here origin is itself to be understood not as some temporal starting point, but rather as that out of which something comes to appearance. Origin is thus already topological—to begin is to begin *in and from out of place*. In Heidegger, this focus on the placed origin of thinking appears very early. It is present in Heidegger's emphasis on the need to turn back to "life" as the proper context for philosophy, in the emphasis on the idea of hermeneutical situatedness, and in the focus on *Dasein*—that mode of being that is constituted in terms of the "there/ here"—as the proper site for the opening up of the question of being as such. No matter the changes in Heidegger's philosophical vocabulary, a key point around which his thinking constantly turns is the idea that thinking arises, and can only arise, out of our original encounter with the world—an encounter that is always singular and situated, in which we encounter ourselves as well the world, and in which what first appears is not something abstract or fragmented, but rather the things themselves, as things, in their concrete unity. Philosophy begins, then, in that same place that is the place for the emergence of world—and so for the appearance of things, the engagement with others, and the recognition of self. This place is one that is constantly before us, in which we are always situated, and yet from which we often seem estranged.

Although there are occasions when Heidegger appears to present this original and originary place of encounter in terms that are suggestive of the unique and the epochal (for instance, in "The Origin of the Work of Art"[4]), for the most part, it is the place of the ordinary and the everyday in and through which what is extraordinary shines forth. In Heidegger's early writing this appears in terms of the continual use of everyday examples for phenomenological interrogation—it is in the engagement with such ordinary things that the world itself comes into view. In his later essays, the happening of the Fourfold—the unitary gathering of earth, sky, mortals, and gods—is presented as occurring not through the work of any individual, not even the poet or artist, and certainly not the statesman or leader, but rather through those ordinary things around which human life and activity is configured and given shape, and in the light of which human existence itself takes on its character as human. What is extraordinary about these ordinary things is the manner in which they provide the focus for the opening of world, which includes, of course, their own opening as things, their own appearing and coming to presence. It is in the encounter with such presencing that we are given over to wonder—a wonder that is not provoked by anything other than the simple happening of being, a happening in which we are ourselves always implicated.[5] Philosophy thus begins in no special place, but rather has its origin in any and every place, and yet also in a place that is everywhere the "same"—the place or happening of place that is the happening of being, that is the opening of world, that is the original and originary presencing of things.

The inquiry into the place of thinking that Heidegger undertakes in *Being and Time*, in particular, and that is couched in terms of the question of the meaning of being, takes the being of *Dasein* as its essential starting-point.[6] *Being and Time* thus makes quite explicit that the place of thinking is itself identical with the place of *Dasein*'s own being—with the place of existence. The fact of such an identification, and thus the fact that *Being and Time* should find its own orientation to the question of the meaning of being in and through the being of *Dasein*, is not a result of any merely "epistemic" consideration—it is not that *Dasein* simply happens to be the only entry point to the question of being that is available to us. Instead, the focus on *Dasein* arises because of the particular way in which the very question of being already invokes the being of questionability as such, and the being of *Dasein* is that very mode of being whose being is always already given *as questionable*.[7] Only in the being of the "there" can the possibility of any form of question or of questioning emerge, and so the being of the question is itself essentially grounded in the being of *Dasein*, while the mode of being of *Dasein* is the mode of being of questionability. That the place in which *Being and Time* opens up its own inquiry is the place of *Dasein*'s own being is thus a necessary consequence of the way in which the question of being can only be taken up in and through the being that belongs to questionability as such—a being that remains always obscure, always itself questionable.[8] The turn toward place, and so toward questionability, is not a turn back into what is comfortable and secure, but quite the opposite. It is a turn into both the questionability of place and the place of questionability—even in its very placedness, thinking is characterized by its being always "on the way" (*unterwegs*).[9]

Our being *in the world* is the same as our "being there/here." To find ourselves always already in the world is to find our existence always already given before us in the very encounter with ourselves, with others, and with things, as that occurs in the place in which we are. This "being placed" is identical with our existence; it is also that which provokes the most fundamental mode of questioning—the mode of questioning that is the very opening up of possibility that is the opening of world. The belonging together of questionability with placedness is clearly evident in the way

Heidegger deploys the notion, developed further by Gadamer, of hermeneutic situatedness (a key theme in much of his early thinking), and in the related idea of truth as disclosedness or unconcealment—as *aletheia*.[10]

The happening of understanding that is the happening of truth is itself the happening of questionability—it is the opening up of that expansive but bounded locale in which our speaking and our acting is revealed as not only true or false, but as capable of being true or false, and so of being addressed as to the grounds of its truth. Moreover, the way in which place and questionability appear together here is indicative of the way in which the emergence of truth itself occurs only in the opening of a dimension that both allows certain elements to emerge as salient while at the same time others are withdrawn—"truth" names, in one sense, just this event of emergence and withdrawal. As an event, this happening of truth takes place as the opening of place into world as an opening-up, a clearing, that allows for the appearance of both truth and error as these attach to specific claims, statements, and beliefs. It is thus an opening that allows for the very possibility of philosophy even as a body of things said.[11]

Heidegger was himself critical of *Being and Time* for its failure adequately to address the problem of subjectivism.[12] This may already be thought to be a problem in the way in which the work begins with a focus on *Dasein* understood as the essence of *human* being, and although this starting point should not be seen to entail any necessary subjectivism, the manner in which the being of *Dasein* is subsequently explicated— particularly the prioritization of existentiality and "projection" over other elements with the structure of *Dasein*, as well as the associated prioritization of originary temporality[13]—suggests that there may indeed be a problem in the way in which *Dasein* is originally understood. In Heidegger's later thinking, *Dasein* comes to be understood rather differently from the manner in which it is analyzed in the earlier thinking. The priority given to existentiality and temporality is largely abandoned as Heidegger's thinking develops further, and although the focus on *Dasein* remains, as does the intimacy of the connection between *Dasein* and questionability, it is the topological character of *Dasein* that comes increasingly to the fore—its connecting of *Sein* with *Da*, of being with place. *Dasein* still encompasses the essence of the human, but it does so precisely because of the way in which the being of the human finds its essence in the being of place—in the belonging together of being and *topos*.

On this reconfigured understanding, questionability can be seen to reside not merely in the asking of questions, but in the essential iridescence—the indeterminacy and multiplicity—that attaches to place and to being as such (which is why it is also tied to listening). Moreover, both questionability and iridescence are bound to finitude. The happening of place is the happening of finitude—which is not merely the happening of that which is opposed to the infinite, but rather the very opening up of that bounded which is the domain of the presencing of things. Place is *Dasein*, the belonging together of the there/here with being, and as such it is essentially singular and bounded even though its boundedness can never be given any absolute determination. Questionability is tied to such finitude, since it is only in finitude that a domain of possibility can be opened up that reaches out to the world, and is itself open to it, and yet does not already determine the world. What happens over the course of Heidegger's own thinking is thus also an increasing recognition of the way in which the finitude that is the focus for so much of his thinking is indeed a finitude that belongs to place *as such* (to *Dasein* as that *in which* human being is founded), rather than as belonging, in the first instance, *to the human* (as that whose essence *Dasein* is).[14]

The most serious problem presented by Heidegger's thinking in *Being and Time* is arguably its ambiguous, sometimes inconsistent, treatment of place or *topos*. Not only does *Being and Time* lack any adequate thematization of place, but it also interprets the "there" in explicitly *temporal* terms. As a result, place as it appears in *Being and Time* is on the one hand downgraded, inasmuch as it is associated with spatiality and so with "falling," and on the other hand, inasmuch as originary temporality itself appears as implicitly topological, so also is place given a certain centrality, but only as removed from the spatial.[15] The attempted resolution of the ambiguity that is apparent here leads Heidegger toward a more direct concentration on place in his later thinking, and, simultaneously with this, a reconfiguration of the thinking of time and space as "timespace"—*Zeitraum*[16] (whether the latter is a wholly satisfactory reconfiguration is another question[17]). This attempted resolution also results in a change in the way in which Heidegger's thinking of being and of place proceeds: there is a shift not only toward a more explicit understanding of place as the proper focus and origin of thinking, but also toward a mode of thinking that itself reflects the character of place as such.

The main line of thinking that is developed in Heidegger's early thinking, and that culminates in his 1927 magnum opus, moves in one direction: toward exhibiting time as the horizon of being. Put in terms of the Heideggerian focus on *Dasein*, this means showing that the "there," for all that it may carry spatial connotations, is fundamentally temporal (in fact, spatiality is itself founded in temporality).[18] Although it is quite clear that this is not intended to imply any reduction of the spatiality or the topological to the temporal—of a multiplicity of elements to a single principle—the way in which Heidegger develops the priority of temporality, and of originary temporality, in *Being and Time* makes it difficult to avoid the conclusion that a form of reduction nevertheless results.[19] Heidegger's employment of a notion of what I have elsewhere referred to as "hierarchical dependence"[20] involves him in what is essentially an attempt to found the unity of *Dasein* in temporality above all else, and so also to "derive" the structure of *Dasein*'s existential spatiality from originary temporality. The latter attempt is one that Heidegger later rejects as untenable,[21] and his later thinking is also characterized by the abandonment of the sort of hierarchical analysis that appears in *Being and Time*. Instead, the approach that predominates in the later work is one directed at the elucidation of a form of unity that retains its irreducible complexity, but whose elements exhibit a reciprocal interdependence.[22] This is perhaps best illustrated by the structure of the Fourfold in late essays such as "The Thing" and "Building Dwelling Thinking."[23] Only within the unity of the Fourfold do earth and sky, mortals and gods come to appearance, and yet only through the gathering together of those elements is the Fourfold itself constituted.

The nature of the unity that appears here, and its importance as constituting a very different mode of philosophical analysis than that found in *Being and Time*, is something that I have discussed in detail elsewhere,[24] but some brief characterization is needed here. The multiple unity that the Fourfold exhibits is an exact mirror of the similarly multiple unity that can be seen in the unity of *topos*, of place, and that is evident as soon as one looks to understand the constitution even of those ordinary locales in which we find ourselves—a town, a stretch of landscape, a countryside. Places find their unity not in any single preexisting element in that place from which the unity of the whole derives, but rather in the way in which the multiple elements of the place are gathered together in their mutual relatedness to one another. Even those salient features within a landscape that may be seen to give focus to it are themselves given their own character through the elements of the landscape that come into focus around it. Thus, in Heidegger's example in "Building Dwelling Thinking," the bridge appears as a bridge not through the exercise of its own qualities in determining an otherwise featureless terrain, but through a coming to appearance in which bridge, river, and the entirety of the countryside around it are gathered together as one and as many, and are thereby determined, in their being, as bridge, as river, as countryside. It is this essential gathering of elements in a mutual belonging together in which they come to presence that Heidegger also describes as the *Ereignis*—an event that is to be understood not as purely temporal, but as the temporalizing of space and the spatializing of time in the single gatheredness of place.[25]

The place that is evident here is the very same place in which not only *Being and Time* but all of Heidegger's philosophy finds its origin and its ground. It is the very same place as that in which thinking itself arises, from which it is often estranged, and to which it must always return. Heidegger is himself quite explicit in his own understanding of thinking as always involved in such a "return" to place—as a *homecoming*.[26] The return at issue here is not, however, a return that is predicated on a genuine moving away from—if that were the case there could be no possibility of return at all. Instead, the return is a "turning back" to that in which we already find ourselves (a turning back, in one sense, to our very placedness). In this respect one might say that it is a turning back to that which is always presupposed by our more specific modes of being. It is like the movement in which, having been engrossed in some activity, we look up to see the place that has been around us all the time, and that has also enabled and supported the activity in which we have been engrossed, or like the analogous movement in which, engaged in conversation, we suddenly realize the way in which our speaking has been sustained and guided by what has remained always unspoken. What occurs in such instances is indeed a turning or a coming back to place, or to a place, in a way that also brings that place itself into view. It is an occurrence that is mirrored in Heidegger's own image of the "clearing" (*Lichtung*) that allows the emergence of things into presence. Such a "clearing" is a place, a *topos*, but as a place, it withdraws at the same time as it allows appearance within it—a place is precisely that which opens up to allow room for what belongs within it. The return to place is thus the turning toward that which allows for, that which gives room, but also that which withdraws.

The movement back to place—back to that which otherwise remains unnoticed and unremarked (as place itself often remains in the background of our activities)—can also be understood as a movement of recollection, of remembering again, and Heidegger draws directly on this idea alongside that of return or homecoming. The conjunction of ideas of remembrance with that of the return home leads to the common charge that Heidegger's thinking contains an essential nostalgia within it—a charge that is correct in its attribution of the nostalgic, but too often mistaken in its construal of what this means.[27] It is the character of thinking as a remembering that is itself invoked in Heidegger's characterization of philosophy as marked by forgetting, and especially by the forgetting of being (*Seinsvergessenheit*)——a forgetting that must now be understood as also a forgetting, not only of finitude and questionability, but of place. Such forgetting is most evident in the denial of limit, in the claim to certainty, and in the assertion of the universal and the timeless—in the loss of any proper sense of the place in which thinking itself belongs.[28]

As a constant turning back to the place in which it already is, a constant remembering of what is being forgotten, a constant bringing forward of what always withdraws, the thinking of place, and so also thinking as such, exhibits an essential circularity that is identical to that which appears elsewhere in both the hermeneutic circle and the circularity of the transcendental. The way in which circularity comes to the fore in these latter two cases—that of the hermeneutic and the transcendental—is indicative of the way in which each is implicated with the question of *ground*.[29] The hermeneutic circle exhibits the way in which understanding always finds its ground within a domain that it has already constituted for itself (hence the interdependence between parts, and between parts and whole, that is characteristic of the hermeneutical). Transcendental circularity, which often appears in critiques of the transcendental project as verificationist, *ad hominem*, or as implicitly presupposing what it aims to demonstrate (but is also present in Kant's characterization of the transcendental as essentially tied to a form of self-constitution[30]), takes on the project of a philosophical grounding of the possibility of understanding or experience as such.[31] In both cases, the hermeneutical and the transcendental, the preoccupation with the question of ground, as well as the movement of circularity, are indicative of the topological character of the projects that are at issue. As such, the hermeneutical and the transcendental move within the same domain that also is the focus in the inquiry into the place of thinking, and the *topos* that they invoke is the same *topos* within which Heidegger's thought also moves. The circularity at issue here is thus, in each case, the same as that which appears in the thinking of place, and so in the thinking of the very place of thinking.

The idea that the topological encompasses the hermeneutic and the transcendental, and that the latter might themselves be understood as forms of the topological, is not itself clear in Heidegger's own thinking on the matter. Indeed, while the hermeneutic and the transcendental are key terms in his early thinking (they play important roles in *Being and Time*), they largely disappear from the later writings.[32] Yet although we can understand the reason for this within the framework in which Heidegger's thinking develops, there is good reason to suppose that Heidegger's abandonment of the hermeneutic and the transcendental itself obscures the essentially topological character of both these modes of thinking, and that the *topos* that emerges so clearly in later Heidegger is actually the same *topos* that was always, even if only implicitly, at stake in the thinking of the hermeneutic and the transcendental.[33]

Circularity, mutuality and multiplicity of elements, rejection of any form of reductionism—these are all key features in any thinking, any form of questioning, that addresses and is attentive to its own placedness. The development in Heidegger's thinking is one in which these elements become clearer as the focus on *topos* also becomes more explicit. The entanglement of place with questionability brings to the fore the finitude of thinking as this arises alongside an essential relatedness to world. Such finitude is not a temporal finitude alone (*pace* some readings of Heidegger's early thought), but is essentially the finitude of placedness—a placedness that encompasses both the temporal and the spatial. The "being-placed" that is at issue here is the very origin, horizon, and focus of thinking, but it also marks its limit. Here, in the sheer givenness of being—which is the givenness of place as well as of world[34]—our thinking finds its proper "end" in that which is also its origin. Here thinking does not come to a stop, but in finding its proper limit or boundary, it thereby grasps its own character as thinking—thinking thus comes into its own, that is, it finds its place.[35] Retaining the focus on thinking as questioning, what becomes apparent here is the radical difference in the *kind* of questioning that belongs to that essential thinking that is philosophy: it is not a thinking that refers us from the questionability of one phenomenon to its answer in another, but instead directs our attention to that which supports and sustains all such questioning, to the very place of questionability as such—its horizon and ground, its origin and its end—a place that is also the place of our own being.

2 The Turning to/of Place

Thinking itself is a way. We respond to the way only by remaining underway.
—Heidegger, *What Is Called Thinking?*

In T. H. White's magnificent retelling of Malory, *The Once and Future King*, the character of Merlin has one especially peculiar characteristic: he lives his life backward, from future to past.[1] It has always seemed to me that a similarly backward trajectory is particularly suited to the reading of philosophers—at least those whose work is sustained by a significant unity of vision—and especially to the reading of a philosopher such as Heidegger (who himself tells us that in essential history the beginning comes last[2]). Much of my own reading of Heidegger (and not only Heidegger, but Davidson too) has thus taken the later works as the key to understanding the earlier, and as the basis on which a broader sense of his thinking as a whole should be developed.

The point at issue here may also be put topologically: if the work of a thinker is construed as the exploration of a certain region of thought—a region that is itself opened up by some sustaining insight—then the more that exploration proceeds, the more will the region itself come into view, and the more will the landscape that belongs to it be made evident. Indeed, the initial survey of a territory is likely to tell more about the character of the explorer than about the territory itself (and perhaps not so much even about the explorer), and this seems to be true of philosophical exploration no less than of the exploration of a physical terrain. It is only as the explorer's own engagement with the territory proceeds that the territory itself comes to light; and so if it is the territory that interests us—in philosophical terms, if it is the problems themselves that are our focus—then we would perhaps do well to look to the explorer's engagement as it is more fully developed, rather than in its early stages.

On these grounds (although they are not the only grounds), it seems sensible to be cautious in our reading of Heidegger's early work as against his later. If what concerns us is indeed the broader direction and domain in which his thinking moves, then the later thinking may prove no less valuable than the earlier. Yet, in fact, the bulk of attention given to Heidegger's writings has tended to focus on the early work rather than the later. Moreover, in comparison with the earlier, the later writings are often viewed as not only lacking the analytical insight of the earlier work, but as increasingly given over to a dubiously founded "history of being" and a mystical obscurantism. In this respect, the opinion voiced by Emmanuel Levinas in a late interview undoubtedly captures a widely shared view: "*Being and Time* is much more significant and profound than any of Heidegger's later works."[3] This is not to say that the later thinking has been simply neglected or that it has been without influence. Some of the most important engagements with Heidegger's thinking begin with the later thinking—certainly this is true of Gadamer, and arguably of Derrida (as well as for those whose engagement with Heidegger takes its point of departure from the work of these thinkers). Yet it remains the case that for many readers of Heidegger's work, not only is *Being and Time* the place where one first enters into his thinking, but it is also a place that many never really leave.

There are obvious reasons for the concentration of so much attention onto the earlier work, not the least of which is the idiosyncratic voice, style, and mode of approach, to say nothing of the density of ideas, which characterizes the later thinking—Gadamer points to the increasing difficulties of language that the later thinking embodies and presents.[4] Yet not only is it the case that the bulk of Heidegger's writing, including some of his most important works—most notably, perhaps, those on Nietzsche and on Hölderlin—comes from the later period, but what is often forgotten, or at least overlooked, is that the later thinking arises out of what Heidegger viewed as a failure of the earlier thinking. This failure is most clearly evident in the fact that *Being and Time* remains, as we all know, an incomplete work, a work that Heidegger rushed into publication and then abandoned. That abandonment did not, as Heidegger reminds us at various places, constitute a disowning or disavowing—the path taken by *Being and Time* is still "a necessary one"[5]—but it was nevertheless grounded in problems intrinsic to the work, and was not the result merely of some arbitrary change of mind.

Although *Being and Time* remains an enormously important and philosophically rich work, we cannot come to any real understanding of the Heideggerian project, or of what Heidegger came to view as lying at the heart of that project, if we remain with the early thinking alone, or if we fail to attend to the path that moves from the earlier thinking to the later—a path to which Heidegger himself directs our attention on more than one occasion. To engage with Heidegger philosophically is thus to engage with the path of his thinking as it moves not only through *Being and Time*, but also beyond it—and that means coming to a clearer recognition of how the later thinking is indeed required by the path that *Being and Time* already opens up, and also of the nature and significance of the later thought. Attending to that path means attending to the shift in Heidegger's thinking that occurs as he attempts to rethink *Being and Time* during the later 1920s and into the 1930s (a rethinking that is also, it should be noted, bound up with his political entanglement with Nazism, and his attempt to come to terms with that entanglement).[6] In attending to the path at issue here, one is also forced to attend to the character of the so-called Turning (*die Kehre*) in Heidegger's thought. The Turning is essentially a turning to place, as well as a Turning of (and in) place.[7] In the Turning, and so in the shift from Heidegger's early to his later thinking, the question of place comes clearly into view, not only as a question in its own right, but also as that around which the other elements in Heidegger's thinking are brought together.

The Failure of *Being and Time*

In his 1962 letter to William Richardson, Heidegger emphasizes that although *Being and Time* is a problematic work, it is a work that nevertheless has to be *worked through*.[8] The working through of *Being and Time* is necessary for Heidegger's own path of thinking, but one might also argue that it represents, at least as Heidegger sees it, a necessary stage on the path of thought as such. One of the reasons for this is that *Being and Time* is a central element in the engagement with Kant, and so also with certain elements that are foundational to the German idealist tradition, that characterized much of Heidegger's work in the ten years from the mid-1920s to the mid-1930s—more or less coming to a conclusion with the publication of *What Is a Thing?* in 1935. It also represents an attempt to engage in a certain sort of *systematic* thinking (itself exemplified in Kant's own work) directed at the analysis of that structure that underpins, and is constitutive of, human engagement in the world, and that also may be said to underpin the structure of world as such.[9]

One of the central difficulties in *Being and Time*, however, is the lack of the conceptual resources in the work needed to enable it adequately to take up that task. Most importantly, *Being and Time* lacks an adequate grasp of the distinction between *space* as it appears in Cartesian thought and *place*. Directly connected with this is the fact that *Being and Time* nevertheless implicitly construes temporality in topological terms at the same time as it also claims to eschew the spatial and the topological in favor of the temporal. The problem can be summarized, in condensed form, as follows: on the one hand, *Being and Time* aims to provide an account of the proper unity of *Dasein*, and so also of world, that reflects the unity of the "*Da*," the "there/here" as founded in the unity of temporality; on the other hand, *Being and Time* also demonstrates that the unity of temporality, which is not itself temporal, can only be topological in character, and so cannot found the unity of the "there/here," but is already given in it (although this latter conclusion is not one that appears in the pages of *Being and Time* itself).

The problems that surround the topological character of *Being and Time* come to a particular focus, as I read matters, around Heidegger's attempts to derive the structure of existential spatiality from originary temporality—an attempt that Heidegger soon came to recognize was "untenable" (as he put it in 1962).[10] The difficulty here is connected to a general problem concerning the argumentative methodology of *Being and Time*. Heidegger's analysis begins with *Dasein*—understood in *Being and Time* as identical with the essence of human being (although the nature of this identity is somewhat equivocal). The taking of such a starting point is already questionable, since it suggests that the inquiry Heidegger undertakes is one already disposed toward a certain privileging of what might otherwise be understood as subjectivity.[11] The key focus for Heidegger, however, is not on *Dasein* understood in some general way, or even on *Dasein* as subject, but rather on *Dasein* in its *unity*. The unity at issue here cannot be external to *Dasein*, but must belong essentially to it,[12] and yet at the same time, that unity is not simply given in the everyday structure of *Dasein*—it is instead a unity that must be uncovered. Heidegger thus attempts to peel back the structures of *Dasein*, through successive layers, as it were, to reveal the core of *Dasein*'s unity as given in the unitary structure of originary temporality. What this means, however, is that the layers that are successively peeled back are taken to be, in some sense, derivative of, or secondary to, the layers that are thereby revealed. Yet in that case, the unity of each of the derivative layers belongs not to that layer as such, but rather to the layer that underlies it—in the case of existential spatiality, for

instance, one might say that what this means is that the unity that belongs
to it is not a unity that belongs to existential spatiality as such, but is rather
the unity imparted to it by temporality. This is why, as I say, the aim of
Being and Time is to show that the unity of the "there/here" is to be found
in the unity of originary temporality.

Even if we leave aside the question concerning the nature of the unity
that belongs to temporality itself, a significant problem nevertheless
emerges here. By attempting to derive the unity of the entire structure of
Dasein from the unity of temporality alone a tension arises that threatens
the irreducible plurality of that structure—everything threatens to collapse
into temporality alone. Moreover, because the unity of temporality is a
unity from which the unity of other structures is supposed to be derived,
so it becomes questionable as to whether the unity that allegedly belongs
to those other structures can properly be said to belong to them, and in
that case, their unity turns out to be itself a secondary form of unity—a
unity "imposed upon" rather than "belonging to."[13] Indeed, one might
argue that the unity of *Dasein*, and perhaps also the unity of world, is itself
a secondary, derivative unity of this sort.

When we move from the position that is set out in *Being and Time* to
that which is apparent in Heidegger's later thinking, a very different picture
emerges. In the later thought there remains a preoccupation with the
problem of unity—a problem that gradually comes to be more clearly
focused on the unity of *topos*—but this is no longer articulated in terms of
the successive uncovering of more originary layers or structures. Instead it
is worked out though the identification of a set of elements whose differentiated unity encompasses the entirety of the structure of world, and
whose overall unity is articulated through the essential belonging together
of the elements themselves. There is then no underlying structure or principle that alone *unifies*, but only a single structure that *is unified* in and
through the mutual belonging together of its components.

Place and the Problem of World

The appearing of *topos* as a more explicit theme in Heidegger's work is
directly connected to Heidegger's rethinking of the concept of world and
the problem that it presents. The problem of world is already present in
Being and Time—a large part of the work is devoted to an elucidation of
the worldhood of the world—but in the years immediately after *Being and
Time* the problem of world is also the focus for Heidegger's rethinking of
the framework developed in his earlier work. This is particularly evident

in the lecture course from 1929 to 1930 that has been published in English as *The Fundamental Concepts of Metaphysics*.[14] In these lectures, "world," understood as the "manifestness of beings as such as a whole,"[15] is the main focus of Heidegger's discussion, but Heidegger is also at pains to emphasize the limitations of his characterization of world in *Being and Time*. The focus of the analysis of world in the earlier work was on the structure of equipmentality (*Zeug*). World thus appears as given in the teleological structure of the useful, the instrumental, the ready-to-hand. Yet, according to Heidegger, this cannot constitute the final word on the matter—such analyses can only be preliminary, and must be moved beyond.[16] As a result, much later, he will say that although the analysis of the worldhood of the world (and so the analysis of equipmentality) in *Being and Time* is "an essential step," still it remains "of subordinate significance."[17] Heidegger understands "world" to refer to no mere assemblage of things, nor even to their instrumental ordering, but to the unity of their belonging together in which any and everything is encompassed—a meaning that elsewhere he claims to be present in the original Greek sense of *kosmos*.[18] This means that the problem of world is also the problem of the *unity* of the world. The question is: what is the nature of that unity? The question of unity is also at issue in the question of being—as Heidegger tells us: "The impetus for my whole way of thinking goes back to an Aristotelian proposition which states that being is said in many ways. This proposition was originally the lightning bolt that triggered the question, What then is the unity of these various meanings of being?"[19] Consequently, the question of unity that emerges with respect to world and the question of unity with respect to being may well turn out to be the same.

Heidegger's focus on world *as a problem* is clearest in the period immediately after *Being and Time*. This is for at least two reasons (aside from the independent centrality of the issue): first, because the treatment of the problem of world in the earlier work is indeed so preliminary (and yet was, and still is, often read in ways that ignore this fact); and, second, because the problem of world is connected, in the early work, to the problem of *Dasein*'s own capacity for "transcendence" (the "passing over" of thought toward its object,[20] and in the direction of world), understood as essentially determined by its existentiality—its projecting of its own possibilities (*Dasein*, as understood in the framework of *Being and Time*, is essentially constituted by its capacity for transcendence). Part of what occurs in the years following *Being and Time* is a gradual rethinking of world that is also accompanied by a rethinking, and finally abandonment, of the idea of transcendence (as such, it leads away from the focus on world as constituted within an essentially "projected" structure—even if one determined by modes of practical comportment).[21]

The problem of transcendence can itself be seen to arise out of the attempt to address the unity of world, or of *Dasein* as being-*in-the-world* (transcendence describes a relation that brings together *Dasein* and world by grounding the latter in what is essentially a capacity of the former). Heidegger's later thinking undertakes a rethinking of world that can also be understood as directed toward a rethinking of the problem of unity that itself lies at the heart of *Being and Time*. Yet whereas *Being and Time* largely overstepped that problem as it relates to world as such, moving instead to the unity of being as given in and through temporality (so that, as I noted earlier, it is hard to avoid the conclusion that, in *Being and Time*, the unity of world is actually a secondary unity), the later thinking takes up the problem of world in a way that is not only more direct but also retains the focus on world as such.

The problem of world, which is the problem of the unity of world, is thus central to understanding the shift in Heidegger's thinking from early to late. Indeed, in what is perhaps the key essay from the transitional period of Heidegger's thinking during the 1930s—"The Origin of the Work of Art"—the problem of world, together with that of truth, lies at the very center of Heidegger's inquiry. In that essay, originally delivered as a lecture three times over the period from 1935 to 1936, Heidegger provides an account of the "worlding of world" as it occurs through the strife between world and earth. In this strife, world and earth can be understood as two aspects of the one structure that is the concealing–revealing of truth. Within this structure, not only are individual entities able to appear as the entities they are through appearing in a certain way (entities thus appear under a certain aspect or "look"), but earth and world are themselves brought to appearance so that earth comes to be *as earth* and world comes to be *as world* (although, once again, this appearance always takes on a particular form). The happening that is at issue here, the "worlding of world" that is also the "setting to work of truth," is what Heidegger refers to in the *Contributions*, which he begins writing in 1936, as the *Ereignis*, the "Event."

The Event plays a similar role, in Heidegger's later thinking, to that played by originary temporality in *Being and Time*. But whereas the structure of originary temporality was that which underlay the other structures of *Dasein*, including the structure of spatiality and perhaps also of world, and from which those structures were somehow "derived," the Event does not underlie nor is it that from which any sort of "derivation" is possible.

Instead, the Event encompasses earth and world, as well as mortals and gods, even as they come to appearance in the Event. At the same time, the dynamic interrelatedness of earth and world (what Heidegger refers to in "The Origin of the Work of Art" in terms of strife) is itself constitutive of the Event as such.

The structure that appears in "The Origin of the Work of Art" and that also seems present in the *Contributions* might be thought to be an early version of what appears later, in essays such as "Building Dwelling Thinking," as the Fourfold (*Das Geviert*). There is undoubtedly a lineage here, but the former structure is built around what is properly a "Twofold" rather than a Fourfold, since it is constituted around one key axis, that between earth and world. There can be no doubt, however, that the structure at issue is very different from that which is set out in *Being and Time*. Whereas the earlier structure is indeed one that moves through a succession of ever more fundamental layers, the later structure is one of mutually related elements that are together constitutive of the overall structure at issue— that being the "there/here" that is surely best understood as *topos*—in which no one element takes absolute precedence over any other.

Nevertheless, the way in which Heidegger presents this structure in "The Origin of the Work of Art" (which was given in its final version in the same year, 1936, as *Contributions* was begun) still seems to suffer from a shortcoming similar to that which Heidegger also saw as a problem in *Being and Time*: it fails adequately to think the relation between the happening of world, the "setting to work" of truth, and human being. Thus, in "The Origin of the Work of Art," Heidegger gives a founding role to the poet and even to the statesman in a way that has led some, most notably Jacques Taminieux, to argue that the essay is "decisionistic" in its fundamental orientation.[22] In his 1956 "Appendix" to the essay, however, Heidegger puts the problem in terms of an ambiguity in the talk of truth being "set to work" since it remains unclear "who or what" does this setting and in what manner.[23] The possibility is that the setting of truth to work is somehow an achievement of human being.[24] The problem with *Being and Time* is not merely that it seeks to derive the structure of *Dasein* from the structure of originary temporality, or to do so in a way that neglects the topology that is at issue there, but that it attempts to do this in a way that threatens to found the structure of *Dasein* as a whole in *Dasein*'s own capacity for transcendence, which is to say, in *Dasein*'s own projecting of possibilities.

This projection of possibilities, in the language of *Being and Time*, lies at the heart of the notions of *existence* and *existentiality*, and appears within the structure of temporality in terms of the prioritization given to futurity (*Zukommen*—"coming toward"). Such projection seems to be a possibility within the structure set out in "The Origin of the Work of Art." One might argue that the difficulty of language of the *Contributions* arises, in part, from Heidegger's concentrated attempt to overcome the tendency to give priority to such projection, and so to articulate a mode of thinking that is more adequate in its thinking of being, and does not, even if inadvertently, attempt to found being in the human or in some capacity of the human. It is thus notable that, in the *Contributions*, we find Heidegger using the term *Dasein* in a way that is no longer focused on the essence of human being as given in projection. Instead it designates what might be understood simply as the "there/here of being"—a "there/here" that can still be said to be the essence of the human, but only inasmuch as the being of the human is itself to be found in the place of being that is also the being of place.

The rethinking of world that Heidegger undertakes in the period following *Being and Time* is thus directly connected with his attempt to clarify the problem of world in a way that does not take world as somehow a projection of human activity, and yet nevertheless also recognizes the essential entanglement of the world with the human—the essential entanglement of being with human being. By the late 1940s, the twofold structure that appears in "The Origin of the Work of Art" and in *Contributions* has given way to the fully developed notion of the Fourfold that is familiar from a number of Heidegger's postwar essays, including "The Thing" and "Building Dwelling Thinking." The structure of the Fourfold is analogous to that found in *Contributions* and in "The Origin of the Work of Art," but whereas the earlier structure had a central earth–world axis, the later structure is built around two axes, earth–sky and gods–mortals, while "world" now designates not one element within the structure, but rather the dynamic unity of the structure as a whole—a unity that is also designated in terms of the Event, and that is, as I read it, essentially topological in character.

Here we have a level of analysis that looks to understand both world and place (for in his late work it is quite clear that Heidegger understands the two as standing in an essential relation to one another) through a set of encompassing and schematic terms—earth, sky, gods, mortals—that themselves stand in a relation of reciprocal dependence to one another, and together form two equal axes of a single unitary world. The four terms that make up these axes do not designate some set of principles that lie "behind" the things of the world or that are more originary in the sense of being that from which all else is derived. The language of "derivation" has entirely disappeared from the later thinking—it had already disappeared by 1936—and although the notions of "origin" and the "originary" remain, they do not designate something that comes before or lies beneath. The elements of the Fourfold are "originary" in the sense that they are the fundamental and essential elements of world—that out of which world comes—even while they themselves only come to be inasmuch as they are gathered into the happening of world as such (the happening that is also the happening of the Event).

The Fourfold and the concept of the Event, as well as the notions of *topos* and world, lie at the very heart of Heidegger's later thinking. Yet these ideas, especially the idea of the Fourfold, seem often to have been misunderstood, and their nature and significance have not been fully appreciated in much of the Heideggerian literature to date. The Fourfold represents a radically different mode of analysis from that which is evident in *Being and Time*. In spite of the attempt of *Being and Time* to maintain a focus on the unity of *Dasein* and to refrain from any dissolution of that unity into some simple underlying ground or principle (the later commitment expressed in the idea of *Gleichursprünglichkeit*—"equiprimordiality"), the way in which Heidegger gives priority to temporality inevitably leads to a situation in which the unity of *Dasein*, and so also the unity of being, is understood as a unity given in and through temporality alone—which is why one might say of *Being and Time* that it leads us to a position that understands being *as* time. Such an idea appears completely out of place in the later thinking not only because there time is conjoined with space as timespace (*Zeitraum*), but also because that thinking is so clearly focused on a unity that is irreducibly plural, and in which each of the key elements that articulate that unity stand in necessary and reciprocal relations to one another.

This is not to say, however, that there is no difference in the way in which the individual elements of the Fourfold are related or that those relations are so simple and schematic that they require no comment—that there is no possibility of finding an analytical structure in the later thinking. Since part of the problem with *Being and Time* is the very mode of analysis that it attempts—a mode of analysis that looks to uncover a systematic structure through the uncovering of levels of ontological dependency and that is evident in the style of Heidegger's thinking and writing in the earlier work—so the later thinking is characterized by an abandonment of that mode of analysis and a very different manner of approach. It is an approach in which one can find Heidegger exploring, across many essays and lectures, a single complex structure of relations that nevertheless bears comparison with the structure evident in *Being and Time*[25]—in the case of the Fourfold, for instance, the relation between earth and sky draws upon a set of primarily spatial elements that also sets up an important connection to language, while the relation between gods and mortals is fundamentally temporal in its orientation in a way that invokes notions of fatefulness and history—notions that, it should be emphasized, do not fall outside of or stand in opposition to the project of Heideggerian topology.

Place and the History of Being

The history of being in Heidegger is not so much a descriptive account of the stages in the development of philosophical thought, but is rather closely tied to Heidegger's attempt to think the character of the happening of world, as well as of philosophy's own relation to that happening. Heidegger's thinking on the history of being revolves around two "events," or perhaps better, two *topoi*. The first is the beginning of philosophy among the Greeks and the thinking of being that is evident in the pre-Socratic philosophers. It is often assumed that Heidegger has a conception of pre-Socratic thinking as standing in some privileged relation to the question of being such that, for the pre-Socratics, being was somehow directly evident to them in a way that is now lost. It seems to me, in fact, that what Heidegger finds among the pre-Socratics, or at least among certain of them, is a sense of the unity and complexity of being that has not yet succumbed to the tendency to explain that unitary complexity through the posting of some ground or principle that stands apart from it.

That there is a question about the unity of being is evident to the pre-Socratics; that it is a question to be answered by looking to a unity that underlies or is apart from beings is not a possibility to which they succumb. Here, then, is the beginning of philosophy: in the recognition of the fundamental questionability of things. This recognition of questionability can itself be understood as given in the recognition of the ontological difference, since the recognition of that difference is just the recognition of the possibility of a question about beings that is not addressed by looking to beings alone. Yet the recognition of the ontological difference also opens up the possibility of an answer that will look to being as something other than and apart from beings as their underlying ground and principle, and that will, in treating being in this way, inevitably reduce being to something other than it is, and, in so doing, will also lose sight of the questionability that is essential to being and to thought as such.[26] In the beginning of philosophy we thus see that which impels us to philosophize and is the proper ground of philosophy, and that nevertheless also moves philosophy on a path that will bring the second of the two *topoi* at issue here into view—that which is the *end* of philosophy.

Neither philosophy's beginning nor its end are properly to be understood merely as temporal "stages" in some intellectual chronology of being—they are instead *topoi* for the happening of being. Heidegger's own comments on the "end" of philosophy make this quite clear: "The old meaning of the word 'end' means the same as place: 'from one end to the other' means: from one place to the other. The end of philosophy is the place, that place in which the whole of philosophy's history is gathered in its most extreme possibility. End as completion means this gathering."[27] The place that is the end of philosophy is not in sight because philosophy appears now to be coming to a stop, but because the possibilities that were already evident in its beginning have now drawn together in their most extreme realization—one consequence is that philosophy has exhausted a proper sense of the questionability of things that has sustained it, and, in losing that sense of questionability, has also lost a sense of its own historicity. In this respect, Francis Fukuyama's famous claim about the "end of history" may have proved to be premature so far as world history is concerned (especially in the light of the contemporary rise of new forms of competing fundamentalist and nationalist ideologies, to say nothing of the possibility of the sort of economic collapse that we have witnessed more recently). However, that prediction was, in a sense, correct, if belated, with regard to philosophy, and so also with regard to the understanding of the world that philosophy sustains and expresses. As used here, not only does "end" carry a particular meaning, but so too does "philosophy." The latter term (which, like many other key words, operates equivocally in Heidegger's thinking[28]) here names something that is inextricable from the particular form of technological modernity that is dominant across the earth—and remains dominant in spite of those movements that claim to be opposed to it. The end of philosophy is thus to be seen in that mode of ordering of the world as well as the mode of thinking that accompanies it, that understands itself no longer as a stage in human history, but as instead a transformation in the historical (the modern thus understands itself as radically disjoint from its own past), that sees the only questions as essentially technical or "rational" in character. This is why Heidegger claims that the present age is the age of nihilism—it is the nihilism that comes from the collapse of questionability, the end of history, and the closing off of the openness of the future.

One might suppose that Heidegger's concern with the history of being—which is clearest, it should be noted, in the writings from the later 1930s and early 1940s—represents a continuation of the concern with temporality that characterized *Being and Time*. Yet the understanding of the history of being, though historical, is not thereby exclusively temporal. The happening of place and of world is, in every instance, a happening that both allows things to come to presence as the very things they are and yet does so in a way that also allows them to come to presence in a distinctive fashion. Indeed, things never come to presence in their generality, but always in a way that is singular and distinctive—and that happening of presence is not random or ad hoc, but is rather determined by the particular historical determination of the place as such. The historical is thus not opposed to the topological, but encompassed by it. The history of being is itself a history of place, both in the sense that the philosophical history of place correlates with key movements in the history of philosophical thought as such,[29] and in the sense that the history of being is a history of the successive formations of place—a history of successive *topoi* (of which its beginning and its end are only the most salient)—in which the ending of history is to be found in the nihilism of the almost complete forgetting of being that is also a forgetting of place.

Heidegger's critique of technology, which is strongest in his postwar writings (although already adumbrated even in *Being and Time*), represents a drawing together of the history of being into the explicitly topological frame of the later thinking. Technological modernity is thus understood not only as the culmination of the metaphysical tendency toward nihilism, but also in terms of a specific modification of time and space that reduces the thing to mere resource and place to simple location. Yet in its essence—which Heidegger calls *Gestell*, the "Enframing" or "Framework"—technological modernity remains a mode of the happening of place, albeit one that refuses to recognize its own character in this regard. This means that technological modernity, while it gives to things the look of mere resource, nevertheless continues to allow things to appear, and so also allows (if "inadvertently") for the possibility that they might appear in ways that disrupt their character as resource.[30] It is the tension between the appearing of things *as things*, even in their appearing *as resource*, the appearing of place *as place*, even in its apparent reduction to simple location or "site," that constitutes both the "saving power" of technology as well as its danger.

Place and the Turning

The character of Heidegger's later thinking as attending to things in their multiple unity—and so also, I would say, in their essential and abiding *questionability*—can be seen as the articulation of a mode of thinking that stands in sharp contrast to the character of the thinking that is associated with technological modernity. Technological modernity understands things as unified through their reducibility to a single ordering from which nothing is excluded. Although *Being and Time* was intended to overcome the forgetting of being that is instantiated in technological modernity, one of the lessons of Heidegger's own path of thinking is that the tendency that drives us toward such forgetting, of which technological modernity represents the most extreme form, is one that is evident even in *Being and Time*'s own desire to understand the happening of world in terms of the pure unity of temporality. *Being and Time* (like philosophy and metaphysics more generally) thus points in two directions: on to the later thinking as well as back to the thinking that it aims, unsuccessfully, to overcome.[31]

The transition from Heidegger's early to his later thinking turns on Heidegger's thinking and rethinking of place and its relation to being. That Turning is already underway in the early thinking, and in *Being and Time*. The turn to place is thus not something that occurs only following the failure of the early work, but is instead a turning within the turning that was already underway. A large part of the radicality of Heidegger's philosophy, right from the start, lay in his attempt to engage with the fundamentally situated, placed, character of being and existence. But place, as Aristotle famously observed in a passage Heidegger repeats, is "something overwhelming and hard to grasp."[32] It is perhaps not surprising, therefore, that Heidegger's own turning to place remains often unstable and uncertain. Although one might say that this is especially true of his early thinking, the inevitability of such instability and uncertainty to any thoughtful engagement is surely itself part of what is at issue in Heidegger's thematization of the turning that belongs to thinking as such, as well as to Heidegger's own thinking, and together with this, his emphasis on the centrality of questioning to thinking.

Although the Turning is a turning back to place, it is also more immediately understood in the Heideggerian context as a turning back (in the sense of a returning or reorienting) to being. Being is *presence* (on this point Heidegger remains insistent[33]), and so the turning back to being is also a turning back to presence. Yet the presence at issue here is merely not the determinate appearing of things in the present, though this is one aspect of presence. More properly, it is the appearing of things in a sameness and multiplicity that always goes beyond any single determination—a constant unfolding of things as things. This is why being and questionability belong together, and why the question of being is one with the being of the question, since for something to be present is for it to appear *as questionable*, as standing within a free play (*Spielraum*) of possibility that can never be exhausted. Yet this inexhaustibility of appearance, this dynamic indeterminacy of presence, though it always remains, is nevertheless also constantly solidifying into the simple unity of a determinate aspect. For this reason, thinking, as a turning back to presence, is also an overcoming of the forgetfulness that takes presence to be nothing other than that simple determinate unity as it already stands before. It is thus that we return once again to Heidegger's characterization of thinking as a remembering or recollection, and also, since he takes remembrance to be a form of thanking (as it is an attending to and recognition of what is already given), as a form of giving thanks.[34]

The turning back to being, to presence, to the thing, that is at issue in the Turning is also, of course, a turning in relation to place. The very understanding of being as presence already indicates the topological orientation that is at issue here and that underpins all of Heidegger's thinking whether explicitly or implicitly. Certainly the understanding of being as presence carries with it a specifically *temporal* connotation, and it is this connotation that comes to the fore in Heidegger's early thinking, but presence is better understood as encompassing both a sense of the temporal *and* the spatial that is only properly expressed in terms of the notion of place or *topos* (and place can never be simply identified with the spatial alone). Presence always calls upon place—presence is a being-here/being-there—just as place also calls upon presence. Thinking is then a turning back into the place in which we already find ourselves and to which we are given over; thinking is a putting in question of our own place as we turn back to it. The turn *to* place in Heidegger's thought, which is itself a turning *in* and *of* place, is also indicative of the way in which all of Heidegger's thinking itself turns around the single question of place, and in which, in this place, all of the other elements in his thinking are brought together. The question of place may thus be said to be all that Heidegger's thought addresses—not in the sense that this is *only* what is at issue, but in the sense that this question *encompasses* every other question, and is that to which every other question must be brought back. In this respect, it is especially significant that the foundational role given to the work of art in "The Origin of the Work of Art" has disappeared from his later writings—the thing gathers the elements of world in a single place, but no one thing does this in an epochal or unique fashion. The gathering of place that is the happening of presence and of world is a constant and multiple occurrence rather than a single founding or positing, whether by any human act or in any single preeminent element or thing.[35]

Topos as Surface and Structure

The style and approach of Heidegger's later thinking, especially the language it employs, presents itself as much less analytical, perhaps less rigorous than that of the earlier, and is often more declamatory in its presentation. It is thus that his later thinking is frequently characterized as "poetic" (or even "mystical"—the latter characterization being one of which Heidegger seems to have been particularly dismissive). It may be, however, that the stylistic and methodological shift that occurs between his early and later thinking (and properly there is not one shift, but a number) is best understood as Heidegger's response to the need to find a way of thinking, and especially of writing, that is attentive to the complex unity of the presencing of things—the worlding of world, the happening of truth—and that does not dissolve that complexity into something that is other than it. One might say that in this regard, the "poetic" character of Heidegger's later thinking—if we are to use this characterization at all— refers us to the way in which Heidegger aims at a certain attentiveness to "surface," and so to just appearing or presencing as such. It is worth noting that this focus on "surface" allows us to glimpse another way in which Heidegger's approach is properly characterized as topological, since "surface" is one sense that might be attached to the notion of *topos* (a sense evident in Aristotle's use of the term,[36] as well as its use within the early history of geography and in modern mathematical topology).

What may also be indicated here is an important difference between the sense in which Heidegger's early thinking was "phenomenological" and the sense in which this term might be used in relation to his later thinking. In *Being and Time*, phenomenology is directed toward uncovering those structures or conditions, obscured by everydayness, that make possible the appearing of things.[37] The aim is, in one sense, to "see into" things, to the true "phenomena" that are obscured or disguised by our usual modes of engagement. But in his later thinking, it is not so much a matter of seeing *into* things in this way—a mode of seeing that, against Heidegger's own admonitions, can easily be read as a seeing through or beyond—but rather a seeing that remains *with*, allowing things to shine in their very presencing, and in that shining to light up the structure of the world that shelters and sustains them. Rather than "seeing through" a disguise, it is a matter of the proper *placing* of things. If this is phenomenology, it is a different sort of phenomenology than is evident in the early work, so much so that, like Heidegger, we may chose not to call it "phenomenology" at all—alternatively, we may well be led to rethink what phenomenology itself might be.[38]

Not only does Heidegger abandon talk of his later thinking as "phenomenology," but the notion of the transcendental disappears from his later thinking as well, both terms having a close connection to one another. The abandonment of the language of the transcendental is a direct consequence of the problems that he takes to surround the notion of transcendence (the transcendental being viewed by Heidegger as that which enables transcendence).[39] What we can see here, however, is the way in which the focus on the transcendental in terms of a focus on "conditions of possibility" can be construed as also potentially problematic precisely through the way in which it separates the conditions from what is conditioned, through the way in which it requires a form of "looking through" rather than "remaining with."[40]

The fact that there is no single work that stands as the counterpart in Heidegger's later thinking to *Being and Time* in the earlier is itself an indication of the shift that has occurred. Yet across the many essays and lectures in which the later thinking is set out and developed we can see a philosophical vision and an analytical structure that is no less complex nor less differentiated than that in *Being and Time*—and it is, of course, a vision and structure that is continuous with that of *Being and Time* even while diverging from it. It seems to me that the key to understanding the structure that stands at the heart of Heidegger's later thinking is to understand that Heidegger is indeed attempting a "topology of being," and that means that we have to understand structures like the structure of the Fourfold or of the Event as themselves essentially topological in character—the Fourfold is the structure of *topos* and the Event is the happening of place.

I have talked frequently of "structure" in the account offered here, and topology itself might be thought to appear as a sort of "structural" analysis. In discussing one of my earlier works, Ed Casey takes issue with such talk in relation to the later Heidegger (as does Ingrid Stefanovic elsewhere).[41] Yet when Heidegger sets out the interplay of earth, sky, gods and mortals as constitutive of the Fourfold, what else is he doing but setting out and elaborating a structure? It is certainly a different structure from that to be found in *Being and Time*, but it is a structure nonetheless. The question is not whether there is a structure, but what kind of structure it is. If what Heidegger does in his later thinking is to think being through place, and if the structure that is set out in essays like "Building Dwelling Thinking" is the structure of place, then this seems to me to force us to recognize the way in which what is given here is indeed a structure that is constituted through the mutual interplay of multiple elements, a structure that encompasses the entities and elements that appear within it rather than underlying them, a structure to which belongs a unity that is given only in and through the mutual relatedness of the elements that make it up. This place is not one that is to be grounded in the human alone, since only in such a place can the human even appear, and yet it is a place that cannot appear apart from the human—just as it cannot appear apart from the divine, apart from that which is of the earth and of the sky.[42]

In understanding the structure at issue here as topological, we must understand that the structure of place, and the unity that belongs to that structure, is not something apart from the place itself. If we were to use the language of the ontological difference, this means that the unity of the place, although different from it, is not something apart from the place. This is where the notion of the ontological difference can itself mislead—it may be taken to suggest that being is something apart and aside from beings. But being and beings belong together, and it is the increasing recognition of this that leads Heidegger not only to rethink the issue of unity as such, but also to regard the ontological difference itself as suspect. Thus in a later comment on his earlier writings he notes that "Da-sein belongs to beyng itself as the simple onefold of beings and being," and this emphasis appears in a number of places in the later writings.[43] It is this "onefold" that is also articulated through the unity of *topos*—a unity that encompasses the unity of time and space, as well as of existentiality and facticity, of thing and world, of concealing and revealing.

Conclusion: The Significance of Heidegger's Later Thinking

There can be no doubt that there is a way of approaching Heidegger's thinking that focuses on *Being and Time* as the central work in that thinking. Yet if Heidegger's own dissatisfaction with *Being and Time* was well founded, then there will always be certain insuperable difficulties in the attempt to fully articulate what is at issue in that work. That is not to say that the task of such articulation and exploration should not continue to be attempted, but that we need to keep in mind the fact that such an attempt, if it is concerned with the philosophical problems themselves rather than with issues of historical scholarship alone, must inevitably lead us beyond *Being and Time*, and on to Heidegger's later thinking. Unfortunately, the power of the earlier work, both the intrinsic power of its concepts and of its philosophical influence, as well as the fact that it remains within a much more traditional philosophical framework, has meant that the earlier work rather than the later has dominated philosophical discussion of Heidegger's philosophy. Yet the later Heidegger does not fade away into mysticism or poetry—indeed, in one important sense, a move *away* from mysticism is achieved precisely through the more explicit thematization of *topos*.[44] The development of the later thinking is directly tied to the problems evident in the earlier, and so an adequate engagement with the earlier thinking must require an engagement with the later thinking also—and such an engagement demands a respect for the later thinking as well as an appreciation of the way in which it both breaks with and nevertheless also continues the project of which *Being and Time* is merely a part.

3   The Place of Topology

The idea of philosophical topology, or "topography" as I call it outside of the Heideggerian context, takes the idea of place or *topos* as the focus for the understanding of the human, the understanding of world, and the understanding of the philosophical. Although the idea is not indebted solely to Heidegger's thinking (it also draws, most notably, on the work of Donald Davidson and Hans-Georg Gadamer), it is probably to Heidegger that it owes the most. Moreover, one of my claims (a claim that underpins many of the essays here) is that Heidegger's own work cannot adequately be understood except as topological in character, and so as centrally concerned with place—*topos, Ort, Ortschaft* (which, I should emphasize again, is not the same as a concern with space nor with time taken separately from one another). I do not regard myself as the only person to make this claim, or something like it. In the 1980s, both Joseph Fell and Reiner Schürmann, from very different perspectives, advanced topological readings of Heidegger (or elements of such readings) that contain important points of convergence with my own.[1] More recently, Edward Casey has also discussed Heidegger from the perspective of place,[2] while a number of writers, including Theodore Schatzki and Stuart Elden, have provided important investigations of Heidegger's treatment of place and space.[3] If my work represents, in any way, an advance on the work of other writers such as these, it is primarily in that I have attempted to set out a definitive case for the topological reading of Heidegger's thinking in its entirety, as well as to articulate an account of topology or topography as itself central to philosophical inquiry. On my account, the attempt to think place, and to think in accord with place, is at the heart of philosophy as such.

Yet the taking of place as a central concept here is not without its difficulties, and the most immediate and obvious of these concerns the very understanding of place that is at issue. Place is an opaque and evanescent concept, resistant to standard forms of philosophical analysis, often seeming to dissipate like smoke at the first breath of inquiry, leaving us to turn to what may appear to be the more substantial and substantive notions of space and time. It is the Heideggerian concept of place, with its difficulties and obscurities, that lies at the center of a set of critical responses to my development of Heideggerian topology that have been offered by Steven Crowell, Miguel de Beistegui, Julian Young, and Edward Relph. For each of these responses, a different aspect of place is the focus: for Crowell, it is the relation between place and *subjectivity*, and together with this, between topology and *phenomenology*; for Beistegui, it is the relation to *temporality* and also *historicity*; for Young, it is its relation to the notion of *Heimat*, as well as to the experience of *wonder*; and for Relph it is the way place is taken up in the concept of dwelling (a notion of which Relph is critical) and the significance of place for the understanding of technological modernity.

Phenomenology and Subjectivity

One of the key philosophical questions, the very first question, in fact, concerns the origin of our thinking—where does thinking begin? This is already a question raised in the discussions above, and to which I shall return below.[4] It is, however, a question that also seems to arise within the more explicitly phenomenological frame that Crowell invokes when he asks: "is transcendental topology phenomenological?"[5]

To ask after the origin of thinking is already to place oneself within the ambit of the topological. The reason for this is simple: to ask after the origin of thinking—to ask after the "where" out of which thinking comes— is already to ask after the "place" of thinking. Here the connection of "origin" with "ground," and of both these with place, also becomes apparent. The question of origin is thus not a question about the temporal or historical *starting point* for thinking, nor is it a question about the *cause* of thinking (at least, not in the modern sense in which this term is usually employed, and not in terms of such a cause either psychologically or physically construed). To ask after origin in a genuinely philosophical sense, in the sense, for instance, in which it is surely at issue in phenomenology, is to ask after that on and in which thinking finds its footing and support, from which it takes its orientation and direction.[6]

The topological character of the question at issue here may not always be explicit, but the question is nevertheless one that certainly appears within phenomenology. In fact, one might well argue that the question of the origin of thinking lies at the very heart of phenomenology (something indicated by phenomenological concern with *phenomena*—with what appears), as well as at the heart of Heidegger's thinking (whether or not that thinking remains itself phenomenological). So far as Crowell's overarching question is concerned, "is transcendental topology phenomenological?," my immediate answer is thus in the affirmative, but my reason is that phenomenology is itself essentially topological. In saying this, however, I mean also to suggest that what Crowell takes to be characteristic of phenomenology, namely the concern with subjectivity, and especially first-person subjectivity, does not take us in the direction of the *atopic*, as Crowell argues, but itself returns us back to *topos*. My answer thus depends on a somewhat opposed concept of the phenomenological to that which appears to be operative in Crowell's work.

The question about the place in which thinking has its origin is the central question of philosophical topology or topography—topology is, as we already saw in chapter 1, an attempt to think the place of thinking. But it attempts to think that place in its original and originary character— that is to say, it does not begin with a philosophical *interpretation* of the place in which we first find ourselves, but rather looks to that place as it is given in and of itself. That means that the appearing of place, and what appears with it, cannot be treated as the appearing of an already recognized subject that stands against some object (nor in terms of the appearing of some array of impressions, sense data, or whatever else we may come up with after the fact). What first appears is just the appearing of a place that is a certain definite region, *bounded* and yet also thereby *gathered*, in which we and the things around us are given *together* (it is this that I take to be at the heart of Heidegger's notion of the *Ereignis*[7]).

The concern with the thinking of place *as* the place of thinking immediately brings topology and phenomenology close together. That this is so seems to me evident from Heidegger's own entry into phenomenology as itself a way of reengaging with life, with our immediate immersed experience—something also evident in the emphasis on hermeneutic situatedness in his early work. But it is also apparent in the very nature of phenomenological analysis as developed by both Heidegger and Husserl. There are two points that I would make here.

First, although the phenomenological *epoché* is often taken to be a bracketing-off of the world, and so as a move that gives priority to pure consciousness (whatever that may be), it can also be read as a bracketing-off of those attitudes and presuppositions that remove us from our primary experience of being already in the world. In fact, this reading of the *epoché* returns to something of the original meaning of the idea as it appears among the early skeptics, for whom the *epoché* was essentially a putting into abeyance of the philosophical desire to judge the natures of things—rather than first engaging with things through an attempt to determine *what* they are (in the sense of their "real" natures), we engage with things on the basis of the fact *that* they are (on the basis of their immediate "appearances"). In Heidegger, this way of understanding the *epoché* (although not made explicit, and certainly without any reference to its skeptical deployment) seems to me to underlie those early expositions in which he emphasizes that our very first encounter with things is indeed with the things as they appear. It can surely also be seen to underlie the phenomenological exhortation to return *to the things themselves*—to what is given, rather than to what, after the fact, we think is given.

Second, the way in which Husserl understands the structure of meaningful experience is in terms of a set of notions that are themselves essentially topological in character, so that the structure of phenomenological presentation is identical with the structure of place. This should be no surprise. To be is *to be in place*, and to be a phenomenon, an appearing, is similarly to be placed, or, one might say, to *take place*. This is not merely to say that appearing must be somewhere, but that the form of the appearing will be such as to occur within a certain domain that is open so as to allow for that appearing, and yet also bounded so that the appearing is indeed an appearing of some thing.[8] Here is the basic structure of *horizon* and *intention* that we find in Husserl—a structure that is both fundamental and also topological (and that remains so no matter what might be claimed regarding the extent to which this structure is a structure of consciousness). It is significant that for all that Heidegger distances himself from phenomenology in his later work, the topological elements that are present at the core of phenomenology remain—so in the *Country Path Conversations* (*Feldweg-Gespräche*), from 1944 to 1945, in which topological themes predominate, so too does the idea of horizon play a central role (horizon is itself directly connected with the notion of region, and so also to "gathering").[9]

The concern with the place of thinking also determines the "transcendental" character of topological inquiry, since understood in this manner, such inquiry is always an attempt to think the ground of thinking (the resonance of ground with place is not to be overlooked here), which is just to say that it is the attempt to think that out of which the possibility of thinking emerges. Inevitably, to take topology as transcendental in this way is also to commit to a particular understanding of the transcendental—transcendental thinking itself has to be understood topologically, and this involves some significant shifts in how the transcendental is to be understood.[10]

Heidegger's own critique of transcendental approaches is tied to the increasingly topological character of his thinking. The transcendental is an idea he comes to see, by the 1930s at least, as entailing two problematic elements. First, because he takes the transcendental to be concerned with the conditions that underlie the possibility of transcendence, and transcendence as a structure of subjectivity, he views the transcendental as already given over to a form of subjectivist thinking. Second, because the transcendental sets up a contrast between that which conditions and that which is conditioned, so he also sees it as inadequate to address the proper unity of that which is the coming to presence of what presences—since the contrast at issue here is itself related to the ontological difference, Heidegger comes eventually to regard that difference as also problematic.

Can one understand the idea of phenomenology without recourse to the notion of the transcendental? My own view (and I realize that this is not a view universally shared) is that one cannot—that part of what is distinctive about phenomenology is its properly transcendental orientation—and so one cannot inquire into the nature of phenomenology without also inquiring into the nature of the transcendental (although, having said this, I should emphasize, in a way that preempts some of the following discussion, that what I mean by the "transcendental" here is not a project directed at the erection of some philosophical susperstructure of categorial machinery, but rather an inquiry that looks to uncover the proper "place" of appearance).[11] The transcendental is itself often understood in terms of a concern with subjectivity, and with the self-constituting power of subjectivity—the latter being something explicitly thematized by Kant.[12] I do not disagree with this characterization, so long as we acknowledge that part of what is at issue in such transcendental inquiry is the nature of subjectivity as such. What, we may ask, is subjectivity if it is self-constituting in the required way? This is not a question whose answer I think we can simply assume, and subjectivity is thus a concept as much in need of interrogation as is the transcendental.

Since the transcendental and the phenomenological are so closely entangled, Heidegger's shift away from the transcendental can be seen, as he himself saw it, as entailing a shift away from phenomenology. In Heidegger, of course, this also coincides with a shift away from the approach set out in *Being and Time*, a work that explicitly set itself within a transcendental and phenomenological frame. The shift at issue here is one that can be seen to be driven by Heidegger's increasingly explicit thematization of topological elements in his thinking, and, as a result, the movement away from the transcendental and phenomenological appears as a shift toward topology, thereby setting the transcendental and the phenomenological in apparent opposition to the topological (with the complication that later Heidegger seems to view *all* his thinking as a mode of topology—as a *Topologie des Seyns*).[13]

Although at times I have found myself tending to favor the contrast that appears in late Heidegger between the topological and the transcendental and phenomenological, and so to argue for the former as replacing the latter, my more considered view is that once one arrives at a topological perspective what is required is not an abandonment, but a rethinking of the transcendental and the phenomenological in topological terms—and I tend to think that Heidegger would not have been averse to such a view himself. What this means is that one also has to rethink the way in which those two elements that Heidegger identifies as problematic—the tendency toward subjectivism and the inadequate thinking of unity—can themselves be thought.

In fact, this was already a key aspect of my work on the transcendental even before I began to think of it in more developed topological terms.[14] Thus, I have always argued that it is a mistake to think of the transcendental as primarily an argumentative structure in which there is a clear separation of conditioning from conditioned elements, and a movement from one to the other. Instead, the "circularity" of the transcendental is a reflection of the essential unity that the transcendental itself sets forth and aims to make explicit. The unity at issue is, however, not a simple, but rather a complex unity—a *differentiated* unity.[15] Moreover, although the transcendental is often interpreted as attempting, in Kantian terms, to ground the unity of experience in the unity of the self-constituting subjective (in the Heideggerian terms of *Being and Time*, to ground the unity of world-projection in the unity of *Dasein*'s own temporalizing), it is better understood as attempting to exhibit the already prior unity of experience and subjectivity, or better, of world and self. Moreover, the unity at issue here is nothing other than a unity given in the differentiated interplay of the elements—and this is the very same form of unity that is exhibited in later Heidegger in terms of the gathering of the Fourfold. It is a form of unity that I argue belongs essentially to place.

Crowell's approach to the question of the relation between topology and phenomenology focuses specifically on the phenomenological concern with experience, and especially its first-personal character, as well as with the character of subjectivity. Already some of what I have said should indicate that I do not see topology as ignoring such concerns. One way of thinking about topological analysis, in fact, is precisely in terms of a rethinking of subjectivity in terms of *topos* (I would argue that this is just what is presaged in Husserl's own analysis, and in its reliance on notions like that of horizon, as well as in the critical philosophy of Kant—although the latter claim is perhaps harder to explicate and defend[16]). Place or *topos* is certainly not a univocal concept on my account, but like most significant concepts in philosophy, and especially in Heidegger, it carries with it an essential multivocity—what I referred to in *Heidegger's Topology* as *iridescence* (since the multivocity here is one of overlapping and shifting aspects rather than a set of distinct and easily denumerable senses).[17]

In *Place and Experience*, I explicitly draw attention to what I refer to as the *complexity* of place. This complexity is evident in the "folded" character of place (which, it should be clear, is not intended to refer in any way to the "fold" that appears in Deleuze)—the way any place encompasses other places within it while also being encompassed by other places in its turn. It is also evident in the way in which place names both that which supports and grounds the appearing of any and every place as well as the various appearances of place as such—it refers to both *this* place and to the very place or placedness of which this place *is an instance*. The distinction at issue here is, not surprisingly, an analogue of the ontological difference. However, whereas the ontological difference can give rise to the mistaken apprehension that what is at issue is indeed a twofold structure that relates two different and distinct elements—being *and* beings—it is harder to think this way in relation to the difference at issue in regard to place. Place cannot be other than what is given in the multiplicity of places—to suppose otherwise would be to envisage the possibility of place, *topos*, as itself *atopic*, and although there may be circumstances in which this is a form of words to which we are drawn, the immediate oddity of such a mode of speech and thought ought also to indicate its problematic character (and indicate it in a more direct way than is evident in talk of ontological difference). One might say that the difference at issue in these two senses of place (which represent only one aspect of the differentiating unity of place) is like that between a surface and the plane to which that surface belongs—a difference that itself insists on the sameness of that which differs.

I will come back to this difference below, since it is also relevant to certain issues raised by Julian Young. For the moment, the difference is significant because of the way it stands opposed to what seems to me to be a tendency in Crowell's discussion not only to read place in a more univocal fashion than I indicate here (and I say this is a *tendency*, because I do not think that this is a straightforward element in Crowell's discussion), but also to treat place in a way that overlooks its role as ground for the appearing of place, at the same time as place is positioned apart from subjectivity, and in a way that seems to take it as identical with *world* or something given *within* the world.

Consider Crowell's claim that "within the *topos* of what is disclosed—the world wherein is found the claim-responsive human being together with all the other things that are—the being who is 'claimed by being' is not dependent on the world in the same way that the world is dependent on it."[18] What this passage seems to suppose is that *topos* names "the world wherein is found the claim-responsive human being together with all the things that are." But *topos* cannot be unambiguously identified with the world or with what the world contains. Certainly, specific *topoi* are within the world, but *topos* as such names the very happening of world as that occurs in and through the happening of place. Moreover, the *topos* that is invoked here, in its multiplicity, is constituted in many different modes, including that mode that we encounter in our own selves—in the "withinness" of experience that itself occurs within and in relation to the *topos* (and *topoi*) of worldly locatedness.

At this point, it should be evident that part of the complexity that surrounds topology is a complexity that reflects the dual operation of topology as a mode of philosophical thinking—a mode of analysis—that employs topological structures, figures, and distinctions (and which I would argue is implicated in all thinking), and as a substantive focus for such thinking. Place is thus that which thinking essentially addresses and also that which determines the mode of that address. The thinking of place is always a thinking in and through place, and this itself makes for a complexity in the thinking of place over and above even the complexity that attaches to place as such. Moreover, the complexity that appears here is a complexity that runs throughout Heidegger's own thinking, and is one of the reasons for its often dense and opaque character—all the more so since Heidegger never directly thematizes nor attempts explicitly to articulate the implications of the topology in which he is engaged.

Crowell's attempt to set subjectivity off from *topos*, as in some sense prior to it, is surely inconsistent with *topos* understood in the multiple and complex fashion set out here, and which I would argue also underpins my work elsewhere. It may be that Crowell would want to contest this way of understanding *topos*, or contest its adequacy for addressing the philosophical issues that concern us, and this would be quite reasonable, but it would raise an additional set of issues, and move us into a further conversation that cannot properly be embarked upon here. There are, however, two related issues that are already present in Crowell's original discussion that deserve some further comment: one concerns the notion of priority, and the other normativity.

Let us take normativity first, since this is a topic that is increasingly at the center of much contemporary philosophical thinking. Advancing what may be viewed as a defense of certain aspects of Heidegger's approach in *Being and Time* (of which my account in *Heidegger's Topology* is highly critical), Crowell argues that the dependence of practices of normativity on human subjects, coupled with the centrality of such normativity to the very possibility of the disclosedness of things, implies that, within the structure of disclosedness, priority has to be given to human subjectivity. Leaving the issue of how priority itself is to be understood here (an issue to which I shall return below), the difficulty that I have with this argument is that it seems to presuppose the idea of normativity at the same time as it also seeks to elucidate the grounds of normativity.

One reason for saying this is that it is not at all clear that Crowell's conception of subjectivity can itself be elucidated without reference to notions of normative practice. For instance, if one adopts the sort of externalist conception of human subjectivity that I set out in *Place and Experience* (and that is to some extent presupposed, if not much thematized, in *Heidegger's Topology*), then the subject cannot be understood independently of the world in which the subject is located (or independently of the places in which the subject acts), but normative content and normative practice cannot be understood independently of the world either. Normative content and normative practice are dependent on subjects *and* on the objective world in which those subjects are embedded.[19] Against such a background, the idea that normativity, as operating through the structure of existential responsibility, might provide the basis for a notion of the atopic makes little sense. Indeed, it seems that this can only be meaningful if we already presuppose much of what is supposed to be elucidated.

To some extent my concern here could be expressed by saying that subjectivity and normativity are not sufficiently distinct concepts such that one can provide an elucidation of the other, and inasmuch as both are externalistically determined and constrained, so neither can be elucidated without reference to the subject's prior embeddedness in a world, and in an already given structure of normative practice. To use the ideas of Donald Davidson as an example here, the structure of Davidsonian triangulation depends on the capacity of the triangulating speaker to engage in normative acts. In a certain sense, triangulation depends on the possibility of subjectivity and normativity. However, the structure of triangulation provides the frame within which normativity and subjectivity are both constituted: to be a subject and to be subject to norms is to be enmeshed within a certain triangulative structure. Without expanding on the point here, this triangulative structure is also, I would say, topological.[20]

Crowell's argument for the priority of subjectivity obviously raises a question as to the notion of priority that is in play here. Priority is itself an important topic in *Heidegger's Topology* as well as in *Place and Experience* (although it is perhaps less to the fore in the latter work). Priority has also been a key element in my discussions elsewhere, especially in my treatments of the transcendental. One of the recurrent themes in my thinking has been the idea that traditional philosophy has been preoccupied not only with understanding certain key concepts univocally, but also with establishing relations of reduction or derivation between those concepts (or between the entities, elements, or principles to which those concepts refer). In contrast, the idea of philosophical topology or topography is intended as a way of doing philosophy that, although it does not eschew analytic concerns, looks to understand the structures that are the focus of its inquiries in ways, first, that deploy concepts in their multivocity, and so in their complexity and multiplicity, and second, that look to uncover relations of what I term *mutual* rather than hierarchical dependence. This is in keeping with the idea of *topos* as itself a *surface*, and so as constituted in terms of the relatedness of the elements that make up that surface (much as elements in a landscape are determined through their relative location[21]), rather than by anything that lies beneath or above that surface. Yet as Crowell correctly notes, and as I have myself acknowledged,[22] some notion of priority may still be operative even where reductive or derivative approaches are not (one may thus distinguish between strong and weak senses of priority). It is thus that Crowell finds a space still to argue for the priority of the subject, who stands at the center of practices of normativity, over the *topos* in which those practices, as well as the subject herself, are located.

In *Being and Time*, Heidegger holds to the presence of certain relations of priority exist even within structures whose elements stand in relations of mutual dependence. Thus, within the structure of originary temporality, the future has a priority with respect to the other temporal modalities.[23] The priority at work here is a weak sense, just inasmuch as it implies a primacy to the future, but does not allow of any derivation from it or reduction to it. In *Heidegger's Topology*, I take the presence of such weak priority to be an inevitable part of what is involved in the very idea of any form of structural analysis that would lay bare the ordering of a domain— weak priority is thus a matter of the order that obtains within that domain. One has to be extremely careful, however, about just how even this notion of priority is understood, and in some ways, considering Crowell's comments, and looking back at my own account in *Heidegger's Topology*, I am tempted to say that priority, even weakly construed, may be the wrong concept to employ here—that it may simply mislead in ways that are too difficult to avoid.

This seems especially so in the case of Crowell's discussion. Although priority, as Crowell deploys it, is explicitly shorn of any connection with derivative or reductive modes of analysis, it is hard to see how it can be anything other than the priority associated with hierarchical dependence. The way in which Crowell formulates the notion of priority is fairly general—it requires simply the notion of one-way or asymmetrical dependence. Thus subjectivity is said to be prior to our worldly placedness on the grounds that although we cannot speak of our place in the world without reference to subjectivity, we can speak of subjectivity without reference to our place in the world. It is, of course, partly because of my externalist conception of the self that I am led immediately to deny that there is any asymmetrical dependence here, but the more pertinent observation is that priority understood in terms of such asymmetrical dependence almost exactly accords with the definition of hierarchical dependence I advance in *Heidegger's Topology*.[24] The latter definition does not itself call upon the notion of derivation or reduction, although it does argue that relations of hierarchical dependence are typically associated with derivative or reductive approaches. In fact, in very many cases of asymmetrical dependence, some relation of derivation, even if not of reduction, does seem to apply. In the asymmetrical dependence exemplified in generation, for instance, the generated entity or element derives from that which generates, as the child derives from the parent, or the statue is derived from the sculptor.[25] In the relation between universal and particular, also a case of asymmetrical dependence, a relation of derivation can be understood to obtain at least in regard to the formal or intelligible character of the particular (the idea of participation can be seen as one attempt to articulate the particular sort of derivation at issue here). In the case of the asymmetrical dependence between subjectivity and placedness in the world advanced by Crowell, it remains unclear whether the dependence at issue may indeed entail some form of derivation—Crowell asserts that it is nonderivative, but given that Crowell's account does continue to draw on elements from *Being and Time*, one might be forgiven for harboring the suspicion that some form of derivation may still be in play.[26]

Significantly, asymmetrical dependence does not seem to be a good way to describe the ordering of elements within a "transcendental" structure, since, within any such structure, all of the elements are given together— one cannot have any one element without having all (and this is true, I would argue, of the "transcendental" structure that is set out in *Being and Time* and in Kant's first *Critique*, as well as of the Fourfold in late Heidegger and triangulation in Davidson[27]). Moreover, asymmetrical dependence as deployed by Crowell, cannot even be said to apply, within a "transcendental" frame, to the relation between condition and conditioned—that which conditions is not something other and apart from than that which is conditioned, but is intimately bound up with it. Although one might argue that the conditions obtain irrespective of any particular formation of what is conditioned (so the conditions that make possible experience obtain irrespective of any *particular* experience), it is nevertheless also the case that those conditions do not obtain irrespective of the obtaining of *any* experience. If asymmetrical dependence holds here, then it does not hold in a way that establishes any absolute priority, nor that establishes asymmetrical dependence as the primary sense of priority.

To understand the nature of the ordering that obtains within a structure of mutual dependence, consider the relation between intention and horizon in the structure of meaning-constitution. To suppose that intention comes prior to the horizon is to suppose that intentionality somehow generates the horizontal structure, but it does so only in the sense that intentionality itself always brings horizontality with it, and vice versa. Both are elements within the same structure. Similarly, I would argue that within the structure of temporality, it is mistaken to view the future as prior to the other temporal modes—the idea that it is prior arises only because of the topologically orientational character of temporality. The different orientations that belong to each temporal mode are themselves associated with different orientational priorities in much the same way as we prioritize different orientations in relation to our own bodily orientation. Thus we tend to give priority to that which we face over that which is behind over the very spot in which we stand (and here we can see the same structure of temporal priority as set out by Heidegger). The priority of the future is thus no more "absolute" than is the priority of the forward projection of the body—that forward projection is part of the structure of attention, movement, and action, but since such forward projection itself depends on and is always accompanied by a larger set of bodily capacities and orientations (by, among other things, an overall body-schema, and a larger environmental sensibility), it cannot be said to be "prior to," in an unqualified sense, the other elements of the structure in which it is embedded. Here one can also see how there can be an ordering that belongs to the structure at issue without any need to specify an absolute priority within that order, and so without any real need to resort to the notion of priority at all.

The fact that it is an explicitly *topological* structure (which does not mean merely *spatial* structure) that emerges as a way of explicating the structure of mutually dependent ordering at issue here is not, of course, accidental. It reflects a key aspect of topology as including, in addition to the thematization of place as a philosophically central concept, the adoption of a conception of philosophical inquiry as itself structured by and in relation to the structure of place. Place thus appears both as determining the "methodological" structure of inquiry and its "substantive" focus.

To return to Crowell's discussion, the prioritization of subjectivity over *topos* is not only inconsistent with the character of place itself, but actually depends on a problematic notion of priority. Indeed, it is hard to avoid the conclusion that, contrary to what I take to be Crowell's intention, the priority of subjectivity that he asserts will be hard to distinguish from more traditional forms of metaphysical subjectivism. This seems almost straightforwardly so, in Heideggerian terms, since Heidegger takes subjectivism to consist in just the assertion of some single entity, structure, or principle as underlying the presencing of things—as a *subjectum* or, in the Greek, *hypokeimenon*.[28] In Crowell's account, subjectivity is such a *subjectum*, and it is so in virtue of the insistence on its ontological priority. In contrast, *topos* does not underlie in the same way, but is instead deployed so as to undermine the very idea of anything that might lie "beneath." *Topos* refers us not to a *subjectum*, but rather to that domain of interrelatedness in which the very things themselves come to appearance, and which does not itself appear other than in and through such appearing. There is a sense in which *topos* is prior to certain other concepts, not as underlying them, but rather through being that in and to which each and every other concept is related, and in and through which each and every concept finds its relatedness to others. Place thus encompasses, even though it is not fully encompassed by, the bodily *and* the environmental, the spatial *and* the temporal, the objective *and* the subjective. It does so, moreover, not only through the way in which all of these may be said to stand in a relation to place, but also inasmuch as all of these share a similar "topological" structure.

Temporality and Historicity

Miguel de Beistegui describes *Heidegger's Topology* as concerned to explore the "place of place" in Heidegger's thinking, as well as in philosophical thinking more generally.[29] It is a description that nicely captures some of the ideas at issue in the discussion of Crowell above. In particular, the phrase "the place of place" indicates something of the multivocity that is at work in talk of place (since the first sense of place—"*the place* of place" is not straightforwardly identical to the second—"the place *of place*"), and so gestures toward the complexity and multiplicity of the structures at issue here. Beistegui's account of the argument of *Heidegger's Topology* provides a neat synopsis of many of the work's key ideas, but his discussion also provides, at least to me, something of a reminder and a corrective. I have to admit to having very mixed responses to Heidegger's massive work from 1936 to 1938, the *Beiträge zur Philosophie (Vom Ereignis)—Contributions to Philosophy (of the Event)*. The work seems to me to present too many difficulties, obscurities, and inconsistencies to warrant the adulatory attention that has often been given to it by contemporary readers. As a result, however, in *Heidegger's Topology*, I almost certainly give the *Contributions* less attention than it deserves from a strictly topological perspective. Beistegui's brief discussion indicates how rich a text the *Contributions* can be for explorations of the concepts of space and time in Heidegger's thinking—concepts that are, of course, closely bound up with place. Yet it is also significant that the *Contributions* does not yet take up the notion of *topos* in the explicit fashion of the later work (a clear indication of its transitional character), even though it is quite clear, in hindsight, that the work is a crucial step on Heidegger's way toward a closer engagement with the topological.

Beistegui uses the *Contributions* account to demonstrate the close and intimate belonging together of time and space as developed through the idea of *Zeitraum*—timespace—a concept to which the *Contributions* gives considerable attention. The idea of *timespace* has its first real appearance in the lectures from 1935 that appeared under the title *What Is a Thing?*, although the notion is one that seems to be adumbrated by Heidegger's use elsewhere of the terms *Spielraum*, literally "play-space" (usually translated as "leeway"), and *Zeit-Spiel-Raum*—time-play-space.[30] The way Heidegger treats the notion of *timespace* in the *Contributions*, and to which

Beistegui draws attention, has close affinities with aspects of Heidegger's account of the happening of truth in the 1935–1936 essay "The Origin of the Work of Art"—as one might expect, given that the works were both written in the mid-1930s. Indeed, the *Contributions* seems to be a development of the ideas already set out in somewhat less enigmatic form in "The Origin."[31]

Within the structure set out in the *Contributions*, as Beistegui points out, time is associated with rapture, with world, with clearing (and also a danger of dispersal), and space with earth, captivation, and self-concealing (and the danger of self-enclosure or alienation). It might be thought that this structure is further developed in Heidegger's late work, in the Fourfold, in which there also seem to be temporal and spatial axes within the structure of the Fourfold. In the later thinking, however, the axis of earth and sky appears to be more closely associated with space (and also language), while that of gods and mortals suggests an association with time. Yet the structure set out in "The Origin of the Work of Art," and in the *Contributions*, is significantly different from that which appears in, for example, "Building Dwelling Thinking." In the later work, the Fourfold is itself both an opening *and* a concealing; it is properly a *worlding of world*; moreover, in the later work, world is no longer associated with opening alone, nor with time, and is not set in opposition to a concealing found only in earth or connected solely to space.

In Heidegger's later thinking, the happening of world is properly topological—the concealing and opening of world corresponds, in fact, to the bounding and opening up that is characteristic of place. Moreover, the way in which the earlier work, particularly the *Contributions*, takes temporality to be at work in opening and so also in the worlding of world, suggests a continuation of a similar understanding of temporality as was evident in *Being and Time*. Although the *Contributions* abandons the language of projection and transcendence, it retains a conception of the happening of world, and so of the opening up in which things come to presence, as essentially temporal in character. To some extent, one might argue that this is a tendency that Heidegger never entirely overcomes. The late essay "On Time and Being" retains an emphasis on the priority of temporality over spatiality that is expressed in the fact that time comes before space in the very term *timespace*. In this respect, the idea of *timespace*, though it does indeed express the belonging together of time with space, also continues to assert the priority of the temporal.[32]

One might argue that the priority of temporality that is at issue here is not itself problematic: the temporality at issue is no longer explicated in terms of any attempt to "derive" spatiality from temporality (an attempt that Heidegger refers to as "mistaken"), and so it is indeed a "weak" sense of priority; it also enables us to understand how time and space may indeed be ordered in relation to one another even when the two are conjoined in the structure of *timespace*, and even when *timespace* is itself understood as part of the very structure of *topos*. It should already be obvious, however, that such a conclusion is unlikely to be one to which I am drawn, and it should also be obvious, at least to some extent, why I might think such a conclusion mistaken. Some of the reasons are similar to those I set out in the discussion of priority above—reasons that concern the understanding of the notion of priority that might be at issue here—but there are also reasons that connect with ideas of time and space, the relation between them, and with the idea of place.

If we look to the account of time and space that Heidegger gives in the *Contributions*, and to which Beistegui draws our attention, then one of the odd things about that account is the way in which it systematically overlooks the possibility of a reversal of the analysis it sets out. Time, for instance, is associated with rapture, world, clearing, and the possibility of dispersal. But in fact, this surely applies to time only insofar as priority is given to that modality of time that is the future. As it is given in the modality of the past, time carries those very tendencies and associations that are supposed to belong to space, namely, earth, captivation, self-concealing, and self-enclosure (this is clearly evident as soon as one reflects on the way, for instance, that the past relates to notions of identity and belonging—to time appearing as itself a form of *ground*). The analysis of space too can be similarly reversed. Understood not in its character as *ground* (the perspective that seems to dominate in the *Contributions*), but rather as *openness* (a connotation or modality perhaps more strongly indicated by the German *Raum*—"room"—than the English "space"), space is aligned with those same elements that the *Contributions* connects solely to time (one of the oddities of the analysis in the *Contributions* is the association of dispersal [*Zerstreuung*] and dissemination with time rather than space, given that, in *Being and Time*, one of the crucial underlying claims is that *space* disperses, which is why the unity of *Dasein* cannot be spatial, whereas *time* unifies and gathers). What becomes evident, in fact, once one escapes from the sometimes intoxicating atmosphere of the *Contributions*, is that time and space, earth and world, clearing and self-concealment, do not constitute distinct strands, but rather twine in and through one another, each rupturing the purity of the other, their entanglement such as to destroy the possibility of any simple alignment between them.

It is not clear to me that Heidegger ever arrives at a fully satisfactory account of the relation between time and space, and is constantly seduced by the idea that it is time that plays the crucial role in the happening of world, and in the opening up of space that allows for presence (it is time, in other words, that Heidegger seems always tempted to understand as belonging most properly to *topos*). Part of the problem, of course, is that the very ideas of time and space that are at work here seem not only to be inextricably entangled with one another, but also remain irreducibly obscure. We still await an adequate way of conceiving of time and space (whether or not such a conception can be achieved), being always pulled in the direction of privileging one over the other, of forgetting the way in which each always implies the other, even when we try to disentangle them. This is especially so in the context of contemporary thinking. The movement of modernity has thus been one that seeks to pull time and space apart, and to do so as it also tries to collapse both into a single homogeneous measurability—a collapse that often appears as a collapse of time into space. As a result, the relation of time to space, and the relation of both to place, is made even more obscure; and yet the clarification of this relation becomes even more urgent.

The urgency that appears here is an urgency that undoubtedly belongs to *our time*, yet if what I have said about the obscurity of time and space is correct, then what it means even to speak of a time that is ours must be similarly obscure. Thus, while Beistegui argues that the question of place is itself determined by time in its historical dimension—by the danger of the time in which we now find ourselves—I would contend that this is itself to overlook the way in which the historical is itself configured topologically rather than temporally. History works itself out only in and through the concrete formations of place in which it also becomes evident—and this means that the places of which I speak in *Heidegger's Topology* are to be understood in terms of the *histories* they themselves invoke, and by which they are also constituted, and not merely their geographies. The topological character of the historical—or the historicality of the topological—is itself obscured, we might be tempted to say, by the character of "the time" in which we seem to find ourselves. But this way of putting things itself obscures, since it both reifies and abstracts the "time" that is at issue here. "Our time" is thus all too readily understood as something that stands somehow over and above the concrete sites and situations in which that "time" is itself made evident.

Heidegger's "history of being" should be understood as essentially a history of place. This is not, however, to be understood as solely to do with a history marked out by a set of shifts in the philosophical appropriation of place (an appropriation that is explored, not only in the work of such as Ed Casey,[33] but also in Heidegger's own thinking). More than this, the history of being is a history of place that is contained within, and unfolds from, the places in which we find ourselves. In this respect, the dominance of the technological—which consists not in the prevalence of technological devices, but rather in the holding sway of the system of ordering with which they are associated (more specifically, the globalized system of technological-bureaucratic, corporatized "economism")—occurs through certain specific transformations of place. Technological modernity gives priority to certain modes of place as it also covers over both the topological character of its own functioning, as well as the topological character of being as such. The tensions and obscurities that characterize modernity's appropriation of the concepts of time and space can thus be viewed as themselves reflections of the topological working out of modernity's own tensions and contradictions—tensions and contradictions that modernity cannot itself recognize or admit. Thus in the globalized world in which we live—a globalization that is itself invoked problematically invoked by talk of "our time" as a time that encompasses the entirety of the world—globalization appears only in and through the countless places by which the world is constituted, and yet it is those same places that it also seeks to efface.

Heimat and the Experience of Wonder

It is probably almost twenty years now since Julian Young and I first began talking with one another about issues of place in relation to Heidegger and beyond. For the most part, we share a great deal of common ground, but as is so often the case in such conversations, the commonality that exists sometimes serves to make the points of difference that much sharper. One of those points undoubtedly concerns the way we each understand the notion of Heimat—a term that has no exact English equivalent, but that is loosely translatable as "home" or "homeland." A large part of Julian Young's discussion of my work focuses on how Heimat is to be understood, and connected to that is the relation between place and the experience of wonder. In addition, Young raises questions concerning the way in which we should view death and the gods in light of the later Heidegger. So far as the last of these is concerned, death and the gods, I am not so sure that Young's position is as far away from my own as it might first appear. Let me take the question of death first, and then go on to consider the issue concerning the gods.

Young presents an account of my position that takes death to be a "dark limit" (the phrase is from Joseph Fell) that is also an annihilation. This is the view that Young takes to characterize Heidegger's position in *Being and Time*, but *not* in his later thinking. There, according to Young, one finds a conception of death, not as annihilation, but as "a moment of passage: a bridge."[34] Young is certainly correct that I view death as a limit, but this reading derives from Heidegger's own particular understanding of the notion of limit, taken, as one might say, in the Greek sense, and so as productive rather than merely restrictive.[35] In a number of places Heidegger emphasizes the positive rather than purely negative character of limit—as that which enables something to come to presence.[36] This is how I have always understood the limit-character of death. Death is not a restrictive limit, and so cannot be understood as the signifier of a simple negation or nullity, but is rather constitutive of the life that it also marks off.[37] This way of thinking of death does not seem to me incompatible with the idea of death as also what I would think of as a "threshold"—which I take to be another way of capturing Young's talk of death as a "gate" or "bridge." The threshold is a threshold through the way in which it brings to presence both that from which it allows passage and that to which it gives entrance. Similarly, as Heidegger says of the bridge that serves as his example in "Building Dwelling Thinking," "The bridge . . . does not connect banks that are already there. The banks emerge as banks only as the bridge crosses the stream."[38] In the terms Heidegger employs, to speak of death is not to rule out the character of death as indeed constituting the sort of limit—limit as positive and constituting—that is also found in the idea of the threshold. Perhaps Young would not be averse to this way of putting matters, but I also want to retain the possibility of adopting a more critical attitude to some ways of understanding death—including some traditional religious conceptions—than Young seems to allow. For instance, the religious fanatic, whether Christian, Muslim, or of any other creed, who understands death as the gateway to another life, a life *against which* this life pales into insignificance and relative worthlessness, seems to hold to a position that does indeed treat death merely as a restrictive limit, rather than a constitutive one, and as a restrictive limit that is best overcome sooner rather than later. Young himself refers to "Orthodox Christians (and Muslims)" and so I take him to exclude the fanatic. But the fanatic nevertheless provides us with an exemplification of a problematic mode of relating to death that is also to be found, in less extreme forms, among at least some of the "Orthodox." The contrast here is not, I would argue, between those who treat death as a "dark limit" and those who view it as a "gate" or "bridge," but between those who view death as that which establishes the possibility of a genuine life on earth, and those who view it as a means of escape to something that is valued over and above any such earthly life.

Again, when it comes to the gods, much of what Young says can be read in a way that is quite compatible with my own position. His insistence on the gods as "personalities" is certainly not in opposition to my own account, nor indeed to the account found in Walter Otto's work on which I draw—for Otto the gods are worlds (I would prefer to talk of aspects or forms of world), but they are also the personalization of worlds. Here it is perhaps worth noting that Otto's approach is itself indebted to that of Schleiermacher, a thinker with whom Heidegger was also familiar, and Otto's view of the Greek gods can be seen as echoing Schleiermacher's understanding of the divine as "a particular intuition of the universe."[39] Where I think Young and I do differ is on the question of the relation of the gods who figure in the Fourfold to the "heroes" of Being and Time. Young claims that the latter, thought of "in modern jargon," as "role-models," are the precursors to the gods of the Fourfold. Yet although the figure of a god may well provide a model for an individual life, the idea that Heidegger's late understanding of the gods is primarily as role models seems to me to be mistaken. The gods encompass much more than this, and any exemplary role they play is very much secondary to the way the give shape and form to certain modes of the world. Heidegger's comments in the Parmenides lectures—that the Greek gods "are not 'personalities' or 'persons' that dominate being; they are Being itself as looking into beings"[40]—would seem to give support to this reading. Young argues that we must rule out those comments as coming too soon before the working out of the Fourfold in the later essays (can it be too soon—when some of the elements of the Fourfold seem already to be present in the twofold structure evident in Contributions?[41]) Yet if that were so, the same argument could surely be applied, a fortiori, to Heidegger's comments on heroes in Being and Time—all the more so when one reflects on the way the idea of the hero seems itself to be evocative of many of the elements of Being and Time (the emphasis on projection, transcendence, and also resoluteness) that are most problematic.

The real focus for Young's discussion is not, however, death or the gods, but rather the concept of Heimat, and the question concerning the very nature of place as it relates to human dwelling. Perhaps the very first point that I should make here is that although I have talked, in my response to Crowell, of one sense of *topos* as associated with subjectivity—so that one way to understand subjectivity is as itself a form of *topos*—place certainly does not consist in "a state of mind." Indeed, given the extensive attention I give, not only in *Heidegger's Topology*, but also in *Place and Experience* and elsewhere,[42] to arguing against construals of place in purely "subjective" terms (as "constructed," as a form of "emotional reminiscence," as a human "projection"), I am perplexed as to how Young could arrive at such a view. Place, and our relatedness to place, can, of course, figure in "states of mind," which is to say that we can encounter particular places as we can also have a sense of our own placedness. The encounter with such placedness, and so one might say with place, is what I argue underpins the experience of wonder. Here, however, I do not treat wonder as *any* experience so called, but rather take wonder to be that particular mode of encounter with the world in which our own placedness in the world, and the strangeness of that placedness, becomes the focus for attention.[43]

We are not "in place" only when in the throes of wonder. Just as, to use Heidegger's terminology, dwelling is the mode of human being, so human being is essentially a being in place, just as it is also a being in the world. If the relation to place is an essential one, then it is not a relation that we can ever leave without also leaving our very humanity. Indeed, it makes very little sense even to speak of such a departure. We may become estranged from place, we may forget or cover over our essential placedness, but these are all forms of concealing, disguising, or denying a relatedness to place that nevertheless perdures. Even under the reign of technological modernity, our relatedness to place is not obliterated, but is rather covered over, ignored, made invisible. If this were not so, then there would be no basis on which to mount any critique of the placelessness of modernity—such a critique depends on the contradiction, within modernity itself, between its refusal of place (a refusal that refuses to recognize itself as a refusal) and its own inescapable placedness.

Place is a complex and multiple concept. When we talk of our own relatedness to place, our own placedness, as well as our encounter with such placedness, then place appears in at least a twofold way—and this twofold character corresponds to a twofold character that belongs to the idea of *Heimat*.

Place refers us, first, to that underlying structure of placedness that is essential to our being as human. This underlying, one might say, *ontological*, structure, although properly *topological*, is everywhere instantiated differently, and yet everywhere it is the same. This is why it is indeed correct to say that place "consists neither in Wordsworth's Lake district, nor in John Clare's native Northamptonshire, nor in the Aborigines' central Australian desert, nor in Heidegger's Black Forest. Rather, it is to 'be found in all or any one of them.'"[44]

Place refers us, in a second sense, not merely to placedness as such, but to the placed character of our own being as that is worked out in and through the specific places in which we live and move—as our lives are shaped and formed in relation to *this* place and *these* places. Although there is no privileged place in which placedness—or being—is made pre-eminently apparent (even if some places are perhaps better attuned to enabling such appearing than others), there is nevertheless a privileging of places in relation to the singularity of ourselves as persons. Here is the second, and almost certainly more familiar, sense of *Heimat*—a sense that refers to just this idea of the place-bound identity and determination of human being. If the concluding emphasis on *Heidegger's Topology* is on the appearance of place in and through place (in and through *any* such place), then the emphasis of *Place and Experience* is on the dependence of human life on the singular places in which it is lived. It is this idea that I referred to, in the earlier book, as "Proust's Principle"[45]—the idea of persons "*being who and what they are* through their inhabiting of particular places." The two senses of place, and of *Heimat*, that appear here are in no way incompatible with one another—if anything, each can be said to imply the other.

Young suggests that it is my concern with the "problem of place"—the tendency to treat place-oriented thinking as inevitably given over to reactionary and exclusionary forms of politics—that leads me to refuse any privileging of places in relation to the experience of placedness that I discuss at the conclusion of *Heidegger's Topology*.[46] In fact, my refusal of any generalized privileging of particular places is, as I see it, a direct consequence of my attempt to explore and to articulate Heidegger's own topological mode of thinking. Such thinking is not exclusively reserved for those who live in certain special places—although, for each one of us, since we are ourselves formed by specific places rather than others, the possibilities of our own thinking will be similarly and specifically place-dependent. As in Heidegger's own case, each of us may well find that certain places provide the preeminent sites for thinking, and for the encounter with the "nearness of being." "The problem of place" does not motivate the concluding comments in *Heidegger's Topology*, yet that problem can adequately be addressed only on the basis of a recognition of the complex and multiple character of place. It is precisely the way in which place encompasses both the singular and the multiple that it can indeed allow both the foreign as well as the familiar to appear within it; that it can allow a genuine encounter, both with oneself and with others. It is this placed encounter that is surely the proper source of wonder, and that is also named, in all the equivocity of that naming, by Heidegger's use of the word *Heimat*.

Dwelling and Technology

There can be no doubt, as Edward Relph acknowledges, of the crucial role that Heidegger's thought has played in the contemporary turn to place within the humanities and social sciences, as well as in the philosophical inquiry into place as such.[47] Moreover, Relph provides a strikingly apt and vivid image of the way the concept of "place" has, in recent years, "exploded" across many different areas and disciplines, in a proliferation of different forms and uses. Undertaking a review of recent work on place is, says Relph, "like walking into the aftermath of an academic explosion. What had once been a reasonably coherent body of thought, grounded in phenomenology and mostly the concern of humanistic geographers and environmental psychologists, seems to have flown off in all directions."[48] The "exploded" and expanded character of the current discussion of place is particularly problematic for any attempt to think place theoretically. Not only is there a proliferation of topological ideas and tropes whose relationship to one another remains often obscure and uncertain, but, in the midst of this explosion, place sometimes seems itself to have been rendered almost invisible.

Although there are many works that deploy various senses of place and also delineate the detailed textures and forms of particular places, when it comes to the theoretical inquiry into place, the focus, for the most part, is not on place as such, but either on the effects of place or else on place as itself an effect of other processes. Thus David Harvey, as Relph notes, treats place as a social construction, claiming that the only interesting question then concerns the social processes that give rise to place[49]—here place is *itself* nothing more than an effect; Doreen Massey, on the other hand, treats place, which she refuses to distinguish from space, as significant largely in terms of the consequences of our imagination of place[50]—here it is the effects *of* place that are given priority. Even the work of a theorist such as Henri Lefebvre,[51] so often cited as a key figure in the literature on place, turns out to be important less for his elucidation of the concept, than for the prioritization of space and place as acceptable terms within critical discourse (moreover, in Lefebvre, of course, one also finds much the same treatment of space and place as effects of social and economic factors as is evident in Harvey's own Lefebvrian-inflected writing); and much the same is true of other prominent theorists such as Foucault, and even Deleuze and Guattari.

Part of Heidegger's importance is thus not only the way in which his work has played an important role in enabling the appearance of place, as well as space, as a key theoretical concept in writers such as Lefebvre, as well as Foucault (a point that Stuart Elden's work has done much to establish[52]), but that Heidegger is also one of the few philosophers, and the only major twentieth-century thinker, to thematize place as such, and to provide an analysis of its structure and significance—so much so that the later Heidegger referred to his own work as a "topology of being." For anyone interested in the attempt to say more about place than is available in the work of Harvey and Massey, or, indeed, in Lefebvre and Foucault, Heidegger must be considered essential reading.

Yet although Relph and I seem to be in agreement on the importance of Heidegger as a central figure in the thinking of place, we disagree in our assessments of just what is most significant in Heidegger's treatment of place. Focusing on the concept of dwelling that looms so large in Heidegger's later thinking, Relph observes that while he finds this aspect of Heidegger's philosophy "appealing because it reinforces my own doubts about modern placelessness," he nevertheless also views it as "the most superficial" aspect of Heidegger's thought. Relph takes the turn toward the concept of dwelling in later Heidegger as indicative of a shift from "rigorous phenomenological description to a selective historical judgment."[53] There is no doubt that there is a move away from a certain conception of phenomenology in Heidegger, although as I have already noted in the discussion above, reiterating a point from *Heidegger's Topology*, there is an important sense in which a form of "phenomenological seeing" remains central to all Heidegger's thinking,[54] but I would certainly dispute Relph's claim that what characterizes the later Heidegger is a shift to a "selective historical judgment," just as I would also take issue with Relph's own judgment as to the superficiality of the Heideggerian account of dwelling.

It is important to note, as Young acknowledges (though with reference to a different context),[55] that the concept of dwelling is already present in *Being and Time*. In a brief and highly condensed passage in §12 (some of the main elements of which reappear in "Building Dwelling Thinking"), Heidegger distinguishes the way in which *Dasein* is "in" its world from the way in which a physical entity is "in" space (a sense of spatial-physical "containment" that allows one thing to be said to be "in" another as the water is "in" the glass or the glass is "in" the room). Heidegger refers to this first sense of "in" in terms of dwelling.[56] As deployed in *Being and Time*, the concept of dwelling remains obscure and problematic,[57] but in the later thinking it becomes one of the central ideas in Heidegger's articulation of the enriched conception of place, one that actually includes within it both spatial and temporal elements, to which human being is tied. In this respect, it is a mistake to see the notion of dwelling as tied to some pre-modern mode of life—not only does it render the concept itself superficial, but it also constitutes a highly superficial reading of what Heidegger has to say about it.

What is at issue in Heidegger's talk of dwelling is not a comparison in the "quality of life" between different historical periods, but rather the nature of human being as intimately tied to place. Dwelling is thus Heidegger's name for the topological mode of being that belongs to human being—and not merely the human in some selected historical period, but to the human "as such." It is precisely because humans *dwell* that the technological transformation of the world that occurs in modernity is such a challenge, an affront even, to what it is to be human—the essential character of human life as dwelling is contradicted and obscured by the representation of the human in terms of consumption, productivity, preference, and utility. Moreover, just as Heidegger's critique of technology is directed at a pervasive tendency that underlies technology rather than being necessarily instantiated in any particular technological device, so too is Heidegger's account of dwelling intended as a description of a fundamental mode of being, rather than something to be instantiated only in certain lives rather than others.

Although Relph rejects the Heideggerian concept of dwelling as "superficial," he is rather more sympathetic toward Heidegger's critique of technology—a critique that Relph reinterprets as a critique of "rationalism." I think that the use of the latter term here is ill advised—although there is a certain calculative rationality that Heidegger views as problematic, it is a serious mistake, even if a widespread one, to treat Heidegger as an "antirationalist" in any more general sense. However, there are undoubtedly important points of convergence between Heidegger's account of modern technology and its essence (which Heidegger refers to as "*das Gestell*"—"the Framework"), and the accounts to be found in the work of a number of other twentieth-century thinkers including Foucault's analysis of the rise of governmentality[58] and of the biopolitical, Weber's description of the processes of rationalization and bureaucratization, and Adorno's account of instrumental rationality. Such convergence is perhaps unsurprising given the prevalence of ideas concerning the problems and limits of technology in prewar European thinking. What marks Heidegger's account as distinctive, however, is the way in which the critique of technology is tied to a topological analysis of which Heidegger's account of dwelling is an integral part. Nowhere is this more evident than in the essay "The Thing"—itself part of the original lecture sequence from which "The Question Concerning Technology" also came—which begins with Heidegger's announcement of the phenomenon that has come to be known as "time-space compression."[59] Relph himself assumes a connection between "rationalism" and the loss of place—not only does he see such "rationalism" to be associated with placelessness, but he also sees evidence of the decline of "rationalism" in the resurgence of interest in place—but it remains unclear how or why such a connection should obtain.

If my account is correct, then Heidegger provides an answer here—one that works through the elucidation of place in relation to being, and, in terms of dwelling, to human being, and through his analysis of the way in which technology itself operates in relation to place. The fact that Relph seems not to have appreciated this aspect of Heidegger's topological thinking may indicate a deficiency in my own presentation of these ideas in *Heidegger's Topology*—it may well be that much more needs to be said in order to bring out the complexity and detail of Heidegger's later thought—although I suspect that part of the difficulty here is that any writing on the later Heidegger still stands under the shadow of the often partial and superficial readings that have dominated much of the literature to date, and that pervade the broader appropriation of Heideggerian thinking (especially in fields outside of philosophy).

Relph finds the Heideggerian response to the danger of technological modernity, at least as I articulate that response in *Heidegger's Topology* in terms of the importance of ideas of openness, indeterminacy, wonder, and also, though not mentioned by Relph, of questionability,[60] to be "insubstantial," and Heidegger's own comment in the *Der Spiegel* interview that "only a god can save us"[61] to be disingenuous and evasive. I can sympathize with Relph's dissatisfaction here, but I think it also misses the point concerning what is at issue. Once we analyze the operation of technological modernity topologically, then we can see how it actually transforms our experience of place in ways that are at odds with the underlying character of place, and the underlying character even of that mode of being that belongs to technological modernity itself, but which it also conceals. My emphasis on the importance of concepts such as openness, indeterminacy, wonder, and questionability, and the modes of comportment associated with them, is intended to direct attention toward key elements in an experience of place that obscures neither its own embeddedness in place, and the nature of that embeddedness, nor the character of place as such. Moreover, that we should look for a more concrete solution to the problems of technological modernity, while unsurprising, is also mistaken. Our contemporary situation is not the result of a process over which we, either collectively or individually, have mastery. Indeed, the desire for mastery, and the appearance of the entire world as potentially subject to control, is itself an integral element in the particular formation of the world that is technological modernity. The relinquishing of the desire for control, and the recognition of the extent to which all-encompassing solutions are beyond us, will themselves be key elements in that "other beginning" that might presage the shift to a truly "postmodern," "post-technological" world.

The later Heidegger's apparently weary insistence on the limits in our ability to change the course of the world should not be construed as indicating a failure of vision or some lapse into quietistic resignation. It follows directly from a recognition of the essentially placed character of human being, and the limitation and fragility that follows inevitably from it. If it were possible to reconfigure our current forms of social and political organization around a recognition of such placedness, then we would have a solution to many of our contemporary ills. Yet there is no concrete way in which such a wholesale reconfiguration can be brought away in a directed and purposive manner. What we can do is work, as Heidegger suggests, in the many small ways that are available to us, to reorient ourselves to our actual situation, to reorient ourselves to the proper place in which find ourselves—beyond this, however, there is no "saving power" that we ourselves can exercise.

Heidegger's Topology attempts to provide an account of the way in which place provides a starting point for Heidegger's thinking as well as an idea toward which it develops. Indeed, it is only in the very late thinking, from perhaps 1947 onward, that Heidegger's topology emerges in a fully developed form (though a form that can only be appreciated when viewed in terms of the problems in the earlier thinking to which it is also a response). If we are to take Heidegger as making a significant and positive contribution to the philosophical analysis of place in the twentieth century, then it must be primarily on the basis of the *later* thinking rather than the earlier. But the later thinking also makes demands on the reader that are much greater than those of the earlier work—demands that follow, in part, from Heidegger's own attempts to think topologically—and as a result the later thinking is more prone to being misread and misconstrued.

I had hoped that *Heidegger's Topology* would go some way toward correcting this latter tendency, but if Relph's comments are taken as an indication then the work would seem to have fallen short of at least one of its objectives. On the other hand, if the sort of topology or topography in which I take Heidegger to have been engaged, and to which I take my own work to be a contribution, does indeed constitute a different, if not entirely unprecedented, mode of thinking, then perhaps one simply has to accept certain inevitable difficulties in the communication and elucidation of that thinking. *Heidegger's Topology* does not, however, stand alone. Not only does it seem to me to be supported by the work of others in the same field, including some of the writers already referred to at the beginning of this chapter, but it should also be read against the background of my work elsewhere. In this respect, *Heidegger's Topology* should be read as one part of a much larger topological project that does not include Heidegger alone, but other thinkers such as Kant, as well as Gadamer and Davidson, and that also attempts to rethink the character of philosophy as itself essentially topological in character. It is toward this larger project, which is not restricted merely to some form of Heideggerian exegesis, that the essays that make up this volume should also be seen as contributing.

II Topological Concepts

4 Ground, Unity, and Limit

[P]hilosophy has always and constantly asked about the ground of beings. With this question it had its inception, in this question it will find its end, provided that it comes to an end in greatness and not in a powerless decline.

—Heidegger, *Introduction to Metaphysics*

With Heidegger, philosophy seems to have remained in greatness: although Heidegger's treatment of the question concerning the ground of beings undergoes important shifts in the course of his philosophical career, still the question of ground remains always near the center of his thinking.[1] Heidegger saw the question of ground as the determining question of philosophy—and in this respect the question of ground is one with the question of being[2]—yet he also saw philosophy as persistently misunderstanding and covering over the true nature of this question or, at least, of what this question contains within it. In this respect, the "forgetfulness of being"—*Seinsvergenssenheit*—that, according to Heidegger, characterizes the history of philosophy, cannot be separated from philosophy's misunderstanding of the question of ground.

One particularly important form in which the question of ground appears within the philosophical tradition is in terms of the transcendental project concerning the ground of knowledge or experience that first sees clear formulation in the work of Kant. Of Kant himself, Heidegger declares that he was "the first one since the philosophy of the Greeks to again pose the question of the being of beings as a question to be developed"[3]—in which case, Kant was also, perhaps, the first since the Greeks to pose the question of ground as a question to be developed. Certainly Kant's transcendental approach to the question of ground marks a striking new development in the history of philosophy—a development taken further in the transcendental phenomenology of Husserl, and that is also reappropriated and reinterpreted by Heidegger in relation to his own project, especially in the terms in which that project is set out in *Being and Time*. Indeed, the idea of the transcendental provides us with perhaps the clearest expression of the concern with ground in modern thinking, that is, as a concern with "conditions of possibility," in particular, with the conditions for the possibility of "knowledge of experience," or, to use the idea of which Heidegger makes much in his *Kantbuch*, explicitly in terms of a "laying of the ground" for metaphysics.[4] What is especially important about the Kantian approach, from a Heideggerian perspective, is precisely the way in which it reopens the question of being and the question of ground with it. Kant provides a new framework for the thinking of the question of being and the question of ground, and it is this new framework that we can call the "transcendental."

Reflection on the question of ground is crucial for an understanding of the idea of the transcendental, as well as for what Heidegger calls "the question of being" (it is thereby also crucial for an understanding of Heidegger's relation to Kant), but it is significant too in that such reflection directs attention explicitly to issues of philosophical methodology and approach that might otherwise be taken for granted. Such issues are especially important in the Heideggerian context, and yet, perhaps surprisingly, the question of ground receives relatively little explicit discussion in the Heideggerian literature, or even in the literature that deals with questions concerning the nature of the transcendental. In this chapter, I aim to explore the question of ground, and the nature of ground itself, as it arises in Heidegger, with particular reference to the apparent transition in Heidegger's thinking from the transcendental character of the early thought to the "topological" orientation that is characteristic of the later. The matter I intend to pursue concerns the way in which both the transcendental and the topological entail a similar conception of what it is to ground—a conception in which notions of unity and limit play central roles—and so the exploration in the pages that follow can be taken as a further elucidation of both the transcendental and the topological.

The Concept of Ground

Notwithstanding Heidegger's insistence on its centrality, exactly what is involved in the question of ground may seem, from the outset, quite obscure. Certainly talk of "ground" is not a common term in the contemporary philosophical vocabulary. In *The Principle of Reason*, Heidegger provides an exploration and elucidation of the question of ground by reference to Leibniz's statement of the principle of sufficient reason: the principle that nothing is without reason, without "why." Leaving aside, for the moment, Heidegger's own account of what is at issue in this principle, we may explicate the idea at stake here by saying that it amounts to the idea that it ought to be possible, with respect to any and every feature of the universe, and with respect to any and every "thing" that "is," to provide a reason for the being of that feature or thing. And when asked philosophically, the question of ground moves us in the direction of a reason, not merely for this or that, nor a reason that refers us to something else about which the question of ground could be asked once more, but a reason for all and everything beyond which nothing more could be asked.

Heidegger's discussion in *The Principle of Reason* specifically takes up the role of reason as both that which demands grounding (inasmuch as it is reason that makes the demand for ground) and which also provides such grounding (inasmuch as it is through reason that any ground comes to light, as the giving of ground is a giving of reason, and as reason may itself function as a ground). In contemporary thinking, the emphasis on reason is evident in the demand for explanation—often explanation takes the form of derivability from mathematically formulated laws or generalizations. Moreover, given that much contemporary metaphysics tends to assume a physicalist or materialist ontology, so it can also be viewed as tending to treat the question of ground as answerable in ultimately physicalist or materialist terms. The explanation of the existence of any particular thing is thus to be given by looking to its physical causes or perhaps its material constitution. The question of ground has thus not disappeared from contemporary thought, even if some of the language of ground as such has. Indeed, so long as philosophy concerns itself with the inquiry into the first principles of things—with questions concerning the fundamental explanation of what is—so long will it remain concerned with the question of ground.

The question of ground asks after the ground of what is, that is, after the ground of beings. It is thus that the question of ground always implicates, and is implicated with, the question of being—one might say, in fact, that the question of being is one with the question of the ground of beings. It is significant, however, that it is *beings*, and not *being*, for which a ground is sought; it is beings, rather than being, that call for grounding. "[B]eing qua being grounds," says Heidegger, "Consequently, only beings ever have their grounds."[5] Here Heidegger presents what he elsewhere terms the "ontological difference" in terms of the distinction between that which grounds and that which is grounded. To speak of being is already to speak of ground, and as a consequence, it would be mistaken to suppose that one could ask after the ground of being, as if one could ask after the ground of ground.[6] Moreover, this is not because being is somehow its *own* ground. The question of ground asks after the ground or reason for *what is*, but strictly speaking "what is" is not being. As Heidegger comments: "Only a being 'is'; the 'is' itself—being—'is' not."[7] The point here is a simple one: being is not a being, and it is only of beings that one can ask after their ground, because only beings can be questioned as to their being. Being cannot be so questioned, but is itself that to which we turn when we attempt to answer such a question. "Insofar as being 'is' what grounds, and only insofar as it is so, it has no ground/reason."[8]

It is, however, characteristic of the history of metaphysics (and, more generally, of philosophy[9]), as Heidegger describes it, for being to be understood in terms that identify it either with something common to all beings or with some particular being—in terms that run exactly counter to the "ontological difference" as expressed above. Being is thereby treated as that which supposedly functions as ground—as the one "thing" that grounds the rest—and yet, in being treated as a "being," being is itself opened up to the question of its own ground. Here not only is being misunderstood, but so too is the idea of ground. Ground is seen as identical with some particular aspect of beings, or some particular being or mode of being, and in being so understood, the question of ground is able to be turned back on to ground itself, with the result that the role of ground as ground is itself brought into question. The difficulty that is apparent here may explain the disappearance of talk of ground in much contemporary philosophy, but the difficulty only arises, of course, out of a way of understanding being and ground that is deeply problematic, and rather than having disappeared, that way of understanding is itself perpetuated within contemporary thought.

Metaphysical inquiry continues, in fact, to exemplify the tendency that Heidegger identifies as characteristic of the history of philosophy: contemporary thought takes a particular mode of the being of things, most often their physicality or materiality, and turns that mode into the touchstone for the understanding of being as such. The being of things becomes, on this account, nothing more than being physical or material. And, for Heidegger, of course, this physicalist or materialist understanding is closely tied to the disclosure of things as "resource" (*Bestand*) that lies at the heart of technological modernity.[10] Thus, although contemporary metaphysics stands at one extreme in the history of philosophy, it nevertheless exemplifies a general metaphysical tendency—a tendency that Heidegger characterizes as "onto-theological"—to understand being always and only in terms of beings and so to obliterate the ontological difference between being and beings.[11] Moreover, it should also be noted that as this onto-theological tendency characterizes the history of metaphysics, so it also characterizes the interpretation of that history. The tendency is always to read past philosophers in a way that is itself governed by such an onto-theological understanding. The forgetting of being is, in this respect, a double forgetting: the forgetting of being occurs in both the thinking of being and in philosophizing about such thinking. This makes the task of a retrieval of the question of being a task that must be pursued, not only in relation to the question as such, but also in relation to the way that question appears within the history of its forgetting.

Although the details concerning Heidegger's own understanding of the question of ground change with the turnings in Heidegger's *Denkweg*,[12] still there are certain important continuities in the way in which the question of ground appears in his thinking, and it is the exploration of those con-tinuities—continuities that also extend to the Kantian transcendental project—that is a large part of the aim of this discussion. A number of concepts stand out as especially important in that understanding, in par-ticular, concepts of unity and limit. The aim of this chapter will be to explore the way in which unity and limit figure as central concepts in relation to the question of ground, and so to the question of being, and along with this, to explore the nature of the ideas of unity and limit that might be at issue here. The latter task is especially important, since the understanding of these concepts is as much at issue here as is the idea of ground that stands in proximity to them. Indeed, in each case there is a "metaphysical" understanding of these concepts that is more or less influ-ential within the philosophical tradition and that mirrors the metaphysical tendency to understand being in terms of beings, to understand presence in terms of what is present. Yet the meaning of the concepts at issue here is not exhausted by such metaphysical understanding. Heidegger's own thought can be seen as essentially concerned with retrieving the meanings of terms in cases where those meanings are otherwise obscured by, and yet are still evident in, their metaphysical uses. Understanding the question of ground thus involves a retrieval of a "premetaphysical," or equally "postmetaphysical," understanding of ideas of unity and limit, along with the idea of ground itself, and of their interconnection. Together such ideas provide an elucidation of the question concerning the ground of what is, while they also lead toward an understanding of the way in which any adequate response to that question must take the form of a topology of being—indeed, as we move, in Heidegger's thought, from the transcendental to the topological, so the way in which the Kantian transcendental project must itself be understood in topological terms should also become clearer.

The question of ground originally emerges in Heidegger, at least according to Heidegger's account of his own genesis as a thinker, specifically in relation to the problem of the unity of being as it arises out of Aristotle. Heidegger famously claimed that it was Brentano's dissertation, *On the Several Senses of Being in Aristotle*,[13] that first awakened philosophical stirrings within him. Indeed, he writes that "The quest for the unity in the multiplicity of being, then only obscurely, unsteadily and helplessly stirring within me, *remained*, through many upsets, wanderings and perplexities, *the* ceaseless impetus for the treatise *Being and Time* which appeared two decades later."[14] In Aristotle, of course, the question of ground, which in Aristotelian terms can be seen to arise in terms of an inquiry into the fundamental *archai* or principles of being, leads Aristotle to insist both on the irreducible multiplicity of being, as well as on the ontological primacy of substance (*ousia*), and ultimately of essence (*to ti en einai*) or substantial form. Indeed, being turns out to be articulated through a complex, but nevertheless unitary structure—a structure whose unity is not the unity of a single genus or class, but rather of what might be termed a differentiated "teleology" (inasmuch as the notion of essence is itself understood in relation, not only to the idea of form, but also to notions of *telos, ergon, energeia* and *entelecheia*).[15] So the question of ground is seen, from this perspective, as a question that requires an articulation of the multiple meanings of being in their unitary interrelation. The grounding of beings is thus achieved through a demonstration of the unity of being, that is, through a demonstration of the unity of that the basis of which any being can be the being that it is (the demonstration of the unity of being thus amounts to a demonstration of the unity of any and every being *qua* being).

Even Aristotle, however, is not immune to what Heidegger views as the inherent tendency of metaphysics toward onto-theology—toward the identification of being, and of ground, with some being or aspect of beings. This is so, not only because one might view Aristotle's ontology to be based in a certain theology, but also because of the way in which the Aristotelian question of being is ultimately seen as a question concerning being as substance or *ousia*, while substance is itself understood in terms of that which is most fully present, namely, the intelligible determination of the thing that is its essence. The problem here, however, is not so much that there is a prioritizing of the senses of being in Aristotle's account (to unify the various senses of being is precisely a matter of establishing the proper ordering that obtains among those senses), but rather that the horizon within which that account operates already gives precedence to a particular mode of being and so determines a particular orientation. According to Heidegger, being is already understood, in Aristotle and for the Greeks in general, in terms of the present intelligibility of things, and it is this that determines the way in which the unity of being is then articulated. Nevertheless, this should not blind us to the fact that, for Aristotle, the question concerning the ground of beings cannot be divorced from the problem of understanding being in the complex unity of its multiple senses.

The Aristotelian problem of the unity of being, understood as a problem concerning the unity of the many senses of being, is thus not a problem that directs us toward finding a single univocal meaning for being. Any approach that took the unity of being to consist solely in the unity of a single sense of being—a single being or class of beings—would fail to address the unity of being *as a whole*. The question of the ground of "what is" addresses itself, from the very start, to the whole of what is (or better to the whole of the being of what is), and only through exhibiting its own entire unity can that question be adequately answered. So although Aristotle does maintain that the primary sense of being is being as substance (and ultimately as essence), in doing so he nevertheless also maintains the idea of being as having an irreducible multiplicity of senses that is unified precisely through its relation to that primary sense.

Though essential to the understanding of ground within an Aristotelian frame, the focus on unity is also a determining feature of the way in which the problem of ground emerges in Kant and in the Kantian idea of the transcendental. Kant's self-appointed task in the *Critique of Pure Reason* is to find a secure footing for knowledge—which means establishing the conditions that make possible not only natural scientific knowledge, but also metaphysical knowledge ("laying the ground for metaphysics"). The way in which Kant approaches this task is through a question concerning the possibility of *a priori* synthetic judgments. As puts it in the introduction to the first edition, what must be done is:

> To uncover the ground of the possibility of synthetic *a priori* judgments with appropriate generality, to gain insight into the conditions that make every kind of them possible, and not merely to designate this entire cognition (which comprises its own species) in a cursory outline, but to determine it completely and adequately for every use in a system in accordance with its primary sources, divisions, domain and boundaries.[16]

To present the problem of knowledge in terms of the problem of a priori synthetic judgment is already to indicate the way in which the problem of knowledge is essentially a problem of unity, but of unity understood in terms of the a priori *synthesis* of the elements that are constitutive of knowledge.[17] The Kantian concern with unity appears, however, in a number of forms that run throughout the *Critique*. It can also be put, for instance, in terms of a concern with the unity of *experience*, and, in this form, the problem of unity emerges as a problem concerning the unity of the experienced object, of the unity of the experiencing subject, and the relation between the two.

The Kantian focus on the being of the object, and the correlative turn to the subject, is what marks Kant, at least in Heidegger's eyes, as a specifically modern thinker—it is the concern with objectivity, and with the foundation of objectivity in subjectivity, that is the mark of the modern.[18] Nevertheless, the focus on the problem of ground and unity that lies at the heart of the idea of the transcendental represents an important point of continuity with premodern thinking: the idea of the transcendental can be viewed as a modern appropriation of the concern, already evident in Aristotle, with that which transcends, and so also unifies, the multiple "meanings" of being as articulated through the Categories. The question of the unity of being across the Categories is just the question of the unity of the being of things, which, in the "Copernican" turn undertaken by Kant, is transformed into the question of the "transcendental" unity of the object as it stands in relation to the subject in the structure of experience (that is, to reason) and as it is prior to experience.[19] Moreover, in spite of the fact that there is, in Kant, no explicit statement of anything like the equivocity of being that we find in Aristotle, the Kantian transcendental structure is nevertheless exhibited as a complex unity of elements in which, even though some elements may take priority, no single element can be singled out as that from which all else can be simply derived.[20] Thus Kant gives a special emphasis to ideas of system, writing, for instance, of the unity of the pure understanding that it is

a unity that subsists on its own, which is sufficient by itself, and which is not to be supplemented by any external additions. Hence the sum total of its cognition will constitute a system that is to be grasped and determined under one idea, the completeness and articulation of which system can at the same time yield a touchstone of the correctness and genuineness of all the pieces of cognition fitting into it.[21]

It is thus only through the systematic unity of a number of elements— sensibility *and* understanding, experience *and* reason, subjectivity *and* objectivity—that knowledge is even possible, and it is only through exhibiting that system that the ground of its possibility can be established.

Kant's use of the term "transcendental" as a way of describing his project, and the manner of his approach, is intended to indicate a concern "not so much with objects but rather with our mode of cognition of objects insofar as this is to be possible *a priori*."[22] The aim of the *Critique* is to provide knowledge that is transcendental in just this sense, that is, knowledge that concerns "the mode of our knowledge of objects insofar as . . . it is possible *a priori*." We can therefore characterize transcendental knowledge as knowledge concerned with the grounds of the possibility of our knowledge of objects, or, more broadly, of experience, and this is, of course, how Kant does himself describe it. According to Kant, however, the only guide in arriving at such transcendental knowledge concerning the ground of experience is experience itself.[23] Thus he says of the principle that "everything that happens has its cause," that, although it can be proved "apodictically," it also has the peculiar character that "it first makes possible its ground of proof, namely experience, and must always be presupposed in this."[24]

Kant's mode of proceeding here might seem immediately to suggest a circularity in his approach, and circularity has, indeed, often been taken as characteristic of transcendental philosophy and transcendental reasoning—both in Kant and elsewhere.[25] In fact, Heidegger discusses the apparent circularity that Kant acknowledges in the proof of the principles of the understanding, and connects it directly with the character of the transcendental project as fundamentally concerned with the issue of unity:

> The unity of thought and intuition is itself the essence of experience. The proof [of the principles] consists in showing that the principles of pure understanding are possible through that which they themselves make possible, through the nature of experience. This is an obvious circle, and indeed a necessary one. The principles are proved by recourse to that whose arising they make possible, because these propositions are to bring to light nothing else than this circularity itself; for this constitutes the essence of experience. . . . Experience is in itself a circular happening through which what lies within the circle becomes exposed [*eroffnet*]. This open [*Offene*], however, is nothing other than the between [*Zwischen*]—between us and the thing.[26]

A similar circularity appears in Heidegger's own work,[27] particularly in *Being and Time*, where it is seen as identical with the basic structure of care.[28] Notwithstanding the absence of explicit reference to circularity in Heidegger's later thinking,[29] the phenomenon at issue nevertheless remains central—as it must—since what is at issue in the "circularity" of the transcendental is simply the way in which thinking is always already given over to the world and so the way in which thought and world always constitute an already given unity.[30]

For Kant, of course, the structure at issue here, which for early Heidegger is the structure of care, is understood as part of the essential structure of subjectivity, which is to say of reason. The apparent circularity of the transcendental in Kant, which has also been seen by some commentators as actually a form of self-referentiality,[31] can thus be understood as referring to what might be understood as the self-constituting character of reason or subjectivity itself. Kant characterizes transcendental thinking as based in just such a notion of self-constitution: "transcendental philosophy," he says, "is the capacity of the self-constituting subject to constitute itself as given in intuition."[32] At this point, of course, the question of the relation between transcendental philosophy and idealism comes directly into view. One might wonder, moreover, whether talk of self-constitution does not suggest a conception of subjectivity as "self-grounding"—something that would be problematic indeed. Much depends, of course, on exactly how transcendental subjectivity is to be understood; and, though this is not the place for a detailed discussion of the matter, two points should be noted. First, the Kantian focus on subjectivity need not entail any necessary reduction of the structure by which experience is possible to one element, namely, subjectivity, since that focus can be taken to indicate only a certain ordering of elements within that structure. Second, the idea of transcendental subjectivity ought not to be understood as referring us to some substantive "subject" that performs the work of constitution upon itself.[33]

From the perspective of the present discussion, however, what is crucial is simply the idea of the transcendental as concerned with a form of grounding that is not achieved by reference to anything other than what is to be grounded. This need not imply any form of "self-grounding," but only that the ground not be some further "thing" that stands behind or beyond that which is to be grounded. In Kant's case, this means grounding experience through exhibiting its own "internal" structure of possibility. The emphasis on the self-constituting character of the unity that is at issue in the Kantian conception of the transcendental—on the self-constituting unity of subjectivity or reason—thus gives special emphasis to the way in which the unity of being is only to be worked out in terms of the structure of being as such and cannot involve appeal to anything other than this. It is this that can be seen to underlie the frequent appearance of circularity in connection with the transcendental.

The emphasis on some notion of "self-constitution," "self-referentiality," or "internality" is not peculiar to the question of ground as it arises only within a transcendental frame, however, nor is it peculiar even to the question of ground as it arises in relation to being. The appeal to such notions is characteristic of the question of unity wherever it arises. The real unity of a thing is to be found in the internal articulation of the elements that make it up, and their interrelation, rather than in anything that "imposes" unity from "outside." Any attempt to provide a principle of unity that stands outside of being, if one could even make sense of such an idea, would fail to address the unity of *being*—directing attention only to the unity of what is other than being or providing a unity that was essentially derivative of that "other" (and so a unity in a similarly "derivative" sense). Aristotle makes much the same point when he says that things that are one "by nature" are more properly unitary than those things that are one "by art"—unity is primarily unity of form, such that the unity of artificial things, whose unity of form is imposed from without, are unities in only a derivative sense.

From Kant and Aristotle, then, we can take two important points concerning the understanding of unity as it arises in relation to the question of ground (and also with respect to the idea of unity as it relates to the idea of transcendental). First, the unity at issue when we talk of ground is a unity that, even though it gives priority to some notions over others, nevertheless preserves an ordered multiplicity of elements within it. Second, the unity at issue is not to be found anywhere outside of that which is unified. Thus, in looking to establish the ground of beings, we must look to the unity of the being of beings, but in doing this, we cannot look beyond that being, nor to any other beings. In summary, we might say that the question of ground, understood in terms of the question of unity as expressed in Aristotle and in Kant, thus concerns the "internal" articulation of an otherwise differentiated structure.

It is characteristic of Kant's project in the *Critique of Pure Reason*, however, that the task of *grounding* knowledge that is identical with the articulation of its proper unity is also seen as a matter of determining the *limits* of knowledge. Thus, in the preface to the first edition of the *Critique*, Kant says of the very project of a critique of pure reason that it will address "the decision about the possibility or impossibility of a metaphysics in general, and the determination of its sources, as well as its extent and boundaries."[34] Indeed, the task of determining the extent and limits of metaphysics, and more generally of reason and knowledge, is one that cannot be undertaken independently of the determination of its sources. The point can be put quite generally, in a way that is not restricted to Kant: to determine that in which the possibility of something rests is, at one and the same time, to determine what is possible for it—to determine ground is also to determine limit.

That there is a close connection between the ideas of ground and limit, and so also between limit and unity, is evident in Aristotle, as well as in Kant. Thus, in *Metaphysics* Δ, Aristotle writes:

Limit [*peras*] means [*legetai*] (a) the furthest part of each thing, and the first point outside which no part of a thing can be found, and the first point within which all parts are contained. (b) Any form of magnitude or of something possessing magnitude. (c) The end [*telos*] of each thing . . . (d) the reality [*ousia*] or essence [*to ti en einai*] of each thing, and the essence of each. . . . Thus it is obvious that "limit" has not only as many senses as "beginning" [*arche*] but even more; because the beginning is a kind of limit, but not every limit is a beginning.[35]

Thus, every principle of unity—every "beginning" or "origin"—is to be construed as also a limit, since to unify is to limit. But Aristotle here distinguishes the notion of limit as tied to origin, and so to unity, from another sense that is not so tied, and this latter sense encompasses, most obviously, the notion of limit that figures in the first of his definitions: "the last point of each thing . . . and the first point within which any part is." The idea of limit given in this first definition seems to be more properly spatial than the ideas specified in the succeeding definitions and to be exemplified by notions of limit as used to mark out the area of a thing within space. Significantly, such a "spatial" conception of limit brings no strong notion of unity with it beyond the idea that, in marking something as a limit, what lies within the limit is thereby demarcated from what lies without. In such an idea, however, there is no sense of the limit as derived from and determined by the nature of the thing limited—the limit is simply that at which something stops and so we might characterize it, in distinction from the concept of limit as origin, as a notion of limit as terminus.[36]

In the concluding chapter of the *Prolegomena*, entitled "On the Determination of the Bounds of Pure Reason," Kant himself discusses two different senses of limit (in the German these two senses are marked by two different terms—*Grenze* and *Schranke*—which are sometimes taken to correspond, in English, to *bound* and *limit*[37]). These two senses are distinguished in that one involves something positive whereas the other contains only negations. The positive sense of limit leads Kant to posit the existence of *noumena*, and it is by means of this positive sense of limit that we are able to determine "the bounds of reason," which is, in Kant's words, "the spot where the occupied space (namely, experience) touches the void (that of which we can know nothing, namely, *noumena*)."[38] The negative sense of limit is simply the sense that is exemplified by the always incomplete character of empirical knowledge. These two senses of limit do not match up exactly with the two senses we distinguished in Aristotle—the sense of limit as that at which something merely stops, as its terminus, and the sense of limit as the determining nature of a thing, that is, as its origin— but there is nevertheless a correspondence here, even if a slightly complicated one.

Although Kant uses spatial metaphors to characterize the positive sense of limit, that positive sense is actually much closer to the idea of limit as origin than to limit as terminus, whereas the negative sense of limit is closer to the idea of limit as terminus than as origin. The positive sense of limit is closely tied to the character of that which is thereby limited, in this case reason, as also unified. The positing of the *noumenon* follows from the very character of reason itself and from the necessity of the distinction, drawn on the basis of the whole Kantian transcendental structure, between the thing "as it appears" and the thing "in itself."[39] Indeed, there can be no other access to the idea of the *noumenon* at all, since we can have no knowledge of such a "thing-in-itself," but must posit it purely as a requirement of the understanding of reason, and of knowledge, in its unity and so together with its proper limits. The complication, of course, is that the negative concept of limit, as applied to empirical knowledge, is itself able to be grounded, when properly understood, in relation to the overall unity of reason, and so the negative sense of limit turns out to be grounded, at least in Kant, by reference to the positive sense—this is just what is indicated by the idea of *phenomena* as distinct from *noumena* (although matters are further complicated by Kant's introduction of a distinction between a positive and negative concept of *noumenon* in which the negative conception is given primary emphasis as the sense in which the *noumenon* operates as a limit[40]).

The idea of the *noumenon* thus plays an important role in the Kantian grounding of reason and knowledge, but not through being that in which reason is itself grounded. Indeed, even talk of the *noumena* as "cause" of the phenomena should not be taken to imply any simple causal grounding. Kant says of the realm of the *noumena* that it is, to us, a "void,"[41] an "empty space,"[42] whereas in the *Opus postumum*, he is emphatic in talking of the *noumenon* as a "mere thought-object (*ens rationis*)."[43] Although this is, once again, difficult and contentious territory, the crucial point for the purposes of this discussion is that the way in which the *noumena* function as limiting reason (in the positive sense of limit) is directly tied to the way in which the concept of *noumena* is part of the overall transcendental structure wherein the unity of reason is delineated and the articulation of which constitutes the proper grounding of reason. In this respect, the role of the *noumenal* in the Kantian transcendental structure is not to function as some realm of "things" from which all else is derived and on which all else rests, but as one element in a much larger framework.

Throughout the *Critique of Pure Reason*, and also in the *Prolegomena*, Kant makes use of spatial, cartographic, and topographic metaphors and images to describe his project and the ideas central to it. In the famous opening to the chapter on the distinction between *phenomena* and *noumena*, for instance, Kant describes his achievement in the first part of the *Critique of Pure Reason* in explicitly cartographic terms: "We have now not merely traveled through the land of pure understanding, and carefully inspected every part of it, but have also surveyed it, and determined the place for each thing in it."[44] The use of such metaphors is not merely a reflection of Kant's own geographical interests (he was, after all, one of the founders of modern geography within the university), but relates directly to the way in which he conceives of the question of ground and his own response to that question. Knowledge and reason are not to be grounded in anything that lies outside knowledge and experience; instead the task is one of mapping out the very territory at issue—the territory that he refers to in the above passage as "the land of truth—enchanting name!"[45] The idea of the *noumenal* plays a role in that mapping, but not through appearing on the map itself; rather it names the void into which no such map can ever take us—a void that must be posited, on the basis of what we know of the territory itself, in order that we can indeed make explicit the proper boundaries of the territory in question. Moreover, the map Kant provides for us is one that is constructed only by an investigation and survey that proceeds from *within* the territory that is thereby mapped out (and here there are echoes of the same emphasis on "internality" or "self-referentiality" that are also to found in the ideas of the circular and "self-constituting" character of the transcendental). The transcendental project is thus one that can be characterized as an attempt to describe and delineate a particular place—the place of reason, of knowledge, of experience[46]—and as with all such attempts at such topography or "topology," the place to be described here cannot be other than the very place in which the topographer or topologist is herself situated.

Just as Heidegger's approach to the question of being and ground is heavily indebted to his reading of Aristotle, so something analogous to the Aristotelian equivocity of being appears as a central element in Heidegger's own thought. In *Being and Time*, for instance, Heidegger can be seen as taking the multiple senses of being, there understood in terms of the complex array of elements that are constitutive of the structure of *Dasein* (a structure that is identical with the structure of being understood as presence—*Anwesenheit*) to be unified through the relating of those elements in ecstatic temporality in which the primary *ekstasis* is that of the future.[47] Although the role of temporality is modified somewhat in his later thinking,[48] still we find there the same type of analysis in which a number of different elements are seen as together constitutive of the single structure that is the structure of being. Moreover, the equivocity that is first clearly set out in Aristotle, and which applies not only to Aristotle's talk of being, but also to a range of other key terms, can be seen to carry over into the Heideggerian vocabulary. This is partly what makes for such difficulty in reading Heidegger, since the same term may be used in a range of different and yet connected senses, while different terms can sometimes refer to much the same structure, depending on the aspect of that structure that is to be given emphasis. Thus being is seen as closely tied (and sometimes almost identical) with a range of different notions such as presence, truth, clearing, opening, and so forth, while it can also refer to the totality of beings, to the being of beings (and this too in more than one sense), to being as such. One might say that just as metaphysics, in its problematic forms, attempts to construe being (and ground with it) as identical with some particular being or aspect of being, so it also strives to eliminate the equivocity that attaches to terms such as being and to find some univocal sense to which they can finally be reduced. Heidegger's own approach is to maintain such equivocity, although at the same time he avoids any presentation that would suggest that the various notions at issue here could be simply aligned one beside the other in some comprehensive hierarchy. The equivocity of being brings with it a certain necessary opacity.[49]

The way in which the equivocity of being is articulated in Heidegger's thinking naturally changes as Heidegger's own thought shifts. One of the distinctive features of the investigation of the equivocity of being in Heidegger's early thinking is its joining of the Aristotelian question of the unity of being with the problem of meaning as Heidegger inherits it from Dilthey and from Husserl. For Dilthey, meaning is the fundamental category for the understanding of the human world—for the understanding of that which we might say prefigures the Heideggerian concept of *Dasein*. For Husserl, too, the problem of meaning is central: phenomenology can be viewed as an attempt to uncover the structure of meaning through the analysis of the structure of consciousness, that is, of the structure of acts of meaning-constitution, *noesis*. On this basis, the inquiry into meaning can be viewed as an inquiry into that which makes possible the unitary field that is the field of intelligibility or meaningfulness—where the unity of that field is understood in terms of its own internal differentiation and integration, and so in terms of the "internal" relatedness of the elements that make up that field. Meaning is, then, the unity of the "field" or domain within which what is meaningful can "show up" as meaningful. As Heidegger tells us in *Being and Time*, meaning "is that wherein the intelligibility [*Verständlichkeit*] of something maintains itself. That which can be articulated in a disclosure by which we understand, we call "meaning.""[50] Meaning is thus the structure wherein things can show up as meaningful; the inquiry into the meaning of being is the inquiry into that wherein things can show up as things that are, and thus the uncovering of the structures that make such intelligibility of being possible—the uncovering of meaning—is identical with the uncovering of the structure of being itself. Understood as a question that asks after the ground of "what is," the inquiry into meaning aims to uncover such a ground by exhibiting the unity of the structure within which things are—by exhibiting the internal relatedness of the domain in which anything meaningful appears (and thereby also marking it off within its proper bounds). In *Being and Time*, Heidegger reinterprets this problem of the unity of meaning in a way that integrates it, indeed shows it to be continuous with, the Aristotelian inquiry into the complex unity of being as well as with the Kantian inquiry into the conditions for the possibility of experience. It is in this fashion that Heidegger is able to transform ontology into phenomenology, the phenomenological into the hermeneutical, and the hermeneutical into the transcendental.

The unity of meaning that is identical, in *Being and Time*, with the unity of being is, of course, a unity that is worked out through the articulation of the complex interplay between a number of different elements. Inasmuch as this constitutes a response to the question of ground, it does so not by identifying a single element as primary, but rather by exhibiting the connectedness of those elements, albeit a connectedness that also requires a certain ordering. In *Being and Time*, Heidegger refers to the mutual relatedness of the elements at issue here in terms of their "equiprimordiality" (*Gleichursprünglichkeit*).[51] Within a structure of equiprimordial elements, a form of grounding is not arrived at, according to Heidegger, by reference to some "simple primal ground" from which all else is derived. Instead such grounding is achieved through the complex interconnection of the very elements themselves—elements whose plurality remains irreducible. Heidegger's rejection of the idea of any form of reduction or derivation here is closely tied to his conception of the analytic of *Dasein* as not a matter of dissolving or breaking *Dasein* up into its parts, but rather of demonstrating its essential unity. Elsewhere, commenting on the concept of such an "analytic" in *Being and Time*, Heidegger draws explicitly on Kant to reinforce this point. In the "Analytic of Concepts," Kant emphasizes that the analytic at issue there does not entail what usually passes for analysis, but rather involves "the much less frequently attempted analysis of the faculty of understanding itself, in order to research the possibility of *a priori* concepts by seeking them only in the understanding as their birthplace and analyzing its pure use in general."[52] In relation to this Heidegger notes that the concept of the "analytic" at issue here is "is not a reduction into elements, but the articulation of the [a priori] unity of a composite structure [*Strukturgefüge*]," and he adds that "this is also essential in my concept of the 'analytic of Da-sein.'"[53] Even though the idea of the transcendental largely disappears from Heidegger's later thought, along with other Kantian notions such as that of an "analytic," still one can discern the same emphasis on the articulation of unity over reduction into elements. The idea of equiprimordiality referred to in *Being and Time* is thus exemplified, not merely by the structure outlined in that work, but also, much later, by the idea of the Fourfold (*das Geviert*),[54] in which Earth, Sky, Gods, and Mortals are jointly constitutive of "World," and of the Opening that is World, and yet it is only within the unity of the Fourfold that Earth appears as Earth, Sky as Sky, Gods as Gods, and Mortals as Mortal.

Heidegger's discussions of the Fourfold also bring the connection between unity and limit clearly into view. The Fourfold is the gathering together of world-constituting elements into a single but complex unity. That gathering-together does not happen in some indeterminate "nowhere," but always occurs in a determinate location, a place, and with respect to the particulars of that place. The descriptions of the gathering of the Fourfold in "Building Dwelling Thinking," for instance, or in other later essays, focus on the way in which the elements of world are brought together in and through particular things, such as, famously, a bridge, and so also in particular locales or "places."[55] The unity that is established in the gathering of the Fourfold is thus the same unity to be found in the opening up of a place and in the establishing of the boundary or horizon that is part of the structure of such a place. Here we find Heidegger referring explicitly, as he does in so many places (and in a way that also echoes Aristotle and Kant), to the concept of boundary or limit as itself tied to origin and to ground: "A space is something that has been made room for, something that is cleared and free, namely within a boundary, Greek *peras*.

A boundary is not that at which something stops but, as the Greeks rec-ognized, the boundary is that from which something *begins its presencing*. That is why the concept is that of *horismos*, that is, the horizon, the boundary."[56]

The sense of limit as origin that appears in the talk of the Fourfold is not peculiar to Heidegger's later thinking, but, as I have noted elsewhere,[57] runs throughout Heidegger's thought. Not only is it a key idea in Hei-degger's thinking about death (in *Being and Time* as well as in the later work), but it also connects with Heidegger's understanding of *aletheia* (unconcealment) as the happening of truth, the coming of things into appearance, the event of presencing. In "The Origin of the Work of Art," Heidegger talks of the happening of truth as *aletheia* in terms of "clearing" or "lighting" (*Lichtung*). Thus he writes that

In the midst of beings as a whole an open place comes to presence. There is a clear-ing [*Lichtung*]. . . . The being can only be, as a being, if it stands within, and stands out within, what is illuminated in this clearing. Only this clearing grants us human beings access to those beings that we ourselves are not and admittance to the being that we ourselves are. Thanks to this clearing, beings are unconcealed in certain and changing degrees. But even to be *concealed*, is something the being can only do within the scope of the illuminated. Each being which we encounter and which encounters us maintains this strange opposition of presence in that at the same time it always holds itself back in a concealment.[58]

Truth or *aletheia*, understood as the unconcealment of beings, thus turns out to be inextricably bound to what is not truth, that is, to concealment, so much so that Heidegger is led to write that "Truth, in its essence, is un-truth."[59] Elsewhere, Heidegger makes a similar point by emphasizing the privative character of the Greek term *aletheia* in which the word-stem *leth-* or *lath-* (referring to concealment) takes primacy.[60] In fact, one should think of *aletheia* as itself encompassing the play of concealment and unconcealment in exactly the same way that limit or boundary involves a play of closing-off and opening-up (if the latter term is more often emphasized in talk of limit, this is because it is more common to think of limit as primarily a closing off—analogously, Heidegger's emphasis on the connection of truth to concealment can be seen as a response to the ten-dency to think of truth primarily in terms of unconcealment). The connection of truth as *aletheia* with the idea of limit is strongly evident in "The Origin of the Work of Art." There Heidegger notes two ways in which beings remain concealed even while they are also revealed: first, beings remain concealed inasmuch as they refuse themselves to us in such a way that what we know of them is always limited; second, beings remain

concealed inasmuch as their appearance also obscures ("Beings push themselves in front of others, the one hides the other, this casts that into
shadow"[61]). Truth is thus itself a delimitation just insofar as it is also an
unconcealing; inasmuch as it delimits and unconceals, so truth can also
be understood as an originary *placing*.

Heidegger's emphasis on the primacy of concealment in relation to
unconcealment, of untruth to truth, echoes the Husserlian emphasis on
the aspectual character of appearance;[62] it also prefigures the Gadamerian
emphasis on the positive role of prejudice, literally, "prejudgment," in all
understanding—prejudice is a closing off that thereby also opens up.[63] The
coming to appearance of things is thus a matter of their coming out of
their prior concealment, but such revealing is precisely a matter of demarcation and limitation, since "Where demarcation is lacking, nothing can
come to presence as that which it is."[64] Limit is part of the very structure
of unconcealment or presence—thus truth is possible only on the basis of
"untruth," and the being of the thing is possible only in relation to its
"nonbeing."[65] Although there is much more at issue in the Heideggerian
account, the interplay between the hidden and the unhidden that Heidegger describes, when considered in connection with the idea of limit as
origin, may suggest a further link with the Kantian notion of the *noumenon*.
As Kant presents matters, the *noumenon* functions as a positive limit
through marking off the thing-in-itself from the thing as it appears, but in
this respect the *noumenon* can be thought of as standing in much the same
relation to the phenomenon that it thereby marks off as does the idea of
the hidden, in Heidegger, stand to the unhidden, as untruth stands to
truth. Yet if we think of matters in this way, then we must recognize that
the *noumenon* cannot be thought of as an object that is somehow not
intuited (the "positive" sense of *noumenon* Kant warns against), just as the
"hidden" does not name some thing to which we simply do not have
access.

The conception of ground that can be found in *Being and Time*, along
with the ideas of unity and limit with which it is necessarily connected,
continues through into Heidegger's later thinking in spite of other shifts
in his thought. Whether we look to the evocative descriptions of the Fourfold in essays such as "Building Dwelling Thinking," to the depiction of
the working of truth in "The Origin of the Work of Art," or to the analysis
of *Dasein* in *Being and Time*, the question of ground remains at issue, as
does the working out of that question, and with it the question of being,
in connection with the ideas of unity and limit. Equally, however, there is
a clear shift in Heidegger's thinking from the explicitly transcendental

framework of the early work to the "topology" that characterizes his later thinking. Such a topology—a "saying of the place"—is already evident in "The Origin of the Work of Art," in which the focus on unconcealment, and so on the "clearing of being," is immediately suggestive of *topos*: the clearing of being is the *topos* of being, and the "saying" of the clearing is thus also a saying of the *topos*, the place, of being.

The idea of topology gives special emphasis to the nonreductive character of Heidegger's thinking—to its refusal to think being by way of beings—even while it aims, nonetheless, to "speak" being and so to articulate the "structure" within which any being comes to be. In addition, and unlike the explicitly transcendental approach of *Being and Time*, the topology of Heidegger's later thought does not take the analysis of the being of *Dasein* as its central focus, or even its starting point. Instead it presents the being of *Dasein* (that is, the being of mortals—those beings capable of death), as a part of that more encompassing structure that is the truth, the clearing, the place of being. This does not mean that the analysis of *Dasein* is thereby abandoned, but only that it needs to be moved through (as *Being and Time* is similarly a work to move through rather than to remain with)[66]—it is a necessary stage in the thinking of being, even though it cannot represent the culmination of such thinking. The focus on the structure of *Dasein* is characteristic of the transcendental inasmuch as the transcendental can itself be seen to be characterized by a concern with the structure of transcendence (the "passing over" in the direction of object and world), and the essence of *Dasein* is taken to be identical with the structure of transcendence, and this is certainly how Heidegger sees matters.[67] The project that makes up the first two parts of Division One of *Being and Time* thus takes the question of being as a question that concerns the structure of transcendence, and what that project was unable to accomplish was the shift, the turning or reversal, that would have moved from the problem of transcendence understood as a problem concerning the being of *Dasein* to the problem of the structure within which transcendence itself must be located and in which transcendence has its origin. In Heidegger's own thinking, this shift back to the truth or place of being was accomplished only through a reworking of the framework within which the inquiry into being was to proceed, and such reworking was required not merely because of the philosophical need to move beyond the transcendental framework employed in *Being and Time*, but also because of the readiness with which the language and approach of the earlier work was able to be assimilated back to a metaphysical perspective—that is, to a perspective from which being, and so also the notion of ground (as well as of unity and limit), is once again understood in terms of beings.[68] The thinking of the *Ereignis* that appears in Heidegger's work from the late 1930s onwards can be seen as aiming at just such a more originary thinking of the unitary and unifying ("gathering/appropriating") happening of the truth of being.

Herman Philipse asks: "What, we may wonder . . . justifies Heidegger's assumption that there must be one fundamental meaning of 'to be'? Why does his question of being have a pole of unity?"[69] The question is not altogether clearly put, since it could be seen as asking why the various senses of being must be unified in relation to one primary sense, or why the senses of being should be thought as having any unity at all. In fact, the latter question is clearly the more basic. If the various senses of being are to be unified, then this can only be through establishing some ordering of those senses, and so through the establishing of a certain priority among them, but this does not explain why any such unity should be sought in the first place. Philipse's question can thus be viewed as asking after the reason for the association of the question of being with the idea of unity. The answer to that question, however, should already be clear: the question of being is a question concerning the ground of being and this question is precisely a question that asks after the unity of being—to ground is, in fact, to unify. Indeed, once we understand the connection between the question of being and the question of ground, and the way unity is implicated in both such questions, then we can also understand why being might be thought in terms of unity itself (although in saying this we must be careful not to misconstrue the unity that is at issue here), as well as the way in which the articulation of such unity necessarily requires a certain marking out of limits.

In fact, leaving aside the details of the Heideggerian understanding of what is involved here, the idea that to ground is, in some sense, to unify is an implicit presupposition evident in almost all philosophical inquiry. Any attempt to understand or to explain is already a matter of establishing a certain unity or integration, and so also a certain demarcation, with respect to some particular range of phenomena or some particular domain. Thus one may look to explain some particular range of physical phenomena, for example, by reference to some set of underlying physical laws— laws that may achieve the requisite relating and integrating of the phenomena in question by showing how one level of description of those phenomena is actually dependent on (or reducible to) another level of description. In this respect, although the way in which Heidegger understands the philosophical concern with ground and with unity may diverge from that which is common with the tradition, it is not discontinuous with it—the Heideggerian focus on ground, and on unity, is a focus that arises out of the tradition itself.

Perhaps what really perplexes Philipse, however, is not merely the Heideggerian concern with unity, but rather the Heideggerian concern with being as such—why should it be thought that there is some single encompassing question about being? The question of being, however, is inextricably bound to the question of ground. Asking why it should be thought that there is a question concerning being is thus the same as asking why it should be thought that there is a question concerning the ground of beings. But as soon as one puts matters in this latter form, in terms of the question of ground, then it should immediately become apparent that to ask why we should ask the question is to ask after nothing other than the very ground for questioning itself. To question the question of ground—and so also to question the question of being—is thus already to acknowledge the force of that question; it is already to take a step in asking the very question that is in question.[70] As soon as we allow ourselves to come into the vicinity of the question of being, so we also draw near to the question of ground, and as soon as we raise the question of ground, which is to say, as soon as we begin to question, so being is also raised as an issue.

Following the path of Heidegger's thought, we can clearly see the question of ground as a continuing concern that moves from the transcendental framework of his early work to the explicitly topological approach of the later. Moreover, the concern with ground, and the working out of that concern in relation to concepts of unity and limit, turns out to provide an important illumination of what is at issue in both the transcendental and topological projects. Indeed, although the topological can be seen as a turn away from certain aspects of the transcendental—even, perhaps, as a "reversal"—it does not represent an abrupt break. It is rather a continuation and deepening of the concerns that motivate and underlie the transcendental project. One can thus view Heidegger's thought, inasmuch as it always remains focused on the question of ground, as showing both the way in which the transcendental must give way to the topological if that question is properly to be addressed, and also the way in which the transcendental itself must already constitute a form of topology (a particular "appropriation" of the topological). Of course, while the transcendental may thus be taken to stand in a special relation to topology, it is also the case that all thinking is topological precisely in the sense that it aims at a "saying" of that place—a place that constantly opens up before us and that is therefore never to be reduced to what is merely "present"—in which we always already find ourselves; a place in which we are given over to the mortals among whom we ourselves are, to the gods, to the earth and to the sky. It is this that is the place, the *topos*, of being. To ask after the ground of what is—after the ground of beings—is thus, whether knowingly or not, to ask after this very place; it is indeed to ask after the place of being.

5 Nihilism, Place, and "Position"

Certainly a *topography of nihilism* is required, of its process and its overcoming. Yet the topography must be preceded by a *topology*: a discussion locating the locale which gathers being and nothing into their essence, determines the essence of nihilism, and thus lets us recognize those paths on the ways toward a possible overcoming of nihilism.

—Heidegger, "On the Question of Being," in *Pathmarks*

According to late Heidegger, the contemporary world is suffering from an "oblivion of being"—we live, he says, in a "desolate time," a time of destitution, a time of the "world's night."[1] He sees this desolation and destitution as most accurately diagnosed by two key thinkers, one of whom is the poet Friedrich Hölderlin and the other the philosopher Friedrich Nietzsche. It is Nietzsche who provides Heidegger with much that is foundational to his analysis of the nihilism that he takes to be characteristic of modernity, yet it is Hölderlin who provides him with a way of thinking that is possible even in the face of such nihilism. Not only does Hölderlin mark the way toward the later Heidegger's attempt to reengage with the piety of thinking, namely its properly poetic character, but it is also Hölderlin who plays a crucial role in Heidegger's recognition of thinking as essentially a form of topology. It is as topology that thinking is poetic (which has implications for how we understand the notion of the poetic itself); it is also as topology, and only as topology, that thinking is able to recognize and to begin to understand the nihilistic character of modernity. The nihilism of modernity is, above all, a denial of the very *topos* in which thinking itself comes to pass; and the possibility of finding a way to think in the face of such a denial (a denial that refuses even to recognize its character *as* denial) is thus essentially dependent on maintaining a proper sense of the topological character of thinking, and so of thinking's proper *place*, as well as our own orientation within it.

The idea that the Heideggerian response to the nihilism of modernity is indeed to be understood in terms of a turn to the topological might seem an unsurprising claim, and to be characteristic of a whole series of "anti-modernist" reactions that emphasize place, rootedness, and community, of which Heidegger's is merely one, albeit highly influential, example. On such an view, the turn to *topos* is also entirely consistent with Heidegger's political entanglement with Nazism in the 1930s—Nazism being understood as itself drawing heavily on a conception of German identity as rooted in "blood and soil" (*Blut und Boden*), in *Heimat* and Fatherland, and thereby standing opposed to the decadent excesses of a nihilistic and cosmopolitan modernity.

In fact, the thematization of *topos* in Heidegger's thought, and the emphasis on Hölderlin as opposed to Nietzsche (and so on the resistance to nihilism rather than merely its proclamation), is increasingly explicit as Heidegger moves away from, rather than toward, the engagement with Nazism. Moreover, the Heideggerian critique of nihilism, especially as it develops in the 1930s and early 1940s around the thought of Friedrich Nietzsche, and which is there articulated in terms of a critique both of "subjectivism" and of metaphysics, is itself directed at what also appear as potential tendencies in Heidegger's own previous thinking, including the thinking that moves Heidegger in the direction of Nazism.[2] Rather than simply a form of reactionary romanticism, then, the Heideggerian turn to topology can be taken as constituting a critical response to a destitution and nihilism at the very heart of modernity—a nihilism and destitution that is not marked by any single political ideology of the right or the left, and that Heidegger saw as exemplified in Nazism,[3] but which, today, is perhaps more clearly evident in the worldwide dominance of a technological-bureaucratic, corporatized "economism."[4]

The exploration of the interrelation between the themes of nihilism and topology in Heidegger's thought, with respect to which I will address only one small part here, cannot be separated from the shifts in the development of Heidegger's thinking both in terms of his engagement with the philosophical tradition (and the larger history of the West of which it is a part) and in terms of certain problematic elements within his own thinking. This is not an engagement that is ever finally settled, however, but one that always remains unstable and to some extent uncertain. Thus, as I have argued elsewhere in this book,[5] Heidegger's thinking can be understood, in topological terms, as a constant turning to place that is also a turning in and of place.

The issues that are at stake in Heidegger's thinking of nihilism, and of modernity in general, as it connects with his thinking of place (and less directly, with the matter of questioning in his thought) come to a particular focus in the 1935–36 essay "The Origin of the Work of Art," or more specifically in the "Appendix ("Zusatz") to that essay, written in 1956. In his clarificatory comments on the earlier essay, Heidegger focuses on an issue that is at the center of his turn to topology and at the center of the problem of nihilism: the question of the proper understanding of the relation between being and human being, which is also the question of the human relation to place, and the underlying question of the nature of place as such. It is on these comments, and particularly the manner in which they thematize the Greek term *thesis*, or "position," that I will focus my discussion here. The aim will be to lay bare one part of the larger development of Heidegger's thinking, and the problems with which it is concerned, particularly as these connect with the matter of both nihilism and topology.

Place and "Position"

"The Origin of the Work of Art" is situated at a key point in the development of Heidegger's thinking. It is in this essay that Heidegger first presents the "event" of truth in terms of the gathering of elements around a single "thing"—the artwork, the temple—allowing the opening up of world on the closedness of earth.[6] It is also in this essay, in a way directly connected with its thematization of the event of truth, that the topological themes present in Heidegger's thought from the start take on a new and more explicit character.[7] Thus, for all that "The Origin of the Work of Art" constitutes something of a *Holzweg* (a forest path that leads nowhere unless to a woodsman's clearing), it nevertheless harks back to important elements, including certain problematic elements, in Heidegger's earlier thought, while also pointing the way forward, as Gadamer recognized,[8] to key aspects of the later work.

One such pointer forward that is of particular relevance to the issue of topology and nihilism is the appearance in the essay, and in Heidegger's appended comments, of the term that figures in later writings as designating the essence of technology, namely, *Gestell*. In his 1956 discussion, Heidegger notes that the way in which *Ge-stell* (which Heidegger hyphenates here) is used in the 1935–36 discussion is in the Greek sense of "the gathering together of the bringing forth" and so as enabling a mode of appearance or unconcealment. The sense of *Ge-stell* that Heidegger employs later, as "the summoning of everything into assured availability" that is the essence of technology, is a sense that he tells us is "thought out of" this earlier use even though it is distinct from it.

Consequently, although "The Origin of the Work of Art" does not itself take up the problematic character of modern technology (and so does not take up the movement of nihilism as it occurs in relation to modernity), the essay nevertheless already operates, through its initial deployment of the term *Ge-stell*, within a framework out of which the later thinking can emerge. Equally significant, however, is the way in which the notion of *Ge-stell* as it appears in "The Origin of the Work of Art" is explicitly presented by Heidegger, in his appended comments, as deriving "not from bookcase [*Büchergestell*] or installation" (a derivation often cited in discussions of the term[9]), but rather from this Greek sense of a gathering that also brings forth, which is itself understood in terms of a "placing" or "positioning." *Ge-stell* is the "positioning" that allows something to stand before us, to appear, in a manner that has a bounded shape and character, an orientation, one might say, belonging to it. It is thus that Heidegger's use of *Ge-stell* in "The Origin of the Work of Art" is translated by Young in the Cambridge edition of the essay as "placement." As a result, *Ge-stell* has to be seen as itself carrying a set of topological associations that are themselves central to the analysis that "The Origin of the Work of Art" develops.

Inasmuch as "The Origin of the Work of Art" provides a "topology" of truth and of the artwork, so it is a topology that focuses on the happening of truth as occurring in and through the "placed" work. The happening of truth is therefore an establishing and opening up of *place* as much as it is an establishing and opening up of *world*. Moreover, although terms referring directly to place (terms such as *Ort* or *Stätte*) appear only occasionally in the discussion in "The Origin of the Work of Art," whereas they become much more central in later essays, the earlier essay already seems to draw upon a similar notion of place as itself a *gathering*—a gathering focused in the placed work—to that which appears so prominently in Heidegger's later explications of place.[10]

The topological character of Heidegger's thinking of *Ge-stell* is reinforced by Heidegger's comment, again from the 1956 "Appendix," that *Ge-stell* "as the essence of modern technology, comes from letting-lie-before experienced in the Geek manner, λόγος, from the Greek ποίησις and θέσις." The last of these, *thesis*, can mean position, but also orientation, setting, or placing, and the verb from which it is derived, *tithemi*, has almost exactly the same connotations as the German *stellen* that recurs throughout "The Origin of the Work of Art" and is present in *Ge-stell* as well as a range of other terms such as *vorstellen* (to represent), *aufstellen* (to set up or to install), *feststellen* (to fix in place or make determinate), *herstellen* (to produce). Heidegger also takes the Greek sense of *thesis* to be at work in his use, in phrases such as "the *setting*-to-work of truth," of the German *setzen* (meaning "to set")—quoting himself, he writes, "So one reads on p. 36: 'Setting and taking possession [*Setzen and Besetzen*] are here always (!) thought in the sense of the Greek, θέσις, which means a setting up in the unconcealed.' The Greek 'setting' means: placing as allowing to arise, for example, a statue."[11] *Ge-stell, stellen, setzen,* and *thesis* with these, all seem to be understood in explicitly topological fashion as tied to a sense of place or being-in-place—although it is a sense of place that is also connected with a notion of *setting-in-*place, which is perhaps also a *setting up* of place, or positioning.

Partly because of the use of *Ge-stell* in his later thinking, but also because of the possible tension between the ideas of "placing" or "setting" and "letting happen" as these relate to truth and the artwork, Heidegger devotes considerable attention to an analysis of what is involved in the key terms at work here, "to place" and "to set" (*stellen* and *setzen*), arguing for an understanding of these terms that does indeed connect them with a reading of *thesis* as a "bringing *hither* into unconcealment, bringing *forth* into what is present, that is, allowing to lie forth."[12] The topological character of *thesis* comes clearly to the fore in this discussion (especially in the emphasis on bringing *hither* and the bringing forth *into* what is present), and it is further given prominence through Heidegger's explication of *thesis* (and with it *stellen* and *setzen*) in relation to the notion of boundary (*peras*). The "fixing in place" of truth, which is also a setting of truth to work, is a matter of the establishing of a boundary or outline, but in a passage that closely parallels Heidegger's comments elsewhere, notably in "Building Dwelling Thinking,"[13] Heidegger says that "the boundary, in the Greek sense, does not block off but, rather, as itself something brought forth, first brings what is present to radiance. . . . The boundary which fixes and consolidates is what reposes, reposes in the fullness of movement."[14]

Heidegger's discussion of the concepts of placing and setting is a complex one. He is concerned both to preserve an original Greek sense in which these terms may be employed, and yet also to maintain the continuity between this sense and the transformed sense that belongs to them as they appear in the analysis of technological modernity. *Ge-stell* is thus related to the Greek *thesis* and yet it has to be read as encompassing both the original Greek and the modern sense. The matter is further complicated, however, by the fact that the Greek term *thesis* has itself been taken up into contemporary discourse. Heidegger notes this, commenting that "In the dialectic of Kantian and German idealism . . . thesis, antithesis, and synthesis refer to a placing within the sphere of the subjectivity of con-sciousness. Accordingly, Hegel—correctly in terms of his own position—interpreted the Greek θέσις as the immediate positing [*Setzen*] of the object."[15] As Heidegger will have been well aware, the use of *thesis* evident in Hegel also occurs in Husserl, who employs the German *thetisch*, or "thetic" (which he explicitly understands in relation to *Setzen*) to refer, in general, to the intending of some object *under a certain determination*.[16] The sense of thesis as a positing (often understood as a "position" in the sense of a "claim") is probably the one most familiar to us today—and it is also one in which any topological connotation has been more or less lost or else subsumed under the idea of the posit or the projection (although in the German, of course, a project itself carries a sense of "throw," *Ent-werfen*, a casting *outward or away from*—a sense also present in the Latin from which the English term derives).

Significantly, there is another place in Heidegger's work in which the notion of thesis is discussed "topologically"—where, in fact, it is the rela-tion between *thesis* and *topos* itself that is at issue. In his 1925 lectures on Plato's *Sophist*, Heidegger considers the concepts of *thesis* and *topos* in the course of his exposition of Aristotle's understanding of mathematics.[17] What Heidegger tells us about *thesis* in the *Sophist* discussion is not incom-patible with his comments thirty years later in the appendix to "The Origin of the Work of Art." However, the earlier comments tend implicitly to draw attention to what the later comments seem concerned to downplay, which is precisely the connection between *thesis* and the modern sense of posit or projection. *Thesis* is distinguished from *topos* in that place is absolute (every being has its proper place), and there is an ordering of such places within the *cosmos*, whereas position is absolute as it pertains to the cosmos (so "above" is that to which fire and air move) and relative as it pertains to us (so "above" may change as we move our bodies).[18] Thus geometrical objects have position (*thesis*), but they have no place (*topos*). They are essentially abstracted from place and from body (even though they can be reapplied to particular places and bodies), yet nevertheless retain a direc-tionality and orientation, albeit one that is relative to us. So the abstract geometrical figure is not in any place, but nevertheless has, for instance, a left and a right.[19]

One might say that *thesis* is revealed as having two modes, one of which is almost identical with *topos* (the sense in which *thesis* is positionality in the *cosmos*) and also belongs to the thing, and the other of which is sepa-rate from *topos* (inasmuch as it is fundamentally a matter of human *bodily* orientation, or perhaps better, of the orientation of human *activity*), and therefore belongs to *us* rather than to the thing itself. The possibility of separating position from place in this way opens up the possibility that position, *thesis*, may indeed be understood in the sense of posit or projection—specifically in the sense of a *human* posit or projection, although in Aristotle it has not yet acquired the full implications associated with it in its modern usage.

We might say, then, that the idea of *thesis* already carries within it, in the very possibility of the distinction between the positionality of *place* and the positionality of *human activity*, the possibility of a subjective understanding of positionality, in the sense of a mode of positionality determined on the basis solely of the human, and so also, perhaps, of a "subjective" understanding of place itself. All that is required to arrive at the latter destination is to lose the sense of absolute determination of place belonging to the thing itself, and all that will be left is the relative "place" of "subjective" positionality—indeed, even the thing might be said to disappear in such a relative positionality. This is precisely what seems to happen within the subsequent history of Western thought, and to some extent, this development marks the history of metaphysics, and can already be seen to mark the movement toward nihilism (both in the sense of the denial of value and in the sense of the dominance of *Gestell*)—although the exact nature of this development requires further elucidation.[20]

The sense of *thesis* as posit, as Heidegger would insist, is still more nascent than fully realized in the Greek use of the term, yet it indicates how the Greek sense of the term is not discontinuous with the modern. In this respect, Heidegger's own use of *thesis* to distinguish between the two uses of *Ge-stell*—one referring to the Greek and the other to the essence of technology—might be thought to be somewhat misleading. *Thesis* already contains an ambiguity or equivocation similar to that which is present in *Ge-stell*. Consequently, in his insistence, at least in the his 1956 comments, on reading *Ge-stell* in relation to *thesis* as a way of understanding *Ge-stell* differently, Heidegger may be thought deliberately to overstate and obscure the difference between the Greek and the modern.[21] At the same time, however, the ambiguity at issue here is itself closely related to a difficulty that Heidegger himself recognizes as lying at the very heart of his own thinking, not only in "The Origin of the Work of Art" but also in *Being and Time*. This difficulty cannot be resolved merely by clarifying the ambiguity that surrounds *thesis*, since that ambiguity is itself an expression of the difficulty at issue. It is to that difficulty that I now turn.

Place and "Subjectivism"

If the appearance of the notion of *Gestell* in "The Origin of the Work of Art" points forward into Heidegger's later writing, another reference points back to the earlier. In a particularly important passage from the 1956 "Appendix," Heidegger directs attention to a "distressing difficulty" that is evident in the 1935–1936 essay, and that he tells us has preoccupied him since *Being and Time*. He writes:

According to pages 44 and 33 [of "The Origin of the Work of Art"], it is the art*work* and the art*ist* [*Kunst*werk and *Kunst*ler] that that have a "special" relationship to the coming into being of art. In the label "setting to work of truth," in which it remains undetermined (though determin*able*) who or what does the "setting," and in what manner, lies concealed the relationship of being to human being. This relationship is inadequately thought even in this presentation—a distressing difficulty that has been clear to me since *Being and Time*, and has since come under discussion in many presentations (see, finally, "On the Question of Being" and the present essay p. 36 "Only this should be noted; that . . .").[22]

The difficulty to which Heidegger alludes here (a "difficulty" that surfaces in a number of chapters above and will resurface below[23]) can be construed in terms of the notion of *thesis* we have just been discussing, since what is at issue is the extent to which being itself may be considered a "posit" or "projection" (perhaps even a "product" or "result") of the human.[24] The problem here is thus the tendency to treat *thesis* as already tending toward a form of human-centered *subjectivism*.

In another of his late essays (from 1954), Heidegger discusses the idea of *thesis* in a way that makes this quite clear, and argues, once again, for a distinction between the Greek and modern senses of *thesis*. Beginning with the notion of "work" (a notion that also appears in "The Origin of the Work of Art" in terms of the "working" or truth), Heidegger writes:

"To work" means "to do" [*tun*]. What does "to do" mean? The word belongs to the Indo-Germanic stem *dhē*; from this also comes the Greek *thesis*: setting, place, position. This doing does not mean, however, human activity only; above all it does not mean activity in the sense of action and agency. Growth also, the holding-sway of nature (*physis*), is a doing, and that in the strict sense of *thesis*. Only at a later time do the words *physis* and *thesis* come into opposition. . . . *Physis* is *thesis*: from out of itself to lay something before, to place it here, to bring it hither and forth [*her- und vor-bringen*], that is, into presencing. That which "does" in such a sense is that which works; it is that which presences, in its presencing.[25]

In asserting the identity of *thesis* with *physis*, and so appearing to deny the ambiguity that seems so self-evident here, Heidegger is resisting the tendency to think of *thesis* as indeed something accomplished primarily by human beings. Moreover, in asserting the coincidence of *thesis* with *physis*, a coincidence that is not accidental, Heidegger also asserts the character of *physis* as itself a positioning or placing, as a happening of *topos*, and of presencing as therefore something essentially tied to such placing—as essentially *topological* in character. To take matters even further, we can say that what is implied here is a conception of *topos* according to which *topos* must indeed possess a "power" of its own, and cannot be identical with any form of simple "location" or already determined "site" that arises primarily out of human activity or intervention. *Topos*, no less than *thesis*, is thus not to be construed as any form of "construction," neither in the sense of a "social" construction nor a construction based on scientific "projection," and yet it is precisely toward its understanding as such a construction that the modern appropriation of *topos* and *thesis* inevitably tends, an appropriation that is itself made possible by the ambiguity in the very notion of *thesis*.

The understanding of presencing that emerges in Heidegger's discussion of *thesis* is the very same conception that becomes clearest in his later thinking and that leads him to characterize that thinking as a saying of the place of being—a *Topologie des Seyns*.[26] The story behind the development of this topology is one that I have expanded upon elsewhere.[27] What interests me here is just the way this topology is connected to Heidegger's thinking of *thesis* as that connects to his reading of the nature of *Ge-stell*, and so to the nihilistic character of the modern age. Central to this is the difficulty concerning the relation between being and human being that Heidegger identifies in his 1956 comments—what might be termed the question of "subjectivism"—which is, at its most general level, a question of *thesis* or posit in the sense of *foundation*, but more specifically, is the question of the role of the foundation of presencing, and so also of place, as it stands in relation to the human.

It is important to recognize, however, that the "difficulty" referred to here has a twofold reference: it indicates a difficulty that Heidegger experiences in his own thought and which extends at least from *Being and Time* onward (something indicated by Heidegger's own frequent reference to the problems of "subjectivism" and "anthropologism" that emerge in relation to *Being and Time* itself);[28] but it also indicates a problematic tendency within the history of Western metaphysics that is identical with the rise of the technological and the dominance of the human, with the loss of any sense of value in the very insistence on the preeminence of value, and which is also made salient by Nietzsche's valorization of the

"will-to-power" and his proclamation of the "death of God." It is nonetheless the same question of place that can be seen to underlie this twofold
set of issues, and it is thus that in Heidegger's later thinking both sets of
issues come together, and are to some extent subsumed (and thereby also
transformed) under the single task that is the saying of the place of being—
the *Topologie des Seyns*.

If the "difficulty" at issue here is inadequately thought, as Heidegger
claims, "even" in 1935–1936, then it is inadequately thought in 1927, in
1930, and in 1933 (it undoubtedly plays a role in Heidegger's own entanglement with Nazism[29]), and is likely also to be inadequate even in the
Contributions to Philosophy on which Heidegger works from 1936 to 1938
(which should give pause to those who would give this work a more privileged status).[30] What is at issue in this difficulty is *the* fundamental difficulty in both Heidegger's thinking and in modern philosophy. It is the
fundamental question that underlies what Heidegger calls nihilism and
also *Gestell*, and that is central to the project of topology.[31] It is the question as to how we are to understand the happening of presence, which is
also a happening of place, in light of the realization that this topological
happening also inevitably implicates the human. The happening of place
is a happening of world, and as such it is always the happening of a particular formation of world, a particular formation of place, but it can easily
appear as if this formation is itself something *posited* on the basis of human
being. The question is how to understand the happening of place and
world, the happening of presence, so that it is not understood as founded
in any merely human act (nor, indeed, in *any* foundation in the usual
sense), even though it is only in relation to human activity that such a
happening arises.

In "The Origin of the Work of Art," the difficulty is evident in a particularly acute manner in Heidegger's attempt to think of the work of art as
itself having a founding role in the establishing of world, and not only the
architectural work of art, but also the founding act of the statesman or
the originary saying of the poet (here Heidegger surely has Hölderlin—"the
poet of the Germans"[32]—in mind).[33] Within the history of thought, this
difficulty is intensified as place comes increasingly to be understood as
falling under the sway of human activity, and as human activity itself
increasingly appears as nothing more than an endless "positioning" and
"placing" (*Ge-stell*) that encompasses even the human.[34] Within such a
framework, in which the "positional" has been rendered as identical with
the measureable and the calculable, and in which the thing itself has all
but vanished,[35] the original separation of *thesis* from *topos* that was already

indicated in Aristotle (but that in a way did not give undue emphasis to *thesis* alone), transformed with Descartes, and heralded by Nietzsche, is revealed as itself leading to the seeming obliteration of place. *It is this that is properly the movement of nihilism—a movement in and of place that cannot be adequately thought independently of place.*

So far I have talked of "subjectivism" and "subject" (at least in this chapter) without any additional clarification of what these terms might mean. In fact, as we have seen in the discussions above and will be reiterated below, these terms have a very specific meaning for Heidegger that is related to their more commonplace contemporary usage in philosophy, but also differs from that usage. The difference at issue is itself indicated by the fact that even while Heidegger often admits a subjectivist tendency in *Being and Time*, he also always views *Being and Time* as a work that is intended to take issue with subjectivism. This apparent tension arises largely from the fact that the subjectivism that appears in *Being and Time* as the target of Heidegger's critical engagement actually appears as a form of *objectivism*—that mode of static presentation of things, and of the world, that takes things as merely present-at-hand, and so as essentially *spatialized* (this latter point being especially significant from a topological perspective).[36] It is this objectivism that Heidegger identifies with the Cartesian conception of the world as *res extensa*, and that it is so identified also indicates the implication of such objectivism with subjectivism.

As Heidegger sees it, subjectivism has a twofold reference: it draws first upon a tendency at the heart of metaphysics, namely, the demand for a foundation (and as such, a form of "subjectivism" can already be discerned in Greek as well as medieval thought); but it also names the particular mode of thinking that construes the foundation at issue always in relation to the human. More specifically, subjectivism is that mode of metaphysical understanding that takes things as appearing always as objects standing in relation to a subject, and so as also standing within the frame of the representational (where representation translates the German *Vorstellen*—literally a "standing-before"). Subjectivism is a particular way of taking up the "positive" (or "thetic") character of presence—which is its being always placed—according to which the placing is always a placing of some object in relation to or by a subject. It is just that way of understanding *thesis* that arises, as I indicated above, once *thesis* is understood as separate from the world (from *cosmos*) and relative to activity. The sense of "subject" at issue here is also a sense derived from the notion of *thesis*, and *topos*, in another way, not merely as "positioning," but of "place" or "placing" understood as that *in* or *on* which something *is placed*—which is why "subject" is also to be understood as *sub-jectum* (from the Greek *hypo-kei-menon*), that which underlies, which stands beneath, which grounds.[37]

What makes Descartes so important in Heidegger's account of the development of metaphysics and in the movement toward nihilism, and that connects Nietzsche directly to him,[38] is the way in which Descartes, through taking certainty as the objective of scientific and philosophical inquiry, already gives a certain priority to the human, but in a way that also privileges the purely "objective." He does this not in the sense of the human as that from which everything is causally or substantively derived, but as that which provides the fundamental and all-encompassing *criterion* (the "measure") of what is—being thus becomes that which can be represented to a knowing subject, that stands over against the knowing subject, and whose existence can be ascertained by a knowing subject.

What occurs here is perhaps complicated by Heidegger's own description of this development as "metaphysical." The way in which thinking is reoriented to the human subject is certainly a development within metaphysics, but it is also a development in which there occurs a bifurcation within metaphysics between the epistemological and the ontological. What occurs in Descartes is actually a shift within metaphysics from subjectivism as the attempt to identify a single underlying foundation, or *sub-jectum*, for both what is *and* what is known (the two being held together in both ancient and medieval thought), to a modern form of bifurcated subjectivism (based in the primacy of the *cogito*, but in a way that uncovers the world as essentially *materia* and *extensio*), that consists in an epistemological foundation located in the human *as subject* and an ontological foundation located in the world *as object*.

In this context, it should be noted, the terms "subject" and "object" appear as quite particular metaphysical designations that rest within subjectivism as a more general phenomenon (although understood in a way specific to the "modern"), but which also give rise to the more generally recognized and specific forms of *both* "subjectivism" (in the sense of "idealism," "emotivism," "constructionist," or whatever) *and* "objectivism" (including "scientism," "materialism," "physicalism," and so forth).[39] Significantly, even when this tendency toward subjectivism, in all its various forms, is understood, it is often understood within a narrowly subjectivist frame, and so is understood as something *brought about* by the human subject (a tendency characteristic of much contemporary discussion of our current situation), and so as a result, for instance, of the particular interventions of specific thinkers (the privileging of the name "Descartes" here itself encourages such a view). To repeat a familiar Heideggerian formulation, although to a slightly different point, subjectivism is not something subjective, but is instead a mode of presencing, a mode of the happening of truth, a mode of *Ereignis*—subjectivism as a general tendency of thought is thus already given in the very character of being, of presence, of place.

Subjectivism, both as the desire for an underlying foundation and as the modern bifurcation of that desire into forms of "subjectivism" and "objectivism" (the latter being Heidegger's main target in *Being and Time*), is, according to Heidegger, that which underlies and is expressed in nihilism. The devaluing of even the highest values that Nietzsche identifies as characteristic of nihilism is itself a consequence of the reduction of the human to mere subject and of the world to object. Thus Heidegger writes, in 1943, that

The human uprising into subjectivity makes beings into objects. However, what is objective is that which, through representation, has been brought to a stand. The elimination of beings in themselves, the killing of God, is accomplished in the securing of duration [*Bestandsicherung*] through which man secures bodily, material, spiritual and intellectual durables [*Bestände*]; however, these are secured for the sake of man's own security, which wills the mastery over beings (as potentially objective), in order to conform to the being of beings, the will to power.[40]

The death of God is a complicated idea in Heidegger and in Nietzsche; nonetheless, we can view it, in the frame established here, as itself an assertion of modern subjectivism, and so also as the completion and culmination—the "end"—of metaphysics. Heidegger's identification of Nietzsche as the last metaphysician is thus well founded: it is in Nietzsche that the nihilistic essence of metaphysics becomes fully evident in thought (even though it is only in the following century, perhaps, that it can be said to become fully evident in the concrete formations of world history). The death of God thus appears as the consequence, even as identical with, the triumph of the human (it is, as Nietzsche declares, "we" who have "killed" God), and yet this apparent triumph is also the very obliteration of the human—what appears, if at all, is only the subject that stands against an object, or, even more radically, the human is transformed, along with the thing, into that which merely "stands ready" (what Heidegger calls *Bestand*, a term I have also translated as "resource"). Place itself disappears into even less than this: nothing more than a point or mere "site" within a globalized network of relations that are themselves in constant "flow." One might say that here *topos* and *thesis* have become completely disconnected from one another, with *topos* replaced by *thesis*; but one might also say that *topos* is now understood as nothing but *thesis*, while *thesis* has itself been reduced to a pure "position" within a system of such positions defined relative to each other.[41]

The examination of the relation between "subjectivism" and nihilism, and also between *topos* and *thesis*, as these emerge in Heidegger's thought, and in the history of philosophy more generally, is a complex task. What the brief discussion undertaken here has done, however, is to sketch out some of the issues at stake, and to substantiate, in part, the claim concerning the topological character of Heidegger's approach to those issues, including the issue of nihilism, as well as of the issues themselves. In Heidegger's postwar thinking, his approach to these issues undergoes further development—a development that is discussed elsewhere in this volume,[42] but which is also worth commenting briefly upon here.

By the late 1940s and 1950s, the focus on nihilism that is such a feature of Heidegger's essays from the late 1930s and early 1940s has largely been incorporated into the questioning of the essence of technology that is *Gestell*. The relation between being and human being, or, as we might also understand the matter, between *place* and human being, is itself addressed largely through the exploration of the more fully developed concept of "dwelling" that appears in Heidegger's later thinking, together with an analysis of the character of the Fourfold as encompassing, yet not simply determined by, mortals. Mortals *build*, and such building can be construed as constituting a positionality of its own; but building is itself founded in dwelling, while dwelling is itself based in the prior belonging of mortals to the Fourfold that also encompasses Earth, Sky, and Gods, and so in a prior belonging to world and to place—moreover, inasmuch as the happening of the Fourfold requires mortals, the coming to presence of mortals also requires the Fourfold.

The account of place, presence, and being that emerges in these late essays,[43] though it is clearly in continuity with the earlier writing (including "The Origin of the Work of Art"), also constitutes an attempt to think of these in a way that does not succumb to the "inadequacy" that seems constantly to plague much of Heidegger's earlier thought—it seeks to think presence and place in a way that does not look to found them in something apart from and independent of them. The saying of place—the *topology*—that increasingly comes to the fore in Heidegger's later thinking is the name Heidegger gives to the task at issue here. It is also a task that can be understood in terms of an attempt to rethink the concept of *thesis*, and its relation to *topos*, in a way that does not fall victim to "subjectivism" or to nihilism. *Gestell*, as the essence of technology, cannot be understood as if it were some form of anthropologistic instrumentalism, but it also cannot be separated from the prior implication of being with the human, nor from the entanglement of *topos* with *thesis*. An adequate thinking of being, of presence, and of *topos* (and these three can only be thought together), has both to acknowledge the implication of the human without allowing that implication to be misunderstood. Whether Heidegger's later thinking achieves this, and whether, in accord with its intentions, it provides a fully adequate account of *topos* as such, is perhaps a question that must remain open to debate. It seems to me that there are grounds on which one may argue that even Heidegger's later thinking remains obscure as to how this matter is to be addressed or the exact manner of its resolution.[44] Heidegger is certainly clear, however, on the need to refuse any account of *topos* that founds it in something other than itself (including the human), and yet he sometimes appears reticent in regard to the explication of the "structure" of *topos* and the exact manner in which the human relation to place is to be construed. Nevertheless, it is only in the direction of the thinking of *topos*, itself an essential form of questioning—of holding open a free-play of possibility (a "play-space")[45]—that any proper response to the overpowering movement of nihilism can be found. Any such response must take the form of a returning to place, a refinding of oneself, a reorientation (even, perhaps, a repositioning)—as Heidegger himself refers to it, a form of *homecoming*, although a coming-home to that from which we never really departed.[46]

6 Place, Space, and World

That is why I regard space and spatiality as very important—because from here the phenomenon of the world can be elucidated in connection with openness [*Offenheit*] and clearing [*Lichtung*]. . . .

—Heidegger, *Zollikon Seminars: Protocols-Conversations-Letters*

The way in which the question of world is implicated with the question of space is already indicated by Heidegger's very characterization, in *Being and Time*, of the essence of human being, *Dasein*, as being-in-the-world. Here the nature of "being in" is as much at issue as is the nature of "world," and although Heidegger himself moves fairly quickly to assert, in §12 of *Being and Time*, that "being in" as it figures in relation to world is not a matter of spatial *containment*, but of active *involvement*,[1] the analysis that follows constantly invokes the spatial at the same time as it also seeks to move away from it.[2] The rethinking of the framework of *Being and Time* that Heidegger undertakes in the late 1920s and early 1930s (the rethinking that lies at the heart of the so-called Turning in his thought)[3] involves a rearticulation of the concept of spatiality along with that of world, although it is a rearticulation that is not directly addressed, nor does it come properly to fruition, until the late 1940s.

Contemporary work in cognitive science has also increasingly come to recognize the complexity of spatiality, as well as its centrality to accounts of cognition and behavior and to the understanding of world. Thus, in the introduction to a groundbreaking volume published in 1993, Naomi Eilan, Rosaleen McCarthy, and Bill Brewer take as their guiding question: "What is the connection between the capacity for spatial thought and grasp of the idea of a world out there, an external world we inhabit?"[4] The answer evident in the volume's essays (an answer already, of course, adumbrated in Kant) is that the two are intimately and inextricably tied together. Yet although work in cognitive science elsewhere often draws on what are supposedly Heideggerian ideas, surprisingly little attention has been paid to the way spatiality emerges and develops in Heidegger's thinking, nor to the way in which shifts in Heidegger's understanding of spatiality might be connected with shifts elsewhere in his thought. Moreover, although Heidegger is often seen to be especially relevant to contemporary cognitive science in virtue of his understanding of being-in-the-world as based in a mode of "practical" rather than "theoretical" comportment (largely as a result of Hubert Dreyfus's influential reading of Heidegger along just these lines[5]), there has been relatively little appreciation of the limited character of such a reading of Heidegger's work, even when applied to *Being and Time*, and especially of the way such a reading is itself rendered problematic by close consideration of the issues surrounding spatiality.

Once one inquires more closely into the interconnection of the problem of world with the problem of space, it soon becomes apparent that one cannot understand world independently of spatiality, nor can one understand either spatiality or world on the basis of any form of purely "practical" comportment or mode of "involvement." Indeed, an undue emphasis on practice can easily threaten the same sort of one-sidedness in thinking that is also engendered by the focus on pure theoreticity. In the discussion that follows, I will explore the way space and world appear in Heidegger's thinking, including some of the problems that accrue to Heidegger's treatment of space in *Being and Time*, in order to sketch out, first, something of the complex and nonderivative structure of spatiality (especially the way in which it cannot be treated as somehow derivative of the "practical" or the "involved"),[6] and, second, the way spatiality is tied to the concept of world, and especially the way in which Heidegger's own attempts to clarify the concept of world also lead inevitably to an increasingly spatialized analysis.

Space and Spatiality in *Being and Time*

The treatment of spatiality in *Being and Time* is not a merely peripheral element in the work. If time and temporality are the focus for the second part of the book (Division, I, Part II), space is arguably the focus, even if problematically so, for the first part (Division I, Part I). Inasmuch as *Being and Time* takes up the question of being, in large measure, through the question of world, so *Being and Time* can be seen as pursuing a two-stage analysis in which world is explored first in its *spatial* character (and in which spatial concepts such as "being-in" and "being-alongside" play a central role, but in which spatiality is shown to be derivative of or "founded in" the care-structure of *Dasein*), and then in its more primordial *temporal* determination (temporality being that in which both the care-structure and existential spatiality are founded—and so, one might say, in which world itself has its ground).

One of the reasons for the problematic status of spatiality in *Being and Time* is Heidegger's evident difficulty in severing the connection between the idea of spatiality and the particular understanding of space as homogeneous extension that he takes to be a key element in Cartesianism[7]—one consequence of this is that spatiality in *Being and Time* is presented as an entirely secondary structure. Although Heidegger does advance an account of an existential mode of space that is tied to the teleological ordering of equipment and project,[8] this is not a *sui generis* mode, but is instead derivative of temporality—a derivation for which Heidegger argues explicitly, if not altogether successfully, in *Being and Time*, §70 (Heidegger seems implicitly to be alluding to this in his 1935 comment noted above[9]). The derivative construal of spatiality is an expression of Heidegger's implicit methodological commitment to what I have elsewhere termed a structure of "hierarchical dependence" according to which *Dasein* exhibits an ordered structure of successively derived or dependent unities themselves founded in an originary unity.[10] As a result, Heidegger's prioritization of temporality in *Being and Time* takes the form of an assertion of temporality as the originary *foundation* for the unity of *Dasein* in its entirety. It is this assertion of temporality as foundational, itself evident in the teleological understanding of the structure of world that is developed through the idea of equipmentality, that gives rise to problems in the Heideggerian account of space, and that also, of course, makes for difficulties in the account of world as such.

The problematic status of spatiality is itself connected to the uncertain role of the body in Heidegger's analysis. Heidegger's account of existential spatiality in *Being and Time* is developed in a way that sets it apart from, and actually opposed to, any notion of *objective* spatiality (and we should be careful not to prejudge what might be involved in such a notion), but in addition it is developed in a way that separates it from any notion of a distinctive *bodily* spatiality. The claim that Heidegger ignores or neglects the body is a frequent complaint of readers of *Being and Time*. In fact, Heidegger does not quite ignore issues concerning the body but instead, while explicitly acknowledging the importance of the problems that are raised by it, sets those problems deliberately to one side.[11] There is good reason for this—at least within the structure of Heidegger's thinking in *Being and Time*: given the interconnection of the bodily with the spatial, and given also Heidegger's derivative construal of spatiality, he has no option but to regard the issue of the body as already encompassed, inasmuch as it is relevant, by the treatment of spatiality, and so also by the account of temporality. This approach is also to some extent reinforced by the way in which Heidegger, quite correctly given the nature of his analysis, sees our being embodied as a consequence of our character as existing rather than as determining the character of our existence—in much the same way that our having sense organs is, as Heidegger points out in his 1929 *Kantbuch*, a consequence of our finitude rather than itself being determinative of it.[12]

Significantly, the issue of the body has emerged as an increasingly important theme in contemporary cognitive scientific approaches to the question of space—although usually drawing on the ideas of Merleau-Ponty rather than Heidegger.[13] This is not always without its own problems, however, since the body cannot be simply assumed—what the body *is* must be acknowledged to be itself in question here. Moreover, this is a point that Heidegger himself seems implicitly to recognize—it may partly contribute to the uncertain treatment of the body in *Being and Time*, and undoubtedly emerges as an element in Heidegger's later thinking. An indication of the latter is given in the Le Thor Seminar, in 1968, in which Heidegger argues for a difference between what he there terms "body" and "lived body": "when we step on a scale, we do not weigh our 'lived-body' but merely the weight of our 'body.' Or further, the limit of the 'lived-body' is not the limit of the 'body.' The limit of the body is the skin. The limit of the 'lived-body' is more difficult to determine. It is not 'world,' but it is perhaps just as little 'environment.'"[14] The body cannot then simply be appealed to as an alternative foundation for spatiality—nor, indeed, as a "foundation" for anything else—since, quite apart from the problems that attach to the very notion of "foundation," the body is itself part of the larger structure, which we may refer to as being-in-the-world, the nature of which is at issue. The way spatiality emerges as an issue in Heidegger is thus not a result of his supposed neglect of the body alone, nor is it resolved simply by reintroducing the body. Certainly, once the question of space is reopened, the question of the body also reemerges. It does so, however, not in terms of some reassertion of corporeality, but rather through the way in which the body itself serves to refocus the question of spatiality, and so also to refocus the question of world.

One of the main features in Heidegger's account of spatiality in the first part of *Being and Time* is that, as I noted above, it attempts to construe spatiality in terms of *Dasein*'s practical situatedness as that is teleologically understood (in a way that ultimately founds it in temporality), and, more particularly, as it is given through *Dasein*'s involvement within a particular equipmental structure—so *Dasein*'s own spatiality is understood as founded in *Dasein*'s worldly "involvement" rather than vice versa. Quite apart from any methodological issues that might arise here, there is also a substantive problem in any such derivative construal of spatiality. Any such equipmental array presupposes an extended and unitary dimensionality within which each item of equipment can be juxtaposed alongside other such items. Such a dimensionality can only be understood as spatial (which does not mean that it is therefore to be understood in the terms supplied by the physical sciences alone)—we might say, in fact, that the dimension that enables such juxtaposition is just what space itself is.[15]

The way in which spatiality is implicated in the very possibility of *differentiation*, which is actually the point that emerges here, is something to which I shall return shortly, but for the moment I want to remain focused on the role of spatiality in the structure of equipmentality. That structure requires the spatial *ordering* of items of equipment. It also requires that any such ordering be an ordering that relates the things themselves, and at the same time allows them to stand in a relation to each and any individual *Dasein* for whom that equipmental structure can be accessible as ready-to-hand (or, indeed, as present-at-hand).[16] The structure of equipment thus requires a complex space that belongs to equipment as such (it is a space in which each item of equipment stands in relation to other items) and that also belongs to *Dasein* both individually (it is a space in which each *Dasein* finds itself) and "collectively" (it is also a common, "public" space in which *Dasein* encounters others, and within which *Dasein* can act with others)—a space that is "objective," "subjective," and "intersubjective."[17]

What this means, of course, is that, contrary to the direction of argument that Heidegger pursues, the unity of the equipmental cannot explain the unity of the spatial, since the unity of the spatial is already presupposed by the unity of the equipmental. The fact that this point is not immediately evident in Heidegger's account in *Being and Time* is partly due to Heidegger's own lack of clarity in the deployment of spatial and topographic concepts in that work, and partly by the almost exclusive concentration of attention on the teleological (and so, ultimately, temporal) ordering of the equipmental as developed within the structure of hierarchical dependence that he assumes.[18] Significantly, Heidegger is himself aware of some of the difficulty here, and in particular, of the extent to which spatial concepts seem constantly to intrude into his analysis. As a result, he frequently reiterates his assertions concerning the secondary and derivative character of space, and in §70, in which he sets out the argument for the supposed derivation of space from time, he claims that the "the well-known phenomenon that both Dasein's interpretations of itself and the whole stock of significations which belong to language are dominated through and through by 'spatial representations'"[19] is a consequence of Dasein's inevitable tendency toward "Falling," and so toward the covering up of its essential being.

The way in which the spatial ordering of equipmentality includes a spatial ordering that relates to Dasein itself—something indicated, as I noted above, in the very idea of the "ready-to-hand"—is a particularly salient point that immediately relates back to the brief discussion of the body above. For Dasein to be able to engage with some equipmental structure, it must be able to locate itself in respect to that structure, and so with respect to the spatial ordering that belongs to it. For this to be possible, Dasein must already have a sense of the spatial ordering of that equipmental structure as its appears in relation to Dasein's own spatiality, which means, to Dasein's own body and sphere of action. This is crucial to the understanding of spatiality as it relates not only to practical activity, but to any form of self-locatedness, and it indicates why the emphasis on "involvement" *as opposed to* spatial containment is not sufficient to achieve the shift in the understanding of being-in that Being and Time attempts.[20] "Involvement" itself presupposes some sense of containment, just as the equipmental array presupposes a sense of spatial extendedness—which is not to say that containment supersedes the notion of "involvement," but rather that "involvement" cannot be construed in a way that overrides or takes precedence over the sense of spatiality, as that is expressed, in one very important form, in the very idea of containment as well as that of extendedness.

Heidegger claims that things that are merely "in" space cannot stand in any relation to one another—which is another way of saying that spatiality alone cannot unify or "order".[21] But this claim already depends on construing space in a way that begs the questions at issue, and treats "involvement" as removed from spatial containment or extendedness. Being "in" space means being connected, and in the case of Dasein, being able to connect oneself, to that which surrounds. This is where the Aristotelian analysis of *topos* becomes relevant, since it emphasizes the character of the space (and also place) as a matter of containment by an enclosing body, thereby understanding space as essentially tied to a form of horizonality.[22] For Dasein to have a sense of its own "being-in" requires, as should already be evident, Dasein's ability to locate and to *orient* itself.

In its original sense, the ability to orient oneself means being able to identify the direction that is east, and so to identify the other cardinal directions also, but it more generally involves an ability to grasp the differences
between the regions that make up that space, or the directions within it,
and to do so in such a way that those differences can be related back to
one's own bodily differentiation—so, if we were to employ the sense of
orientation to the cardinal points, east is over there, to my right as I now
stand, west is to my left, north ahead of me and south behind.[23]

The essential tie between the sense of space in general and the sense of
spatiality that one has in one's own body, or better, in one's own sphere
of action, is a matter on which Kant is especially clear (he is perhaps the
first philosopher to give explicit attention to this point).[24] In *Being and
Time*, however, Heidegger misconstrues as *subjectivist* the way in which
Kant ties orientation to the body in this way.[25] It is only subjectivist,
however, if one takes the differences in space that are at issue here to be
reducible to differences in the body *alone*, so that bodily differentiation
becomes the fundamental ground on which spatial differentiation rests—
and one can see why this would be especially problematic within the
framework of *Being and Time*, not in virtue of the problematic character of
the very attempt at such a foundation, but because it would constitute a
competing foundation to that given by temporality.

In fact, the relation between bodily differentiation and spatial differentiation is complex. Spatial differentiation is not *produced by* bodily differentiation, but instead bodily differentiation is what *enables* spatial
differentiation to become relevant in behavior and cognition, in action
and perception.[26] This is a simple but crucial point, since the space that is
opened up through one's being able to connect regions and directions in
that space with one's own bodily orientation is not subjective, but *objective*—as it must be if action and perception are to be effective in our engagement with *things*.[27] Not only is the Kantian point at issue here often
misunderstood, and not only by Heidegger, as implying some form of
subjective foundation for spatiality (as well as being assumed to be associated with a view of space as essentially Newtonian[28]), but what is also often
missed is precisely the way in which subjective and "objective" elements
are inextricably bound together in this way, as well as the fundamental
role spatiality must play for *any* mode of engagement, and not only for
the "involved" or the "practical."

We can only locate ourselves inasmuch as we can also orient ourselves,
and such orientation requires having a sense of the space in which one
finds oneself as it relates to oneself and to one's own spatiality—the latter

being necessarily the spatiality of one's body, and so also the spatiality of action. To be oriented is therefore to be capable of action (or at least to have a sense of the possibility of such action), but this does not mean that our capacity for action can be taken as the foundation for our other capacities nor for our being in the world as such. If that were so then it might appear as if "involvement" could be, after all, the foundation for the rest, but, as we have seen, the capacity for action already implies notions of both space and world—the capacity for action requires orientation, as orientation requires a capacity for action. This point can be applied not only to the idea of involvement or action, but also to the supposed "primacy of practice." It is not that our practical mode of engagement underpins other modes, but that any mode of engagement must already be an engagement that is located and oriented—and that is, therefore, spatial and spatialized—and must be so in a way that encompasses "subjective," "intersubjective," and "objective" aspects. Indeed, even supposedly "theoretical" engagement, of the sort involved in contemplation or deliberation, must be "spatialized" in a similar way—even theory requires its own location and orientation.[29]

"Subjectivity," understood in terms of the spatial ordering associated with action and so also with the body, opens out into, and in fact already implicates, the world in its "objectivity," that is, in terms of the spatial ordering of things and regions. The way in which these different orderings, which I have referred to as "subjective" and "objective" orderings, are inextricably bound together is an important idea in Heidegger's thought even though one might argue that it is not adequately or clearly addressed, at least not in spatial terms, in *Being and Time*. It is an idea that can be seen to lie at the heart of the Heideggerian insight into what might be termed the "productive" character of finitude (and of the boundedness associated with it): our finitude does not cut off or somehow reduce our access to the world, nor to the things that appear within it, but is rather that by means of which the world is itself opened up and things are made accessible.

All too often, of course, as should already be evident from the immediately preceding discussion, the path that is opened up from our own subjectivity to the objective ordering of things is mistakenly understood in a way that in effect takes such "objectivity," as well as the idea of world itself, to be founded in subjectivity—to be founded in our "practical" activity and "involvement." To some extent (although, as will be evident below, the matter is by no means straightforward), Heidegger's own attempt to present "involvement" as more primordial than spatial "containment" can be seen as one example of such a tendency, as can his attempt to found "being-in-the-world" in originary temporality. Although the subjectivism at issue here, both in Heidegger's case and more generally, is not a subjectivism that looks to the individual alone, encompassing, as it does, the social context within which activity is meaningful, and so also the teleologically ordered structures of the equipmental, it is a form of subjectivism nonetheless, since, in simple terms, the foundation that it identifies is, in a certain sense, in us and *only* in us. Admittedly, this is not unambiguously so, but whether the foundation at issue here is to be found in our bodily organization or structure, habits, our conventions, our practices, our "ways of coping," or, indeed, our essential temporality, it is nevertheless a foundation that is to be found in *us*, rather than anywhere else (including any larger or more encompassing structure).[30]

There should be little doubt, however, in spite of the attention given to this prioritization of the practical and the subjective, that such an approach involves a misunderstanding of the nature and direction of Heidegger's thinking—even, to some extent, of his thinking in *Being and Time*. That this is so is evident from Heidegger's own attempts to clarify the matter following the publication of the work as well as in the subsequent revision and modification of his position in the period thereafter.[31] The reworking that Heidegger undertakes in the 1930s and early 1940s, in particular, is largely provoked by the shortcomings Heidegger himself identified in *Being and Time* that were associated with, among other things, the subjectivist tendencies present in the work, which were themselves connected with the emphasis on the "practical" in the early work as well as its reliance on a structure of hierarchical dependence. As I indicated above, the reworking that occurs is not only focused on the problem of world, but it also develops in a way that essentially implicates spatiality. Indeed, in some respects, Heidegger's rethinking of space and spatiality in the years after *Being and Time*, a rethinking that is undertaken in close connection with the retrieval of the concept of *topos*—the turn toward place—leads Heidegger to an understanding of space that is much closer to that of Kant. It is, however, an understanding that is arrived at after working through Kant in a way that, ironically, never properly engages with the concepts of space or spatiality as Kant himself developed them. In particular, Heidegger comes to recognize, as Kant already had, that the possibility of the ordered structure of coming-to-presence that is the world is inextricably bound not only to time, but also to space.

Subjectivity, Objectivity, and Agency

The essential interconnection between what we might call subjective and objective modes of spatiality or of spatial ordering (as well as the intersubjective, although I shall leave this to one side for the moment) is clearly evident in the Kantian emphasis on location as tied to orientation in one's own "sphere of action." The fact of this interconnection has the consequence, since action requires location and orientation, that there can be no mode of action that does not involve a grasp of both subjective and objective modes of spatiality. Moreover, the connection between subjective and objective modes also means that there can be no mode of location or orientation, no mode of spatiality, that does not also implicate both subjective and objective modes.

The necessary interconnection between "subjectivity" and "objectivity" within the complex structure of spatiality is often overlooked—and the early Heidegger is not alone in this. Just as it is relatively common, then, to find the practical and the "involved" being treated as the foundation for spatiality, and especially for any notion of objective spatiality, neither is it unusual to find spatiality being treated as if it could indeed be construed entirely "subjectively" (which often means, in this context, as entirely a matter of practical involvement). On such a view, a purely subjective space is not seen to present any problems for action or orientation in that space—an agent can simply react to features of a situation as they are presented to it from within the situation and as they are differentially located within a spatial field that is entirely relative to or centered on the agent (which is what subjective can be taken to mean in this context). Such a capacity for reaction, so it is sometimes supposed, does not require anything other than a capacity to distinguish spatially between those representations, a capacity to grasp those presentations as soliciting a response, and a capacity to so respond.

The idea of a purely subjective space that appears here is, however, a deeply problematic one. To begin with, it involves a misconstrual of the way in which a space may be said to be subjective. As Kant emphasizes, space is essentially unitary,[32] and part of what this means is that, strictly speaking, there are not different spaces that are to be aligned with different modes—the subjective, intersubjective, and objective—but instead there is but one space that itself encompasses these three modes. It is this space that is properly objective, that is also intersubjective (and so equally accessible to all), and yet is always and only accessible subjectively (and so by means of our own individual location within it). Any agent, insofar as it is capable of action at all (that is, insofar as it is, indeed, an agent), acts in a space that is an objective space, in which other agents also act, and yet which is always immediately configured subjectively in terms of the agent's own oriented locatedness. Moreover, as Kant also points out, for subjectivity to have any content at all—for it to be determined in any way, as opposed to a bare possibility—subjectivity *requires* objectivity.[33] In Kant, this point is developed through the way in which inner sense, the form of which is time, is only determined through outer sense, and so in space (it is also tied, as we shall see below, to the necessity of spatiality to the possibility of differentiation). Kant takes time to be the form for all representations, and yet it is space that is necessary for representations to have content. Space and time thus turn out, within the structure of experience, to stand in a relation of mutual implication or dependence (or, as it may also be put, of "mutual priority").[34]

Although every agent stands in this same basic relation to space—such that the very idea of agency presupposes spatiality in all its complexity—there are also important differences in the way in which agents may have access to the space at issue here that are directly correlated with differences in the basic capacities of agents, both their behavioral capacities and the cognitive capacities with which such behavioral capacities are intimately connected. Thus, while every agent acts *in* an objective space that is subjectively accessible *to* it, the range of action available to each agent, and by means of which that space is articulated cognitively and behaviorally, will vary between agents. The most important difference here concerns the capacity of agents to act in a way that takes the objectivity of the space as a directly thematized and determining element in cognition and behavior. Put simply: all agents must have some access to the space in which they act, but not all agents have the access that comes from being able to represent or conceptualize that space or their access to it—to recognize or acknowledge it *as such*.

It is this difference that undoubtedly underlies the tendency to think of subjective space as if it were a separate space in its own right, and that also leads to the tendency to suppose that there could indeed be a mode of spatial involvement that would be to some extent distinct from and perhaps even independent of any objective mode of spatiality—as the ready-to-hand might be thought to be independent of, as well as prior to, the present-at-hand. In contemporary discussions these ideas are sometimes further articulated through the idea of nonconceptual content. The subjective, "involved" access to space, and to the world, is thereby supposed to be nonconceptual in character, not only in the sense that it does not rely on concepts or representations, but in a more basic sense according to which the very content of what is grasped is not conceptual.

The idea of nonconceptual content has been the focus of much attention in recent years (and has also been deployed by Dreyfus in his own work—sometimes in ways that indicate he takes the idea to be applicable to Heidegger[35]), and the introduction of the notion here threatens to open up a large area of discussion. Two points, however, are worth making in relation to what is at issue here. First, not only is the idea of nonconceptual content problematic in its own right,[36] but if we take seriously the point made above about the unity of space—and I would make a similar point in relation to the unity of agency and of experience—then it is difficult to see how radically different content could belong to one and the same space. The same space, and so the same content, may well be grasped differently (so that perhaps one may talk of a "nonconceptual" grasp), but that the content itself could differ seems an unjustified claim that also creates additional difficulties without any obvious explanatory gain.[37] Second, and perhaps more importantly, the idea of nonconceptual content has most often been introduced in the Heideggerian context, as I indicated above, as another way of elaborating upon the ideas of the "practical" and the "involved" that are supposed to found *Dasein*'s being-in-the-world. Yet once the move toward such a foundation is recognized as already problematic in itself, the additional characterization of that foundation in terms of the idea of the nonconceptual can do nothing by way of alleviating the problems that are associated with such a foundation—although it may well provide additional reason to be suspicious of the move to the nonconceptual as such.

World and "World-Formation"

The difference between the two modes of access to space that emerge here appears in Heidegger's own lectures—specifically in the lectures from 1929 to which I referred briefly above—in terms of a distinction between the modes of access to world that belong to the nonhuman animal and to the human. Heidegger says of nonhuman animals, not that they have *no* world, nor that they have a world in the same sense as the human, but rather that they are *poor* in world (*weltarm*).[38] "The animal does relate to something else, does therefore have access to something," writes Heidegger; "Not only that, we can even say that the animal has access to beings. The nest that is sought out, the prey that is seized, is surely a being that is, and not nothing; otherwise the bird could not settle upon the nest and the cat would never catch a mouse—if these were not beings."[39] The animal thus appears to stand in an ambiguous relation to world, but the difficulty for Heidegger is to say just what that relation is, and, more importantly, to distinguish the manner of that relation from the relation that obtains to world in the case of the human—the latter relation being one that Heidegger characterizes as "world-forming."[40] Much of the second half of Heidegger's lectures are given over to the attempt to clarify both what it means for the animal to be "poor" in world and for the human to be "world-forming."

In considering this issue, Heidegger takes as a central example the behavior of the honey bee, considering, among other things, the honey bee's capacity for orientation and navigation—something particularly pertinent to the discussion here. By way of a preliminary comment, Heidegger notes that

In the strict sense, there is orientation only where space is disclosed as such, and thus where the possibility of distinguishing different regions and identifiable locations within these regions is also given. We recognize of course that the bee flies through space as it returns home to the hive from the meadow, but the question is whether in behaving in this way the bee opens up a space as space and flies through it *as* its *spatial flight-path*.[41]

The honey bee has a remarkable capacity, as Heidegger acknowledges, to find its way to and from its hive, doing so on the basis of distance and direction largely as determined by the position of the sun. Yet, as certain experiments show, the bee's capacity for spatial orientation and direction is relatively inflexible in this respect. As Heidegger himself explains, if a bee is allowed to fly from its hive, is caught, and then held in a darkened box long enough so that the position of the sun has changed by the time the bee is released, then the bee will attempt to fly back to its hive according to the direction in relation to the sun that was relevant at the time of its capture. Once the bee has flown the distance originally traveled on its outward journey, it will begin looking for its hive by flying more or less randomly about until the hive is located (which it will be so long as the distance flown is not too great).

Heidegger takes the relative inflexibility in the bee's navigational capacities as showing that

The bee is *simply given over* to the sun and to the period of its flight *without being able to grasp either of these as such*, without being able to reflect upon them as something thus grasped. The bee can only be given over to things in this way because it is driven by the fundamental drive of foraging. It is precisely because of this *driven-ness*, and not on account of any recognition or reflection, that the bee can be *captivated* by what the sun occasions in its behaviour. . . . The *captivation* of the animal therefore signifies, in the first place, essentially *having every apprehending of something as something withheld from it.*[42]

Given Heidegger's characterization of what it is to be oriented ("there is orientation only where space is disclosed as such"), the bee has no proper orientation in space, being largely determined in its behavior by its "captivation" in relation to the sun. We might say that the bee has no proper sense of space, even though it has a capacity for behavioral response that correlates to features of the bee's environment. The problem is, of course, that it can only respond in this way, having no real capacity to free its behavior from the environmental circumstances in which it finds itself. It is because its response is so restricted, and because of the "withholding" of any other capacity for response (which is a withholding of any capacity to grasp space or things as such), that Heidegger characterizes the honey bee's, and the animal's, relation to world as "impoverished."

The captivation of the organism by its environmental circumstances is also addressed in Jakob von Uexküll's concept of *Umwelt* or "environing world." Heidegger makes explicit reference to von Uexküll in his 1929 discussion, since Heidegger takes von Uexküll's work as possibly providing a counter to Heidegger's own claim regarding the nonhuman animal's impoverished relation to world. Indeed, von Uexküll's work is often taken to provide a parallel to that of Heidegger—both are treated as advancing a similarly "ecological" conception of the relation between living organisms and their world.[43]

The key point about von Uexküll's account for the discussion here is the way in which his concept of *Umwelt* is understood as based in the internal, biologically determined character of the animal's "species nature." In this respect, the concept remains thoroughly subjectivist—as might be expected given the essentially neo-Kantian background against which it arises. The character of any particular *Umwelt* (and von Uexküll does not restrict the applicability of the concept, taking humans, as well as animals, to have an *Umwelt* of their own) is always relativized to the creature whose *Umwelt* it is, constituting a sphere of sense and action that encloses the creature, and that is essentially its own. Thus, in one of his best-known passages (which, although published later than Heidegger's lectures, develops in more popular form ideas already present in earlier works[44]), von Uexküll requests of his readers that they

first blow, in fancy, a soap bubble around each creature to represent its own world, filled with the perceptions which it alone knows. When we ourselves then step into one of these bubbles, the familiar meadow is transformed. Many of its colourful features disappear; others no longer belong together but appear in new relationships. A new world comes into being. Through the bubble we see the world of the burrowing worm, of the butterfly, of the field-mouse; the world as it appears to the animals themselves, not as it appears to us. This we may call the *phenomenal world* or the *self-world* of the animal.[45]

The subjectivist character of von Uexküll's analysis is particular evident in his discussion of space and time. So a few pages on in the same essay he writes that

We are easily deluded into assuming that the relationship between a foreign subject and the objects in his world exists on the same spatial and temporal plane as our own relations with the objects in our human world. This fallacy is fed by a belief in the existence of a single world, into which all living creatures are pigeonholed. This gives rise to the widespread conviction that there is only one space and one time for all living things. Only recently have physicists begun to doubt the existence of a universe with a space that is valid for all beings. That such a space cannot exist is evident from the fact that all men live in three distinct spaces [operational, visual, and tactile], which penetrate and complement, but in part also contradict one another.[46]

Thus, even space, and perhaps also time, appears to be subjectively—which, in von Uexküll's framework, means biologically—determined.

Significantly, von Uexküll also emphasizes the way in which the *Umwelten* of certain animals, including humans, is structured in terms of the functional character of the objects presented within those *Umwelten*. Von Uexküll thus distinguishes between the perceptual presentation of an object (the "receptor image") and the presentation of the object as it relates to action (the "effector image"). To illustrate this point von Uexküll uses the example of "a young, very intelligent and agile Negro" who supposedly lacked any knowledge of European tools. On von Uexküll's account, when asked to climb a ladder, the young man responded by asking how he was to do that given that he saw nothing but "rods and holes." Once shown how to use the ladder, however, his perception of the rods and holes changed, and he saw the object as something climbable, as a ladder.[47] Von Uexküll comments on this example as follows:

This experience with the Negro indicates that we have developed an effector image for each of the functions which we perform with the objects in our specific *Umwelt*. This effector image we inevitably fuse so closely with the receptor image supplied by our sense organs, that in the process the objects acquire a new quality, which conveys their meaning to us, and which we shall briefly term their *functional tone*.[48]

In their functionally oriented character, von Uexküll's *Umwelten* thus appear in a way that suggests obvious affinities with the equipmentally ordered structure of world as developed in *Being and Time*. It is perhaps no surprise, then, that Heidegger was so concerned to distinguish his account of world from the sort of account evident in von Uexküll.[49] Moreover, in distinguishing his account from von Uexküll's, Heidegger can also be seen to be looking to develop an account of the human relation to world that can be correlated with the second of the two modes of access to space that was identified in the discussion above—a mode of access that does indeed allow access to the things and to the world, not merely in terms of their "functional" tone, as von Uexküll might put it, nor as some overarching functional array, but in a way that allows them to appear *as things*, and *as world*; a mode of access in which it is also the case that "space is disclosed as such."

Much of the contemporary discussion of Heidegger's inquiry into the difference between the human and the animal as it arises in these 1929 lectures has focused on what is often taken to be the problematic nature of Heidegger's assertion of this difference, and its characterization in terms of a lack or privation that afflicts the animal, together with the humanistic and anthropocentric bias that this supposedly entails.[50] Yet the difference at issue in Heidegger's discussion, and the manner of its characterization, is not of only secondary importance in Heidegger's thinking, but stands at its very heart. What concerns Heidegger more than just the capacity to engage with things in the world *in some way or another*, is that particular mode of engagement that allows, as we have already seen, the "emergence" of the world *as world*, of things *as things*, and of space *as space*—a mode of engagement that Heidegger claims is not available to the nonhuman animal. It is precisely this emergence of world that is at issue in the central Heideggerian concern with the question of being, and that also implicates the being of the human—the being that is, as Heidegger emphasizes, our own[51]—in an essential way.

As Heidegger presents matters, the human does not have an *Umwelt*, or perhaps better, does not remain captive within its *Umwelt*. Instead, the human is defined in terms of its possession of *Welt*, of world, and more specifically, in terms of its character as world-forming.[52] The idea of world-formation is itself interpreted by Heidegger in terms of an understanding of world as "the manifestness of beings as such, of beings as beings" [53] (although he will also modify this to emphasize that it is the manifestness of beings as such and "as a whole"[54]). The character of human being as world-forming is presumably, then, a matter of the character of human beings as participating, in an essential way, in an opening up of world as just such a manifestness of beings.[55] In his discussion of the idea of world as "the manifestness of beings, as such, of beings as beings" Heidegger focuses on the "as" in this phrase, noting that "bound up with world is this enigmatic 'as,' beings *as* such, or formulated in a formal way: 'something *as* something,' a possibility which is quite closed to the animal. Only where beings are manifest as beings at all, do we find the possibility of experiencing this or that particular being as determined in this or that particular way."[56] The focus on the "as" leads Heidegger in the direction of an investigation of *statement* or *assertion* as that in and by means of which things are manifest *as* the things they are, and so are manifest *as* having a certain character, as being thus and so—"Our explication of the problem began with the 'as.' We found that it is a structural moment of the statement, or more precisely that it expresses something which is always already understood in every propositional statement."[57] The question of world-formation thus seems to direct us inevitably toward the question of language, and that is indeed the direction in which Heidegger himself moves.[58]

Yet as is already indicated in the passage just quoted, the implication of language in world-formation should not be taken to mean that world-formation is brought about *by* language, any more than world-formation is simply brought about *by* human beings. That human beings are world-forming, or even that language might be said to be world-forming, means that human beings and language participate in world-formation, but not that they enable it or that they are somehow prior to it. Indeed, the human only appears *as* human, and language *as* language, in and through the forming of world. Such world-formation, which nevertheless stands in an intimate relation to the essence of language understood as *logos*, has its ground in the original opening up of the world as a whole that enables the accessibility to things in order that they can be grasped as thus and so, and in order that statement and assertion about them can be possible. The argument here is a familiar one in Heidegger—it is much the same argument that also appears in Heidegger's account of truth as the original concealing/revealing that must be prior to any possibility of truth as a matter of the correspondence or *adequation* of statement to thing.[59]

World, Space, and Time

So far it may appear as if this excursion into the problems of world and world-formation has taken me away from what was hitherto the main theme of my discussion, namely, the question of space. It is at just this point, however, that space and spatiality reenter the picture—although still, in 1929, the way they do so remains somewhat obscure. Toward the end of his discussion of language and *logos* in *The Fundamental Concepts of Metaphysics*, Heidegger summarizes the issues he has explored as follows:

The λόγος can point out beings as they are, and in such pointing out point *toward* whatever pertains to those beings or direct *away* whatever does not pertain to them, only if it already has the possibility in general of measuring this point out and whether it suitably conforms to those beings. However, in order to be able to decide about the conformity or nonconformity of whatever the λόγος says in pointing out, or more precisely, in order to be able to comport himself in general within this "either/or," man in his propositional discourse must have *leeway* [*Spielraum*] in advance for the comparative to-and-fro of the "either/or," of *truth or falsity*. He must have leeway within which those beings that assertion is to be about are themselves manifest.[60]

In spite of the fact that Heidegger does not thematize the concept here, space nevertheless forces its way into his account in terms of an essential spatiality, an openness, an extendedness, a mode even of enclosedness, that is presupposed by the very possibility of the appearing of things, and their being accessible to propositional statement. It is surely not insignificant that the idea of *Spielraum* that Heidegger employs here reappears in his work as *Zeit-Spiel-Raum*, "time-play-space" or "the play of time-space," as a means to designate the essential play of time and space that constitutes the *topos* of being.[61] Indeed, this very phrase reappears in the 1966 appendix to *The Fundamental Concepts of Metaphysics*, in which Heidegger writes, "Perhaps thinking must first open the time-play-space for poetizing, so that through the poetizing word there may again be a wording world."[62]

The final section of *The Fundamental Concepts of Metaphysics* attempts to inquire more closely into the character of the "occurrence" of the original manifestness of things that has become evident through the inquiry into *logos*. That occurrence is one that Heidegger recognizes as having an essentially unitary character, and yet it is a unity within which the multiplicity of beings is manifest; it is an occurrence in which we find ourselves oriented toward beings, and so bound to them, and yet at the same time beings are "freed up" so as to be able to be revealed as the beings they are. Heidegger uses the term "projection" to characterize that which enables this occurrence of world: "projection," he says, "is world-formation."[63] The idea of projection already appears in *Being and Time*, where *Dasein*'s existentiality is itself understood in terms of *Dasein*'s projecting of possibilities. As part of the structure of human being, projection can be seen to present a problem for Heidegger's account. It can too readily be seen as something that is achieved or brought about by the human, or by the *Dasein* within the human, and indeed, by the mid-1930s, Heidegger tells us that "being itself projects the human."[64] In many respects, as developed in *The Fundamental Concepts of Metaphysics*, "projection," although still associated with *Dasein*, simply names the complex structure of world-formation understood as a "unifying" and "binding" that also "frees up," and that does so precisely through the opening up of possibility.[65]

Significantly for the concern with spatiality, however, Heidegger's attempt to clarify the nature of such projection inevitably turns to a set of concepts that seem, once again, to be inevitably dependent upon spatiality and forms of spatialization. Even projection itself is analyzed etymologically in such a way. Thus Heidegger writes that

> What is *most proper* to such activity and occurrence [of projection] is what is expressed in the prefix "pro-" [*Ent-*], namely that in projecting [*Entwerfen*], this occurrence of projection *carries* whatever is projecting *out and away from themselves* in a certain way. It indeed removes them into whatever has been projected, but it does not as it were deposit and abandon them there—on the contrary: in this being removed by the projection, what occurs is precisely a peculiar *turning towards themselves on the part of whoever is projecting* [*Zukehrung des Entwerfenden*].[66]

The very idea of projection as a "throw" (a meaning embedded in the original German term, *Entwerfen*) connotes a sense of space or *room* (the latter term itself being closely related to the German *Raum*), while the constant employment of ideas and images of movement and of *turning*,[67] toward and away from, provides a reiteration of the same sense of movement in space that is carried by Heidegger's employment of the term *Spielraum*.

One might object that it is a mistake to take what is surely nothing more than the employment of a set of spatial *metaphors* to license the claim that there is an implicit emergence of space and spatiality as fundamental concepts in Heidegger's analysis of world. Indeed, one might even point to the fact that, in *Being and Time*, as I noted in the discussion above, Heidegger himself acknowledges the inevitable intrusion of spatial metaphors or images into our thinking, and warns against taking these too literally or giving them undue weight. There is, however, no such warning to be found in the later Heidegger. Moreover, in the "Letter on Humanism," in which there appears a different sort of spatial or topographic idea, that of language as the "house of being," Heidegger explicitly objects to any simple reading of this idea in metaphoric terms.[68] In fact, as we have already seen, spatial and topographic concepts play key roles throughout Heidegger's later thinking: in the increasing emphasis on the *Da*, the

"There," of being; in the ideas of the clearing (die *Lichtung*) of being, and of the Open (*das Offene*) as well as of the "between" (*das Zwischen*); in the conjoining of time with space (*Zeitraum*); in the strife of world and earth in the working of art;[69] and in the happening the Fourfold as that occurs in the thinging of the thing and the worlding of world.

The spatialized character of thinking that opens up in *The Fundamental Concepts of Metaphysics* (and which is, of course, already presaged in so many earlier works) thus cannot be set to one side as merely a feature of this work alone nor as an artifact of some spurious metaphoricity or stylistic idiosyncrasy. Instead, it reflects the deep-seated role that space plays in all thinking, and especially in any thinking that would inquire into world and our being *in* the world. In fact, even without looking to the emergence of the spatial in Heidegger's later thinking, one might well ask how else one is to understand the original occurrence of world-formation that Heidegger describes in *The Fundamental Concepts of Metaphysics* other than by drawing on notions of space and spatiality (which, to reiterate the point once again, does not mean drawing on a notion of space as this may be identified with physical space alone—one of the lessons of the engagement with Heidegger, and of Heidegger's own engagement with the spatial, is the need to rethink what space itself might be). On this point it is instructive to return to the Kantian understanding of space and spatiality, according to which space and time are seen both as fundamental to the possibility of experience and also as standing in a relation of mutual dependence.

As the form of inner sense, *all* representations have a temporal ordering, and yet time itself, as I noted earlier, cannot be represented other than spatially. Thus Kant writes that "The possibility of things as quantities . . . can only be exhibited in outer intuition, and . . . only through the mediation of outer intuition can it be applied to inner sense,"[70] and he illustrates the point by reference to quantity as represented through the use of "fingers, in the beads of the abacus, or in strokes and points which can be placed before the eyes."[71] This is not, moreover, just a matter of the dependence of *representation* on outer intuition, but also involves the necessity of outer experience if inner experience is even to be possible. This is a key point in the "Refutation of Idealism" that appears in the B edition of the *Critique* (and in this respect, it shows how relevant the issue of spatiality is to Heidegger's own concern with subjectivism), and is tied both to the way in which subjectivity requires objectivity and also to the way in which that tie necessarily implicates spatiality also. This is because, on the arguments Kant adduces (arguments alluded to in the discussion above), objectivity and spatiality are themselves closely tied together.

What Kant provides us with, in fact, is one of the few sustained inquiries into the nature of space and spatiality in the history of philosophy—an inquiry, moreover, that does not merely assume a concept of space as it might be taken up within physical science, but rather adopts a properly *critical* approach to space and spatiality that enables them to be understood in what Kant would have thought of as their *transcendental* character, that is, in terms of the role they play in the possibility of experience, or, as Heidegger has it, in the possibility of world or world-formation.[72] Space and spatiality emerge here as having a unitary and complex structure that is not separable from time and temporality, and yet is not reducible to or derivative of it either.

I mentioned the possibility, in the discussion above, that one might understand space, as distinct from time, as precisely that mode of dimensionality that enables *juxtaposition* and so also *differentiation*. One might argue that this is just what is evident in the Kantian treatment of spatiality, although it is not a conclusion that Kant himself draws (and probably, given that he holds open the possibility of a mode of intuition other than that of sensibility, it is a conclusion he could *not* have drawn). Such an understanding of space and spatiality, although also worked out in close connection to the concept of *place*, is one that I have explored elsewhere in a way that draws not on Kant, but on Marcel Proust's "phenomenological" investigations of space and time as developed in his monumental *In Search of Lost Time*.[73] There the loss that occurs in the displacement of time is overcome precisely through the juxtaposition of elements alongside one another in space (and also in relation to place), in such a way that those elements are copresent and are thereby brought together in their difference.[74]

The direction in which this understanding of space inevitably moves is one that, though present in late Heidegger, is perhaps even more clearly evident in the work of Jacques Derrida. Derrida's concept of *différance* as a primordial differing and deferring has an essentially spatial as well as temporal aspect. *Différance* is thus understood as tied to *spacing*.[75] As is well known, Derrida argues for *différance* as having priority even over the ontological difference.[76] Yet if one takes Heidegger's own work seriously, attending to the increasing focus on the interplay of unity and difference in his late thought, as well as to the way in which this interplay is itself played out in the space or "leeway" (*Spielraum*) that belongs to the essential happening of place—the *Ereignis*, the Fourfold—then one can see how even Derrida's *différance* may be presaged in late Heidegger's own spatialized and topological mode of thinking. Indeed, it is significant that, like Derrida,

Heidegger comes to see the unity and difference that are played out within the timespace (*Zeitraum*) of place as more primordial even than the ontological difference itself.[77]

Space and spatiality cannot be understood as derivative of any other structure—and certainly neither of "practice" nor of temporality. Moreover, any attempt to investigate the concept of world cannot neglect spatiality. This is not simply because the world encompasses both space and time, but because the very structure of world can only be articulated and understood through an essential *spatialization*. The centrality of space and spatiality to the understanding of world, and so to the understanding of our own mode of being, is especially evident in Heidegger. Indeed, the development of Heidegger's thinking is such that the spatial and topographic elements that occur in such pervasive and fundamental ways throughout his thinking—and that are present even in the concept of *Dasein*, as well as in the idea of our essential existential and hermeneutical situatedness, as these appear in his early work—are gradually taken up in increasingly direct and self-evident fashion, with the centrality of space as well as place becoming ever more evident, until Heidegger is finally able explicitly to characterize his thinking as itself *topological* in character.[78]

Conclusion: Rethinking Space and World

From the perspective of contemporary cognitive science, the considerations regarding the nature and significance of space and its relation to world that have been explored here are indicative of certain key aspects of the framework within which the scientific investigation of cognition and behavior must operate, as well as of the limits of any such investigation. No investigation of the way in which organisms act in and respond to their environment can be adequate that does not attend closely to the spatial character of such action and response. Moreover, the way spatiality enters into the sort of action and response that is characteristic of human beings in their relation to the world involves a mode of conceptual and representational engagement that cannot be neglected nor ignored, and that is also itself tied to a particular mode of spatial engagement.

For just these reasons, Heidegger's work remains of relevance to contemporary cognitive science. Yet if spatiality does indeed have the fundamental and primordial character that is presaged in Kant and also developed in Heidegger, as well as in Derrida, then the concepts of space and spatiality, as well as spatial and topographic images and modes of thought, will always remain essential to any cognitive scientific understanding and yet also essentially resistant to any such understanding. In the end, space and spatiality belong, as does the concept of world, not so much to the domain of strict physical science nor even of a certain "empiricist metaphysics," as to the domain of properly *philosophical*, and perhaps also *poetic*, critique and reflection. Such a conclusion is, significantly, not one for which *Being and Time* provides an adequate basis, but rather becomes evident, at least as far as Heidegger is concerned, only through the rethinking of the project of which *Being and Time* is part, and, in particular, through the rethinking of the concepts of both world and of space.

7 Geography, Biology, and Politics

To what extent are those forms of contemporary thinking that adopt a holistic or ecological conception of the relation between human being and the environing world associated, even if only implicitly, with a conservative and reactionary politics? That there is such an association is often claimed in relation to a number of thinkers, but most notably perhaps in relation to Heidegger.[1] Sometimes the claim is extended to encompass broader movements in contemporary thought, with environmental thinking being the most common, but by no means the only target here.[2] Seldom, however, is much consideration given to the way such a claim relates, in any detailed way, to twentieth-century intellectual history in general, nor, indeed, is much account taken of the possible differences that might obtain between different forms of holistic or ecological thinking as such. Moreover, the same holds even more strongly for those particular forms of holistic or ecological thinking that give a special role to notions of place or *topos*. Although such place-oriented approaches have a special prominence in contemporary thinking across a number of disciplines, including both geography and history, there is a tendency to argue (sometimes simply to assume) that such approaches do indeed bring problematic political associations along with, and yet also to neglect any real consideration of the details of those approaches.

I want to pursue these issues here by considering the way they emerge in connection to Heidegger, especially as he may be positioned in relation to the geographers Friedrich Ratzel and Paul Vidal de la Blache, as well as the ethologist Jakob von Uexküll. The contrast between Heidegger and von Uexküll is particularly important, as I argue that although they both adopt a holistic or ecological conception of the relation between human being and the world (in von Uexküll's case, this is part of a broader account of the relation between the animal and environment), the place-oriented character of the Heideggerian approach, which also unites Heidegger with

Ratzel and Vidal de la Blache, marks a crucial point of difference with the subjectivist and biologically oriented approach evident in von Uexküll. As it turns out, this difference is itself crucial to the political issues that might also be thought to be at stake. Moreover, getting clear on these differences is important not only for our understanding of Heidegger or the other thinkers at issue here, or for our understanding of certain aspects of intellectual history, but also for our understanding of a set of place-oriented ideas that have become important and influential in much contemporary thinking concerning the world and our relation to it—whether that be in philosophy, environmentalism, geography, or history.

From the Historical to the Geographical

Heidegger is often thought of as a philosopher—perhaps *the* philosopher— of temporality and historicality. His best-known and most influential work is, after all, *Being and Time*, in which temporality plays a central role, and in which human being is understood as fundamentally determined by its temporal and historical character. Yet, although it is undoubtedly true that *Being and Time* prioritizes time and history, the way it does so is also quite problematic, and is undoubtedly one of the factors that underlies Heidegger's failure to complete the work as originally projected.[3] A large part of the difficulty here is that *Being and Time* is essentially a work that operates within a *topological* framework that cannot adequately be articulated with respect to temporality alone (although that is precisely what Heidegger attempts). Both the temporal and the spatial have to be theorized together, and in a way that does not reduce one to the other. One somewhat provocative way to put this is to say that such a topology must do justice to the "geographical" alongside the "historical," since it must be attentive to the way in which human being is always spatially situated on the earth (*geo-*), and not merely temporally located in relation to a past and a future. Indeed, if we look to Heidegger's later thinking, the idea of the Fourfold that appears there—and that incorporates Mortals, Gods, Sky, and *Earth*—appears, almost explicitly, to give recognition to this sense of the geographical, alongside the historical, within a single account of the place, the *topos*, of being.[4]

Additionally to its focus on *topos* as such, the place-oriented mode of thinking that is to be found in Heidegger (and which is present in problematic form in *Being and Time*) is characterized by a particular *mode* of analysis—one that looks to a single integrated conception of the phenomenon at issue as it stands in relation to the larger context in which that phenomenon appears.[5] This aspect of the approach, which reflects the character of *topos* itself, is clearly evident, in *Being and Time*, in Heidegger's understanding of the essence of human being, *Dasein*, as being-in-the-world (*In-der-Welt-Sein*)—human being is thereby understood in terms of its prior and necessary relatedness to the world within which it appears[6]—and it is also evident, in his later thinking, in the idea of the Fourfold as that within which not only human being, but any being, can come to appearance. The integrative aspect of Heidegger's topological approach can be seen to be mirrored in holistic and relational analyses of human being, as these arise in twentieth-century thought in particular, that look to understand the human in close interconnection with its worldly surroundings, and to understand the world itself in similarly interconnected fashion. Such analyses often give particular emphasis to the interconnection of spatial and temporal elements, in terms of the interconnection of condition with process, of the environmental with the developmental, of the geographic with the historical.

The rise of this sort of integrative spatiotemporal analysis, one that seems inevitably to draw upon and to move towards place or *topos* as a key concept (even if this is not always acknowledged or made explicit), is especially evident within twentieth-century historiography. Although Marxism and Weberian sociology have both played important roles in shaping historical thinking over the last hundred years or more, that period has also seen the rise in what might be termed a more geographically inflected mode of historiography that has explicitly thematized the interconnection between climatic, geological, and topographical factors and human action, society, and culture—between, in the words of Lucien Febvre, "the earth and history"[7]—and that also thinks these issues in an explicitly relational, holistic, or "ecological" fashion. The engagement of the historical with the geographical, as well as with philosophical ideas derived from Heidegger (and originating with Husserl), has also been evident in the rise of a form of "humanistic geography" that is itself attentive to the interplay between the human and the environmental.[8] Significantly, the thinkers who have been foundational in the rise of such "humanistic geography," most notably Paul Vidal de la Blache, also played a key role in the rise of geographically oriented history. Thus, Marc Bloch and Lucien Febvre, the founders of the influential *Annales* school of French historiography, were both heavily influenced by Vidal de la Blache, as well as by Friedrich Ratzel, himself an influence on Vidal.

The impulse toward a focus on something like place or *topos*, and so also toward more integrated or "holistic" modes of understanding, can be seen not only in geography or in geographically inflected historiography, but also, particularly in early twentieth-century Germany, in the psychological and biological sciences.[9] In biology, the most significant exponent of such a holistic approach was Jakob von Uexküll, the founder of modern ecology and ethology. Heidegger himself compared his own position with that of von Uexküll in an important series of lectures from 1929, published in English as *The Fundamental Concepts of Metaphysics*. In those lectures Heidegger is specifically concerned with rethinking the problem of world and the relation of human being to it, and it is in just that context that he takes up the work of von Uexküll, but also draws on the work of other holistically inclined thinkers of the time such as the experimental embryologist Wilhelm Roux, the Czech biologist Emmanuel Radl, and the neovitalist biologist Hans Driesch.

A Problem of Politics

At this point, however, a problem arises—a problem that concerns the implication of the general approach that is at issue here, no matter where it appears, whether in philosophy, geography or biology, with the sort of reactionary politics that, in twentieth-century Germany, is paradigmatically exemplified by Nazism. It is, moreover, a problem that comes to a particular focus around Heidegger and von Uexküll.

In his essay, *The Open*, Giorgio Agamben discusses von Uexküll's work, in particular, with specific reference to Heidegger, but, significantly, he also connects that work, both that of von Uexküll and Heidegger, with the work of the geographers Paul Vidal de la Blanche and Friedrich Ratzel. Agamben writes:

The studies by the founder of ecology follow a few years after those by Paul Vidal de la Blanche on the relationship between populations and their environment (the *Tableau de la géographie de la France* is from 1903), and those of Friedrich Ratzel on the Lebensraum, the "vital space" of peoples (the *Politische Geographie* is from 1897), which would profoundly revolutionize human geography of the twentieth century. And it is not impossible that the central thesis of *Sein und Zeit* on being-in-the-world (*In-der-Welt-sein*) as the fundamental human structure can be read in some ways as a response to this problematic field, which at the beginning of the century essentially modified the traditional relationship between the living being and its environment-world. As is well-known, Ratzel's theses, according to which all peoples are intimately linked to their vital space as their essential dimension, had a notable influence on Nazi geopolitics. This proximity is marked in a curious episode in Uexküll's intellectual biography. In 1928, five years before the advent of Nazism, this very sober scientist writes a preface to Houston Chamberlain's *Die Grundlagen des neunzehnten Jahrhunderts* [*Foundations of the Nineteenth Century*], today considered one of the precursors of Nazism.[10]

Agamben refrains from making it explicit, but the clear implication of his comments is that the shared commitment to a holistic or ecological conception that is such a key element in place-oriented thinking is also associated with a shared political tendency. This tendency is taken to be explicit in the case of Ratzel and von Uexküll, and also Heidegger (although Agamben does not draw attention to it), through the way their ideas are themselves implicated with Nazism.

There can be little doubt that Agamben intends such an implication, but whether and to what extent the implication can be restricted to just the thinkers Agamben mentions is not so clear. If the mode of thinking that is to be found in von Uexküll, Heidegger, Ratzel, and Vidal de la Blache is indeed politically problematic in a way that is connected with its holistic or ecological, and so also its place-oriented, commitments, then surely this should also hold for the broader intellectual trends and movements of which their thought is a part. In that case, the geographical tradition that derives from Ratzel and Vidal, as well as the developments in historiography that are influenced by them, and the line of philosophical thinking that comes through Heidegger (though it can be seen as beginning in Husserl) would have to be viewed as having the same potentially problematic political tendencies.

Agamben is not alone, of course, in drawing these sorts of connections between Heidegger's philosophy and the ideology of Nazism. Heidegger's preoccupation with ideas of rootedness and belonging, his apparent preference for the world of peasant and farmer, and his frequent appeal to notions of origin and home have all been seen as tied to a conservative and even reactionary politics of a sort evident not only in Heidegger's personal entanglement with Nazism in the 1930s, but also in his admission late in his life, in the interview with *Der Spiegel* magazine in the 1960s, of his lack of faith in democratic politics (although exactly how this admission should be interpreted is by no means obvious). With such ideas clearly in the background, the historian Troy Paddock draws connections that are similar to those to be found in Agamben, but that focus directly on Heidegger in connection with Ratzel, and specifically on the place-oriented aspects of their thinking. Arguing that Heidegger distinguished between two concepts of space, the mathematical or geometric and the "geographic," Paddock claims that, taken in this latter sense, Heidegger does not consider space as an abstract entity but as part of a larger environment. Borders help give space a specific location, and consequently a specific function, creating a space that is grounded in the specific building, bridge, or jug. . . . Heidegger's conception of space bears striking parallels to views expressed in the late nineteenth century by the geographer Friedrich Ratzel, who suggested that there was a connection between the physical space that a people inhabited and their culture.[11]

Although Paddock seems to equivocate on the connection between such views and fascism,[12] he nevertheless claims that Heidegger's adoption of such a view of space reveals "a continued ideological affinity with basic tenets of Nazi ideology."[13] Moreover, Paddock makes quite clear that part of his interest in Heidegger's "geographic" conception of space derives from the way in which Heidegger's thinking has been taken up outside of philosophy, especially within contemporary environmentalism.

The clear implication here is that such "geographic" or place-oriented thinking has dangerous affinities with key elements of Nazi ideology, and should, therefore, be treated with extreme caution, if not shunned altogether. Once again, as was also the case with Agamben, it is hard to see how this argument could be restricted to Heidegger and Ratzel—or to contemporary environmentalism—alone. If Heidegger's geographic conception of space is deemed politically problematic, then so too must the "geographic" conception of space that surely also appears in the geographically inflected historiography of such as Bloch, Febvre, or, indeed, in the work of their immediate successors such as Fernand Braudel, as well as of the many historians, geographers, and social theorists who have been influenced by the tradition stemming from Ratzel as well as Vidal de la Blache (a tradition, it should be said, that might well be said to include thinkers such as Henri Lefebvre and Michel Foucault[14]).

The question to be addressed here is whether and to what extent Agamben and Padock are correct in seeing Heidegger, von Uexküll, Ratzel, and Vidal de la Blache as sharing a similar mode of thinking that leads them into proximity with Nazism. I shall argue that the arguments advanced by Agamben and Paddock (arguments that reflect assumptions and ideas that are quite prevalent if not always clearly articulated in the wider literature) considerably oversimplify the matter at issue, while also omitting important and relevant facts, and that, more to the point, there are differences between the positions that Heidegger, Ratzel, and Vidal de la Blache hold on the one hand, and von Uexküll holds on the other, that are crucial to the political affiliations to which each may be thought to be prone.

Whereas Heidegger can be seen as sharing with Ratzel and Vidal de la Blache a similar place-oriented or "geographical" conception of the relation between human being and the world that is inconsistent with key elements in Nazi ideology, this is not so for von Uexküll. A large part of what connects von Uexküll with Nazism, or at least with certain elements in the thinking to which Nazism as a movement was committed, is actually a form of subjectivism that gives priority to the racially determined "mind" or "soul" over the environment or world in which it is located. In contrast, Heidegger, Ratzel, and Vidal de la Blache, in accord with the topological character of their approach, view human being as standing in a relation of necessary interdependence and interconnection with the environing world, and as articulated in terms of the complex interplay of both environment and action as that occurs in and through place.

Heidegger and von Uexküll

Leaving aside, at least for the moment, some of the broader issues that are at stake here, it is worth recalling that in the case of Heidegger himself the simple fact of his connection with Nazi politics is straightforward and indisputable—Heidegger was a paid-up member of the Nazi Party from 1933 onward, and was appointed by the Nazis as Rector of Freiburg University in that same year, resigning one year later. What remains open to dispute is exactly how that connection should be interpreted, what significance should be given to it, and, more particularly, how deeply it can be connected with Heidegger's philosophical thought.[15] In the early 1930s, Heidegger certainly seemed prepared to use ideas and images of autochthony and rootedness that appeared to bring his thought into close alignment with Nazi ideology and rhetoric.[16] Yet in terms of the specific claims advanced by such as Paddock, it is notable that although a "geographic" conception of space is indeed present in Heidegger's work up to and including the early 1930s (though usually expressed in terms of notions like that of "rootedness"), it is actually in the works after his resignation from the Rectorate in 1934, and so at a time after his attempt to establish himself as the intellectual leader of a National Socialist Germany had clearly failed, that such a conception, as developed explicitly in terms of place, seems to become much more important.[17]

There is undoubtedly a clear shift in Heidegger's thinking that first occurs in the 1930s, and intensifies around the late 1940s, toward an explicit concern with place and related concepts—concepts that include those of "dwelling" (already present in *Being and Time*), the "Fourfold" and the Event, *das Ereignis* (itself a concept that connects with the idea of *topos*[18])—and this shift toward the "geographic" or "topological" is itself closely tied to the so-called Turning in Heidegger's thought[19]). There is good reason to suppose that this change in thinking is itself connected to Heidegger's own failed engagement with Nazism, not in the sense that it derives from Nazi ideology, but that it is instead formed in reaction to it.[20] Significantly, it is in his engagement with Hölderlin in 1934–1935, imme- diately *after* his resignation of the Rectorate, that ideas of place and dwell- ing that lie at the heart of the "geographic" conception of space that concerns Paddock begin to emerge more explicitly (though still in a rela- tively undeveloped form) as a focus for Heidegger's thinking. Thus, one finds, at the same time as Heidegger's thought orients itself more toward more clearly "place-oriented" or "geographic" conceptions, a shift away from, and sometimes direct criticism of, key elements of associated with Nazi ideology. One might argue, of course, that this shift is simply a result of the failure in Heidegger's own political ambitions, and so treat it as a kind of "sour grapes" response; while there may be some truth in this from a biographical perspective, it should not be allowed to obscure the philo- sophical issues that are nevertheless also involved. Indeed, as I have already indicated above, and as we shall see in more detail below, there is a deep tension between "geographic" modes of thinking and the type of thinking that is characteristic of Nazi ideology, and this tension becomes apparent not only in Heidegger's thinking, but also in relation to the work of Ratzel and Vidal de la Blache.

Just as a closer examination of Heidegger's own involvement with Nazism complicates the attempt to discern a simple line of connection between Heidegger's fascist politics and his thinking of space and place, so too a closer examination of the intellectual history that implicates Heidegger, along with figures such as Ratzel, Vidal de la Blache, and von Uexküll, leads to a more complex picture than that which Agamben or even Paddock suggests. Agamben takes Heidegger's concept of "being-in- the-world" to be a close correlate to von Uexküll's concept of *Umwelt*— literally the environing world—according to which the organism is understood as always enclosed with, almost as a part of, its environment. To what extent Heidegger's concept of "being-in-the-world" is actually indebted to or influenced by von Uexküll's concept of *Umwelt* seems debatable—there does not appear to be any evidence that would demon- strate a direct influence from one to the other as opposed to some conver- gence of what were otherwise independent lines of thought. Heidegger was certainly familiar with von Uexküll's work at the time he wrote his 1929 lectures, *The Fundamental Concepts of Metaphysics*, and, as Harrington points out, von Uexküll himself drew attention to apparent similarities between his thought and that of Heidegger in a 1937 paper.[22] Yet even though the exact nature and extent of any influence of von Uexküll on Heidegger may be uncertain,[22] there can be no doubt of the connection between von Uexküll and Chamberlain. Indeed, what Agamben omits to tell us, somewhat surprisingly, is that not only did von Uexküll write a preface to Chamberlain's book, but he was himself a close and long-time friend of Chamberlain, holding similar anti-Semitic and racist views (views that were not usually apparent, however, in von Uexküll's academic writing).[23]

Heidegger directly cites von Uexküll's work in 1929, but he does so, as I noted earlier, along with a number of other prominent biologists and zoologists with similar holistic commitments. Significantly, the discussion of these thinkers is part of Heidegger's own attempt, following *Being and Time*, to rethink the idea of world, and the relation between the world and human being, that is so central to Heidegger's magnum opus (Heidegger claimed, in fact, that his discovery, or rediscovery, of the problem of world was one of the unique achievements of his thinking in the 1920s[24]), and can thus be seen as already on the way toward the more radical reorientation of Heidegger's thought that would occur in the 1930s. Heidegger's interest in von Uexküll is in the context of this attempt to reinvestigate the concept of world. Moreover, it arises not so much because of the possibility of a convergence between von Uexküll's view of the relation between animal and environment and Heidegger's conception of being-in-the-world, but rather because von Uexküll's approach may be thought to provide a scientific counter to Heidegger's claim, also evident in *Being and Time*, as to the uniqueness of the human relatedness to world. What von Uexküll's work may be taken to show is that the animal does indeed have a world, contrary to Heidegger, albeit a different world from the human. While Heidegger is generous in his estimation of the significance of von Uexküll's work, as of that of the other biologists he discusses (and that generosity may well derive from Heidegger's own sympathies toward their holistic and antimechanistic approach), he also concludes that there remains "a fundamental question whether we should talk of the world of the animal—of an environing world or even of an inner world—or whether we do not have to determine that which the animal stands in relation to in another way."[25]

Although part of a rethinking that began almost immediately following the publication of *Being and Time*, Heidegger's discussion of von

Uexküll in 1929 nevertheless stands within the essentially Kantian frame that determines much of Heidegger's thinking from the 1920s, especially as it is worked out in *Being and Time*, but also as evident in *Kant and the Problem of Metaphysics* (published in 1929). One of the problems that leads Heidegger away from that Kantian frame is what he comes to regard as its incipient tendency, in spite of Heidegger's own efforts to counter that tendency, toward a form of subjectivism or idealism. Thus, in commenting on a passage from the 1936 essay, "The Origin of the Work of Art," Heidegger writes that "Here lies concealed *the relationship of being to human being*. This relationship is inadequately thought even in this presentation—a distressing difficulty that has been clear to me since *Being and Time*, and has since come under discussion in many presentations."[26] The inadequacy of the presentation seems to lie in the possibility that the relationship at issue might be construed as one in which being is somehow grounded or based in human being—as Heidegger writes elsewhere concerning the way *Dasein* appears in *Being and Time*, the presentation "still stands in the shadow of the 'anthropological,' the 'subjectivistic,' and the 'individualist,' etc."[27] In *Being and Time*, this problem can be seen in the emphasis given to *existentiality* (the character of *Dasein*'s being as grounded in its own projection of possibilities) over *facticity* or *thrownness* (the already determined actuality of *Dasein*'s being) in the structure of *Dasein*, and so also to the priority given to the *future* over the *past* within the structure of temporality.[28] One might add, of course, that this is also tied to Heidegger's prioritization of temporality.

Heidegger does not himself formulate any criticism of von Uexküll, in 1929, as standing "in the shadow of the 'anthropological,' the 'subjectivistic,' and the 'individualist'" (and at that stage, he was only on the verge of formulating such a criticism of elements of his own work). Von Uexküll is nevertheless clearly situated within exactly the sort of Kantian, or better, neo-Kantian frame that Heidegger came increasingly to view as problematic precisely because of what he saw as its subjectivist and related tendencies. One can certainly view von Uexküll's concept of the organism in its world as moving toward a more integrated understanding of the relation between organism and environment, but that concept nevertheless stands in clear distinction from the more fully "ecological" conception of the relation between mortals and their world that appears in later Heidegger, and may even be viewed as already standing somewhat apart from early Heidegger's conception of being-in-the-world. Indeed, for all that

Heidegger comes to regard *Being and Time* as hampered by certain problematic Kantian or neo-Kantian tendencies, it should be quite clear that
part of his intention in thinking of *Dasein* as being-in-the-world is to avoid
any idea of the world either as standing apart from *Dasein* (as some pregiven realm of "objectivity") or as being constituted or constructed by
Dasein (as a function of a pregiven "subjectivity"). Von Uexküll's account
of the animal in its environment, however, stands in significant contrast
here, since it gives priority to the animal as determinative of its world,
treating each such world as a self-enclosed domain that is strictly speaking
inaccessible from the outside, and so von Uexküll's account remains, as we
have seen, essentially subjectivist or phenomenalist.

Harrington draws explicit attention to the subjectivist character of
von Uexküll's work, citing von Uexküll's account of his sudden recognition, on seeing a beech tree in the Heidelberg woods, that "this is not *a*
beech tree, but rather *my* beech tree, something that I, with my sensations,
have constructed in all its details. Everything [about the beech] that I see,
hear, smell or feel are not qualities that exclusively belong to the beech,
but rather are characteristics of my sense organs that I project outside
of myself."[29] As we saw previously in chapter 6, the same subjectivism is
also clearly evident in von Uexküll's published work. Moreover, inasmuch
as this subjectivism gives priority to the subject *as biological organism*,
so it understands each surrounding world, each *Umwelt*, as itself a
function of the organism's own biological nature, and so each world is
understood to be determined biologically, one might say, rather than
geographically.

This determination of the world by the organism is an important idea
that undoubtedly fed into von Uexküll's racism and anti-Semitism: different races form the world in different ways, and the world of the Jew is
therefore a different world from the world of the Nordic Aryan, just as the
Nordic Aryan landscape is also different from that of the Slav. Indeed, in
the 1940s, similar ideas underpinned attempts on the part of Nazi planners
to reshape the conquered landscapes of Poland in ways that would accord
with German identity and the German soul.[30] It is thus not merely the idea
of a connection between the organism and its space, between the human
being and the world, that is at issue here, but the exact nature of that
connection. The emphasis in von Uexküll, and in many racial theorists
from the same period,[31] on the determining role of the organism in its
species nature—which, in the case of human beings, also means its *racial*
nature—stands in sharp contrast to those positions that see the organism

as determined by its environment, and those positions that see organism and environment as mutually determining or interdependent.

Ratzel and Vidal de la Blache

It has been common to assimilate racialist thinking of the sort exemplified by von Uexküll, with its emphasis on the difference between the racial types associated with different regions or "spaces," to Ratzelian geographic "determinism." In fact, Ratzel stands quite apart from writers such as von Uexküll, and other racial theorists in general, simply on the basis of his very different understanding of the nature of the connection at issue here. It is indeed as an *environmental* or *geographic* determinist—one who puts the emphasis on the human as determined by the environment or geography—that Ratzel has been most commonly read, if not entirely accurately, within English-speaking circles; and it is notable that Ratzel also placed himself in clear opposition to the racialist doctrines that were common in the latter half of the nineteenth century. Indeed, he seems to have viewed racial differences as having little relevance to geographical or ethnographic inquiry, writing that "The task of ethnography is . . . to indicate, not in the first instances the distinctions, but the points of transition, and the intimate affinities which exist; for mankind is one though very variously cultured."[32]

Ratzel's notion of *Lebensraum*, "living space," was an expression of his commitment to the idea that the forms of human organization were always bound to their own geographic space, and could not be understood in separation from that space. As Robert Dickinson writes:

Ratzel . . . thought of the anthropogeographic unit as an areal complex whose spatial connections were needed for the functioning and organisation of a particular kind of human group, be it the village, town or state. The concept of lebensraum deals with the relations between human society as a spatial (geographic) organisation and its physical setting. Community area, trade area, milk-shed and labour-shed, historical province, commercial entity, the web of trade between neighbouring industrial areas across state boundaries—these area all subsequent variations of the concept of the "living area."[33]

Ratzel believed that the development of states would imply an increase in the state's *Lebensraum*, but he did not take the idea of *Lebensraum* as providing any justification of territorial expansion as such. It was the later deployment of the term within the geopolitics of Rudolf Kjellen and Karl Haushofer that led to its instrumentalist use within Nazi ideology. Moreover, Ratzel's opposition to racialist theory can be seen, in fact, as a direct consequence of his emphasis on the role of the environment and on geographic space—something that presented problems for those, like Haushofer, who wished to assimilate his ideas to the ideology of Nazism[34]—although Ratzel also held, quite independently, it seems, that ethnic mixing itself contributed to the vigor of a society (a view that he may have developed during his early experiences in the "new" societies of Mexico and the United States).

Ratzel's emphasis on the importance of geographic space in social, cultural, and ethnographic analysis can be seen as an important precursor to the ideas of many more recent writers, including such as Gilles Deleuze and Felix Guattari,[35] concerning the spatialized character of social, economic, and cultural formations. Within French geographic thought, Ratzel was especially influential, and the work of the founder of French "regionalism," Paul Vidal de la Blache, can be seen to arise out of Ratzel's geographical approach to human history and ethnography, and as a continuation of the Ratzelian idea of "human geography" or anthropogeography. Like Ratzel, Vidal de la Blache also rejects biological determinism, but whereas Ratzel tends, not always consistently, to emphasize the role of the physical environment in human history and culture, Vidal de la Blache takes a more explicitly interactive approach (although the differences between them on this point are often overstated). The regional geography that he initiated was based on the study of the interplay between the cultural and the environmental, but the place or region was to be defined in ways that attended to cultural factors, rather than to natural features alone.[36] The physical environment is seen as opening a range of possibilities for human interaction rather than as determining that interaction—hence Vidal de la Blache's oft-cited commitment to a geographical "possibilism" rather than "determinism." Interestingly, Henri Lefebvre was strongly influenced by Vidal de la Blache, and his early work on the Pyrenees can itself be seen as containing important elements of Vidalian geographic practice.[37]

In both Ratzel and Vidal de la Blache, the emphasis on a conception on geographic space is crucial not only to the theoretical positions they advance, as well as to their significance within the history of geography, but also to the differentiation of their thought from that of von Uexküll and others like him. It also marks, of course, a key point of differentiation from Nazi ideology, and, in this respect, Heidegger must also be positioned alongside Ratzel and Vidal de la Blache. Moreover, it is not just the emphasis on the role of the "geographic" as opposed to the "biologistic" that is at issue here. What characterizes the work of von Uexküll, as well as Nazi racial theorists, is the tendency to understand the nature of the animal or human "world" as based in certain general forms of species-nature, "racial stock," or racialized "soul." Such a tendency is already one that diminishes the significance of geographic space or place—it is the *general type* that is important in such thinking, in contrast to which the thinking that is oriented toward place typically gives emphasis to the regional and the local.

This latter issue turns out to be a crucial point of difference when one looks to the way Nazi ideology is related to the German "*Heimat*" tradition. The idea of *Heimat*—a term usually translated as "Homeland" (though the translation does not capture the richness of the original German)—is connected with ideas of one's place of origin, the place in which one belongs, not only in the sense of the region from which one comes, and in which one may still dwell, but also in the sense of one's childhood home (it is the same notion that occurs in the discussion of Young in chapter 3) In its academic form, the focus on *Heimat* and *Heimatskunde* was part of the same orientation toward an understanding of human life and culture as it stood in relation to space, and so to region and landscape, as is evident in Ratzel and Vidal de la Blache. Thus Ratzel's *Deutschland: Einführung in die Heimatkunde*,[38] which was a standard text in German schools in the early part of the twentieth century, essentially consisted in a regional ethnography of Germany.

Elements of the *Heimat* tradition were themselves appropriated by the Nazis, appearing in Nazi propaganda and rhetoric as well as the work of Nazi ideologues—elements of local and regional tradition and culture could be seen as a reflection of the racial stock associated with that locale or region. Yet the emphasis here is not on the local and regional as such, but rather on the local and the regional as they stand in relation to the racial and the national. The totalizing politics of the Nazi state was not about strengthening local or regional associations and culture, but rather about the creation of a political apparatus geared to the satisfaction of a set of universalizing desires and ambitions, and far from being strengthened, the idea of *Heimat* took on a much diluted and abstract form during the Nazi period.[39] It is thus that Nazism, for all its Romantic antimodernist elements, can also be seen as the instantiation of something essentially modern—the attempt to reshape the world with respect to a single ideal image, and at the same time to impose one's will upon that world, and to make it one's own.

In this latter respect, what marks out Nazism as a mode of engagement with the world is its desire for domination and control—its desire to subject the world to its own will. It is thus that Heidegger, in his Nietzsche lectures from 1936 to 1940, developed his own critique of Nazism as the contemporary instantiation of what he saw as the Nietzschean "will to power" (a critique that might also be thought to be relevant to tendencies within his own earlier thinking).[40] Indeed, one might argue that in Nazism one finds a version of the "subjectivism" that is present in von Uexküll now developed into a determinate political form—the geographical becoming itself subject to the racial and the psychological. Moreover, the subjectivist character of such a development is not accidental, nor does it always remain implicit. Within German geopolitical thinking in the 1930s and 1940s, the geographer Otto Maull embraced just such a subjectivism as a direct response to the problem apparently presented by Ratzelian thinking. Discussing the 1941 edition of Maull's *Das Wesen der Geopolitik* (The Essence of Geopolitics), Mark Bassin writes:

Maull now categorically rejected geographical determinism as "materialist,: insisting that true Geopolitik was "idealist" in its inspiration and that it identified the rooted Völkisch "spirit" itself as "the cause of all political developments." . . . The Volk [People] itself now became the "quintessential agent of activity and determination" to which the natural-geographical milieu was correspondingly subordinated and by which it was instrumentalized as nothing more than "a task, a goal and a purpose." Far from being constrained by the natural conditions in which it exists, a Volk demonstrates its worthiness through its success in an endless struggle to overcome, and, eventually, to conquer them.[41]

As it is the *Volk*—the People as determined by their racial character—who are given priority here, so too are the geographical, the topological and the spatial correspondingly deemphasized. Moreover, in giving priority to the *Volk* as the active principle in the formation of the world, so too is a form of subjectivism, and as the later Heidegger would argue, of a modernistic nihilism, also enacted.

The "Uncanniness" of Place

It is often claimed that to take human being as standing in an important relation to place or geographic space is already to presuppose a homogeneity of culture and identity in relation to that place, as well as to exclude others from it. This is the core of the argument that is often used to demonstrate the supposed politically dangerous character of place-oriented or "geographic" thinking (an argument that appears, for instance, in Levinas,[42] but is also assumed, apparently as self-evident, in many other writers). Yet this claim typically depends on already construing such thinking in a way that assumes its problematic political associations rather than exhibiting or proving them (and seldom delves too deeply into the actual historical and philosophical details that might be relevant here). What the work of thinkers such as Heidegger, as well as of Ratzel and Vidal de la Blache, and the broader tradition of humanistic geography, brings to prominence is the very question of place or geographic space as such, and, along with it, the question of our own being that is itself necessarily implicated here.

In Heidegger's work, the questionability of place is already evident, if indirectly, in *Being and Time*, in terms of the problematic status accorded to spatiality within the structure of being-in-the-world at the same time as ideas and images of space and place constantly emerge as central elements within the overall analysis (in, for instance, the very idea of "being-in," as well as the notion of the *Da*, the "There," of *Dasein*).[43] As I have repeatedly argued here and elsewhere, much of Heidegger's later thinking can be seen as a sustained attempt to elucidate the nature of place or *topos*; hence Heidegger's own characterization of his thinking as a "topology" of being.[44] In his thinking of place, Heidegger can also be seen as urging a rethinking of space. Thus, in the very late essay "Art and Space" (written in conjunction with the Basque sculptor Eduardo Chillida, whose contribution was in the form of series of lithographs), Heidegger urges an understanding of space, in terms not of the "physical-technological" space of "Galileo and Newton," but rather of "clearing away" (*Räumen*)—the sort of "clearing away" that opens up a region for settlement and dwelling.[45] While space is that which Galileo and Newton theorize, it is also that clearing away and opening up, that "spacing," that allows for the possibility of appearance, and that occurs always and only in relation to specific places. It is this sense of space, itself closely associated with geographic rather than purely geometric space (to use Paddock's contrast), that turns out to be so important in the later Heidegger's meditative thinking on the happening of the Fourfold.

The space and place at issue here is not, however, a space or place already determined by, nor simply determinative of, human being. Instead, it is that within and on the basis of which human being is itself brought to articulate and meaningful appearance. Thus, in the account of the Fourfold in late essays such as "Building Dwelling Thinking," place is that which is established in and through the gathering together of Earth and Sky, Gods and Mortals in the thing, while it is also that within and on the basis of which the thing itself appears, as it is also that which allows the appearance of the elements of the Fourfold as such—the Sky is that very sky that arches above us, and the Earth that which lies beneath our feet, here, now, in this place, and it is also here, in "this" place, and only here, that the encounter between Mortals, and between Mortals and Gods (whether in their absence or presence) also occurs. Mortals thus play a role in the coming to be of places, although not exclusively so, and places themselves play a role in the appearing of Mortals. On this basis, place might be viewed in terms somewhat reminiscent of Plato's conception of the *chora* (a term sometimes equated with space, but also with place) as the very matrix of becoming—although unlike Plato's *chora*,[46] which remains always indeterminate, place itself comes to appearance, and so appears in a singular and determinate form (as just "this" place) in the happening, the *Ereignis*, of place that is also the happening of the Fourfold.[47]

Although there has sometimes been a tendency within humanistic geography to treat place in ways that assume a certain "subjectivism" in relation to place—place is thus viewed as a function of human experience (a tendency that is sometimes evident in, for instance, Yi-Fu Tuan's work,[48] and one might also worry about the emphasis on *mentalités* within some French historiography)—there is nevertheless a complexity and indeterminacy that has also merged as a key element in the geographical understanding of place as that has developed over the last century or so, particularly in the line that derives from Ratzel and Vidal de la Blache, and that encompasses thinkers such as Tuan, Relph, and others. J. Nicholas Entrikin, for instance, emphasizes the "betweenness of place"[49] (an emphasis also present in Heidegger), while Doreen Massey, at the same time as she has been critical of a certain rather caricatured version of the Heideggerian position,[50] has nevertheless also argued for the centrality of a conception of place articulated through notions of process, interconnection, and diversity.[51] Places are thus understood as dynamic structures that allow for the interaction between the human and the environmental, and as themselves determined in and through such interacting, at the same time as they also participate in it. Such a view is far removed from the conception of place as determined by the racial and the biological that is to be found in the work of thinkers such as von Uexküll, and to which, to reinforce the point, Heidegger must be seen as opposed. The rise of place as a central concept in contemporary thinking within cultural and human geography—a rise to which Heidegger has himself contributed—should thus be seen not as a function of the increasing dominance of a reactionary and deterministic conservatism, but quite the opposite—as the opening up of place as the proper site for the questioning of ourselves, our world, and our locatedness within it.

In the *Parmenides* lectures from the early 1940s, Heidegger says of the Greek *topos* that it consists essentially "in holding gathered, as the present 'where,' the circumference of what is in its nexus, what pertains to it and is 'of' it, of the place." It is thus that he argues that place is always "a manifold of places [that are] reciprocally related by belonging together, which we call a settlement or a district [*Ortschaft*]." That "place" in which "the essence of Being comes to presence in an eminent sense" is, Heidegger tells us, a δαιμόνιος τόπος (*daimonios topos*)—an *uncanny* place (*unheimliche Ortschaft*).[52] That place might appear as uncanny or "unhomely" in this way ought to indicate how far Heidegger is from viewing place, and especially the place that belongs to being, as merely some "given" that is already secure and determined. It is thus that Heidegger comments in the "Letter on 'Humanism'" from 1947, that as he has used it, the term "homeland" (*Heimat*) is to be understood in "an essential sense, not patriotically or nationalistically, but in terms of the history of being." And he adds that "the essence of the homeland . . . is also mentioned with the intention of thinking the homelessness of contemporary human beings from the essence of being's history. . . . Homelessness . . . consists in the abandonment of beings by being. Homelessness is the symptom of oblivion of being."[53] The "homeland" that is invoked here is not some place of safety and familiarity. It is the same place that Heidegger refers to in the passage from the *Parmenides* lectures as that "uncanny district" in which "the essence of Being comes to presence." And why should it be uncanny?—Because the coming to presence of being is not a matter of the coming to be of some being, but is rather the coming to presence of the *questionability* that belongs to being essentially. In Heidegger, therefore, homecoming names the turning back to the questionability of being, which is also the questionability of our own being. It is this return to questionability that is also at issue in the turn to place, and it is what marks off, in particular, the topology that is explicit in Heidegger's later thinking (which encompasses a focus on both the "historical" and the "geographical") from the deterministic subjectivism and biologism of such as von Uexküll.

Conclusion: Place and the Political

It is not the focus on place that turns out to be politically problematic, nor the emphasis on a holistic or relational conception of human being and the world, but rather the tendency to view the human as completely determined by something that is internal to it and prior to its worldly engagement (whether that be in terms of race, "soul," or some other notion), to treat the environment in which we find ourselves as essentially formed by the character of human subjectivity, and to take the world as itself subject to the dictates of the human.[54] In contrast, the "geographical" orientation that is a feature of much twentieth-century as well as twenty-first-century thought is one that can be seen to place human being in the world, and to do so in a way that also draws attention to the mutuality of that "being-in," thereby also opening up a space in which it can be brought into question.

To a large extent, of course, this opening up of a space for the questioning of human being-in-the-world is just what Heidegger's *Being and Time* aims to achieve, and yet that work also presents matters in a way that complicates and obscures what is at issue through its ultimate prioritization of the temporal over the spatial, its understanding of human being as primarily determined by its own projection of its possibilities for being (by what Heidegger calls its "existentiality"), and by its failure adequately to articulate a conception of place as distinct from the space associated with the Cartesian ontology of the world as present-at-hand. Indeed, it might even be argued that it is precisely the *inadequacy* in Heidegger's thinking of place and the topological in his early work, rather than his concern with place as such, that contributes (though not in any determining or necessitating fashion) to his own entanglement with Nazism in the 1930s. In this respect, just as Heidegger's work plays a critical role in the elaboration of a place-oriented mode of philosophizing and thinking, so too does it provide a demonstration of the dangers in thinking of being-in-the-world (or of the *topos* that this can be seen already to mark out) from the perspective of what he refers to as "the 'anthropological,' the 'subjectivistic,' and the 'individualist'"—or, we might also say, from the perspective of an analysis that prioritizes the existential or the temporal.

In *A Geographical Introduction to History*, Lucien Febvre quotes approvingly from Jules Michelet: "Without a geographical basis, the people, the makers of history, seem to be walking on air, as in those Chinese pictures where the ground is wanting. The soil too must not be looked on only as the scene of action. Its influence appears in a hundred ways, such a food, climate, etc. As the nest, so the bird. As the country, so the men."[55] Michelet's comments here could easily be read in a way that would see them as already predisposed to a politically reactionary position of the sort not too far removed from that of Nazism. Yet to do so would be to fail to attend to the full implications of the sort of geographical approach that Febvre takes Michelet to be propounding. Michelet certainly emphasizes the variety of influences that bear on the events of history, but more fundamentally, he gives voice to a conception of the human as inextricable from the complexity of the world, and as fundamentally constituted through the places of human dwelling. Rather than presenting human being as deterministically constrained, such a conception opens up a view of the human as enmeshed in an essentially reciprocal relation with the world in which it is also situated. The human thus cannot be assumed in advance, nor can it be taken to arise out of only one set of structures or elements alone. Indeed, even the movement of history must be understood as arising out of the interplay of activity and environment, of process and context, of temporality and spatiality.

The geographical orientation—the orientation to place—that can be seen to be illustrated by this brief passage from Michelet, and that is also evident in so much twentieth- and twentieth-first-century thinking concerning the relation between human being and the world, is one that forces our attention on the concrete, one might even say the *material*, circumstances of human being in the world. It forces our attention onto the complexities of that concreteness and its necessary spatialized character. Even historiography, on this account, must be understood as itself properly geographical—as oriented to the temporal only as the temporal is worked out in and through place. Moreover, if Heidegger's own preoccupation with the temporal can be seen as enabling, in a contingent fashion, his engagement with Nazism, then perhaps one might, although with some caution, view those conceptions of the historical that similarly give undue priority to the temporal (perhaps through notions of destiny or futurity), and neglect the spatial and the geographical, as being prone to similar dangers.

The sort of geographical orientation that is at issue here can thus be seen not only to be well grounded in the analysis, both conceptual and empirical, of the actuality of human being in the world (a claim that seems amply demonstrated by the vast and growing body of research in the area), but also to operate against the sorts of deterministic, subjectivist, and even nihilistic approaches that are so often claimed to be associated with geographical and holistic (or "ecological") approaches. One might say that such a geographical (or topological) orientation requires us to recognize, and to contend with, the essentially contingent, multiple, and fragile character of human life and being, and, through its emphasis on the inter-relatedness of human being with the world, it also requires us to recognize the limitations of human agency in the world. Such a recognition of limitation, and of contingency, multiplicity, and fragility, is surely fundamental to any properly ethical stance. It certainly runs counter to the politics of domination and control that is characteristic of movements such as Nazism.

III Topological Horizons

8 Philosophy's Nostalgia

. . . weeping, his eyes never dry, his sweet life flowing away / with the tears he wept for his foiled journey home [*nostos*] / . . . all his days he'd sit on the rocks and beaches / Wrenching his heart with sobs and groans and anguish [*algos*].
—Homer, *Odyssey*

What is wrong with nostalgia? How and why has it come to be the case, as it surely has, that to say of a philosophical position that it is "nostalgic" is already to indicate its inadequacy?[1] In this chapter I want to examine nostalgia both as a mood or disposition in general, and as a mood or disposition that is characteristic of philosophical reflection. Part of this inquiry will involve a rethinking of the mood of nostalgia and what that mood encompasses. Rather than understand the nostalgic as characterized solely by the desire to return to a halcyon past, I will explore the nostalgic through the connotations suggested by its Greek etymology as precisely a *longing* for the return home—a return that cannot be achieved—a form of homesickness, and so as *discomfiting* rather than comfortable, as bringing with it a sense of the essential *questionability* of our own being in the world.

The origins of nostalgia or, at least, of the term itself, lie in the seventeenth century and its use to refer to a form of melancholia most often found among soldiers serving away from their homelands.[2] Nostalgia combines the Greek *nostos*, meaning home or the return home, with *algos*, meaning pain, so the literal meaning of the term is a pain associated with the return home—a pain originally taken to arise as a consequence of the unfulfilled desire or longing for such return. "Nostalgia" thus appears at a particular point in history and within a particular technical discourse—it is an invented term, a technical neologism, belonging to the vocabulary of medical diagnosis—even though the experience of loss and estrangement that lies at its heart is ancient.

From its origins in the eighteenth century to its usage today, the meaning of "nostalgia" appears to have shifted. Part of that shift involves the disappearance of the term, along with other terms like "melancholia" itself, from the language of medicine. Nostalgia, like melancholia, is no longer recognized as an illness to be medically diagnosed and treated. But a more significant, although associated shift, is in the way the term is seen as related to the spatial and the temporal. Understood precisely as a pain associated with desire for *home*—and as home is neither a space nor a time, but a place that holds a space and time within it—so nostalgia can never be understood as spatial or temporal alone (this is a point to which I shall return in the discussion below).[3] Yet having originally referred to a condition resulting primarily from *spatial* displacement (the soldier serving in a foreign land),[4] "nostalgia" has come instead to signify a condition usually taken to involve, first and foremost, *temporal* dislocation (our estrangement from our past, and especially our childhood),[5] so that even the migrant who reflects "nostalgically" on her homeland is typically reflecting back on memories of a place that, while perhaps spatially removed, is also more significantly and specifically temporally distant. One might say, then, that understood as a form of homesickness, nostalgia is that particular form of longing for home that arises in circumstances in which the return home is somehow made impossible. In the contemporary world, in which, as the advertisements often tells us, the "home" that is spatially distant is nevertheless only a flight or a phone call away, the only home that is rendered truly inaccessible is the home that lies in the past.

In addition to the shift from the technical to the commonplace and from the spatial to the temporal, nostalgia has also come to be viewed in contemporary terms in a way that effectively shifts the emphasis of nostalgia away from *algos* and toward *nostos*. Nostalgia is thus often associated not with suffering and estrangement, but with familiarity and comfort. In terms of the history of the term, it seems that what "nostalgia" now refers to is not the *pain* that comes with the separation from home, but instead that which was, in the past, often taken as its immediate cause, namely, the experience of familiar sounds, smells, sights that invoke the presence of home even in its absence. Such experiences, in which the longed-for home reappears, briefly perhaps, but often with startling clarity, achieve a certain form of homecoming in which the pain of nostalgia may be temporarily assuaged, even though it may, as a consequence, also be exacerbated.[6] Contemporary nostalgia seems to involve just such a "homecoming" as given in or evoked by some experience associated with home, and so we find a certain respite, or even pleasure, in reexperiencing the sounds, sights, and smells of childhood or of some other place or world from which we are now irrevocably parted.

The "mood" of nostalgia as it is most often manifest today is one in which we are overtaken by a sense of comfort and familiarity that comes from allowing the present to fade into the background as the past or, more specifically, some remembrance of the past, whether real or imagined, comes to the fore, and we allow ourselves to be overtaken by that remembrance almost as if at the edges of a dream. Yet even in this contemporary form, the mood of nostalgia is never taken up only with the sense of "home," but always brings with it some element of pain. The memory of the past, as it is a memory, must always remain in contrast with the present, and so, even when experienced as pleasurable and comforting, it remains an experience tinged with a sense of loss and estrangement. The mood of nostalgia, so closely linked to memory, is thus always one that remains somewhere *between nostos* and *algos*—between the return home and the pain of its irrevocable loss.

The ambiguity or tension within the notion of nostalgia has not gone unnoticed.[7] Nevertheless, the tendency in most contemporary treatments of nostalgia, in keeping with the shift in the meaning of the term that prioritizes the notion of *nostos* or "home," treat nostalgia in terms that elide this ambiguity. Rather than seeing nostalgia in terms that combine remembrance with loss, the usual understanding takes it to be little more than a form of escapist fantasy—a refusal of the demands of the here and now in favor of the seductive embrace of a glowing memory.[8] In the grip of nostalgia, it seems, we are like the Lotus-eaters of Homer's *Odyssey*— cocooned in a cozy dream-world that insulates us from the demands of the everyday. To refer to a view or attitude as nostalgic is consequently to condemn it as a form of passive and acquiescent immersion in remembrance, as unrealistic and backward-looking, and as privileging an idealized past in a way that cripples our capacity to respond to the present as well as the future.

Nostalgia is typically seen as a product of modernity, and, more specifically, of modernity understood as a mode of historical experience that is essentially given over to a process of unceasing change and renewal. On this account, it is not merely the present, but rather the modern, from which nostalgia attempts to escape. Nostalgia seeks a release from the impermanence and uncertainty of the contemporary world in a retreat back into the familiarity of a remembered time that remains always the same. As the fundamental experience of modernity is the experience of temporal discontinuity—in modernity, time itself appears to lose its constancy and connectedness—so nostalgia arises, in a form that seems quite different from its original sense, as a mood or disposition that is both provoked by that experience as well as being a counter to it. Thus the historian Peter Fritzsche writes that:

nostalgia is a fundamentally modern phenomenon because it depended on the notion of historical process as the continual production of the new. . . . it was in the middle of the nineteenth century that nostalgia found a secure place in household vocabularies, its general usage made tenable by the massive displacing operations of industrialization and urbanization, which also standardized its meaning as a vague, collective longing for a bygone time rather than an individual desire to return to a particular place. Nostalgia retains this general and temporal meaning; it distills the "dispirit of the age."[9]

The longing for home becomes, in the times with which we are familiar, a longing for a time of stability and security, a time that cannot be found in the present. It is almost, one might say, a longing for time itself—since, in modernity, it is as if time has become nothing more than a succession of disjoint moments, and in which there is no longer any more encompassing sense of time as that within which one could orient and place oneself.[10] It is easy to see how such nostalgia might indeed come to be seen (though not by Fritzsche) as entailing a denial of or blindness to the present, and as therefore inevitably given over to conservatism and self-delusion.

Within philosophy, in fact, Heidegger's work has frequently been treated as problematic precisely because of the way in which that work is supposedly given over to various forms of nostalgia: to a nostalgia for "being as presence," as Derrida and many others following him (including, for instance, Baudrillard) would have it, to a nostalgia for the thinking of the ancient Greeks, or a nostalgia for the premodern world of the Black Forest peasant.[11] In Heidegger's case, the dangerously conservative character of such nostalgia is often taken to be given concrete demonstration by his problematic political involvement in the 1930s. Thus one writer has it that "Heidegger's nostalgia for a *völkisch* past, which disposed him favorably toward the Nazis, constitutes a basic quality of his rhetoric and thought";[12] Alan Megill writes of Heidegger's nostalgia as "a longing for the immediate Dionysian presence of the origin, from which all division, all separation, all difference, is excluded";[13] and even such an otherwise sympathetic reader of Heidegger as Albert Borgmann can write that "an inappropriate nostalgia clings to Heidegger's account" and that the things he names are "scattered and of yesterday."[14]

Both within philosophy as well as without, nostalgia is most often invoked as a term of critical opprobrium. Yet there is also a less common usage of the term that is more positive and sees it as directing attention to a central and perhaps defining feature of philosophy. Heidegger, in particular, seems to view philosophical thinking as essentially tied to nostalgia, and frequently refers to his own thinking in terms of notions of home and homecoming, and he repeatedly talks of our modern predicament as one of homelessness.[15] Heidegger also cites Novalis's claim that "Philosophy is really homesickness, an urge to be at home everywhere. Where, then, are we going? Always to our home."[16] Elsewhere, in discussing Nietzsche's identification of Zarathustra with "the convalescent," Heidegger specifically refers to the Greek etymology of nostalgia: "But what does 'the convalescent' mean? 'To convalesce' (genesen) is the same as the Greek néomai, nóstos. This means 'to return home'; nostalgia is the aching for home, homesickness."[17] One might take Heidegger's own talk of nostalgia as merely confirming the views of his critics, and yet his emphasis on the Greek, and so on the importance of both *nostos* and *algos*, should also alert us to the possibility of a difference in the sense of nostalgia as Heidegger uses it from that used by many of those same critics.[18]

There can be no doubt that in both its philosophical and commonplace uses, "nostalgia" is usually taken as a pejorative term that refers, often quite generally, to any attitude that privileges the past over the present. But, as should already be evident from our brief explorations so far, nostalgia is more complex, and perhaps more significant, than this would imply. Nostalgia involves both the spatial and the temporal, both memorial recovery and loss, both a sense of home and of estrangement. Indeed, even the history of the term, as well as its contemporary meaning, is rather less straightforward than I have so far made explicit. Fritzsche and other historians have tended to emphasis the novelty of nostalgia and its direct link to modernity. Yet it should be quite clear that even though nostalgia may take on a different character in modernity, and may perhaps arise in a different form, there is a fundamental continuity between the sense of nostalgia that arises out of the experience of the loss of time in the face of the modern, and the ancient sense of nostalgia as the pain associated with the loss of home. Fritzsche talks of the way in which the experience of modernity led to a standardization of the meaning of nostalgia "as a vague, collective longing for a bygone time rather than an individual desire to return to a particular place," and yet the sense of nostalgia associated with the individual longing for home remains. Proust's *A la recherche du temps perdu*, for instance, which is one of the great works of modernity, and carries the imprint of modernity upon it, is nevertheless also a work that is centrally preoccupied with nostalgia understood precisely in terms of a return to, and recovery of, particular places (especially the village of Combray and the places that belong within and around it). Although that return is also construed explicitly in terms of time and memory, it is not independent, as Georges Poulet makes clear,[19] of the spatial.[20]

Nostalgia refers to a mood or disposition that appears as both a generalized historical or cultural phenomenon—something *collective*—as well as a feature of *individual* personal experience.[21] While historians and sociologists have tended to focus on the former, the latter has also been the subject of investigation—investigations that are often tied to particular culturally specific forms. Svetlana Boym, for instance, focuses primarily on the way in which nostalgia arises within the sociopolitical circumstances of Eastern Europe (where the Russian *toska* often stands in for the Anglo-Saxon "nostalgia" though with some different nuances),[22] whereas in Fred Davis's early psychosociological investigation of nostalgia,[23] as well as in the more recent continuation of that work by Janelle L. Wilson,[24] the focus is the appearance of nostalgia within primarily American popular culture and its role as enabling the continuity of identity. In fact, none of the apparently different forms of nostalgia can be completely separated, just as the different cultural manifestations of nostalgia nevertheless exhibit broadly similar features. The individual experience of nostalgia is inevitably entangled with forms of collective memory and imagining, as well as with nostalgia as a more generalized mode of historical experience, while the key features of nostalgia, even in its historically and culturally specific forms, overlap and connect with nostalgia understood more broadly.

If we look to nostalgia specifically as a mood—a *Stimmung*, as it would be put in the German of Heidegger's *Being and Time*—as well as a form of experience (for every mood brings with it a form of experience), nostalgia is a certain mode of appearing of both self and world. That it should be so is characteristic of moods as such. Moods always involve, as Otto Bollnow points out, a common "tuning" (as the German term suggests[25]) of self and world, so that a mood is no mere internal feeling but is always also externalized. Thus in boredom, for instance, we not only *feel bored*, but the world presents itself *as boring*—everything dissolves in the same lackluster meaninglessness in which we may even lose sight of ourselves. The way Bollnow puts this is to say that "in moods in the true sense there is no I, no objects, no border between I and object. One should rather say: the borders of the I fade away and disappear in a peculiar way. I and world are embedded in an undivided totality of experience. Mood is the feeling of I and world together."[26] Nostalgia exhibits the same encompassing character, and the same externalization of the internal, as do other moods, and yet it also presents a more complex phenomenological structure. Although one of the characteristic features of moods is indeed a certain dissolution of the distinction between self and world, in the case of nostalgia, it is the relation between self and world that is brought to the fore as problematic— and together with that, the very relation of the self to itself. What is at issue in nostalgia is our own self-identity, but as the mood of nostalgia is no mere internal feeling, so the way in which identity appears as an issue here is precisely in terms of the way we find ourselves not at home in the world, as longing for home, as homesick.

The connection between nostalgia and the issue of self-identity is something that recurs frequently in discussions of nostalgia, whether philosophical, sociological, or historical, and regardless of whether it is the individual or collective sense of nostalgia that is at issue. It is, for instance, the central focus in the works of Davis and Wilson to which I referred above, and it is significant that both argue for a certain rehabilitation of nostalgia for just that reason. The direct implication of self-identity in nostalgic experience is shown by the way in which, as Edward Casey comments, nostalgia "cannot be sheerly fictitious (Kant would say 'creative') but must incorporate one's sense of being in a given place as conveyed by memories."[27] This comment draws attention not merely to memory, as opposed to imagination, but to a certain sort of memory, namely, autobiographical memory. Autobiographical memory is that form of personal memory that is always self-referential and in which the "I" is always involved. It is worth noting that the access to autobiographical memory becomes more common with age, and so too, of course, does the experience of nostalgia become more common as we get older—it is as if the past places that have formed important parts of our lives, and in and through which our lives have been formed, return to haunt us as our distance from them increases.

Autobiographical memory, inasmuch as it is tied to a sense of self, is also characteristically tied to a sense of place—autobiographical memories typically involve the remembrance of places no less than of events, people, or experiences (indeed, one might say that in memory, persons and events come to be inextricably bound up with the places in which they are encountered, in which they "take place"). This is not merely an empirically contingent feature of the self as given in memory—so that autobiographical memories just happen always to be given in terms of the remembrance of our being in a place—but is a consequence of the very nature of experience and memory as such.[28] In Heidegger's *Being and Time*, this is captured through the explication of *Dasein* as being-in-the-world, and, more fundamentally, in the very concept of *Dasein* itself—*Dasein* is being-there/being-here, such that Heidegger can eventually say (even though it is not made explicit in *Being and Time* itself) that "'Dasein' names that which is first of all to be experienced, and subsequently thought accordingly, as a place—namely as the locality of the truth of Being."[29] To be the sort of being that human *Dasein* is—a being whose own being can be in question for it—is thus to be a being that finds itself only through its being already given over to a world, and its involvement in it, as that is articulated always in and through the singularity of place.[30]

Returning more specifically to the idea of autobiographical memory, and so also to nostalgia, one can say that it is through the remembrance of oneself as a remembrance of one's own being-in-place (which is not the same as remembering a given location such that one could identify or reidentify it) that makes a memory an instance of autobiographical memory. Autobiographical memory is thus always a memory of self and world given as a memory of a specific being-in-a-place. Since nostalgia is itself a certain form of autobiographical memory—or, at least, incorporates autobiographical memory within it—so nostalgia takes the form of a remembrance of, and a longing for, a certain being-in-place that is also, of course, a certain being-at-home. On this basis, we can see why it is mistaken (quite apart from any juxtaposition of the terms in this way) to treat nostalgia, as it so often is treated, as involving time as opposed to place. It is true that there is a shift in the *conception* of nostalgia that has prioritized the temporal, and that this has also been taken to involve a deemphasizing of the spatial as well as the topographic, but this should not be allowed to obscure the nature of the nostalgic as such. Nostalgia remains, as it always was, a matter of our relatedness to place, even though that relatedness also involves, in different ways, both the spatial and the temporal.

Nostalgia is essentially tied to place, then, and it is so tied in large part because of the self-referential character of nostalgia, because of the way nostalgia is connected with the sense of self that itself always implicates the sense of place. The self-referential character of nostalgia that is evident here, as well as its connection to place, is not peculiar to individual nostalgic experience, but holds also for nostalgia understood as a collective phenomenon. What we are nostalgic for as a society, and not merely as individuals, is always that which we already identify as belonging to us and to which we also belong, and that is articulated through characteristic places and landscapes that have collective resonance as part of collective memory. We are not, and cannot be, nostalgic for that which does not belong, or is not already taken to belong, to our own heritage and our own sense of identity.

Of course, this also means that precisely to the extent that collective nostalgia, and the past that is memorialized in it, is removed from the personal and the autobiographical, and so is more abstractly self-referential, then it already refers to a sense of nostalgia that is itself somewhat more abstracted and attenuated. This may turn out to be true of collective nostalgia, in particular, to the extent that it is more prone to deliberate manipulation—certain motifs or images that may draw on nostalgic associations may thus be deployed in order to advance particular collective self-conceptions that are seen as advantageous to certain social, commercial, or political purposes, and yet may not be well grounded in any collective experience or memory as such (although there will always be a certain degree of ambiguity here, since memory and imagination stand in such a close relation to one another)—but it can surely also apply in the individual case. In general, however, and to the degree that it is indeed more removed from our own memory and experience, from our own sense of self, so nostalgia can easily turn into, or perhaps be mistaken for, what should really be understood as a form of *mythophilia*—a longing not for what is remembered, but for what is known only through its retelling, through story and myth. Such longing falls short of nostalgia precisely because of the mythical character of that which it desires and valorizes—a past of which we ourselves have no experience and in which we were never ourselves engaged. Such mythophilia is not nostalgic, even though it may share some features with nostalgia, and even though it may sometimes contribute to a nostalgic sensibility.

The distinction I have drawn here between the properly nostalgic and the mythophilic relates directly to a distinction Svetlana Boym draws between what she terms "restorative" and "reflective" nostalgia:

Restorative nostalgia stresses nostos and attempts a transhistorical reconstruction of the lost home. Reflective nostalgia thrives in algia, the longing itself, and delays the homecoming—wistfully, ironically, desperately. Restorative nostalgia does not think of itself as nostalgia, but rather as truth and tradition. Reflective nostalgia dwells on the ambivalences of human longing and belonging and does not shy away from the contradictions of modernity. Restorative nostalgia protects the absolute truth, whereas reflective nostalgia calls it into doubt.[31]

Boym differentiates between these two forms of nostalgia partly in order to draw attention to what she clearly views as a productive mode of nostalgic experience in contrast to a mode that she viewed as unproductive. Yet one might argue that a mode of nostalgia that does not recognize itself as nostalgia, which is the characteristic feature of Boym's "restorative" nostalgia, lacks what is essential to nostalgic longing, namely, its self-referentiality. This means that such "nostalgia," if it is to be called that, not only lacks any sense of pain, of *algos*, but strictly speaking also lacks any proper sense of home, of *nostos*, since it lacks any sense that what is at issue is what already belongs to it, and to which to might be said to belong, and so lacks any sense that what is at issue is its own sense of itself, its own sense of identity. Such "nostalgia" is scarcely nostalgia at all, but corresponds instead to the mythophilia that remains fixated on a past of which it has no memory of its own, and that loses itself in the attempt to realize that mythical and unremembered past.

Part of what becomes evident here is that the sense of home that is so central to nostalgia only becomes evident to us in the pain of our separation from it. Nostalgia is thus both *nostos* and *algos*, and neither comes to presence without the other. Within the literature of nostalgia, this is most clearly evident in the emphasis on nostalgia as characterized by the experience of temporal discontinuity—which now has to be understood as a discontinuity that is also a form of displacement—which nevertheless also invokes a form of continued connection. Thus Fritzsche characterizes nostalgia, in temporal terms, as involving both a sense of the ghostly presence of the past and its absence and loss:

Nostalgia not only cherishes the past for the distinctive qualities that are no longer present but also acknowledges the permanence of their absence. It thus configures periods of the past as bounded in time and place and as inaccessible. . . . What the ghostly remains of other pasts recall is the fact of other presents and other possibilities. It makes sense, then, to reconsider nostalgia not as blindness but as sightfulness, which completes the modern experience of time with its insistent perception of disaster and its empathy to strangers stranded in the present.[32]

Fritzsche's characterization of nostalgia, which focuses on nostalgia as a phenomenon of collective historical experience, closely matches the characterization to be found in Wilson, who is concerned not only with the collective, but also the individual experience of nostalgia. Thus Wlson writes that "Nostalgia . . . is not simply a 'living in the past,' but rather an active engagement with the past, and a juxtaposition of past and present."[33]

The discontinuity that is encountered in nostalgia, and that gives rise to its pain, is a discontinuity that exists between the self and the world in which it finds itself. Thus the self finds itself out of place, estranged, homeless, and yearning for a home that it cannot reach.[34] Yet this should not be construed as a discontinuity that obtains between a self that is whole in itself and a world that appears to stand apart from it. Rather, the discontinuity here is one that obtains *within the self as such*. This is inevitable given the character of the self as constituted in and through its involvement with the world and the places that make it up. The self is always externalized (as Merleau-Ponty puts it, "The world is wholly inside and I am wholly outside myself"[35]), and so the discontinuity that appears between self and world, or between self and place, is also a discontinuity that must be internalized within the self just in virtue of that externalization.

Focusing on the temporal character of nostalgia (and without relying on any problematic opposition of time to place) as well as the way it implicates the issue of self-identity, Steve Crowell has explored the discontinuity at issue here in terms of a radical discontinuity within what he calls "the time of the 'I.'" The self that is presented in nostalgic recollection is, for Crowell, a self that is at one and the same time my own and yet also a self that is irretrievably past—nostalgia is thus always, for Crowell, an encounter with the dead. As he writes:

To see the way that I am present to myself noematically in nostalgic experience is to see that nostalgic yearning is not a function of the difference between past and present worlds, but arises from a radical disruption in the time of the I, a noncoincidence that thwarts every attempt to figure one's own past as narratively continuous with the present.[36]

Crowell goes on to refer to Goethe's idea of nostalgia as an experience that brings something spectral into the present, concluding that although there is a certain connection between nostalgia and mourning, "Nostalgia does not mourn for what is dead and gone, but experiences the return of the dead."[37] In this way Crowell connects nostalgia with the philosophy of death, and so also with the essential thinking of finitude. To experience nostalgia is to experience, in a very direct and immediate although also problematic and uncanny way, a sense of our own temporality, our own mortality, our own strange finitude.[37]

Nostalgia, on this account, is thus a returning to self—a coming home to what one has been and so also to what one is, and yet a coming home that is fundamentally uncanny—so that what one encounters is a ghostly, spectral self. One might say that nostalgia, in this sense, is the direct reencounter with one's own past, recognized as one's past (and always, I would add, as that past is given as one's own in and through a remembered sense of being-in-place). It is this odd tension between the ownness of what is recollected in nostalgia and the fact of its loss, its pastness, that renders nostalgia as characterized by both a sense of home and a sense of homesickness and loss of home. Such nostalgia is, once again, in marked contrast to what Boym calls "restorative" nostalgia, which we can now characterize in terms of an experience, or attempted experience, of the past, not in terms of an uncanny or spectral presence, but rather as a reconstituted appearance in the present that denies the very pastness of the past—as if the dead could be returned to life through a refusal to recognize their deaths. Nostalgia, when understood in terms of the two elements that make it up—in terms of *nostos* and *algos*—is thus a form not of forgetting, but of remembering; a form not of escapism but of return; not a restoration of the past, but a reflective appropriation of the very temporality that encompasses present, past, and future.

In looking to the character of nostalgia as a mode of temporal discontinuity within the structure of the self, Crowell is led to argue for nostalgia as a form of temporal experience that is nevertheless not an experience that can be structured in narrative terms. Nostalgic recollection does not itself depend on, nor carry within it, a narrativity of its own—nostalgic experience is thus not an experience of a story, but typically of a moment or an image—and it is this that partly explains its spectral and uncanny character. The experience of the self that is given in nostalgia is typically, therefore, an experience of the self, and of its past, that does not present itself in a way that is incorporated within an existing narrative of the self, or within an already articulated history. This coheres with Fritzsche's emphasis on nostalgia, as it arises within the experience of modernity, as tied to an experience of historical discontinuity—a breakdown in the narrative of history itself. It also means that the discontinuity that is at issue in Fritzsche's account, though it may be said to take on a more extreme form in the historical experience of the past two hundred years or so, is nonetheless not a feature of nostalgia that is peculiar to historical modernity. The experience of discontinuity, and so also the breakdown of narrative articulation or integration, is at the very heart of nostalgic experience as such.

Although the experience of nostalgia involves a breakdown in the usual narrativity of time and of self, the response to that experience is often the attempt at a reconstituted narrative in which we try to find ourselves once again. Proust's great work is the classic example of such an attempt to overcome the discontinuity introduced by temporality, as that is given in nostalgic experience, and to use that experience as part of a retrieval of a sense of self that does not deny temporal discontinuity, nor the essential uncanniness of our being-in-the-world. One might even say that, in certain respects, all writing is directed at such retrieval. Writing, and so also narrative, is both the mark of our homesickness, and also the means by which we constantly attempt to come to terms with it. Writing is thus always an act of remembrance—a remembrance of the world in which we are always already placed, to which we belong, and yet from which we are always estranged. Moreover, the estrangement at issue here, while it is that to which writing may be said to respond, is also that in which the very possibility of writing, and indeed, of language and memory, is itself founded.

The connection between nostalgia and philosophy, or the possibility of such a connection, is reinforced by these considerations of the nature of nostalgia, but it is a connection that still remains to be elucidated, although the direction of that elucidation should already be clear. Of particular importance is the notion of remembrance—and not only because philosophy might be construed as a "kind" of writing. As the epigram to his own essay on nostalgia, Edward Casey chooses a line from Adrienne Rich: "Nostalgia is only amnesia turned around."[39] Although it is not *just* this, nostalgia is, as we have already seen, fundamentally tied to memory. In this respect, the nature of Heidegger's thought as itself centrally concerned with overcoming *Seinsvergessenheit*, the forgetting of being, already suggests its nostalgic character. Moreover, Heidegger himself frequently speaks not only of his own thinking, but of philosophy, as a kind of remembrance. Of such remembrance, Heidegger writes:

Remembrance is no historiological activity with the past, as if it wanted to make present, from outside and from what is later, what earlier thinkers "believed "about" being. Remembrance is placement into being itself, which still presences, even though all previous beings are past. Indeed, even talk about placement into being is misleading because it suggests we are not yet placed into being, while being yet remains closer to us than everything nearest and farther than all that is farthest. . . . Hence it is not first a matter of being placed into being, it is a matter of becoming aware of our essential abode in being, and becoming genuinely aware of being beforehand.[40]

On this Heideggerian conception, philosophy is itself, as a mode of *Seinserinnerung*, a mode not merely of abstract recollection of the thought or concept of being, but of our active reemplacement into being. It is a return to our own experience of being, and one might say, our own experience of ourselves. It is also, it should be said, a remembering of place. Of course, the negative construal of nostalgia that is so widespread would suggest that it is precisely this idea of remembrance that involves the idea of a return to the past, or a desire to accomplish such a return, that is most problematic about nostalgia. It is problematic because it seems to imply a turning away from the present and the future, and so a deliberate remaining in and with the past that refuses change, and bases that refusal in an immersion in what is surely nothing but a form of self-obsession or self-contemplation. Indeed, one may argue that nostalgia is, on this basis, always given over to the contemplative and the quietistic, rather than to activity and engagement—and this is, of course, precisely the argument that is often made, especially in regard to Heidegger.

Certainly the nostalgic does not entail any specificity of future action. Yet in being turned toward the uncanniness of our relation to self, time, and place, it does not turn us only toward and into the past, but through the past, and the places from which we come; it also turns us into a future that remains open and unknown. Nostalgia can be seen as always predicated, and always bringing home to us, our facticity and our freedom. Our freedom has its origins in our factical engagement, which is always an engagement that has already been and to which we can return only in and through nostalgic recollection. Similarly, the experience of nostalgia need not constitute a form of self-obsession, since although that experience is an experience that is tied to who and what we are, nostalgia can itself be seen as disrupting and rendering such identity and self-identity uncertain. What is evident in nostalgia is precisely the loss of self and experience that occurs in time, even as that loss is also productive of self and of experience. What is experienced in nostalgia is not and cannot be a return to something that renders us at home with respect to identity or to being. In Heideggerian terms, this means that the remembrance of being always has the character of nostalgia in that it remains a return that is never completed, but is essentially disjoint, even *spectral*. The homecoming that Heidegger so often evokes is thus a homecoming that is never completed and that cannot be so completed.

The ever-present estrangement that is characteristic of nostalgia, an estrangement that can never be satisfied or overcome, means that the mode of temporality that belongs to nostalgia, and to nostalgic experience, is one that exhibits an essential strangeness or discontinuity. Nostalgia is a certain sort of recollection or experience of the past—not any past, but a past that I recognize as my own through the way in which it is given always in terms of a remembrance of my own being-in-place. Yet that past, and the place with it, while it appears in the present, and so is present to me, is not a past that reappears in the fullness of presence—as simply present once more, complete and unaltered, a past in which I find myself once more, back in the place I once knew. The past as given in nostalgia is always a past that, although present, remains past, the place is one from which I always find myself somehow displaced. Nostalgia, at least of the reflective sort that recognizes itself as nostalgia, may transport us back into our past, and into the places that belong to that past, but it does so in a way that nevertheless refuses any escape from the present. In the nostalgic experience of the past we thus also experience something of the continuity and the discontinuity of temporality, and so of past and present; we also experience something of the essential discontinuity, estrangement, and uncertainty that is to be found everyplace—the uncanniness that is to be found even "at home."

What is so often criticized in Heidegger's nostalgic thinking, and in the mode of philosophy to which his thinking directs attention, is not nostalgia in the sense I have defined it here, but rather what I earlier termed "mythophilia"—the love of a mythical or imagined past. Admittedly, in Heidegger's case there is a genuine question as to what extent elements of such mythophilia play a role in his thinking (especially given the cultural historical background against which he writes), yet perhaps this is something from which no philosophy is ever totally immune. Philosophy constantly retells its past in new mythic forms, and its relation to that past is often mythophilic whether or not the past it creates for itself is a past to which it would return or a past that it requires in order to legitimate its contemporary understanding of itself.

In the same passage in which Heidegger talks of nostalgia as a form of homecoming and of convalescence, he writes that "The convalescent is the man who collects himself to return home, that is to turn in, into his own destiny. The convalescent is on the road to himself, so that he can say to himself who he is."[41] Philosophy's nostalgia is not a nostalgia that removes us from the present or the future; it is not a nostalgia that removes us from where or how we are, nor does it hide us from who we are. Yet at the same time it does not present us merely with a comfortable and comforting narrative. Nostalgia remains a form of longing rather than the assuaging of that longing, it retains a sense of home and of return, and yet does not achieve such a return nor realize that sense of home in any final fashion. Philosophy's nostalgia, simply, involves a sense of our own, and so of philosophy's, uncertain place in the world; of our own, and so of philosophy's, uncertain relation to being.

9   Death and the End of Life

What is strange in finding here on earth the union for which Plotinus yearned? Unity expresses itself here in terms of sun and sea. The heart feels it through a certain taste of flesh which constitutes its bitterness and greatness. I learn that there is no superhuman happiness, no eternity outside the curve of the days. These paltry and essential goods, these relative truths, are the only ones that can move me.
—Albert Camus, "Summer in Algeria"

"Eternity is a terrible thought," says Rosencrantz in Tom Stoppard's alternative view on *Hamlet*, "I mean, where's it going to end?" And Guildenstern adds a little later, "Death followed by eternity . . . the worst of both worlds. It *is* a terrible thought."[1] Death, as they say, is forever, but if the same were true of life—if one could live a life without end—would this be any less terrible? Some philosophers have argued that life in the absence of death would indeed be terrible—it would be a life, according to Bernard Williams, of unendurable boredom.[2] I think there is something important, and right, about this view. If it is flawed, it is only so, I will argue, insofar as it does not give enough weight to the importance of death in giving shape and significance to life.[3] It is not merely that a life without end would be a life of tedium—of endless *ennui*—but that to have a life, *and this is not the same as merely to live*, is indeed to be capable of death.[4]

The strong thesis, according to which death and life are indeed necessarily connected, and not in any merely "psychological" fashion, is a central theme in Heidegger's work, both early and late. It is present in *Being and Time*, as well as in essays such as "Building Dwelling Thinking." It has sometimes appeared obscure, however, as to why death should be so important here—why should it be the case, not merely that a life without death would be empty, but that to live a life without death would not even be to have a life? Why could it not be possible to live, and not merely to live, but to have a life, and yet not die? Part of the answer is given in the understanding of death as a *limit*, and more specifically, as an *end*—as the end of life, and so as that "toward which" our lives are lived. "End is place," Heidegger tells us in "The End of Philosophy and the Task of Thinking,"[5] and the idea of end that appears here applies no less to death in its relation to life than to the understanding of philosophy and its history.[6] If death is the end of life, then it is also that which establishes the *place* of life, its *topos*, and to have a life is for one's life to be "placed" in just such a way.[7] The exploration of these issues also has a useful consequence for the understanding of Heidegger's topological mode of thinking, providing a possible way of integrating some key elements of the early thinking with elements of the later. That is to say, it enables us to see how the focus on the unitary constitution of human life in the early thought—in *Being and Time*, the unity of *Dasein* as based in the unity of temporality—might itself be necessarily embedded in the more fundamental unity of place that is the focus of the later thinking.[8] Much of the discussion will thus follow a line of thinking that draws on elements consistent with Heidegger's approach in his 1927 work, and that thereby focuses more strongly on temporality than I have elsewhere, but which gradually moves to a broader and more explicitly topological view.

Living and Having a Life

What do I mean by distinguishing mere living from the having of a life? As a characteristic of the living, life is ubiquitous. We find it exemplified in all things that are capable of sustaining themselves in existence, of nourishing themselves, of reproducing themselves. But in the sense that I intend it here, the having of a life is something much more specific—rather than mere continued, self-sustaining existence, the having of a life involves having a sense (even if poorly articulated) of one's life as indeed one's own, as something that one lives, as something for which, to a greater or lesser degree, one takes responsibility. In this sense of "having a life," my cat asleep on the sofa, though undoubtedly alive (as any attempt to displace her will soon make clear), cannot be said to "have" a life. This does not mean that my cat lacks "interests" or desires or has no strong attachments to places and people (for she certainly has all of these) or indeed that she has no "personality" that marks her out from other cats, but that the having of a life is more than this, for it involves having a sense of one's life as, in some sense, one's own, as to some extent subject to one's own self-formation. And this is something of which, notwithstanding her many other accomplishments, my cat is quite incapable.

It is the having of a life in this sense that is one of the things that marks out creatures such as us from other living things. This is not merely a *biological* difference between us and others, but a difference that is properly *ontological*—human beings, and any beings sufficiently like us in the relevant respects, are *in the world* in a way that is very different from other beings, living or unliving.[9] Indeed, it is perhaps only creatures that can be said to have a life (in the sense I have outlined here) that can also be said to have any sense of the world as such, since to be in the world, and to have a sense of one's being in the world, must involve both a sense of the world and of one's life within that world—a sense both of the world as world and one's life as one's own. It is, indeed, only through being able to locate oneself within the world that one can order one's experience so as to be able to have a sense of oneself as the subject of that experience; equally, it is only through having a sense of the order of experience, and so of oneself, that one is able properly to have a sense of the world, and the objects and events within it.[10] In these respects it would seem that to have a life is to have a world and that to have a world is also to have a life.[11]

Thus, in having a sense of one's life or a sense of the world, one does not merely have a grasp, separately and discretely, of the various elements that are part of the world and that also go to make up a life. My cat has a grasp of aspects or features of the world much as I do—although we have very different reactions to its presence, and may even "understand" its presence in very different ways, we are both, for instance, aware of the wattlebird that drinks from the pool outside the window where I work— but my cat cannot properly be said, on the account I have given here, to have a life or to have a sense of the world. The having of a life or a world involves more than just a capacity to grasp and react to aspects of the world. Instead, it is a matter of having some sense of the whole within which those aspects are placed. In this respect, the sight of the bird drinking is, in my own case, located within a larger horizon that encompasses myself and other persons as well as other events and objects—a horizon that, like the horizon of the visual field, bounds and so unifies that which lies within it, while also stretching out to the manifold possibilities that lie beyond those bounds.[12] Since the having of a life and of world consists precisely in having an understanding of this larger horizon of possibility— of the limits and range of possibilities—then, insofar as my cat lacks any sense of such a horizon, she does not properly have a life or a sense of the world. Moreover, this does not, it should be noted, entail any "lack" or "deficit" on the part of my cat. We have a tendency to think of other creatures and entities, as well as ourselves, as if we stood apart from our defining capacities and potentialities. But we are not first beings, thought in some abstract way, who are then associated with some capacities or other. Our mode of being is itself intimately tied to the capacities and potentialities that belong to us. There is thus no possibility of making sense of a lack or deficit *in that mode of being*, since for a creature or entity to be the being that it is just is for it to be the way that is proper to it.[13]

Unity and the Idea of a Life

Just as the world consists in more than a mere concatenation of features, but has a unity integral to it, so a life is not simply a collection of events or experiences, and nor is its continuity a matter only of the physical continuity of a single body. Events may be unified by being part of a single temporal or causal sequence, and yet those events need not be part of the same life; a body may continue in existence—for instance, in the case of a body kept alive in the absence of significant brain activity—even though the life associated with that body has ceased to be. The unity of a life is something over and above mere causal, temporal, or even bodily continuity. It must be a unity internal to the life—a unity worked out from within it and intrinsic to it[14]—a unity that is paradigmatically expressed through the capacity of the creature whose life it is to have a sense of that life as its own. A life is consequently something that can be understood as a whole, as having a certain shape, and as being in some important sense self-directed. In this latter sense a life is undoubtedly something on which one can "work"—as one can work on the way one's life is oriented, on the way it exemplifies certain ideals or traits of character, on the sorts of possibilities that it enacts—and in working on one's life one also, of course, shapes and molds one's own identity.

The very idea of a life, then, carries with it a sense of self-awareness, self-conception, and self-direction—perhaps something of this is suggested in the injunction, typically directed at someone who seems to have no sense of what is important or who lacks any meaningful or ordered way of living, to "get a life!"—and so the having of a life is also a matter of the having of a sense of self-identity. It is indeed through one's ability to recognize one's life as one's own that one is able to shape and direct that life, and so establish it as a having a unity that is integral to it. Insofar as the having of a life and of a sense of the world are also tied together, so the unity of a life and of the self is a unity necessarily worked out in terms of a particular locatedness and orientation within the spatial *and* temporal frame of the world. Properly understood, it is a *topological* unity that is at issue, and so it is a unity that cannot be understood in terms of the temporal or the spatial alone. Nevertheless, the unity of a life is often thought in terms that give primary emphasis to the temporal aspect that appears here (a tendency of thought that is not accidental), and so to the way in which the unity at issue is one that must be established and maintained with respect to the unity of past and present actuality, together with future possibility. This is certainly the direction in which Heidegger moves in *Being and Time*.[15]

If one is to focus on temporality, then the temporal unity at issue will be a unity that operates both *over* time and *at* a time.[16] Thus, the set of actions and attitudes that constitute a life must be a coherent and integrated set (a coherence and integration partly expressed in the unity and integration of the body), even if that coherence and integration is imperfect (as, in a certain sense, it must be, given that it is a unity that necessarily encompasses multiplicity), and having a sense of the unity of one's life must be a matter of having a sense of the way in which one's past actions and attitudes are connected to and consistent with one's present and future actions and attitudes.[17] Memory and recollection, along with purposiveness and imagination, are necessary elements in this unity, since it is through both one's sense of the past *and* one's projections and anticipations of the future that one's life is integrated and unified over as well as at a time.[18]

The capacity to understand oneself as existing "over time" is necessary not merely in order to have a *conception* of the unity of one's life, and of the unity of the actions and attitudes that are the constituent elements of that life, but also for the very *existence* of such a life and for the existence of those elements. A sense of time and possibility is essential to the capacity for complex, integrated action and to the having of those attitudes on which action of this sort is grounded—that is, complex forms of belief, desire, intention, and so forth. To be capable of belief, for instance, is to be capable of having an attitude that one can recognize as related to other attitudes one holds, an attitude that may be based on past experience, may influence present actions, and may also be open to modification in the light of future events. Indeed, the very concept of attitudes such as belief or desire is closely connected with the idea of an enduring subject to whom those attitudes belong and who is capable both of being acted upon and acting in ways largely determined or mediated by those attitudes; it is also connected with the idea of the world as that which both constrains us and yet also offers new possibilities.[19]

The skein of connections here is tangled: to have a life is to have sense of that life as one's own and a sense of the world in which that life is lived; and these notions in turn mutually imply a sense of oneself as existing in and through time, and so as having a life grounded in past and present actuality and projected into a future of possibility. To this tangled skein we may add two more threads. The first concerns responsibility and self-direction. To have a life is to have a sense of one's life *as one's own*, and part of the having of a life in this sense is that one's life is something for which one takes *responsibility*. But since one can hardly take proper responsibility for that over which one has no control, so one component in the having of a life would seem to be just the ability (always constrained by circumstance) to shape and direct that life.

Here, once more, we are forced to recognize the close interdependence that obtains between the capacity for self-reflection and self-recognition, the capacity for coherent action, and the having of a sense of temporality, possibility, and history. Moreover, since the having of a sense of a life—indeed, the very living of a life—involves some understanding of both past and present actuality and future possibility, so one can say that to have a life is knowingly, on the basis of the already determined actuality of the life, to hold oneself open to the possibilities of that life and to be aware of the possibilities that it presents—including the limits to those possibilities. To have a life is precisely to have a sense of the bounds of that life, of what is part of it and what is not, of what is possible within it and what is not. And since this understanding of possibility and of limit may be put in terms of a capacity to question, so one might say that to have a life is to be capable of putting that life *in question*—a conclusion that can be seen to express much the same point that Heidegger makes, in *Being and Time*, by his characterization of *Dasein* as instantiated in the human as that mode of being whose own being is an issue for it.[20] What is brought to light here is the very close connection between the capacity for questioning and the capacity for recognition of oneself. Only insofar as we have a sense of ourselves can we put ourselves or our world into question. Moreover, only insofar as we can put ourselves into question can we be said to have a sense of ourselves. In the work of Donald Davidson, the way questioning enters in is evident in his characterization of belief as "taking up the slack" between "objective truth" and what is held true.[21] In this respect, the idea of belief opens up a domain not of indubitable certainty, but precisely of questionability.

In having a life, one has a sense of one's self-identity, and to have this is to have a sense of one's life as consisting in more than the bare causal or logical connectedness of the elements that make up that life or the simple acquaintance with those elements. It is precisely to have an understanding of one's various actions and attitudes as unified parts of a single, temporally (and spatially) extended, rationally connected, and (though I have not made much of this point) causally integrated structure. Since the unity that is at stake here is indeed a complex unity, it is also a unity that is able to tolerate a certain degree of disunity. Every life is but imperfectly integrated, and the connections that go to make up a life, any life, always display an element of fragmentation. Even the best of us act foolishly, contrary to our interests, in ways that seem to us irrational or mistaken; we do not always well understand our own desires and motives; we forget, we disappoint ourselves, we feel regret. Conceivably a life could become so fragmented that it would cease even to be a life (and indeed such a possibility will be important later in this discussion). For the most part, however, our lives retain an ordering and unity, even in the face of the always imperfect coordination of those lives. Such unity is exhibited in and maintained by means of our own sense of self—by means of our own capacity for self-conceptualization, self-reflection, and self-direction.

The unity of a life is thus neither pregiven (it does not exist prior to the actual articulation of that life) nor does it consist in the unity of some simple self (it does not consist in anything independent of or apart from such articulation), even though it can be expressed through the idea of the self or person whose life it is. The unity of a life is precisely something to be articulated or worked out through the actual living of that life and the complex ordering in time and space of the actions and attitudes that make it up. As a direct consequence of this, the unity of any particular life is inseparable from the unity of a particular structure of activity. It is because one's actions and attitudes constitute an integrated whole, even though that imperfection is always, necessarily, imperfect, that those actions and attitudes can count as part of a single life.

Although the integration at issue here is not that of mere causal or logical continuity, and necessarily encompasses more than just the behavioral and attitudinal alone, it is nevertheless an integration that is especially evident in, and articulated through, the complex causal and rational interconnection of actions and attitudes: one's attitudes need to be causally related to one's actions and to other attitudes, and also generally consistent with one another and with one's actions. Such integration is most clearly evident in the integrated, organized operation of a living body. Indeed, it is through the way in which we operate as embodied agents that we can be said to be the sorts of creatures that believe, desire, hope, fear, and the rest, since it is the active body that is the primary focus for our involvement with things and other persons—in truth it is the proper "locus" for such involvement—and it is primarily through practical involvement with things in the world that attitudes are themselves constituted.

Attitudes, whether of belief, desire, hope, or fear, are identified through relations to specific contents—one fears that interest rates will rise, one hopes that the weather will be fine, one believes that Fred is an honest man, one desires that one's friends should come to dinner. And those contents are themselves dependent, first, on the interconnection of attitudes themselves—so that the belief that Fred is an honest man depends on other beliefs about what it is to be honest, about who Fred is, and on other beliefs following on from these—and, second, on the interconnection of attitudes in general with the world. Although one may be mistaken in believing that Fred is honest, one cannot believe that Fred is honest if one is mistaken about Fred's identity and about what it is to be an honest man—or, at least, the more error that creeps in here, the less clear it will be just what one does believe. The point is that one cannot divorce questions of the content of attitudes from questions about the relation between those attitudes and their objects—most importantly, one cannot separate questions about the *contents* of beliefs from questions about the *truth* of those beliefs. And not only must our attitudes in general stand in the right relation to those worldly things and happenings that are their objects, but in the case of the vast majority of the contents of those attitudes, those contents are constituted in terms that are quite specific to our particular activities and surroundings. Thus one understands concepts of identity and honesty, of weather and dinner, friendship and finance only insofar as one can apply those concepts to one's own concrete experience and insofar as those concepts can be employed in a coherent fashion in organizing and directing one's own thinking and acting. The understanding of concepts, therefore, and with it the possibility of content, is thus closely tied to the capacity to interact with things and other persons in the world and so to the possibility of organized, embodied agency—an understanding that might be characterized in contemporary philosophical parlance as both "holist" and "externalist."[22]

The conclusion to which this line of reasoning inevitably tends is that the very having of a life is dependent on one's existence as an active, embodied creature. Our self-identity is consequently bound up, as is the possibility of contentful experience, with our organized activity in the world—we might say that our self-identity is bound up with the worldly projects and activities in which we are engaged. Such projects and activities are orderings "of" the world,[23] but they also function to establish a certain ordering that constitutes an identity of self. One should understand a life as given its identity, then, not in virtue of the person whose life it is—for to be a person is indeed, in the sense I am using here, just to have a life—but through its being a particular ordering of the world, a particular way of being-in-the-world, of which the being whose life it is has can be said to have a sense. A life is not something independent of such ordering, but constituted through it. So my own identity and existence is established through my active involvement with the objects and events around me rather than being something given prior to and independently of those objects and events.[24] The active involvement at issue here—what I referred to above as a "structure of activity"—cannot itself be separated off from the larger worldly structure that gives shape to as well as enables that structure and the activity in which it consists. It is thus that we can understand lives, and selves, not as already constituted entities that then shape the world in which they find themselves, but, to adapt a phrase from Lawrence Durrell, as themselves "functions of place,"[25] or of the complex working out of place—a working out that operates through the embedded interaction of bodies and environments. Moreover, the idea of a life as a certain unity of activities or projects can now be seen as not so much a unity given through a projection that is itself unified by the one who projects, as instead, a unity of activity or projection that is given through a certain interconnectedness and unity *of place*.[26]

The unity of my life, and of myself as a person, is the unity, always incomplete, of an ongoing and interconnected set of activities and projects as worked out in relation to an encompassing environment or locale—it is also a unity that is recognized as such by the one whose life it is. Of course, insofar as one's self-identity is indeed tied to one's active, embodied involvement in the world, and so to a certain sort of projective activity, so the idea of a life as involving recognition of future possibility can itself be seen as tied to the idea of a life as a matter of self-aware, projective activity. The capacity to form a conception of oneself and to have a sense of one's life as one's own is thus not a capacity to grasp something independent of or distinct from the particular connection of objects and events that go to make up a particular life—it is indeed just the capacity to recognize those objects and events as being connected in a certain way, namely, as part of that life that is one's own and so as part of the projects that make up that life, and to act in a way that, for the most part, preserves that integrity.[27]

Insofar as the unity of a life is such that it can be represented within that life (through the concept of self) and that representation can itself function in the maintenance and formation of a life's unity (as the concept of self is part of that by means of which one's life is unified), so it seems proper to say that the unity of a life, for a creature that can properly be said to have a life, is indeed a unity intrinsic to that life—it is part of the very nature of the sort of life it is that it be capable of forming a concept of itself as a whole. A creature that has a life in the sense I have used it here is also a creature that has a conception of itself, that can refer to itself using the first-person (and that can also refer to others in a way distinct from this), that can take itself as an object of its own reflections, and whose life can therefore be said to belong to it alone. Such a creature can be said to have a capacity for self-knowledge that is itself closely tied to the creature's having of a life. The idea of the "ownness" of a life—whether put in terms of my life as "mine" or as "belonging to me"—is therefore closely tied to the idea of unity. Precisely because the unity of a life is not a perfect unity, but one that must include within it a degree of disunity, so the unity of a life can only be understood through the idea of the person whose life it is and through that person's own capacity to understand that life as their own. This is not, however, to make the identity of a life dependent on some prior notion of "person" nor to appeal to the sense of "ownness" as the criterion of identity for lives. Rather, it is to point to the way in which the unity of a life is tied to the capacity for a certain sort of self-recognition and self-conceptualization within that life.

Since the unity of a life is not merely a matter of the unity given by certain connections (causal or otherwise) among the elements of a life, but is a unity that consists in the self-presentation of the life as a whole—in the creature whose life it is having a sense of that life as indeed its own—reductionist accounts of the self, of which Derek Parfit's may be taken to be exemplary,[28] and that treat the self as able to be reduced to a mere concatenation of psychological states, cannot be adequate as accounts of the unity of a life. Such accounts cannot, for instance, explain the way in which the unity of a life can be preserved in a manner consistent with the often imperfect integration of the elements of that life—and they do not even attempt to offer such an explanation. This might be taken to be a simple consequence of the fact that these accounts have little regard for the concept of a life as such, at least as developed here, but such disregard itself suggests a failure to understand the way in which that concept, and the unity that it implies, is intimately connected with the very possibility of the having of contentful attitudes and of organized activity. Reductionist accounts of this sort also sever the connection between the notion of a life and of self or person and the use of the first person. Just as the having of a life and the having of a sense of one's life are connected, so too is the notion of a life or of the self closely connected with the use of sentences containing "I," "me," and "mine." In the use of such first-personal language we refer to and also elaborate on a form of self-identity that is not captured in any mere continuity of body, of causal or temporal connection, or of propositional content. Such a focus on continuity alone fails to capture the connected sense in which the having of a life, and presumably the existence of a self, is tied to the capacity to recognize one's life as one's own, and so to the capacity for self-recognition and self-conceptualization. On reductionist accounts there is thus no real sense in which my life is *my own*, and although this enables such as Parfit to argue for the possibility of a mode of continuation beyond death, it is only by having abandoned the very idea of a life or a self of which death is the ending.

Life and the Unity of Narrative

The organization and unity of a life is essentially a matter of the organization and unity of the activities that make up that life and the integration of those activities as part of a larger set of activities that may be understood as the life itself. One way in which such unity is expressed, but through which it may also be constituted, is in the unity and integrity of a particular life-story. Indeed the sort of unity that is at issue in the unity of a life is not the unity of some self distinct from a set of experiences and involvements, but is just the unity of an integrated form of active engagement in the world (what we might well think of as a "project"), and that may also be said to consist in a form of self-conceptualization paradigmatically expressed in the form of narrative. In this latter respect the unity of a life can also be understood in terms of the unity of a narrative, and this is so both with respect to those smaller projects in which we are always engaged and with respect to the project of a life as a whole within which those various projects are integrated and of which they form parts.[29]

Narrative clearly exemplifies the sort of complex unity over time that seems appropriate to the understanding of the unity of a life—for a story to be a story is precisely for it to combine different events and characters in a way that is not a mere relating of causal connectedness, but is a combining of those elements so as to allow them to be seen and to be understood in quite specific ways. Yet not only does the story exhibit its own unity, through its telling it also unifies the events and actions on which it focuses and so exhibits those events and actions as themselves having a certain unity of their own. Through narrative, then, we come to understand not only the nature of a character or of some event, but we also come to see how the character or the event is exhibited, develops, and is articulated through a manifold of particular happenings, relationships, and actions. In fact, one might claim more generally that, when it comes to an understanding of human lives and the human significance of events, it is through narrative that such understanding is primarily to be achieved, for only through narrative can an appropriately rich interconnection of elements over time be achieved.[30]

The idea that narrative may have an important role in the understanding of the unity of a human life can be seen to lie behind the view of many of those historians who have objected to the simple application of deductive-nomological models to historical explanation. Perhaps the idea that notions of rationality have an ineliminable role in explanations of human action, so that those explanations cannot be reduced to purely causal accounts, can also be seen to suggest a similarly ineliminable role for narrative in such explanations—to cite a reason for an action, it might be said, is also to place that action within a particular narrative space and to indicate a particular kind of story that can be told about the actor. But it is not just that narrative is an important tool in the understanding of human life from "the outside." Our own understanding of ourselves would seem to be bound up with our ability to tell stories about who we are and what we have done, and to construct narrative accounts of our lives. Indeed, it may be that only through such stories can we bring order into our lives to begin with. Thus, Bruno Bettelheim, for instance, has emphasized the role of the fairy story in enabling young children to give meaning to the world into which they are growing,[31] while Paul Ricoeur, Alasdair MacIntyre, and others have pointed to the way in which narratives and narrative figures provide the means by which we bring order to our lives and by which we can assign value and significance to events—in MacIntyre's case, they provide the cultural schemata by which we make sense of the world.[32] Thus while Louis Mink and Hayden White tell us that stories are not lived and lives are not told,[33] the truth, perhaps, is that only a life about which stories are told is a life that is lived.

To live a life is also, we might say, to be involved in telling and retelling the story of that life. Of course, since none of us can know the real ending to our lives, and for the most part we have only the haziest memories, if any, of our beginnings, the stories that we tell provide ways to unify our lives on the basis of a particular position within those lives. So the stories we tell ourselves are *projections* of our lives rather than necessarily factual accounts of that in which those lives consist. In this respect we can see how the capacity for storytelling is actually quite closely connected with the capacity for agency, since the coordination and purposiveness necessary for action, as well as the appropriation of a past context that provides the grounding for such action, is dependent on just the ability to understand the way in which actions fit within larger narratives. It is through narrative, then, that we are able to project our lives from the past and present into the future, and in so doing we are also able explore and map out possibilities for action.

In narrative, one is able not only to project one's life forward, but to understand one's life as an ongoing project and so as constituted with respect to certain central aims and values. Indeed, given the necessarily temporal dimension to the project and projection of a life, and the complexity of the connections that go to make up a life, it would seem that only a narrative structure would be sufficient to capture the sort of unity at stake. Understanding a life as a project or as a narrative can thus be seen to be closely related ideas—projects can be seen to have a structure exemplified through narrative, and one may view the project of a whole life as just the formation of a life that carries a certain sort of narrative integrity. In this respect, the having of a life is not only a matter of having a sense of one's life as one's own, but is also a matter of one's own making of that life, both of which converge in the capacity to understand that life within some narrative frame. To have a life, one might say, is to be a creature that makes itself through its ability to tell stories about itself (as well as through the other actions and activities to which those stories relate), and to shape its life through those stories.

Mortality and Finitude

For there to be a life, there must be a capacity to have some sense of the life as a whole—such is indeed implied in the idea that to have a life is to have a sense of that life as one's own. This means having a sense of a whole that extends over a certain time and space—having a sense of the past background to current actions and events, having a sense of the extension of those actions and events into the future, and, although I have not said much about this, having a sense of the located character of those same actions and events (even if the understanding is primarily manifest in action itself). Having a sense of one's life as a whole is thus also having a sense of the perspectival and situated character of one's life—of the *topos* that belongs to that life. For creatures that are finite, having a grasp of their lives as a whole in this way must ultimately mean having some sense, no matter how rudimentary, of the way in which their lives encompass a concrete history from their birth to that end of possibilities that is their death. But what of creatures that have no such end in view—because either they do not die or because, for whatever reason, they cannot grasp their own deaths? What of the possibility of a life that was lived without the idea of its own ending? Can one properly have a life that is understood to stretch endlessly into the future in this way?

At this point, some clarification is required. There is a difference, or so it would seem, between having a sense of one's mortality and the fact of such mortality. After all, one's understanding of the facts of one's life may be mistaken, and it might be that one conceives of one's life as having a finite span, and yet one's life never actually comes to an end. The questions that I put in the preceding paragraph took no account of the difference that is indicated here between knowing of the possibility of one's death and the fact that one can die, and the discussion that follows will also tend to ignore this difference. In doing so, it might appear that an important distinction is being left to one side. Maybe to have a life it is necessary that one have a sense of that life as having a limit in death, and yet it is not necessary that such a limit actually be reached—not necessary for there to be a life that it should indeed come to an end.

In fact, as may already be evident, and as I hope will become clearer in the course of the discussion below, any creature that can have a sense of its life as a whole will be a creature that dies, since the death at issue here is not some arbitrary event that exists independently of the life whose ending it is or independently of the having a sense of that life or its finitude. To have a sense of one's life is also to have a sense of that life *as finite*, and so already to take the fact of mortality into the structure of one's life, and for there to be a life such that one can have a sense of that life is also for that very life to be finite, to be a life that will end. These two—the sense of one's own mortality and the fact of that mortality—are bound closely together.[34] It is this argument, or the details that underpin it, that must now be followed in a little more detail.

For a creature to be said to have a life it must, I have claimed, have a sense of that life as its own. The question before us now can thus be put as the question of whether a creature that does not die or that has no sense of its own death—of its mortality—can be said to have a sense of its own life. We might also ask whether such a creature could be said to properly have a sense of itself. Ordinarily this question might seem peculiar, even arbitrary—why suppose that one's mortality or one's grasp of one's mortality would have anything at all to do with one's grasp of oneself or one's self-identity? Surely, it seems, whether one dies and whether one has any conception of one's own death is a purely contingent matter, unrelated to whether one can be said to have a life or to have a grasp of that life.

Although he raises the matter in a rather different form, Sartre makes a rather similar point in arguing against any attempt to tie finitude to mortality. "Since death is always beyond my subjectivity," he writes, "there is no place for it in my subjectivity,"[35] arguing that:

> Ordinarily the belief seems to be that it is death that constitutes our finitude and which reveals it to us. From this combination it results that death takes on the shape of an ontological necessity and that finitude, on the other hand, borrows from death its contingent character. . . . But if we consider the matter a little more closely, we detect their error: death is a contingent fact which belongs to facticity; finitude is an ontological structure of the for-itself which determines freedom and exists only in and through the free project of the end which makes my being known to me. In other words human reality would remain finite even if it were immortal, because it *makes* itself finite by choosing itself as human.[36]

Death, according to Sartre, is thus a contingent matter, whereas both our finitude and our having of a life are not. Whether we are finite creatures, and whether we are creatures that can be said to have a life, is therefore not dependent, according to Sartre, on whether we are capable of death.

An immediate problem with this account, however, is that "death" may refer to either of two logically distinct events: the ending of the integrated functioning of the body or the ending of a life.[37] Sartre does not himself distinguish between these two events, and ordinarily, of course, the events coincide, but they need not do so. Indeed the fact that we can conceive of the possibility of increased human longevity through the replacement of bodily parts and, in the case of some science fiction possibilities, of a whole body (although the latter raises many more questions) suggests that we do not need to identify the ending of the body with the ending of a life. This is not to say that the identity of a life is in no way dependent on the identity of the body. But one can grant that a particular life is lived always in relation to a particular body (insofar as that body is a part of the set of objects and events with respect to which a particular life is constituted)[38] without having to admit that the span of a particular life through time is logically indistinguishable from the span of a particular body's continued existence through time. The question as to whether a creature can be said to have a life if it is not capable of dying, or if it lacks any grasp of the possibility of its own death, is thus not a question about whether a creature must have a body that can die if that creature is to have a life (although an answer to this question can certainly be inferred).

Rather, the question is whether a life that has no end is indeed a life, or whether a creature can have a sense of its own life in the absence of any sense of the ending of that life.

Once the question at issue is put in these terms, we can begin to see that the connection between the having of a life and the capacity for death need not be so arbitrary or contingent after all, for if the having of a life is the obtaining of a certain unity among the elements of that life (among a set of experiences, behaviors, and attitudes), then it seems reasonable to ask whether such a unity can obtain over an unending span of time. And here we come to another consideration to which the sort of account offered by Sartre apparently pays scant attention: if a life is constituted as an ongoing set or activities or projects, and if such a life, and the activities in which it consists, are constituted through the ordering of objects and events in the world, then it is hard to see how there could be the right sort of unity or integrity to a life that was understood as spanning an unending period of time and as consisting in what would presumably be an unending series of activities and projects. The immortals described in one of the stories of Jorge Luis Borges are indeed creatures in whose infinitely extended lives everything is possible and consequently nothing is significant. As Borges puts it, "No one is someone; a single immortal man is all men. Like Cornelius Agrippa, I am god, hero, philosopher, demon, and world—which is a long-winded way of saying that *I am not*."[39]

How could one conceive of a life without end as constituting a unity—that is, as constituting a single life? Not only might there be quite radical discontinuities between a portion of this "life" lived over one period and a portion lived over another, but it is hard to see how, from within that life, *any* activity or project could possess significance in giving identity to that life as such. Our lives are largely constituted by the activities in which we engage and so are constituted in terms of the particular orderings of the world that we establish. But for a life without end there need be no limit on the orderings that are possible within that life and no sense in which that life need depend on any finite number of choices. Given an endless span of time, the possibilities that a particular life might encompass are themselves endless. In that case it seems that the Sartrean claim that death, as the ending of the span of a life, bears no essential relation to finitude would seem to be simply false. Finitude is the finitude of *my* activities and projects, and this does not mean simply that those projects are finite in the scope of what they encompass, but that they cannot be projected endlessly. The same is true for the "project" that is my own life.

Insofar as I can grasp it as my own, and insofar as this is necessary for me to have a life, such a life cannot be projected forever.

It is precisely because we cannot play through an endless series of choices, an infinite series of possibilities, that the choices we do make become so important to us (and so are part of what is most properly our *own*): those choices establish the character and identity of our lives; they allow certain things to show up as valuable; they establish a certain ordering of and orientation within the world. It is perhaps for this reason that the idea of immortality can seem to entail an emptying out of life, even a form of boredom. A life without end would be a life in which the framework within which value and significance was established or within which it was able to appear was absent. This seems to be one of the inconsistencies in any sort of reductionist approach to the self and so another problem for such an account. Parfit, for instance, argues that death should hold no fear for us, since what is important for identity is just the continuation of certain attitudes and values and these may continue independently of the existence of any particular embodied creature.[40] But by removing any sense of self-identity Parfit also removes any sense in which things can matter just insofar as doing so removes the sense in which they can matter to me or to any other individual. And as content is itself constituted through the unitary activity that makes for a life, so value can only appear within the context of such an integrated, organized unity of activity. But the possibility of such a unity requires a recognition of a unity and identity that is more than just a matter of the persistence of certain attitudes or values. As Paul Ricoeur asks, "really, how can we ask ourselves about *what* matters if we could not ask *to whom* the thing mattered or not? Does not the questioning about what matters or not depend upon self-concern, which indeed seems to be constitutive of selfhood?"[41]

One way of understanding the nature of a life is through the idea of a certain unity of projects. Such a view seems to present problems, however, for any account that takes the temporal finitude of a life to be merely contingent and allows the possibility of a life without end. If we look to conceive of the unity of a life through the idea of the unity of narrative, then similar problems arise: Does a story that lacks an ending, a narrative that goes on forever, really constitute a story? Does it constitute a single story? One can certainly conceive of stories that go on, perhaps, forever. But such stories are surely understood better as sequences of stories, sequences that may be unified in only an attenuated sense that is given warrant, perhaps, by the presence of some connecting thread (perhaps some loose continuity of content or theme), rather than as a single story.

Maybe an unending narrative should be understood as not one story, but an infinite sequence of stories in which there is always, rather like the tales of Scheherazade, another story to come.[42] Maybe a "life" without end should be similarly understood as not a single life, but an infinite sequence of lives. Of course, in such an unending sequence, not only might we be left with a multiplicity of finite lives rather than a single infinite life, but the sense in which we have even a single *sequence* might itself be quite tenuous—perhaps the only unifying principle would be that the various lives are part of a single causal chain, and this hardly seems to make for a unity in any appropriately significant sense.

The existence of a life is a matter of the existence of certain sorts of connections between objects and events—to live a life is to impart a certain ordering to the things in the world. In this respect one cannot divorce a life from the objects and events in the world with respect to which that life is constituted. If a life has its character in a particular way of being in the world—in standing in a particular relation to objects, events, and places and to other persons, other lives—then one cannot separate the life from the relations that constitute it. Thus, the character of a life, and so the life itself, cannot be grasped independently of a grasp of the relations that are constitutive of that life; independently of the concrete particularities of the life that is lived; independently of the particular involvements and commitments in which that life consists. This means that we have to conceive of lives as encompassing more than just the self as narrowly conceived (or perhaps, we have to conceive of the self as encompassing more than just some set of internalized "experiences"). A life must be understood as given in a certain "being-in-the-world," to use Heidegger's phrase, that encompasses self, others, things, events, locales, and environments—a being-in-the-world that should itself be understood in terms of a certain complex, multiple, and active *placedness*.[43]

This is not to say that the relations that are part of a life (or the persons, things, events, and locales that are implicated in those relations) cannot change without the life of which they are a part also being destroyed, but that there must always be a certain continuity in those relations and some sort of integration between them. Too catastrophic a breakdown in the integration of a life or between elements of a life—say, a breakdown that occurs in such a way that it separates what might otherwise have been a single life into two quite separate wholes—may itself constitute the ending of one life and the start of a new. This why the body alone cannot be wholly determinative of a life—the body may remain and yet the life be extinguished—even though body and life are in so many respects almost the same.[44]

We often talk of beginning a new life, of breaking with the past, of becoming a new person (even of being "born again"), when we mean to indicate the way in which our lives, though still the same lives, have undergone some radical or important change. But such turns of phrase can also apply to cases where we really do mean that there has been a change in the seeming identity of the life that is being lived—in relation, for instance, to catastrophic breakdowns or changes in personality or character. Thus someone who undergoes a severe trauma of the sort associated with some form of neurophysiological damage may well be said literally to cease to be the person they were previously. It is hard to comprehend the phenomenology that might be involved in such a breakdown, but it may well be appropriate in such cases, and reactions from relatives and friends may bear this out, to regard such a breakdown as no less the ending of a life than the death of the body. And this may be so even if the person concerned remains a functional human being, simply because the involvements, commitments, and attitudes that previously made up that person's life have been completely altered.

If the ending of a life is essentially a matter of the breakdown in the integrity of the life—a breakdown in the ongoing projects, in the involvements, commitments, and attitudes, that make up that life—then a life may indeed end without the ending of the body with which that life is associated. And similarly, the idea of a life that *never* comes to an end may be better expressed in terms of the idea of a project that never breaks down or whose breakdown can never be envisaged, rather than in terms of the death of some particular body. Yet future possibilities always carry the possibility of ceasing to be because they carry with them the possible destruction of what we are (and we are not just this set of bodily parts or even this set of dispositions), because they carry with them the possible destruction of those objects and events, those projects, with respect to which our identity is established. Thus, insofar as my worldly surroundings and activities are contingent, so my continuity and identity is always uncertain, always fragile, always determined within a finite frame.

That our self-identity is indeed connected with the identity of that which surrounds us—in which we find our place—is indicated by the way in which the desire for a continuation of our projects, and of ourselves—for immortality—can be manifest in a desire to make the world around us as permanent and unchanging as possible. But this desire, common though it may be, represents a failure to understand the nature of our projects themselves and of our involvement in the world. An unchanging world would be a world that made no demands on us, in which we would no longer have any significant involvement, and in which there would be no life to live. It would also, perhaps, be a world in which we could no longer find anything that would require our attention and our care, since it is surely only that which has a certain fragility, and that which therefore must be cared for, that can be worthy of such attention. If there was nothing in such a world to care for, would there be anything to care about—would it even be a world in which there could be anything of worth? On this basis, to wish for a world of unchanging stability and permanence, and for the immortality that such a world might be thought to bring, is actually to wish, paradoxical though it may seem, for a certain kind of "death." The possibility of the kind of ending that comes with the fragility of our projects, the essential changeability of our world (and of the locales within it), and the mortality of our existence is thus intrinsic to the possibility both of our own self-identity and to the having of a life.[45]

The End of Life—the Nothing

The having of a life requires a sense of that life as a whole. To have a sense of one's life requires understanding it through the ongoing unity and integrity of the elements, including the projects and activities, that make up that life. But the very identity of those elements, and of the life as a whole, cannot be separated from the particular entities, events, and locales with which those elements, and that life, are involved. A life that continued endlessly would be a life that was capable of continuous mutation, and yet such a life would not be a single life at all. At most it could be a succession of lives—the realization of something like the "dispersal" (*Zerstreuung*) that threatens *Dasein* and which Heidegger considers in *Being and Time*.[46] Not only would this sort of life lack any sense of genuine of temporal unity (and would also, as a consequence, lack any genuine spatial, or more properly, topological, unity[47]), but it would not be a life about the shape of which one could care—in fact, such a life would have no shape. In that case we can say that immortality (and this includes the sort of quasi immortality that reductionism offers) means a dissolution of identity, a dissolution of self, and this hardly seems like immortality at all.

To suppose that one could have a life that did not end is actually to suppose a mode of living that would not be a life at all. The ending of a life is part of what constitutes a life, and the sense of one's life as having an end is part of the structure of one's life that itself reflects the very character of that life—it is thus not a sense of one's life that can be other than true to the reality of that life. To have a life, to have a world, to have a sense of value and significance, is also *to have a sense* of one's own fragility and mortality, and *to be* fragile and mortal—to have a sense of being given over to death *and* to be capable of death. As Heidegger comments:

The mortals are human beings. They are called mortals because they can die. To die means to be capable of death. Only man dies. The animal perishes. It has death neither ahead of it nor behind it. Death is the shrine of Nothing, that is, of that which in every respect is never something that merely exists, but which nevertheless presences, even as the mystery of Being itself. As the shrine of Nothing, death harbours within itself the presencing of Being. As the shrine of Nothing, death is the shelter of Being. We now call mortals mortal—not because their earthly life comes to an end, but because they are capable of death as death. Mortals are who they are, as mortals, present in the shelter of Being. They are the presencing relation to Being as Being.[48]

To be capable of death is simply to find oneself placed in the world, and to be placed in the world is to be capable of death. The sense of "being placed" that is at issue here is not merely of being able to be located in relation to other things and other places (as one might do using a GPS or a map), but rather in the sense of standing within that open realm in which self, other selves, and things first come to presence. The very possibility of such an opening is essentially dependent upon that opening being bounded in a way that presupposes an end no less than a beginning that is already encompassed in the idea of the placed character of that opening. Such placedness is evident in the embodied character of human being, in its historicality, its fragility, and in its essential mortality. Such placedness is itself grounded in nothing that lies beyond or outside of it. It finds its meaning and significance within the very same relations as appear within it and by which it is constituted.[49] The shrine of nothing is thus also the shrine of home and hearth, of the threshold, of the bounded, of place.

10 Topology, Triangulation, and Truth

Every interpretation is a dialogue with the work, and with the saying. However, every dialogue becomes halting and fruitless if it confines itself obdurately to nothing but what is directly said—rather than that the speakers in the dialogue involve each other in *that* realm and abode about which they are speaking, and lead each other to it. Such involvement is the soul of dialogue. It leads the speakers into the unspoken.

—Martin Heidegger, *What Is Called Thinking?*

Heidegger's *Being and Time* is not primarily concerned with questions of interpretation or understanding. Its driving interest is instead ontological—an interest in the question of the "meaning of being." Yet inasmuch as the work adopts a thoroughly hermeneuticized approach to ontology—the very focus on the *meaning* of being suggests as such—so the inquiry into ontology also involves Heidegger in an inquiry into the "structure" of understanding. Although the explicitly hermeneutic focus disappears from Heidegger's later work, still the concern with understanding, thought in terms of a broader happening of disclosedness—a happening of world—can be seen to continue.[1] Moreover, if we look to the work of Heidegger's one-time pupil, Hans-Georg Gadamer, which takes as its starting point Heidegger's later rather than earlier thinking, we can clearly see how the hermeneuticized ontology pursued by Heidegger readily gives rise to an ontologized hermeneutics. One might say that once philosophy takes the "hermeneutic turn," the inquiry into some form of "fundamental ontology" and the inquiry into the structure of understanding become one and the same. Perhaps something similar is also true within so-called analytic philosophy: following the linguistic turn (the analytic correlate of the earlier turn to hermeneutics within continental thought), the inquiry into the structure of language seems inevitably to lead back to a concern with the fundamental structures in which meaning, rationality, and agency are grounded.

If the move from a hermeneuticized mode of ontological inquiry back to an ontologized hermeneutics can be discerned in Heidegger's work, as well as in Gadamer, then the work of Donald Davidson, and perhaps also the transition to Davidson from Quine, provides an example of how analytic philosophy might be viewed as turning from a concern with the linguistic, the logical, and the semantical, back to an interest in the underlying ontology (broadly understood) that grounds them. Thus, whereas Davidson's earlier work may be viewed as characterized by a focus on semantic and logical issues, his later work has been increasingly concerned with the elaboration of the fundamental structures in which the possibility of meaning and understanding reside (or, as Davidson puts it into "the conditions of objective thought").

Heidegger and Davidson can both be seen, then, as providing an example of how the inquiry into questions of interpretation and understanding may be central to a broader set of more fundamentally "ontological" issues. In addition, and notwithstanding the enormous divergence between them in style and philosophical background, there also seems to be a number of important points in relation to these issues on which the two converge. The exploration of such convergence has come to be the focus for a small but growing body of literature.[2] As I read matters, however, the convergence at issue here cannot adequately be understood except inasmuch as the work of *both* Heidegger *and* Davidson is read as giving a central role (whether implicitly or explicitly) to the idea of locality or place—to the idea of *topos*. Within the framework of the inquiry into interpretation one might say that the structure of interpretation is itself given in the structure of place or location; more broadly, that the very possibility of the disclosing or unconcealing of things, the very possibility of world, is to be found through the disclosing of that same topological structure—through the disclosing or unconcealing of what Heidegger calls "the place or . . . locality of Being [*Ortschaft des Seins*]."[3] Such a topological or topographical approach is one in which the work of a "mapping out" of the "place" of disclosedness is, at the same time, the delineation of a certain "topography" of understanding—and so one in which understanding is also reconfigured.[4] This approach is, so I claim, characteristic of Heidegger's thinking both early and late, and although it appears in a very different form, it is a central, if to some extent implicit, element in Davidson's work as well.

Before going any further, however, one possible source of misunderstanding needs to be cleared away. It might be thought that whatever form of "ontological/topological" analysis in which Davidson might be said to be involved, there is an essential difference between the Davidsonian approach and that to be found in the work of Heidegger or even Gadamer. Whereas Heidegger's analysis, whether in *Being and Time* or in the later work, already begins "in" the world (either through *Dasein* as always already "being-in-the world" or through our being always already given over to the *Ereignis*), and so as already given over to a meaningful context of relations, Davidson might be supposed to assume precisely the abstracted and displaced "Cartesian" starting point that Heidegger thereby rejects—a starting point according to which the world is to be understood simply as a set of spatiotemporally extended, causally interacting physical systems, among which are to be included those particular physical systems that are human beings. On this reading, the *topos* of Heidegger's thought must be very different from the notion of mere "location" that might seem to play a role in Davidson.

Yet to assume such a contrast would be seriously mistaken—mistaken not only because neither Heidegger nor Davidson need be viewed as rejecting a physicalist understanding of the world as that may be articulated in the vocabulary of the natural sciences (what they each seem to reject is rather the idea that such an account is entirely sufficient for an understanding of the way in which human beings are in the world),[5] but also because Davidson's own starting point is the fact of our locatedness in a world that is already grasped as meaningful, a world in which we are already engaged with other persons and other things.[6] Indeed, this starting point is one important feature of his approach that marks Davidson off from Quine (and is also an important element in his "anomalous monism"), much as Heidegger's insistence on starting with "being-in-the-world" (rather than a mode of being with respect to which the world has already been "bracketed off") is one feature that marks him off from Husserl.[7] Moreover, as we shall see below, the structure of the Davidsonian analysis also mirrors features of the Heideggerian, notably in taking the structure on the basis of which understanding and interpretation are possible as a single meaningful structure—a unitary place—that encompasses and defines both the interpreter as well as the worldly context of interpretation.

Reprising Heidegger's Topology

In "The Origin of the Work of Art,"[8] an essay that is significant in being one of the first works in which the topological character of Heidegger's thinking comes more explicitly to the fore, the topological project is undertaken through an inquiry into the nature of the artwork, and through an elaboration of the way in which the setting up of the concrete work of art is thereby also the setting forth of a world. The Greek temple, situated above rocky earth and under the expanse of the open sky, is taken as providing a paradigmatic illustration of the way in which the artwork opens up a world and discloses the various elements within that world.[9] In later essays, such as "The Thing" and "Building Dwelling Thinking,"[10] Heidegger presents an account of the way in which a world and its network of interconnections is brought into view through the gathering of elements—of Earth and Sky, Mortals and Gods (these four making up what Heidegger calls "the Fourfold [Das Geviert]" that is also a Onefold)—around, not a work of art, but rather something more mundane—a jug of wine, a bridge. It is, according to Heidegger, only within the world, within the "spaces" (not the abstract spaces of Galileo, Newton, or Einstein) opened up by such a gathering that human dwelling is possible.

Whether in Heidegger's discussion of art or in his later meditations on the nature of dwelling, a number of crucial points stand out that are worth reiterating here. First, inasmuch as the structure at issue here is a structure that can be seen to underpin the possibility of understanding, it is so through the way in which it makes possible the very disclosedness of things—a disclosedness or unconcealing that is also the opening up of a domain in which things and persons take a stand alongside and in relation to one another. The inquiry into understanding can only take the form of the inquiry into the domain, the *topos*, opened up here. Second, such disclosedness requires a focus around which a multiplicity of elements is gathered. In "The Origin of the Work of Art," that focus is the artwork itself; in "The Thing" and "Building Dwelling Thinking," it is the thing—whatever it may be. The role of the work or the thing in unifying the various elements that together make up a world does not mean, however, that the work or the thing is somehow more fundamental than the elements themselves. In "The Thing," the jug does not come before earth or sky, but rather, through their being gathered in the jug—through their being reflected in the very character of the jug—earth and sky, and the jug itself, are all brought into view. Third, disclosedness requires a certain boundedness, but it is a boundedness that opens up rather than closes off.[11] Presencing, which is also a way to understand disclosedness, thus occurs within certain bounds, that is, within a *locality* or *place* that is proper to it. Such a place, as it is bounded and is also made possible within those bounds, thereby provides a freed "space" within which things can be "sited." Finally, although disclosedness occurs in relation to human beings, it is not brought about by them—it is only within the place opened up by the artwork or the thing that human being is itself brought into view.

Heideggerian topology is essentially concerned with the delineation of the "placed" or "localized" structure within which human beings are brought into an encounter with themselves, and with the world, a structure that is the ground for the possibility of understanding, as well as being that within which things are brought to presence. The four points outlined immediately above exemplify the main elements that characterize such a topology: it aims to delineate a unitary structure that is constituted in terms of a multiplicity of irreducible elements; a structure that is bounded and yet open; a structure that stands in an important relation to human being and yet is not simply a function of it. These elements of Heideggerian topology can be seen to mirror the characteristic features of more mundane forms of inquiry into particular places or localities.

Typically, one comes to understand a place, and so to grasp the more particular localities and places situated within it, through walking around and getting used to the various pathways and sites that make it up. A similar process underlies the more technical practice of the topographical surveyor who, without additional aids beyond theodolite and chain, is able to build up a map of a terrain through repeated triangulation and traverse across the face of that terrain. In both cases, understanding the place is not a matter of gaining access to something that underlies it (just as one cannot derive a topographical map from a geological survey alone), nor is it a matter of finding just one point from which everything else falls into view. The elements within the landscape provide the focus through which the unity of the landscape is grasped, the capacity to grasp the landscape depends on being able to mark out a particular region within which one works, and the unity of the landscape is also grasped through one's interaction with that landscape even though it is not just a product of such interaction. In Heidegger's thinking one finds exemplified the almost exact philosophical analogue of such a topological (or topographical) approach.

Concerned as it is with the structure of disclosedness or unconcealment, the explicitly topological inquiry of Heidegger's later thinking is continuous with the project pursued in Heidegger's earlier work of uncovering (which is to say, disclosing) the structure of disclosedness through the analysis of *Dasein*. Indeed, insofar as *Being and Time* can be construed as attempting an analysis of the being of *Dasein* as "being-in-the-world," so it must already be seen as centrally concerned with the structure of a certain locality or place. And this is reinforced by the idea of the *Da*—the "there"—that is contained within the notion of *Dasein* itself. Thus, in 1949, Heidegger writes of the meaning of *Dasein*, as the term appears in *Being and Time*, that "Dasein names that which is first of all to be experienced, and subsequently thought accordingly, as a place—namely, as the locality of the truth of being."[12]

Part of the shift from *Being and Time* to the later work is undoubtedly to be found in Heidegger's increasing focus on the *Da*, the "there/here," rather than on *Dasein* as such (the latter term, while not abandoned, appears much less frequently in the later thinking). And parallel to this is a clearer recognition on Heidegger's part of the way in which any adequate analysis of the there/here—of locality or place—cannot afford to treat spatiality as derivative of temporality in the way that *Being and Time* attempts.[13] Yet although Heidegger's approach in the earlier work does assign a certain priority to temporality, still it is clear that the ideas that underpin the topology of Heidegger's later thinking are already present in *Being and Time*. In particular, the structure that Heidegger aims to uncover is a structure that is constituted not through reduction down to some single, underlying entity or principle, but rather in terms of the structure of being-in-the-world as a whole—in terms of a multiplicity of elements that are focused and gathered together in relation to one such element. This idea of a unity that also encompasses a multiplicity, already present, even if not adequately worked out, within the structure of *Being and Time*, is a central element in the development of Heideggerian topology, and in the idea of place or *topos* as such.[14]

In taking place or locality as the central notion in any elucidation of the structure of disclosedness—of that by which human beings are able to encounter anything in the world at all, including themselves—Heidegger presents us with an account of the structure of understanding and of interpretation that directs attention to its essentially place-bound character. To understand or to interpret is thus to be engaged with things in the world within a certain open but bounded "space" of possibilities; it is to be located within a unitary but differentiated "region," each element of which is interconnected and mutually defining; it is to encounter oneself only inasmuch as one also encounters others, and inasmuch as one also encounters things.[15] This is part of what is already suggested by the early Heidegger's emphasis on *Dasein* as "being-in-the-world"—such "being-in" is not a matter of one entity, namely *Dasein*, being located in relation to a set of other entities within a simple physical space. Instead, *Dasein* is to be understood as the opening up of a "space" within which things, including the *Dasein* that is the being of the human, are brought to appearance.

The equivocity that might thus be seen already to be present in the term *"Dasein"* as it is employed in *Being and Time* (an equivocity that derives from the complex topology that is at issue here), to some extent remains even in the later thinking. There *Dasein* names first and foremost the "there/here of being" (the *Da* of *Sein*)—the place or *topos* of being—but in naming this it also names the essential place of human being, the "there/here" in and through which human being comes to be, in and through which it comes to presence.[16] The essence of human being, the "there/here" that belongs properly to the human, is thereby understood, not as determinative of disclosedness, but as instead participating in a larger structure of disclosedness (a structure that is properly one of concealing *and* unconcealing[17]) that encompasses the human and the nonhuman and outside of which neither can be understood. The "topological" structure that appears here—or one that mirrors many of its main features—is not peculiar to Heidegger, but can, in fact, also be found in Davidson, and so it is to Davidson's work that I will now turn.

Explicating Davidson's Topography

Although interpretation and understanding are important themes in Davidson's thinking, they do not arise out of any self-evident Davidsonian concern with "the question of being" or the "topology of being"—at least not in the form in which these ideas appear in Heidegger—and the idea of "place" is not explicitly thematized in Davidson's work at all. Davidson begins, at least so far as interpretation are concerned, with a set of apparently quite limited questions in semantic theory—in particular, the proper structure of a theory of meaning for a natural language. It would be a serious mistake, however, were one to suppose that Davidson's interest in the question of meaning was ever restricted to just a set of narrowly semantic concerns. The focus on meaning can be seen, in fact, to arise out of, and to be continuous with, Davidson's early interest in questions of rationality and understanding (already evident in his dissertation on Plato's *Philebus* completed in the late 1940s[18]) and his empirical work on decision theory in the 1950s.[19] Although Davidson abandoned the empirical approach characteristic of the early work in decision theory, that work also demonstrated the impossibility of investigating the relation between actions and attitudes independently of investigation of meaning and linguistic understanding.[20] As a consequence, Davidson's thinking can be seen to be focused not only on questions of meaning nor even of action (the focus of one of his first and most influential papers), but on the problem of developing an integrated account of the sort of "rational" agency characteristic of human beings—an account of that mode of being that is exemplified by "rational" agents such as ourselves.[21]

Much of Davidson's thinking on these matters has developed through consideration of the problem of "radical interpretation." Derived from the Quinean notion of "radical translation,"[22] radical interpretation asks us to consider what would be required for an interpreter to arrive at an understanding of the utterances of a speaker whose language was previously unknown to the interpreter. The idea is that through consideration of this more radical case we will be better able to uncover the structures that govern understanding in *all* cases. As presented in its original Quinean formulation, the example of radical translation is already suggestive of a topographical emphasis: in one of the most famous examples in twentieth-century philosophy, Quine asks us to imagine a field linguist engaged with a native speaker as both see a small furry animal run across their field of view prompting the native speaker to proclaim "Gavagai!"[23] The encounter between speaker and translator that appears here is one that occurs within a certain locale, and it is this common placing that not only allows the encounter, but also enables the possibility of translation as based in the engagement with a common object (although Quine will construe that commonality in terms very different from Davidson).

As set out in many of Davidson's earlier and perhaps best-known papers, interpretation depends crucially on being able to gain some sort of insight into the overall structure of a speaker's utterances—a structure that can be formally characterized by means of a theory of meaning modeled on a Tarski-style truth theory.[24] But although Davidson sometimes expressed different views in the course of his career as to just how much could be expected of such a formalized theory of meaning, for the most part it has been clear that a purely formal theory that satisfied the requirements set out by Tarski would not, on its own, be enough. Any account of what would be required to enable an interpreter to understand the speech of another would have to be adequate to the empirical circumstances at issue. Moreover, as Davidson makes explicit in his later work (and this seems clearly to have been his settled view), no purely formalized theory could ever be adequate to the demands of understanding in any actual linguistic encounter.[25]

Consequently, although Davidson always retains the idea that understanding a speaker requires some grasp of the overall pattern of the speaker's linguistic behavior (a pattern that, in an *idealized* form, may perhaps be described in terms of a Tarski-style formalization), such understanding is seen as grounded in a set of broader interpretative capacities that are not peculiar to linguistic understanding alone ("we have erased the boundary between knowing a language and knowing our way around in the world generally"[26]) and that are not reducible to mastery of some formalized semantic-syntactic theory. Indeed, not only is linguistic understanding inseparable from our more general capacities for understanding, but understanding a speaker's utterances turns out to be inseparable from understanding a speaker's attitudes and actions. Interpretation, particularly as exhibited in the structure of *radical* interpretation, is thus a matter of arriving at an integrated view of the speaker's overall behavior and, in this respect, is characterized by its holistic orientation. Such holism is, furthermore, not merely an "epistemological" requirement of our being able to understand a speaker's attitudes, actions, and utterances; instead, the very identity of attitudes, actions, and utterances is holistically determined, that is, it is a matter of their location within an overall pattern of attitudes, actions, and utterances. To attribute an attitude is thus always to attribute a network of attitudes; to identify an instance of behavior as action is always to identify a pattern of actions; to interpret the meaning of an utterance is always to interpret that utterance as belonging to a language. The intentional domain—the domain of attitude, action, and meaning—is characteristically holistic.[27]

Holism presents, at least initially, a problem for the possibility of interpretation, since it means that there can be no access to any particular attitude, action, or utterance independently of access to the entire intentional system. In Davidson's earlier accounts, the principle of charity provides a solution to this problem through enabling the interpreter to gain access to the complex of attitudes, actions, and utterances through offering a first approximation of the pattern of a speaker's attitudes. Charity has no single formulation (its indeterminacy can be seen to reflect the indeterminacy of interpretation that is consequent upon the holistic character of the intentional), but essentially it depends on the idea that the interpretation of a speaker must proceed through locating the speaker in relation to her, and the interpreter's, surroundings. Inasmuch as both speaker and interpreter are, as agents, always already engaged with the objects and events that make up those surroundings, and inasmuch as attitudes, actions, and utterances form a single system, so the speaker's surroundings can be taken as a guide to the speaker's attitudes and thence to the speakers actions and the meanings of the speaker's utterances.

Interpretation, as exhibited through the structure of radical interpretation, is thus always directed at the speaker as she is located within a particular environmental setting and with respect to the publicly available objects and events with which she is actively engaged and with which she causally interacts. It is, furthermore, the interpreter's own capacity for engagement, and so for causal interaction, with those very same objects and events (irrespective of how they may be *described*[28]) that enables interpretation to proceed. In this respect, the holism that characterizes the intentional is paralleled by a form of "externalism" according to which it is the "external" objects and events to which speakers, in virtue of their capacities as agents, are causally related that are determinative of speakers' attitudes, actions, and the meanings of their utterances.[29] Moreover, as was the case with holism, this is no merely epistemological claim, but a claim about the very nature of the intentional, and of intentional content, such that actions, attitudes, and utterances are constituted only in relation to a worldly background.

In Davidson's later work the role of charity is largely subsumed under what Davidson calls "triangulation"—a process by which the combined interaction between interpreter, speaker, and a common object or objects provides the basis for the interpreter's understanding of the speaker—and which can be viewed as providing a more detailed elaboration of the externalist-holistic character of interpretation, and of the intentional, that was evident in Davidson's earlier account of the structure of radical interpretation.[30] Davidson's talk of triangulation sometimes has a metaphorical air to it, and although it is true that Davidson does not intend to claim that the interpreter must literally employ the methods of the topographical surveyor, it certainly is the case that the triangular relation between interpreter, speaker, and object describes, in perhaps idealized fashion, a real relation that must obtain if interpretation is to be possible. Moreover, the idea that speaker and interpreter are brought together, and brought together with an object or set of objects, though their relative location within a common spatial frame—an idea at the heart of triangulation in the most basic of cases—is itself indicative of the way in which interpretation is indeed dependent on concrete spatial location and also, one might say, on the capacity, on the part of interpreter and speaker, for oriented, embodied agency.[31] Moreover, inasmuch as the idea of triangulation itself refers us back to the very practice of topographical surveying briefly mentioned above (as well as to other practices for the establishing of location), so it is indicative of the way in which Davidson can be seen to provide us with his own "topography" of understanding or interpretation.

The importance of spatial location and embodiment here is not something to which Davidson himself has given a great deal of attention,[32] but it clearly follows from Davidson's view of interpretation, and of intentional content, as dependent on the causal relations that obtain between speakers and between speakers and their surroundings. Moreover, the idea of location must also play a necessary role in any adequate working out of the holism that is such an important element in the Davidsonian account. Consider one of the standard objections that has been advanced against holism of the sort espoused by Davidson: if the identity of some attitude, say, the belief that there is tea in the pot, is dependent on an entire system of attitudes, then it would seem that two people could have the same attitude only if they shared the exact same system of attitudes within which that particular attitude was embedded; since it seems highly implausible that this could be the case, holism appears to be committed to denying that two persons can ever have the same attitudes (and the same would seem to apply to a single person at different times).[33] Holism would be an absurd position if it were understood as requiring such conclusions, but once it is recognized that the holistic structure of the intentional is always organized in relation to particular "localities"—that is, to a certain object or set of objects and to a certain situation in which interpreter and speaker interact—then the idea that holism requires some complete match across an entire system of attitudes can be abandoned. Indeed, as a general point, it would seem that holism must always be married with some form of "localism" if it is to be a viable position.[34] In the Davidsonian case, this also implies, however, that the idea of a "theory" of interpretation (or of meaning), understood as a structure that aims to address the entirety of a speaker's attitudes or behavior, is something of an abstraction, or perhaps at best, a "regulative ideal."[35]

In this respect it is worth noting that Davidson's own talk of "theories" of interpretation or of meaning has been a source of much misunderstanding. Philosophers such as Charles Taylor, for instance, have taken such talk to commit Davidson to a view of understanding as essentially consisting in mastery or knowledge (whether explicit or implicit) of some *theory*.[36] Yet although Davidson is committed to the importance of finding patterns in behavior as basic to the understanding of speakers, and to the idea of attitude, action, and meaning as forming a single system, he is also committed, as I noted above, to a view of understanding as always going beyond anything that can be delivered by means of any purely theoretical articulation. Understanding is, for Davidson, much more a matter of "knowing how to go on" in a way appropriate to a particular interpretive "location," than a matter of the abstract theoretical mastery (something Davidson can be viewed as inheriting from Wittgenstein). We may attempt to formalize a speaker's understanding by means of some theoretical description, but this does not mean that understanding is therefore to be construed as consisting in mastery or knowledge of any such description; understanding is no more a matter of simply applying a "theory" than it is of merely "following a rule."[37]

Of course, where the understanding of another speaker is at stake, "being able to go on"—that is, being able to arrive at some appropriate and ongoing coordination of responses—is often a matter of going on *in language*, and being able to understand another typically means being able to explain, clarify, and elaborate on one's own and the other's actions in linguistic terms—that is, in terms of certain descriptions of oneself and of the other.[38] In this respect, our ability to provide sentences that state the content of a some attitude (some belief or desire) or to provide a redescription of an action, and so of the intention, with which the action is performed, has a crucial role to play in any attempt to understand. This is not because human mentality is "propositional" in its essence, but because, at the simplest level, it is by means of sentences that we can track and structure a speaker's interactions with others and with her surroundings (and this must apply in our own case as much as in the case of others), and, at a more complex level, it is through language that our very mode of being in the world is articulated and formed. The place of understanding is thus a place whose essential openness is inextricably bound to language—the "spacing" on which language depends is also a spacing that itself depends on language.[39]

Rather than a point of disagreement, I take the Davidsonian emphasis on language to represent an important point of convergence with both Heidegger and Gadamer, since it is indicative of the fundamentally linguistic character of understanding even in the face of the fact that understanding also encompasses more than the linguistic alone. There is, however, a widespread tendency to think of the role of language in understanding as if what was at issue was simply one capacity among others, and, especially when it comes to the reading of Heidegger, to see language as tied in some way to a more "theoretical" stance on the world in contrast to a more fundamental level of embodied "practice" as instantiated in the habitual and behavioral. Mark Wrathall writes in a way that is exemplary of this kind of thinking when he claims that Heidegger presents us with an account according to which "we can, through our practices alone, and without the use of language, embody a richly articulated way of dealing with objects within the world."[40] It is quite unclear what sense is to be attached to Wrathall's use of the phrase "without the use of language." It cannot mean that "we" could embody these richly articulated ways of interacting even if we were not language users; and if it does not mean this, what could it mean? The only possibility would seem to be that "without language" actually means "without *using* language"—without speaking, without writing, without forming sentences or words (whether or not it is overt). But clearly, this is not the claim that is at issue when Davidson—or Heidegger or Gadamer—directs attention to the fundamental role that language plays.

The idea that the structure of disclosedness that concerns Heidegger, in particular (and that may be taken to be identical with the *topos* of understanding that is also at issue here), may be given in some form of purely practical or behavioral engagement that underlies the linguistic (that the structure of disclosedness is "pragmatic") is to make a very simple mistake: it is to assume that the linguistic and nonlinguistic can indeed be set in opposition, as if what were at issue were a choice between different *capacities* or *modes of comportment*. Not only does the linguistic suffuse the behavioral just as the behavioral also suffuses the linguistic,[41] but disclosedness is not a structure founded in some capacity or other—even though it can be analyzed by looking to certain capacities as necessary for it. The sense in we can talk about disclosedness as a matter of our *practical* embeddedness in the world is the same sense in which disclosedness is a matter of our *linguistic* embeddedness; and inasmuch as disclosedness may also be said to come prior to any linguistic capacities we may exercise, so too is it prior to any practical or behavioral capacities.[42]

It is, as I noted above, by means of sentences that we can track and structure a speaker's interactions with others and with their surroundings. Sentences enable us to specify the content of attitudes and utterances, and they do so by identifying the objects of those attitudes and utterances. It is a simple and straightforward truth that the same object or thing can support more than one description. The capacity to redescribe things, and to grasp different descriptions as nevertheless capable of being about the same thing, is an obvious and necessary prerequisite for the possibility of interpretation and, more generally, for communication. Since not every speaker will speak in the same way, without the capacity to grasp that different ways of speaking, and different things said, can still describe or be addressed to the same object or the same subject matter, there would be no way of coordinating our linguistic behavior with anybody else's.

Not only, then, does language give us the means to formulate different descriptions of things, and so to grasp the various possibilities that are conjoined in a particular object (something essential to grasping the alternative modes of interaction that may be available to us), but it also enables us to understand *different* modes of behavior through coordinating them (often in ways that are quite automatic and need not call on any explicit linguistic verbalization) with our own. The linguistic is, in this respect, the essential medium of the social, even though the social encompasses more than just the linguistic. Furthermore, the "place" within which interpretation must function is itself social—indeed Davidson claims that rationality itself "is a social trait"[43]—and this does not mean merely that it must involve at least one other speaker, but that it also draws us into a larger web of social interactions and so into a society and a history. Just as a single triangulation is of no use to the topographical surveyor, so the triangulation that is the basis of interpretation and intentionality is not a one-off happening, but must be part of an ongoing process of interaction between interpreters, speakers, and the things around them in which past interaction is as important as the interaction that takes place now. Much of the criticism of Davidsonian triangulation seems to depend, in fact, on construals of triangulation that attend neither to its temporal aspect (to the fact that it is a dynamic rather than a static process) nor to its essentially spatialized character (to the fact that it requires a sense of simultaneous and not merely serial locations). As the analogy from topographical surveying might be taken to show, triangulation requires a sense of both the temporal and the spatial (a genuine sense of the "topographic")—it requires repeated triangulations and traverses which means it requires *movement between* locations as well as *sightings across* locations.

The idea of triangulation as requiring at least two persons, interpreter and speaker, does not, then, represent some minimalist conception of the "social." Instead it describes a basic structure that is fundamental to sociality while not being exhaustive of it. The idea of triangulation takes social interaction as an essential element in the possibility of intentional content (essential, that is, for the possession of attitudes, for the capacity for action, and for the possibility of language), but the conception of the social that is at issue here is itself one that takes sociality to be fundamentally dynamic rather than static—as based in a process of interactive and ongoing coordination rather than of following or acting in accordance with some set of rules or conventions. This suggests that if we view Davidson as also giving an important role to what Gadamer terms "tradition," it is to tradition as the ongoing framework of social interaction on the basis of which meaning is possible, rather than to tradition as providing a set of prior norms or conventions (the way Davidson himself makes use of the notion of "normativity" must be understood along similar lines[44]). Whether this is seen as a point of divergence from someone like Gadamer depends very much on how we view Gadamer's own conception of tradition and the social. Yet there seems ample evidence in Gadamer's writing, particularly his dialogical conception of interpretation and his use of the notion of "play" (*Spiel*),[45] to indicate that he implicitly views tradition and the social in a way compatible with Davidson's dynamic and anticonventionalist conception. Although Davidson may well be viewed as lacking the same sensitivity to the full richness of tradition and historicality that are to be found in Gadamer and Heidegger, this does not mean that there is no room for such concepts within a Davidsonian framework—indeed, it would seem that the historicality of understanding is certainly not rejected by the Davidsonian account, even if it is, as a result of Davidson's own particular interests, somewhat underdescribed.[46]

Davidson's insistence on the way in which intentional content only arises in relation to the interaction of interpreter, speaker, and world within a particular place or location is closely tied to his denial that there can be any such thing as self-evident or intrinsic meaning or content (meaning is always indeterminate, because there is always more than one way of describing the same pattern of interactions). This has given rise, however, to a common line of objection to the Davidsonian position (one that seems to depend on reading him, against his own explicit disclaimers, as enmeshed in some form of empiricism) on the basis of which Davidson is sometimes seen as occupying a position radically opposed to that of hermeneuticists such as Gadamer and Heidegger. Thus, Stephen Mulhall claims that, according to Davidson,

The world we really perceive is radically devoid of any human significance, until we use our interpretative theorizing to organize this primitive data into units of human meaning—words, actions, gestures. Within this generally alien world, we are alienated in particular from language and from human behavior as a whole, for the significance and the humanity we find in those phenomena of our everyday life are a result of our reading our concepts into the data we directly apprehend. . . . Davidson's commitment to the notion of bare sounds and bare movements as the experiential basis from which any understanding of human speech and action must arise is strikingly analogous to empiricist sense-datum theories of knowledge.[47]

Here Mulhall appears to confuse Davidson's rejection of the idea that there are no intrinsic meanings that can provide a self-evident basis for interpretation with an alleged commitment to the idea that outside of interpretation there are only bare sounds or movements that are somehow ordered or given sense by our interpretive activity. Yet this latter idea is clearly a version of the very scheme–content distinction that Davidson famously rejects in "On the Very Idea of a Conceptual Scheme."[48] Moreover, since Davidson sees no problem in appealing to intentional concepts—concepts of belief, desire, and so forth—in his account of the structure of interpretation, so he is explicit in taking interpretation to proceed not by looking to patterns of sensory stimulation or any other surrogate form of empirical content (as is typical of the Quinean approach), but rather by looking to the worldly objects to which speakers' attitudes and actions are directed.[49] Inasmuch as our involvement with things is indeed an involvement with things as they are grasped in terms of our attitudes and actions, so we never encounter things, at least not in any relevantly "meaningful" way, other than in ways that allow them to "show up" in relation to our ongoing concerns and commitments. Consequently, just as Davidson is not committed to any narrowly "physicalist" account of the nature of human "being-in-the-world," neither is he committed to viewing our engagement with things as an engagement with the merely "present-at-hand" nor the purely "empirical" ("sense data," "patterns of sensory stimulation," or whatever).

It is not Davidson's claim, then, that we are only ever faced with bare movements or sounds—indeed, he would deny this just as Heidegger does[50]—but rather that we cannot, even in the domestic case, take meaning as given in a way that is completely determinate and unrevisable. The reason, moreover, that we cannot rely on meaning as being given in this way is to be found in the very fact that meaning is dependent on the entire complex of localized interactions between speakers, and between speakers and their surroundings—because of the way, that is, in which interpretation and understanding are always "in place."[51] Meaning is, as a consequence, necessarily indeterminate and always open to revision—which is to say only that there is always more than one correct way of interpreting (because there is always more than one way of grasping the overall pattern of interaction), not that we ever encounter things in some bare and uninterpreted form. The threefold structure of interpretation that is at the base of such indeterminacy can itself be seen as constituting an important point of convergence between the Davidsonian account of interpretation and

Gadamer's Heideggerian-derived account of the hermeneutic situation. As David Hoy writes:

For both Gadamer and Davidson . . . there would be no way to say what a speaker was talking about unless that speaker could be interpreted by a second person as talking about an object or *Sache* that they held in common. For both Davidson and Gadamer this interpretive three-way relation is the minimal structure of understanding and intelligibility.[52]

Yet clearly this threefold structure, whether in Davidson or Gadamer (or in Heidegger, since it can be seen to be present in implicit form there also), has to be understood as implying a conception of interpretation as necessarily tied to the concrete location of both the interpreter and speaker: the relatedness of this three-way relation is one that can only be worked out within the bounded openness of place.[53]

Topography, Hermeneutics, and Truth

Whether we look, then, to the structure of Davidsonian radical interpretation or to Gadamerian philosophical hermeneutics, the same topological or "topographic" structure seems to emerge. In Gadamer, of course, that structure is clearly identical with the structure of disclosedness that preoccupied Heidegger from *Being and Time* through to the later works and that is always thought, although with varying degrees of clarity, through ideas of locality and place.[54] But the Davidsonian structure itself bears more direct comparison with the Heideggerian, not merely because it calls, albeit implicitly, upon topographic or topological concepts, but because it is thereby also committed to a similar account of the structure that is at issue—rather than look to any single element as "founding" the structure of interpretation as a whole, the elements that make up that structure are themselves defined by means of their mutual interrelation. As a consequence, no single element can be viewed as independent of the overall structure—in the terms Davidson employs in "Three Varieties of Knowledge,"[55] subjectivity can be separated neither from objectivity nor from intersubjectivity (in similar fashion, the linguistic cannot be clearly separated from the nonlinguistic), and this interdependence is reflected in the structure of each of the concepts involved here. Recognition of this interdependence also leads both Heidegger and Davidson to adopt similar positions in regard to the problem of skepticism: since the very capacity for intentional content is dependent on our ongoing interaction with the things and persons around us, so the very possibility of having beliefs that could be put into question or of being capable of meaningful action in relation to things that could be called into doubt presupposes our erstwhile engagement in and grasp of the world. In short, the possibility of querying our "access" to the world itself requires that such access already be given.[56]

The possibility of our access to the world—the very possibility of disclosedness—cannot properly be put in question on either the Davidsonian or Heideggerian account. Moreover, as disclosedness is, for Heidegger, understood in close relation to the concept of truth—truth understood precisely in the sense of *aletheia*—so truth must itself be taken as an absolutely fundamental notion here, and the structure of disclosedness that is articulated in Heideggerian topology must be viewed as identical with the structure of truth. The more usual sense of truth as "correctness" (*adequatio, orthotes*) is not rejected by Heidegger.[57] Instead, as many writers have emphasized,[58] Heidegger looks to explicate the concept of truth *as correctness* through an account of the structure of truth *as disclosedness*—the latter is thus revealed, in language admittedly more appropriate to the early than the later work (but illuminating nonetheless), as the "transcendental condition" for the former.

Although this structure is variously described at different points in Heidegger's thinking, the laying out of the structure at issue here is just a matter of the delineation of that particular *topos*—that complex but unitary place or locale—that encompasses and founds the interplay between human agents and the elements of the made and natural environment that together make up the world. The "transcendental" character of this project of laying out is to be seen in the way in which the relation between truth as disclosedness and truth as correctness, although it can be understood in the terms traditionally associated with the transcendental as a relation between that which makes possible and that which is made possible,[59] is actually to be seen as given in the topological structure that obtains between what is made salient and what remains always in the background as that against which such salience emerges. On this topological reading of the transcendental, the transcendental structure is itself to be understood, in contrast to the usual focus on "transcendence," as a particular appropriation (often unrecognized as such) of the interplay of concealing and unconcealing, of withdrawal and appearance, of closing and opening that is *aletheia* and is also of the essence of *topos*.

As Davidson's similar attitude toward skepticism might itself suggest, truth is no less fundamental a concept for Davidson than it is for Heidegger. Davidson also advances a critique of traditional accounts of truth, whether as correspondence or correctness,[60] arguing that the concept of truth is only to be understood in relation to "the nature of interpersonal understanding"[61]—that is, through an understanding of the topographical structure, along the lines set out above, that is the basis for interpretation and understanding. Unlike Heidegger, Davidson does not distinguish between two distinct concepts of truth, between correctness and disclosedness or unconcealment, but he does insist both on the absolute centrality of truth—truth is, he says, "the key to how mind apprehends the world"[62]—and on the inadequacy of notions of correspondence or coherence in coming to an understanding of truth. Truth, and with it the accessibility of the world to us, is thus taken to be foundational within the Davidsonian account, just as it is in Heidegger, and it is explicated, as Heidegger also explicates it, through a similarly topological or "topographical" mode of analysis. Davidson's own treatment of the issue of truth is particularly relevant to the Heideggerian case, since it enables us to see, in a way that is perhaps obscured in Heidegger's own account, why it is indeed appropriate to talk of disclosedness in terms of the concept of truth. Before considering this aspect of the convergence between Heidegger's topology and Davidson's topography, it is worth setting out, in a little more detail, some of the salient features of the Davidsonian view of truth, since this account has often been misunderstood and misinterpreted.

Truth plays a central role in the structure of Davidsonian triangulation, just as it is also implicated in the earlier principle of charity. It is truth, rather than, for instance, reference, that is the means by which utterances connect to the world.[63] Since utterances are expressive of attitudes, so too are attitudes connected to the world through the way those attitudes stand, directly or indirectly, to truth. Belief, for instance, is a holding true, and there can be no holding true without a concept of what is true. It is also truth that plays a role in the holistic connection (between attitudes, utterances, and even behavior) that makes for the possibility of content, since it is truth that underpins relations of consistency and implication (even when these notions are understood in a somewhat informal sense).

The sense of truth that operates here, both in terms of the way attitudes and utterances individually connect to the world and in which they connect with one another, is the sense of truth in which truth belongs to individual sentences. Inasmuch as truth belongs to sentences in this way, then truth, understood as always the truth of some sentence, will always be a contingent matter (which also means that no sense can be attached to truth as a property of *propositions* taken to stand apart from sentences[64]).

Whether a sentence is true will depend on language and on the world—on what the sentence says or what it means, and whether the world is the way the sentence says it is—and these may vary as language varies and as the world varies.[65] Thus, in a passage that suggests direct comparison with one of Heidegger's famous claims concerning truth, Davidson tells us that "Nothing in the world, no object or event, would be true or false if there were not thinking creatures."[66] Truth, one might say, is embedded in the same topographical structure as are we—and just as we, and the places we inhabit, along with the places we inhabit, do not endure forever, neither is truth eternal or unchanging. Truth changes just as speakers and languages change, and just as the world changes. Yet the contingency that is evident here does not entail any loss of objectivity—truth is objective just inasmuch as the truth of a sentence is indeed dependent on nothing more than whether the world is the way the sentence says it is. That is all there can be to objectivity and all that there needs to be (although there is much that is implied here).

One might suppose that, on a Davidsonian approach, this is where the account of truth ends. There is nothing more to say about truth, and anything more would be to say too much—to attempt to account for or provide a definition of what cannot be accounted for or defined. Yet Davidson does not hold to a strictly deflationist conception of truth, and he does not think that truth is nothing more than a "disquotational device."[67] Truth is first of all a property of sentences—which means that it pertains first to language, and the relation between sentences and the world, rather than to the world as such[68]—and yet what we can say about truth as it stands in relation to individual sentences does not exhaust what can be said about truth. For truth to be a property of individual sentences—for individual sentences to be true—we also need to have some sense of the way in which truth inheres in the larger background against which individual sentences can be true (or false).

Truth, as we saw above, plays a central role in the possibility of content—not only our *access* to content through interpretation, but, since the structure of triangulation is a structure that determines content in the first-person as well as the second-person case, in the very possibility of content as such (which is why the position should be seen as *ontological*, rather than merely epistemological or methodological). But truth, as it operates in this "background" fashion, cannot be the truth of any specific sentence or body of sentences (at least not such that we could then consider the question of the truth or falsity of that sentence or of those sentences). One might put this point by saying that the very possibility of something being true in any particular case depends on many things being true more generally (although just what must be true will not be able to be given any determinate or unique specification). Truth as a property of sentences is thus dependent on truth as a property of the larger system within which sentences (along with other bearers of content) are embedded in a way that is exactly analogous to the way in which the content of any one belief or attitude is dependent on its location within a larger contentful system of beliefs and attitudes (a system of content that can never be completely elucidated or specified) or the way in which, within a Tarskian truth theory, the definition of truth for a language already depends on our prior mastery of the truth predicate as it operates within our own prior language. Although we can determine truth as it applies to individual sentences, we cannot make the same determination of truth as it always already inheres in the background against which sentences are true—a background, moreover, that does not just encompass sentences, or beliefs or attitudes, but in which language is given in a way that is inseparable from world. That is, at this background level, we cannot make sense of that background as true or false, but only as already and always given as true. Thus Davidson insists that "beliefs are by nature generally true,"[69] and that "our view of the world is, in its plainest features, largely correct."[70]

Here the Davidsonian account is itself illuminated by the Heideggerian, since we can now see the direction in which the Davidsonian account appears to move, even though it would have been difficult for Davidson himself to have made this explicit, is toward the account of truth as disclosedness or unconcealment (or better, the interplay between concealment *and* unconcealment) that we find in Heidegger. Yet at the same time, we can also see how the Davidsonian account illuminates the Heideggerian through providing a way of seeing why and how truth might indeed be implicated here (something contested, most notably, by Ernst Tugenhat,[71] and which even Heidegger himself seems to have finally come to doubt[72]).

The fact that the holistic background—what we might think of as the proper *topos* of truth—against which particular ascriptions of content and particular attributions of truth or falsity arise cannot be understood other than as "true" does not mean that there is some problematic limit to critical inquiry or that the Davidsonian position, perhaps contrary to Davidson's personal politics, implies some deep form of conservatism. Apart from anything else, the way truth inheres in the background—the way it is part of our very being-in-the-world—is not in terms of the necessary truth of any particular belief: there is an important sense in which almost any and every belief, taken singly, could be false, and there is no specificable belief or set of beliefs that can be taken to be definitive of the background of belief in which truth inheres. The way in which truth inheres in belief as such (that is, in our comportment as creatures that believe, and that also assert, speak, and act), thereby providing the context within which truth and falsity can attach to specific sentences, utterances, and claims, means that questioning and disagreement—critique if you will—must always operate at the level of those particular sentences, utterances, and claims, and at the level of the particular arguments and evidence that pertain to them. There is no sense to be attached to any form of "critique," political or otherwise, that manifests itself in some generalized attempt to cast all in doubt (skepticism is the paradigmatic example of such an attempt), or that levels the same generalized question (like the child's constant asking "why?") at any and every claim, without regard for the nature of that claim, but simply in virtue of its character *as* a claim.[73]

The point at issue here fares no better when it is rephrased in terms of the claim, identical to the argument just considered, that truth has an essentially normative dimension that the Heideggerian interpretation of truth as *aletheia* ignores. As truth operates within the normative practice in which sentences are evaluated according to their truth (in which, one might say, it is the *truth value* of sentences that is at issue), truth is always paired with falsity, but, in Davidsonian terms, the normative operation of truth is not all there is to truth, since truth always stands in the background of any such normative practice, and in this respect truth has to be understood as prior to falsity, rather than being paired with it. In similar vein, the practice of normativity cannot be based in the rules or conventions that operate within any normative practice, and yet instead presupposes a normativity that resides in a prior and ongoing engagement that can indeed be understood as "normative," and yet cannot be given any determinative specification in terms of particular instances of normative practice (and certainly not in terms of any such instances understood as codified in specific rules or conventions).[74]

Conclusion: Reading across Philosophical Divides

Significant difficulties arise in any attempt to read across the divides that characterize contemporary philosophy—difficulties evident in Davidson's and Gadamer's own largely unsuccessful attempts to engage with one another's thought. Perhaps the task of such dialogue can only be undertaken if one already stands a little outside of the positions (both personal and theoretical) of those with whose thought one looks to engage.[75] Nevertheless, so long as one does not allow oneself to be unduly distracted by the variations in style and approach that are evident in the work of Heidegger and Davidson, as well as of Davidson and Gadamer, significant points of convergence soon become evident that seem to have a particularly strong focus around the topological and topographical character of their respective projects.

While the obvious differences that exist between these approaches should not denied, our understanding of those approaches can be enriched and illuminated through being brought into juxtaposition with one another, especially when that juxtaposition is explicitly oriented toward the concept of place or *topos*. Thus, understanding the way in which the Davidsonian project, with its holistic, externalist approach to intentional content, can be brought within the frame of a Heideggerian topology enables themes that might otherwise remain hidden in Davidson, and especially the topographical character of Davidson's thought, to be brought more clearly into view, while at the same time, it opens new possibilities in the reading of the Heideggerian position as well as resolving some apparent obscurities. Heideggerian topology may thus be viewed, for instance, as instantiating a certain form of holistic externalism (albeit, as with Davidson, in a somewhat idiosyncratic form[76]), just as the Davidsonian theory of interpretation can be viewed as providing, in its own terms, an account of what appears in Heidegger as the structure of disclosedness. Viewing both thinkers from a topological perspective, one could well argue that Davidson's work offers a more important and direct line of convergence with Heidegger's thinking than does that of those analytically inclined readers of Heidegger's work (among whom Hubert Dreyfus is surely the most prominent) who would assimilate Heidegger to some form of pragmatized, behavioralized "phenomenology."

The topological-topographic perspective that emerges in the work of Heidegger and Davidson is significant for many reasons, but two in particular deserve mention here. The first concerns the way in which the move to *topos*, even though often remaining implicit, is itself tied to an explicit concern to overcome the tendency toward what Davidson refers to as the "myth of the subjective" and Heidegger also identifies, although somewhat more broadly, as "subjectivism." The move toward place thus runs counter both to the idea of meaning as residing in some private "inner" realm that stands in contrast to the public world and to the tendency toward meta-physical foundationalism that is manifest in contemporary thought in the prioritization of the human subject. In their different ways, Heidegger and Davidson can thus both be seen to espouse holistic, and perhaps even "externalist," conceptions of human being, and so also of "content" or meaning, while the antifoundationalist and antireductionist character of their approaches is clearly evident in the way each understands the struc-ture of what Heidegger refers to as *aletheia* or "unconcealment" in terms of mutually related elements in which no one element has absolute priority over any other. The second point of significance concerns the way in both Heidegger and Davidson deal with the question of truth. In a way that stands outside of the usual treatments of this concept within much con-temporary analytic and continental thought, both Heidegger and David-son give a central role to truth, even while each contests the standard understanding of that notion, and each maintains a distinction between truth as belonging to sentences and truth as something more than that which belongs to sentences alone. Although the account of truth that each advances has given rise to considerable criticism and misinterpretation, especially in Heidegger's case, those accounts not only one deserve closer consideration, but the criticisms and misinterpretations directed at them may themselves be seen in a different light when the two approaches are understood in conjunction with one another, rather than separately.

In reading Heidegger and Davidson together as topological-topographic thinkers, a mode of philosophical engagement is opened up in a way that suggests that there is a genuine *topos* of thinking at work here that is not restricted to the analytic or to the phenomenological-hermeneutic alone, but that spans the space between these two. Indeed, one might be tempted to say that the idea of philosophical topology or topography that is pre-saged and exemplified in the work of both thinkers should not be viewed (as it surely will be viewed by many) as belonging exclusively to either the "analytic" or the so-called "continental," but as standing outside of that already rather poisonous and dysfunctional dichotomy (a dichotomy that, if truth be told, is more political than genuinely philosophical). In drawing both Heidegger and Davidson into the philosophical *topos* opened up by the topological-topographic, the aim is not merely to engage in an exercise of philosophical "comparison and contrast," but also to suggest the way in which, notwithstanding contemporary philosophical parochialisms, there remains fruitful ground on which genuine thinking can take place in a way that draws on the creative and valuable insights no matter what their source. What such thinking requires, however, is a willingness to enter into the philosophical place that other thinkers open up, and to think with them, and not merely against them. Such willingness is strikingly absent, however, from much contemporary academic philosophy, which shows a remarkable reluctance to engage in any place than the one already marked out, already defined, already secured. In this respect contemporary philosophy often consists in a refusal of dialogue, a refusal of genuine thought or questioning—a refusal, indeed, to enter into the very *topos* that not only other thinkers but thinking itself opens up.

11 Heidegger in Benjamin's City

On the steep slope
of a mountain valley
a little chalet
eighteen feet by twenty

all around
meadow and pinewood . . .
—Kenneth White, "Black Forest—Heidegger at Home"

The work of Walter Benjamin is inextricably bound with the images and ideas associated with the metropolitan spaces and places that figure so prominently in his writing, and in close proximity to which his own life, from his childhood in Berlin to the last years in Paris, was lived. The work of Martin Heidegger, on the other hand, is usually taken to bring with it an almost entirely contrary set of associations—those of the rural and the provincial, of the peasant and the countryside—that can be seen as themselves deriving from Heidegger's own rootedness in the Alemannic-Swabian countryside, and in particular, his connection to the village of Messkirch in which he was born, in which he spent his childhood, and in whose graveyard he lies buried. It would seem that the distance between Benjamin and Heidegger—between Paris and Messkirch—could not be greater. But to what extent is Heidegger's apparent attachment to the provincial and the rural actually tied to the philosophical positions that he developed? Might it be the case that such details of personal attitude and preference are actually secondary to a more basic and philosophically salient set of considerations in which the difference between the metropolitan and the provincial, at least as ordinarily understood, is of much less significance than it might otherwise appear? How might Heidegger find himself in Benjamin's city, and what might be the place of the city in Heidegger's own thought? Moreover, what light might such considerations shed, in turn, on the work of Benjamin, and how might Benjamin be placed in relation to the landscape in which Heidegger locates himself?

Let us start, however, by leaving Benjamin, and the city, to one side for the moment, and looking instead to the provincialism that seems so apparent in Heidegger—a provincialism that is often taken to be most clearly expressed not only in his attachment to his home village of Messkirch, but also by the role played by another place, and a particular building in that place, namely, Todtnauberg, in the Black Forest, and the small three-room hut Heidegger built there.[1] It was to this hut that Heidegger retreated in times of personal crisis, as well as in times of intense philosophical productivity—it was there that the final draft of *Being and Time* was completed—and it was also to the hut that Heidegger invited his most important guests. The significance of the hut, and its rural location, in Heidegger's life, and so also, one might assume, in his thought, is indicated by the short essay, published in 1934 (and first given as a radio talk the same year), "Why Do I Stay in the Provinces?" There he describes the world of Todtnauberg:

On the steep slope of a wide mountain valley in the southern Black Forest, at an elevation of 1150 meters, there stands a small ski hut. The floor plan measures six meters by seven. The low-hanging roof covers three rooms: the kitchen, which is also the living room, a bedroom, and a study. Scattered at wide intervals throughout the narrow base of the valley and on the equally steep slope opposite, lie the farm houses with their large overhanging roofs. Higher up the slope the meadows and pasture lands lead to the woods with its dark fir-trees, old and towering. Over everything there stands a clear summer sky, and in its radiant expanse two hawks glide around in wide circles.[2]

The reality of this world, Heidegger tells us, has a space opened for it by the work undertaken within it, a work that "remains embedded in what happens in the region." He goes on:

This philosophical work does not take its course like the aloof studies of some eccentric. It belongs right in the midst of the peasants' work. When the young farmboy drags his heavy sled up the slope and guides it, piled high with beech logs, down the dangerous slope to his house, when the herdsman, lost in thought and slow of step, drives his cattle up the slope, when the farmer in his shed gets the countless shingles ready for his roof, my work is of the same sort. It is intimately rooted in and connected to the life of the peasants. . . . The inner relationship of my own work to the Black Forest and its people comes from a centuries-long and irreplaceable rootedness in the Alemannic-Swabian soil . . . my whole work is sustained and guided by the world of these mountains and their people.[3]

Heidegger himself draws attention to the contrast between the world of Todtnauberg and the world of the city. In particular, and in contrast with the mountain landscape of Todtnauberg, the city leaves no space for the solitariness of thought that allows things to come near to us in their simple and essential presence. The city, Heidegger tells us, allows for loneliness, but not for solitude; it fosters "a very active and very fashionable obtrusiveness" that brings with it the risk of "destructive error."[4] Given Heidegger's own tendency to employ images drawn from rural life and landscapes, the attitude and feeling articulated in this essay readily appear as giving us a true insight into the sustaining ground and essence of Heidegger's thought—so much so that we may conclude that Heidegger's thought is not merely rooted in peasant life, but actively extols it in opposition to the rise of the urban, the metropolitan, and also, of course, the modern.

Figure 11.1
Heidegger in the hut at Todtnauberg, 1968. Photograph by Digne M. Marcovicz—reproduced by kind permission of the photographer.

The solitude that Heidegger finds in the mountain landscape of Todtnau-berg has, says Heidegger, "the peculiar and original power not of isolating us but of projecting our whole existence out into the vast nearness of the presence [*Wesen*] of all things,"[5] and what dominates in his descriptions of Todtnauberg is indeed a certain clarity and lucidity in the simple being-there of the landscape, and of that which is found within it—a landscape that is not observed, but emerges in and through the active engagement in and with it. The solitude that Heidegger finds in Todtnauberg is thus as much a solitariness of the thing—a standing out into the world—as it is a solitariness experienced by Heidegger himself, and yet it is also not a solitude that is constituted through isolation, but rather the solitude that comes from the letting-be that allows things to be present as what they are, but also, there-fore, in intimate connection with that to which they belong.

If this is the solitude that Heidegger fears is lost in the city, this is perhaps partly because, as critics from Simmel to Soja have often observed, what one finds in the city is never the *thing* as it simply stands forth in its own presence, but rather a constant proliferation of things, or rather, of the appearances of things—in Simmel's words: "the rapid crowding of changing images, the sharp discontinuity in the grasp of a single glance, and the unexpectedness of onrushing impressions."[6] The experience of the city as an experience of multiple images obtained through one's own movement, as well as the movement that characterizes the urban sur-roundings through which one moves, is an essential part of the experience of the *flâneur* as he strolls through the city, taking in its sounds and espe-cially its sights—for the experience of the city in Simmel, as well as in Benjamin, is intimately tied to the visual—as a constantly changing montage in which images are juxtaposed with and overlaid by other images. Thus, as has frequently been observed, the city is itself essentially cinematic, and so Benjamin can imagine the very spatial form of the city as itself transformed into film, and the act of *flânerie* as itself achieving something like such a cinematic transformation: "Couldn't an exciting film be made from the map of Paris? From the unfolding of its various aspects in temporal succession? From the compression of a centuries-long movement of streets, boulevards, arcades, and squares into the space of half an hour? And does the *flâneur* do anything different?"[7]Although Ben-jamin's interest in the *flâneur* is an interest in a phenomenon that belongs, properly, to the nineteenth century rather than the twentieth, the *flâneur* provides both a means to uncover certain aspects of the past, as well as to analyze certain critical elements of the future—the *flâneur* thereby allows access to both the advent of modernity as well as to that which it portends.

Consequently, Benjamin's best-known and perhaps most influential essay, "The Work of Art in the Age of Mechanical Reproduction," while making no mention of the *flâneur* nor of the Parisian arcades, is nevertheless also preoccupied with the image, its multiplication and transformation, as lying at the heart of the experience of the modern.[8]

If we try to place Heidegger in this modern city of images, then it seems that we immediately find Heidegger in a position that must be counterposed to Benjamin. Indeed, Heidegger's own essay on the work of art, which was first given as a lecture the year before the appearance of Benjamin's famous essay, appears to assert the primacy of the artwork in its singularity as a work in a way that seems to be consistent with Heidegger's emphasis on the solitude of the thing in his "Provinces" talk—harking back to a premodern paradigm, that of the Greeks, focusing on a work, namely the temple, as it stands within a natural landscape, emphasizing the character of the work as gathering world and earth to it—and that also stands against what Benjamin declares to be the destruction of the singularity and solitude of the work that occurs as a result of its reproducibility, and the proliferation of its image. It is hard to imagine Heidegger in the role of *flâneur*, but it is perhaps equally strange to imagine him in the cinema, and the reason is surely the same in both cases: neither *flânerie* nor cinema allows for the kind of "dwelling" that is involved in letting things stand forth in the singular presence (a dwelling that appears in contrast to Benjamin's occasional use of that notion), instead they move us constantly onward, away from the thing, into a constantly fleeting set of images and impressions. In terms of the language of Heidegger's *Being and Time*, whether we walk the streets with the *flâneur* or sit before the flickering images of the cinema, we are in each case immersed in the world of the anyone, of the anonymous *das Man*—dispersed, displaced, and distracted—literally, in the case of the *flâneur*, in the world of the crowd.

Inasmuch as the city is seen as essentially tied to such anonymous dispersal, to such movement and proliferation, and inasmuch as such dispersal and proliferation is seen, in Heidegger, as tied to the "forgetfulness" of being, the "forgetfulness" of the presence of things, that is characteristic of modernity, then the city must be the essential locale for such forgetfulness—with Benjamin, perhaps, as one of its most conscientious attendants. Yet one should be cautious about one's conclusions here. It would, I suggest, be grossly mistaken to treat Benjamin as exemplifying the kind of "forgetting" that Heidegger may be said to have in mind here—although it is true that Benjamin's response to, as well as his understanding of, what such forgetting may consist in is rather different from that which is found in

Heidegger. The concern with the presence, the nearness, of things can also be discerned in Benjamin, but it is pursued precisely through the preoccupation with the image, its multiplication, and its condensation, even its remnants as "trace"—"The trace is appearance of a nearness, however far removed the thing that left it behind may be. . . . In the trace, we gain possession of the thing."[9] In Benjamin, the problem of what Heidegger refers to as the "nearness of the presence of things" is not absent, nor is it overlooked; rather, it is explored through the specifically urban spaces and places that do indeed appear to be so characteristic of modernity. Here the presence of things is no less possible, and no less significant, than in the rural landscape to which Heidegger seems to refer us, even though the way in which that presence is formed may appear somewhat differently.

If the focus in Benjamin's work is said to be on the image, then the image can be understood either in terms of a mode of presence of the thing or its absence. Understood as the mode by which the thing is present, then the image, which is never a single image but always multiple, can be said to allow a presencing of the very multiplicity that is already given in the thing. It is when we focus on the image as the surrogate for the thing, as its replacement, and at the same time treat the image as unitary rather than multiple in itself, that the image turns out to lead away from the thing, or, at least, solidifies the thing into a single presentation in which the thing, as always itself multiple, is effectively lost. What the proliferation of the image can enable—whether that proliferation arises through the movement of the city street or of the cinematic projection—is a realization of the manner in which the thing always supports a multitude of images, without the necessary loss of the thing itself. Indeed, it is through such proliferation that the thing as thing is itself made available. In this way, the image may lead us back to the thing in a way in which the mere concentration of attention on the thing in its apparent solitude can also be seen to have the potential to lead us away from the thing through encouraging an identification of the thing simply with the singular appearance that it presents in any one moment of its presence. Heidegger can be seen to argue against the forgetfulness of the thing, whether that forgetfulness arises through the treatment of the thing as merely identical with its presence in the present, and so as present in a single appearance, as well as to argue against the loss of the thing that might be thought to occur through the proliferation of the image. Yet that to which Heidegger seems not to attend, and which Benjamin may perhaps bring to our attention, is the continuing presence of the thing in the midst of the multiplicity of its images, and the potential in such proliferation, therefore, for a reawakening of what the thing itself may be that always exceeds that which is given in the merely present or in the single image.

The way the presence of the thing appears in Benjamin is not only through the proliferation of the image in relation to the thing, but also through the possibility of the recapturing of the thing through its traces. Thus the solidification of memories within the complex and constantly overwritten texture of the city allows for the ever-present possibility of things appearing and reappearing in ways that draw attention to their character as things, precisely through the way in which they remain, even if only as traces or memories. The possibility of things persisting in this way, in spite of the loss that may occur over time, is indicative both of the way the city may serve to preserve things in their traces or remnants (as the city constantly overwrites itself, it also retains something of that which is written over), and also the character of the city as itself built up through the retaining of things in their remnants and traces. Benjamin's project, then, is one that is directed at the constant excavation of such traces, and the recuperation of the lives of things in the life of the city—and in doing so, illuminating the complex character of the thing, and of the spaces and places in which, in a sense that is not entirely disconnected from Heidegger, it does indeed dwell.

The path back to the thing that leads through the city street or the Parisian arcade or, alternatively, by way of the flickering interiority of the cinema, is a path that allows the thing to be seen in the way it is embedded, almost archaeologically, within a dense deposit of things, paths, images. Even in its solitude, then, the thing, like the thinker, never stands alone. One way of grasping the embeddedness of the thing in its world, which may perhaps be clearer to grasp within the densely packed space of the city than in the openness of the countryside, is through deconstructing the separation between the spaces of the interior and of the exterior—not merely between the spaces within which the thing may be located as opposed to the spaces that lie without, but also the space that might be thought to lie interior to the thing as opposed to its own externality. Moreover, this spatial deconstruction must apply both to the thing and to the one who finds herself already standing in a relation to that thing. While the *flâneur* may stand somewhat outside and apart from that which he observes, what he observes is nevertheless also part of his own mental and material mode of being. The attraction of *flânerie* is thus the attraction to be found in the exploration of a dream work in which one caught up even as one already recognizes it as a dream world. In Heidegger's *Being and Time*, the way in which the world emerges for a being that has a sense of its own "there" is through its movement in and through a multiply connected network of things, places, and regions, bound together in the temporality of care, but from which that mode of being can never disentangle itself. In both Heidegger and Benjamin, though in very different ways, the spatial deconstruction of the dichotomy of interior and exterior (which is not to say its dissolution) is integral to allowing the thing and the self to appear in their presence as singular, and yet also as essentially connected within the mutuality and multiplicity of the world.

The idea of the thing that emerges here, and that is tied always to multiplicity in spite of Heidegger's sometime preference for a language of solitariness and singularity, is actually an idea that is essentially bound to a certain conception of the public realm that is exemplified in, though not restricted to, the specific form of the built city. The multiplicity of the thing, and the way in which the thing is present through its multiple character, is possible only through the multiple character of its relatedness to the human. The deconstruction of the space of interiority and exteriority is not only, in this regard, a deconstruction of a certain spatial separation in respect of the thing, nor even of the individual self in relation to the thing, but also of the self in relation to others. The theme of transparency that one finds so prominent in Benjamin (the transparency that he takes to be an essential characteristic of modernity) is, once again, not a transparency that is to be understood in terms of a loss of self, other, or of thing, but rather in terms of the essentially embeddedness of things, their nesting, in relation to other things, of their mutual incorporation and implication. Moreover, the multiplicity of the thing is directly tied to the multiplicity of the public realm, which is itself made possible through its unification in the thing as singular. This is, of course, a theme that is particularly evident in the work of Hannah Arendt,[10] but it is a theme that one can perhaps view Arendt as taking from Heidegger, and that is also present, though in much less clear-cut fashion, in Benjamin. The space of the city, understood as the concrete space of human being, is a space in which we are constantly engaged in a process of negotiation of self and other, through our relatedness to one another in our corporeality, including the corporeality of speech, and as that is enabled through our mutual engagement with the multiply present thing. Thus Heidegger can speak of the city, understood in terms of the Greek "polis," as

the πολος the pole, around which everything appearing to the Greeks as a being turns in a peculiar way. The pole is the place around which all beings turn and precisely in such a way that in the domain of this place beings show their turning and their condition. . . . The πολις is the essence of the place [Ort], or, as we say, it is the settlement [*Ort-schatf*] of the historical dwelling of Greek humanity. . . . Between πολις and being there is a primordial relation.[11]

Here Heidegger's emphasis is on the *polis* as that place in which human being establishes the "there" of its own being, which is always a "there" belonging to the many rather than the one—a "there" that must be always multiple and never single in any simple fashion—and so also as the place in which being, that is, the nearness of the presence of things, also comes to light.

The fact that this "nearness of presence" always occurs in a place, albeit a place that opens into and out of multiplicity, means, however, that such presence always occurs with respect to a certain sort of singularity, even if it is not that of a simple singleness. Moreover, the appearing of things in this place, and the appearing of self, both in terms of an experience of personalized interiority and of public exteriority, is always both an experience of being drawn into and belonging to this place, as well as of being able to stand apart from it. This dynamic of approach and withdrawal, of belonging and alienation, is evident, to some extent, in the experience of the *flâneur*, but it is also what underpins the experience of uncanniness that is such a central element in both Heidegger and Benjamin. Heidegger's own language of the "homely," as well as of the domestic, and the origin, is always a language that sees these as essentially unhomely, as strange and estranging—in Heidegger, then, it is crucial to see the way in which the uncanny emerges even in the midst of that which is most familiar—even in the *Heimat* of Todtnauberg or Messkirch.

The language of *Heimat*, albeit an uncanny *Heimat*,[12] need not be construed as applying only to the world presented to us in Heidegger's images of the rural and the provincial. For Benjamin, the streets of Paris and Berlin also appear as a *Heimat* of sorts, incongruous thought that language might be. Moreover, Benjamin too has a work-world—a version, perhaps, of the Heideggerian hut—that is his own, and in which his work is rooted. One might be tempted to take that work-world to be the city as such, but, as Arendt seems to suggest, the Benjaminian counterpart to the Heideggerian hut is actually the bookroom or library that is itself to be found within the landscape of the city.[13] One might, of course, treat the street as such a library, a library or archive of images, and similarly the space of words that is language can be thought to constitute a library of sorts, and the way both of these may function as part of Benjamin's world should not be overlooked; but the library that is the heart of Benjamin's work-world is surely the actual library, those very book-filled rooms, in which Benjamin wrote and read, in which his work was undertaken, and from which his work emerged.

Figure 11.2
Walter Benjamin in the Bibliothèque Nationale, Paris, Spring, 1937. Photograph by
Gisèle Freud. Reprinted by permission of Estate Gisèle Freund/IMEC Images.

All thinking has a certain solitariness about it, and for Benjamin it is
the library that constitutes the "solitary" space in which thinking becomes
possible—not just the private space of Benjamin's own collection of books
(his single most valued possession), but also public spaces such as the
Bibliothèque Nationale in Paris in which *The Arcades Project* was undertaken. Contrary to Heidegger, thought is possible in the city—although it
is also true that the spaces that the city opens up for thinking may well
impress themselves on the character of that thinking in significant, though
perhaps not always obvious or expected ways.[14] Benjamin himself seems
to have had some sense of the place of his own thinking within the space
of the library, and that stands in contrast to Heidegger's evocation of his
own embeddedness in the mountain landscape of Todtnauberg. As Benjamin writes of *The Arcades Project* and its relation to the Bibliothèque
Nationale:

These notes devoted to the Paris Arcades were begun under an open sky of cloudless
blue that arched above the foliage; and yet—owing to the millions of leaves that
were visited by the breeze of diligence, the stertorous breath of the researcher, the
storm of youthful zeal, and the idle wind of curiosity—they've been covered with
the dust of centuries. For the painted sky of summer that looks down from the

arcades in the reading room of the Bibliothèque Nationale in Paris has spread out over them its dreamy, unlit ceiling.[15]

W. G. Sebald, a writer who has much in common with Benjamin, has one of his characters, Austerlitz, speak eloquently of the same strange place in the rue Richilieu:

In the week I went daily to the Bibliothèque Nationale . . . and usually remained in my place there until evening, in silent solidarity with the many others immersed in their intellectual labours, losing myself in the small print of the footnotes to the works I was reading, in the books I found mentioned in those notes, then in the footnotes to those books in their own turn, and so escaping from factual, scholarly accounts to the strangest of details, in a kind of continual regression expressed in the form of my own marginal remarks and glosses, which increasingly diverged into the most varied and impenetrable of ramifications . . . my mind often dwelt on the question of whether there in the reading-room of the library, which was full of a quiet humming, rustling and clearing of throats, I was on the Islands of the Blest or, on the contrary, in a penal colony.[16]

What matters is perhaps less the character of the particular places in which each thinker—Benjamin and Heidegger, Arendt or even Sebald—locates thinking as the way in which these thinkers see thinking as indeed having a location that is proper to it, that supports, sustains, and also enables it. Heidegger and Benjamin each sees his own thinking as having an essential placedness, but it is the very placedness of thinking that is really at issue— it is therefore not whether thought is placed in relation to the urban or the rural, the street or the forest path, the French metropolitan or the German provincial that should first and foremost command our attention. Although the placedness of thinking that emerges in both thinkers is a function of their own placedness, it is also a reflection of their common concern with the character of place and its philosophical centrality. In both we find a similar topological orientation—an orientation turned toward the *topos* of thinking that is also thereby turned toward *topos* as such.

12   The Working of Art

What is the relation between the "objectivity" of an artwork, that is, its material being *as an object*, and its nature *as an artwork*?[1] The relation is surely not an irrelevant or contingent one, and yet its nature is not at all self-evident. Indeed, in the case of some artworks, namely those that fall within the category of certain forms of so-called conceptual art, it might seem as if the material objectivity of the work (where "objectivity" is taken to refer to what we might also call, a little awkwardly in English, the "thingness" of the work) is entirely incidental to the work as such—as if the artwork consists entirely in a certain idea, or perhaps nothing other than a certain shape or form. Yet even purely conceptual works still have to work through some medium or mode of presentation, and so through something that is materially given,[2] and the question then returns: what is the relation between that medium or mode of presentation—which now becomes another way of understanding the work in its material objectivity (and so also, one might say, in its singular *placedness*[3])—and the work itself?

One might be tempted to say that the relation in question here, at least when understood as indeed a relation between the medium and the work, is, as the use of the term "medium" implies, just that—the material objectivity of the artwork is the medium for the work, which is to say that it is that through which the artwork works. As it happens, although too strong a distinction between the artwork and its "medium" or "mode of presentation" may itself mislead, the latter part of this answer—that the relation between the artwork and the medium is a relation of "working through"—while it may appear superficial, does indeed point in an important and fruitful direction. Yet it is not the direction taken by most answers to the question at issue. For the most part, rather than leading to an investigation of *the way in which the artwork works*, the question about the relation between the objectivity of the work and the work itself has often been treated as a question about *the kind of thing an artwork is.*

Many writers have argued, at least in the case of those works that depend on some form of "text" (a musical composition, a piece of choreography, a poem or a novel) that requires a performance or "reading" for its realization,[4] that the work cannot be identical with its material or objective instantiations, since any one of those instantiations of the work can be destroyed without the work ceasing to exist, while the existence of a different reading or performance of the work need not imply the existence of a different work. Thus, were my copy of Proust's *A la recherche du temps perdu* to be destroyed, the work itself would remain unaffected, while if I listen now to Vaughn Williams's *The Lark Ascending*, I am not hearing a different work, regardless of whether the performance is live or recorded, from that to which someone else may be listening in Melbourne or San Francisco. Moreover, some writers have suggested that the same is true even of artworks such as paintings. Peter Strawson writes, in a famous passage from *Individuals*, that "it is only because of the empirical deficiencies of reproductive techniques that we identify these [particular objects] with the works of art. Were it not for these deficiencies, the original of a painting would have only the interest which belongs to the original manuscript of a poem."[5] Similarly, some writers have emphasized the imaginative or expressive character of artworks. The work, therefore, cannot be the same as its objective or material realization alone, since the imaginative or expressive quality of the work is not the same as any merely objective or material quality. On such an account, artworks are properly imaginative or ideal (though not in the way claimed by those conceptual artists who identify the work with its idea), rather than objective or material entities.[6]

These latter accounts provide us with different ontologies of artworks, but they do so in a particular way, namely, by looking to specify the ontological class or category to which the artwork belongs—which is to say, as I indicated above, by determining the kind of thing with which the artwork can be identified. While such approaches provide one way of thematizing the question concerning the nature of artworks, they also tend toward an understanding of that question as one that concerns the conditions of *identity* for artworks and their *individuation*. But this is certainly not the only question that can be asked concerning the ontology of artworks, and perhaps it is not even the right question to ask when it is the nature of the artwork *as an artwork* that is at issue. Whether an artwork is or is not a certain kind of thing need not have any relevance to the question as to how the kind of thing that is the artwork works as art.

In addition to asking after the generic mode of existence of the artwork, then, we may also ask after the specific manner in which it exists as art; in so doing we focus, one might say, not on *what* an artwork is so much as on *the way that* it is. Such a focus directs attention to the character of the artwork as precisely *a work*, and so to its dynamic rather than static character. To focus on the work-character of the artwork is already to move away from the ontological question as a categorical question to one that prioritizes activity and process. In relation to the idea of objectivity, *this means understanding the objectivity of the work* (though this is to announce the idea in very preliminary fashion) as that *in and through which the artwork articulates itself as a work*. As Andrew Benjamin puts it: "While a work may be art, what is of central importance is the *way* that it is art. The move to activity means that priority is given to a conception of the object as articulated within a process."[7] Priority is given, in other words, to the artwork as a work.

This way of refiguring the ontological question not only has affinities with Benjamin's own approach to the artwork as articulated in Benjamin's detailed engagements with specific works, but it is also close to that suggested by Jeffrey Maitland as part of an explicit argument for rethinking the ontology of the artwork.[8] Rejecting the idea that the question concerning the nature of the artwork can adequately be addressed by focusing on the question of the kind of thing the artwork is (and rejecting, more specifically, the idea that the artwork can be understood as a type or token of a type—the view associated with, for instance, Strawson, and also Richard Wollheim, among others), Maitland argues for a focus on the way the artwork functions or works as an artwork. Yet whereas I have argued for retaining a focus on the objectivity of the artwork, Maitland argues that the ontological question must be reconfigured "in a way that will not prejudice us into thinking that the work of art is some sort of an *object*. Indeed, as long as we persist in viewing art as an object, we will fail to understand the nature of art."[9] In fact, it is precisely to preempt too ready an assumption that the question concerning the material objectivity of the artwork is indeed a matter of the kind of object that it is that I have so far talked of "objectivity" rather than, for instance, "objecthood." As Maitland would certainly agree, the material objectivity of the artwork is at issue here. The point should not be to disregard such objectivity, but to understand it anew. Thus, rather than abandon the notion of the artwork in its material objectivity, my aim is to rethink that in which such objectivity consists. One way of doing this is precisely through emphasizing the character of the artwork *as a work*, something Maitland also does, and to emphasize, in a way that Maitland does not (though I would argue it is nevertheless present in his account), the way in which the work-character of the artwork does indeed operate only in and through the objectivity of the work.

The question of the relation between the artwork and its material objectivity is not a question about the relation between the artwork and the ontological kind to which it may belong, but rather is a question about how artworks work, and the role of their material objectivity in that working. Undoubtedly, any attempt to address this question must attend to the actual working of artworks, and so also to our engagement with them. This requires attending not only to our own experience of individual artworks, but also to the wider critical and interpretative reception of those works. Indeed, given the enormous diversity of artistic practice across not only different creative domains, modes, and genres, but also different media, styles, and methods of approach, it would seem foolish to suppose that one could provide a single account of the way artworks function as artworks that would address the character of their functioning in any detailed way. To this extent, an emphasis on the process or work character of the artwork already predisposes one toward a critical and interpretive practice in relation to art that is focused on individual works, rather than on artworks in general, and that sees the functioning of artworks as exhibited through the functioning of those individual works and our engagement with them—a point that is particularly well exemplified in Benjamin.[10]

Taken to its extreme, however, such a line of reasoning might be thought to amount to a claim that the process- or work-oriented character of the artwork means that there can be no real ontology of artworks as such—no general account of what an artwork is. Any philosophical encounter with art can only take the form of an engagement with particular works and never with the question of the artwork as such. Yet the claim that artworks can only be adequately understood as art through attending to their character as works, though it may be supported by reference to individual artworks while it also provides a way to ground a certain mode of engagement with individual works, cannot itself be substantiated without some more general level of argument. Moreover, there are also likely to be certain broader implications of such an approach that deserve recognition and elaboration inasmuch as they may direct or constrain our approach to individual works in specific ways. Recognizing the diversity of artistic practice, and the importance of attending to the actuality of that practice as evident in and through individual works, does not, then, invalidate any more general ontology of the artwork, and does in fact already presuppose such an ontology. Indeed, inasmuch as one may view the approach adopted here as an application of the phenomenological injunction to return "to the things themselves" to the particular case of the artwork (and, in this respect, the approach itself constitutes the application of a certain phenomenological mode of understanding to the artwork as such), then the fact that the focus on the artwork as a work does not imply the eschewal of any broader ontological commitment can be seen as reflecting something that is more generally true of phenomenology as such—the phenomenological approach is not intrinsically opposed to ontology, but should rather be seen as a particular mode of ontological inquiry. The particular phenomenological approach adopted here is one that is intended to allow the phenomenon of the artwork itself to come forth, thereby allowing the artwork to exhibit its own phenomenology—one that could be said also to underpin the more specific phenomenology that may be instantiated in any particular artwork. It is also, I might add, a mode of phenomenology that I would characterize as actually a form of topology, since it is a mode of attending to things that is also an attending to their proper *topos*.

Allowing that an ontological approach is not ruled out by the focus on the artwork as work, the initial question with which I began can be put once more: What is the relation between the artwork and its material objectivity? The immediate inspiration for Maitland's focus on the artwork in its character as a work is Heidegger's "The Origin of the Work of Art." There Heidegger begins with the question about the nature of art in a way that already brings to the fore the character of the artwork *as a work*, and yet also attends to the character of the artwork *as a thing*. Heidegger's claim is that the being of the artwork as a thing, its being in terms of what I have here called its "objectivity,"[11] derives from its character as a work: "The thingly in the work should not be denied out of existence; rather given that it belongs already to the work-being of the work, it must be thought out of that work-being. If this is so, then the path to the determination of the thingly reality of the work runs not from thing to work but from work to thing."[12] Heidegger's point here is that we cannot understand the artwork through first trying to analyze what it is on the basis purely of its material "objectivity."[13] It is only when we comprehend the artwork's character as a work that we can understand how its material objectivity stands in relation to its character as an artwork.

Figure 12.1
J. R. Cozens, *The Two Great Temples at Paestum*, circa. 1783. Watercolor, Victoria and Albert Museum, London.

Heidegger's account of the artwork is centrally focused on the classical Greek temple—usually taken to be the second temple of Hera, originally thought to be of Poseidon, at Paestum, itself the subject of a number of works by artists, notably Piranesi and J. R. Cozens.[14] His account emphasizes the way in which the artwork stands in a particular place and in specific relation to that which is configured around it. Thus Heidegger begins his description of the artwork that is the temple by stating that "A building, a Greek temple, portrays nothing. It simply stands there in the middle of the rocky fissured valley"; and in what follows, the character of the temple as "standing there" ("Er steht einfach da," "Dastehend ruht das Bauwerk," "Das temple gibt in seinem Dastehend") is repeated again and again.[15] What stands there is the artwork in its material objectivity, and in its standing-there (we may say its "being-there") the objectivity of the work establishes itself in relation to that which also takes a stand around and in relation to it. The temple-work is not the instantiation of something ideal, nor is it a type or a token of a type—it is a singular thing that stands in its singular locatedness. Heidegger claims that the artwork that is the temple "opens up a world," and it does so through freeing up a "space" in which "all things gain their lingering and hastening, their distance and proximity, their breadth and their limits."[16]

Two elements play a role in this "spacing" or "opening up": earth and world. In their most basic form (the terms have several dimensions[17]), "world" refers to that which the artwork opens up as the realm of related-ness in which things appear, and "earth" refers to the material objectivity of the artwork into which the work is set—what we might think of as its very "standing-there."[18] As world is essentially disclosure, so too is earth (as might be indicated by the impenetrability associated with the material and the particular) essentially concealing. Heidegger understands the way the artwork works as consisting in the opposition between these two elements:

World and earth are essentially different and yet never separated from one another. World is grounded on earth, and earth rises up through world. But the relation between world and earth never atrophies into the empty unity of opposites uncon-cerned with one another. In its resting upon earth the world strives to surmount it. As the self-opening it will tolerate nothing closed. As the sheltering and concealing, however, earth tends always to draw the world into itself and to keep it there.[19]

Although Heidegger describes the opposition between world and earth as "strife" (*Streit*),[20] he also emphasizes that it is not discordant or destructive, but rather an opposition in which the two elements come into their own.

It is in and through the artwork that world and earth are brought into productive opposition. Moreover, the opposition between world and earth is an opposition in which the material "objectivity" of the artwork plays a central role. The opposition in question is indeed one that occurs, in part, between the material objectivity of the work, and that which is opened up in relation to that material objectivity, which includes the material objectivity of the work itself (in the same way, earth appears as earth in the opening up of world), but which also includes its character as art. In a brief discussion of his own focus on the work character of art, Andrew Benjamin writes:

The term "work" opens up in two inter-related directions. On the one hand it announces the presence of the object—the object of interpretation or the object of criticism. The object is the work. Equally, however, there is the work's activity. Its self-effectuation as an object. "Work" both as a named presence and as a conceptual motif dominates Heidegger's approach to art . . . work has an active . . . disclosing . . . role. . . . The limit of Heidegger's approach, however, is that disclosure always opens more than the work. In so doing the work has to open up beyond itself. As such the actual materiality of the work comes to be effaced in terms of what it shows.[21]

There are two points I would take from Benjamin's comments here. The first, and perhaps most important, is the distinction he makes between the work as referring to the presence of the object (its material objectivity) and to the work's activity—which Benjamin terms its "'self-effectuation' as an object." We might think of this as a distinction between the *being* of the work "as object" and its *coming-to-be* "as object." The distinction is one that Benjamin explicitly takes as moving toward an essential indeterminacy that belongs to the artwork—although the artwork is a material object, its materiality cannot be assumed, but is instead placed in question though the working of the work as art—its working is its appearing or coming-to-be, and this is never complete, never finished. The second point concerns Benjamin's claim that Heidegger's account leads toward the self-effacement of the objectivity of the artwork (this is specifically inasmuch as the artwork is understood as always opening itself up in a way that goes beyond the work itself—in the terms echoed by Maitland, the artwork opens up a world, and that world is more than just the artwork).

These two points are connected, since the tendency toward the self-effacement of the objectivity of the work is itself connected with the character of the work as objective and as active or disclosive. What is suggested here is, in fact, a tension or opposition within the character of the work that is identical to that which appears, at least in part, in Heidegger's emphasis on the strife that the artwork sets up between world and earth. But in that case, we ought to view the tendency toward the effacement of the objectivity of the work as something that is not peculiar to Heidegger's account (although there may still be elements in that account that are idiosyncratic to it), but rather part of the way in which the artwork itself works. Indeed, one may argue that such self-effacement is possible because of the essential indeterminacy that belongs to the artwork and that arises out of its character as both being and coming-to-be. If the artwork is disclosive, then independently of whether it discloses anything beyond itself, what it must also disclose is its own twofold character as both object and work. This is certainly true of the artwork in Heidegger's account, in which the material objectivity of the artwork, its character as earth, is itself disclosed in the opening up of world. Indeed, the very resistance of earth itself to such opening up (the tendency of earth to concealment) is only evident in that disclosedness. Yet the opening up of world, since it also involves a certain transcendence of the material objectivity of the work through which such opening up is realized, also tends inevitably toward an effacing of that objectivity. Thus, the disclosedness that occurs in the artwork tends to be understood as moving one away from the material objectivity of the work, and so also away from the work in its disclosive role. However much some such effacement of objectivity may occur in Heidegger, the latter shift seems most evident in the common tendency to view artworks as actually constituted by some meaning, content, or idea that the artwork is intended to disclose, embody, or express.

The key idea in Heidegger's account of the nature of the artwork, and in Benjamin's, regardless of the difference that may also obtain, is the idea that the artwork contains or gives rise to a certain tension between the objectivity of the work and its active or disclosive character. But how does this tension arise? It seems, in fact, that we should distinguish between two moments in the disclosedness that belongs to world and that is opened up through earth. The setting of the artwork in its locatedness, its standing forth in its material objectivity, already places the artwork in relation to a context, already brings it into a certain minimal relatedness with that which surrounds it (and that relatedness may, of course, change as the manner of the setting of the artwork into place may change[22]). Yet while the artwork already stands in relation to that context, it also retains its own material objectivity in a way that, in various respects, conflicts with that context. The temple thus does not simply lose itself in the rocky plain in which it is set, but stands out on the plain, already stands in a certain way that is counter to it.[23] We might say that the strife between world and earth thus already occurs in the incipient emergence of the artwork as art, at the very point at which it is first set into and so stands out against its world. It is not simply the tension between the objectivity of the artwork and its disclosive character as a work that is operative in the artwork, but a tension within the objectivity of the work itself. The objectivity of the work both closes off, that is, remains resistant to any disclosure, but it also opens up. The latter occurs through the very way in which the artwork, in its objectivity, places itself within a setting, so that both its own objectivity and the setting of that objectivity become evident, and so that the work in its setting are together opened up as a new space of possibilities. It is this new space of possibilities, open, yet also constrained, that then opens out into what Heidegger calls "world." In its openness and its concomitant constraint, the establishing of that space of possibilities is also the establishing of a certain *topos*—a place.

On this account, it is in and through the material objectivity of the artwork that the disclosedness of the artwork occurs. Since this disclosedness, whatever else it might be, is itself a disclosedness *of the artwork*, so it is also a form of self-disclosure. Moreover, inasmuch as the self-disclosure of the artwork works through the way in which the artwork, like the metaphor, resists and at the same invokes its own setting, so the self-disclosure of the artwork is both a disclosure of the work in its material objectivity and yet also a disclosure that goes beyond that material objectivity. In summary, we may say that the manner in which the artwork works is through the self-disclosedness of the material objectivity of the work, a self-disclosedness in which that material objectivity constantly transcends itself. This self-transcendence does not mean that the artwork transcends itself in the direction of something other than itself; instead it transcends itself in the direction of the possibilities that the artwork itself enables and that belong to it.

Since the disclosedness that is essential to the artwork is only possible in and through the material objectivity of the work, so in any engagement with the work all that there is to be attended to is given in the objectivity of the work as such. For this reason, one might say that to engage with an artwork as an artwork is always to engage phenomenologically and also topologically—it is to allow oneself to be drawn into the working of the work as it works in and through the work's objective character, and so in and through a particular *topos*—similarly, every artwork can also be said to constitute a form of phenomenology *and* a form of topology in its very working as an artwork and so as a working of *topos*. Yet as we have already seen, what counts as that in which the objectivity of the work consists is itself indeterminate. This means that the phenomenological process of self-disclosure that occurs in the artwork can never be conceived as operating at any one level or in terms of just one set of elements. Indeed, the material objectivity of the work, that in and by means of which it first and most immediately presents itself, is never just a matter of any one mode of presentation or, indeed, any one medium. The painting presents itself as paint on canvas, as an array of light and surface, *as a certain history*. Indeed, it is important to note that the material objectivity of the work may indeed be construed, so long as it is not separated from the other modes of its presentation, as including the way in which the artwork already presents itself within a tradition, a history, a culture. Robert Rauschenberg claims that "All material has history. All material has its own history built into it,"[24] and even material may present itself in terms of its history. This occurs most obviously in the case of works that operate through concrete linguistic forms, especially poetry and metaphor, since the very appearance of certain sounds as having a particular linguistic meaning, to say nothing of their appearing as words, is already for those sounds to embody a historicality, a conventionality, and an intentionality.[25]

The focus on the material objectivity of an artwork does not mean, then, that the character of the work as something *made*, and so as standing within a human frame of significance, is rendered irrelevant. But the human significance of the work, its significance as an artwork, has to be grounded in the material objectivity of the work—there can be no appeal to anything that is extraneous to that objectivity. The historicality, conventionality, *and* intentionality of the work can only be given in the work's material objectivity—in what appears in the artwork. This automatically rules out certain approaches to artworks as constituting real engagements with those works in their character as works. For instance, I would argue that certain so-called metaphorical readings of artworks, in which the viewer looks to find in the artwork a metaphor for an aspect of the viewer's life or experience, often import into the work something that may not properly belong to it. Our personal reactions to works are not always to be construed as part of the work itself, and there must always be a question as to whether some reaction is a function of the artwork, or is rather a matter of our own construction of the work in a particular and perhaps idiosyncratic way that is only incidentally connected with the work as such. This applies no less to the artist than to the viewer in the sense that the intentions of the artist are relevant to the artwork just inasmuch as they are expressed in and evident through the artwork itself. What an artist may tell us about the work apart from the work—for instance, the artist's own *post facto* explanations of the work—has no privileged status in determining the character of the work. Once the work has been set into its own space, it is the work itself that is authoritative, in its objectivity, and nothing else. Since the artwork works only through its objectivity, so the artwork exhibits an autonomy that resides in its objectivity.

The autonomy of the artwork is nicely demonstrated in relation to one of Rauschenberg's works. In 1955, Rauschenberg took a quilt, a pillow, and part of a sheet, and, fixing them to a stretcher, proceeded to apply paint of various colors to the cloth surfaces. The resulting work, entitled *Bed*, has been described by Rauschenberg as "one of the friendliest pictures I've ever painted. My fear has always been that someone would want to crawl into it."[26] Most viewers of the work saw it very differently, however, with the almost universal tendency being to see it as a bed in which some horrible crime had been committed—the bed was thus taken as an image of violence and murder. Does Rauschenberg's rejection of the violent reading of *Bed* count against that reading? Only to the extent that it can be grounded in the objectivity of the work itself, and not merely because the rejection is Rauschenberg's.[27] Significantly, the point at issue here is exactly analogous to one found in Donald Davidson's work concerning a more general autonomy of linguistic meaning. Although the meaning of an utterance is dependent, according to Davidson, on the speaker's intentions in the act of utterance, speakers have no authority over the meanings of their utterances beyond that original act of saying. Meaning is given in what is said, in the words as uttered in a specific situation, not in some additional act of meaning or intending.[28] This does not make the intention of the speaker irrelevant to meaning, but it does mean that we have to be clear as to exactly what intention is relevant—it can only be the intention of the speaker as expressed in the utterance itself. Similarly, although the intention of the artist in the work is a key consideration in the interpretation of the artwork, it can be construed as determinative only as it is expressed in the artwork itself. There is thus no special significance that can be accorded to an artist's reading of their own work as that is given independently of the work.[29]

This point also has relevance to the dispute over Heidegger's reading, in "The Origin of the Work of Art," of one of Van Gogh's still-life paintings of a pair of shoes (since Van Gogh painted several works that appear to fit the description Heidegger offers, it is unclear which painting Heidegger had in mind—or whether he had a specific picture in mind at all).[30] Meyer Schapiro claimed that Heidegger simply got the painting wrong since he treated the shoes depicted as belonging to a peasant woman whereas the shoes actually belonged to Van Gogh himself.[31] Part of the problem in adjudicating in this dispute is that it is not at all obvious that the identity of the actual shoes that figured as the models is relevant to the reading of the work. One may argue that the identity of the shoes forms part of the context in which the artwork sits, but this is by no means self-evident. In fact, one might say that the essential point that is in dispute between Schapiro and Heidegger is exactly how the objectivity of the Van Gogh painting should be construed. What is in question is not, contrary to appearances, the actual history of the objects depicted (as if, *contra* Schapiro, the matter could be resolved by methods of historical inquiry), but rather the history of the artwork in which those objects figure. Inasmuch as Schapiro views the matter as indeed a matter of the history of the depicted objects, one might argue that Schapiro fails to address the artwork itself (in which case one might argue that the dispute actually serves not to discredit Heidegger, but to demonstrate the limitations in Schapiro's own "empiricist" approach to art history). On the other hand, inasmuch as one may take the dispute to originate in the irresolvable indeterminacy that attaches to the objectivity of the work, the dispute may be taken as a simple illustration of the way in which the objectivity of the work will always support multiple readings.

The relation between the objectivity of an artwork, that is, its material being *as an object*, and its nature *as an artwork* is not a relation between two different things—there is only the artwork, and the artwork is given *in* its material objectivity. This means that talk of the objectivity of the work as the medium or mode of presentation of the work—of the sort to which I alluded at the start of this discussion—is limited, though not inappropriate, since the objectivity of the artwork is not separable from the artwork in the way in which it may be assumed that a medium or mode of presentation is separable (and which allows talk of the same thing being given in more than one medium or mode of presentation). The material objectivity of the artwork is the "medium" for the work in that it is that in which the working of the artwork—its self-articulation, its self-disclosure, its self-transcendence—occurs, but what occurs is also the working of that very objectivity and nothing else. The understanding of the material objectivity of the artwork is itself transformed here. The material objectivity of the artwork is not its "stuff," not merely some inert "material," but its own dynamic self-disclosure as that occurs in a singular, *placed* occurrence. In this sense, the artwork is identical with its objectivity, but with its objectivity as this self-disclosing, self-transcending occurrence or placing. Yet as the objectivity of the artwork is its own self-disclosing, so one might also say that the artwork is never simply identical with itself, and so never simply identical with its objectivity either, since it is always in the process of self-disclosure, always in the process of its own self-transcendence.

The tension that is evident here is the underlying source of the dynamism that is essential to the way the artwork is art, and so to what Benjamin refers to as the artwork's own self-articulation as object, to its own "becoming-object," its own coming to presence. Especially significant, given the Heideggerian reading of the artwork, however, is the fact that the artwork never comes to a presence that is not also unfolding toward such presence. *The artwork is thus a constant self-presencing.* This is what I take properly to lie behind Maitland's rejection of the idea that the artwork can be understood as an object. Benjamin argues that the artwork need not disclose anything other than itself, and this I take also to point toward the character of the artwork as self-presencing or self-disclosing. Yet precisely in this, the artwork also discloses something that is of ontological significance, independently of the artwork itself, for it discloses something of the nature of objectivity or thingliness—of material presence—as such.

While it is displayed in a particularly significant and self-evident way in the artwork, the self-presenting that occurs in and through the material objectivity of the work is characteristic of such material objectivity as such—no matter whether in art or elsewhere. What appears as material and objective, what appears in its "standing there/here," never appears as a final, complete, or immediate presence, but is instead a constant unfolding and opening up, a constant self-presencing.[32] Yet this self-presencing is itself a self-presencing that occurs in and through that which is materially and objectively given. To attend to things in their self-presencing is thus not to abandon or efface the material objectivity of things, but is instead to understand that material objectivity as itself given only in and through the self-presencing of the thing, and to understand that self-presencing to be a self-presencing as given in and through the material and the objective—in and through the taking place of things there/here, in the place that is itself unfolded in that same presencing.[33]

Epilogue: Beginning in Wonder

In essential history, the beginning comes last.
—Heidegger, *Parmenides*

The Origin of Philosophy

"It is through wonder [*thaumazein*]," says Aristotle, "that men now begin and originally began to philosophize";[1] and as Plato tells us, through the mouth of Socrates, "wonder is the feeling of a philosopher, and philosophy begins in wonder."[2] These sayings are well known, and they are also representative of an important thread that runs through much of the Western philosophical tradition.[3] Nevertheless, in contemporary philosophy at least, they are seldom reflected upon.

For the most part, it seems, such sayings are taken to indicate that philosophy has its starting point, understood in terms of its motivational or psychological impetus, in puzzlement or curiosity at some feature or features of the world. Yet although puzzlement and curiosity are undoubtedly an important part of philosophical experience, to say that it is wonder in the sense of puzzlement and curiosity alone that stands as the origin of philosophy seems inadequate both to the character of philosophy itself and to the character of wonder. If philosophy is to be more than a mere game, but an activity into which one is drawn because of the demanding nature of the issues it addresses—because of the way one is inevitably given over to caring about those issues—then mere puzzlement seems not to be a good description of that out of which philosophy first arises. If wonder is itself something that can capture us—that can enthrall and enrapture—as it surely can, then wonder must be more than puzzlement, more than curiosity.

The way that Plato and Aristotle themselves talk of the phenomenon of wonder seems to confirm that it is, indeed, not just puzzlement or curiosity that is at issue here. "He was not a bad genealogist who said that Iris [the rainbow/messenger of heaven] is the child of Thaumas [wonder]," says Plato's Socrates,[4] and Aristotle goes on, in the *Metaphysics*, to say that "the myth-lover [*philomythos*] is in a sense a philosopher [*philosophos*], since myths are composed of wonders."[5] It is surely not wonder in the sense of puzzlement alone that myth evokes; nor does curiosity seem a likely relative of the rainbow. Moreover, talk of wonder as that in which philosophy has its beginning is unlikely to mean, in the Platonic and Aristotelian context, merely that which serves as the psychological impetus toward the activity of philosophizing. For the Greeks especially, the idea of beginning or origin is not just the idea of a temporal starting point, but that which determines the very nature of the thing whose origin or beginning it is: thus Aristotle tells us that "'nature' [*physis*] is a beginning [*arche*]."[6] The Greek *arche*, which Aristotle employs here, captures just this idea of beginning or origin as also determining "cause" or first principle.

Talk of wonder as the beginning or origin of philosophy does not imply that philosophy is primarily about wonder or that there is a need for a "philosophy of wonder" as somehow the true and proper basis of philosophy, nor does it mean that philosophy can only ever be properly carried on while one is in a state of wonderment or that puzzlement and curiosity have no role to play in philosophical activity. Talk of wonder as the beginning of philosophy should rather be taken to indicate something about the character of philosophy as such, and so about its nature and limit, about that to which it is a response and so that to which it must be adequate. Inasmuch as wonder is taken to be "the feeling of the philosopher," so wonder must be that which is determinative of philosophy and philosophical activity, that which is its proper "measure," and to which it must, in some sense, always return. But what, then, is wonder, such that it may be the origin of philosophy? And what is philosophy, if wonder is its origin?

Appearance and Encounter

Wonder can take many forms. We may wonder *at* things, but we can also wonder *about* them. In this latter sense, our wondering takes the form of a questioning that may itself be a response to an initial astonishment, puzzlement, or curiosity—to wonder about things may thus mean no more than to puzzle over them, to think about them or to seek some explanation for them. The sense of wonder at issue in Plato and Aristotle, however, is no mere wondering about, but is rather the wonder that is indeed a response to things and to the world—the sort of wonder that is experienced, for instance, at the sight of the rainbow as it shines through a wet, cloudy, but suddenly sunlit sky.

Although they may well be associated with it, and so should not be viewed as irrelevant here, mere puzzlement and curiosity are indeed quite distinct from this sort of wonder. A clear demonstration of this distinction is given by the fact that we may be struck by wonder at some phenomenon in spite of being satisfied with our understanding and explanation of it. A rainbow, for instance, can inspire wonder in a way that is quite unaffected by the knowledge that it is produced by the refraction of sunlight through droplets of water in the atmosphere. This is important to note, since Aristotle, for one, clearly does not ignore the role wonder may play in giving rise to a search for explanations of just this sort, and yet wonder also seems to involve more than just this. The point is not that wonder has no connection with this sort of "desire to know" (or with the puzzlement that may be associated with it), but rather that the satisfaction of such a desire does not exhaust the original wonder from which it may have arisen. Wonder proper should perhaps be viewed, then, as standing apart not only from mere puzzlement or curiosity, but also from certain forms of astonishment or amazement, since the latter, though they can be used in ways that make them near synonyms with wonder, often carry a stronger suggestion of a temporary baulking of the ability to explain, understand, or predict. Wonder is, in fact, consistent with both ignorance *and* understanding (this is something, as will become evident below, crucial to the character of wonder as such); it involves a way of seeing the world, and the things in it, that is independent of what one may know or what one can explain, even though it may also have an important role in making knowledge or explanation possible.

Plato, as we have seen, associates wonder with the rainbow (Iris, "the messenger of heaven").[7] And the association seems particularly apt, since the experience of wonder goes hand-in-hand with the experience of things as suddenly illuminated or lit up—with the experience of things as shining forth into the world around them. Emmanuel Levinas comments on this by connecting the experience of wonder directly with the experience of light:

The contact with light, the act of opening one's eyes, the lighting up of bare sensation, are apparently outside any relationship, and do not take form like answers to questions. Light illuminates and is naturally understood; it is comprehension itself. But within this natural correlation between us and the world, in a sort of doubling back, a question arises, a being surprised by this illumination. The wonder which

Plato put at the origin of philosophy is an astonishment before the natural and the intelligible. It is the very intelligibility of light that is astonishing; light is doubled up with a sight. The astonishment does not arise out of comparison with some order more natural than nature, but simply before intelligibility itself. Its strangeness is, we might say, due to its very reality, to the very fact there is existence.[8]

There is a long philosophical tradition—one as old as philosophy itself—that associates light with intelligibility, and there is certainly something powerful, at least to those of us who are sighted, about the use of visual metaphors and images in this context.[9] But Levinas's point here would probably be almost as well served by reference to any other medium or mode of experience—think of the sudden *presencing* of things in a particular taste, a touch, a sound, a movement. What is at issue here is not only wonder at light and sight, but wonder as a response to the often sudden and striking *encounter* with things—whether it be light refracted through droplets of water in the sky, the explosion of taste in a mouthful of wine, the heady scent of blossoms on the still night, the experience of the openness of space and the capacities of the body in the exhilaration of a dance, or the complex interplay of elements in a piece of music. In each case, it is the encounter—and the character of that encounter as a revealing, an opening up, of things and of the world—that seems to lie at the heart of the experience of wonder.

Wonder is thus not so much a response to any particular appearance or set of appearances, although it always requires some such appearance as its focus and its immediate cause, as it is the response that is evoked in us by the very recognition of appearance as such (although that recognition may not always be well articulated). And if that recognition, and the wonder that accompanies it, is most often evoked by the beautiful, the tremendous, the elegant, or the sublime, then this is perhaps because of the way in which these forms of appearance call attention, most immediately and directly, to their own appearing, to the fact of their being encountered. One is brought to a halt by the appearance, and forced to attend to it, not because it shows something else (as it may indicate some use, purpose, or cause), nor because of anything that explains how it is (the processes or conditions that give rise to it), but merely by the fact *that* it is. The wondrousness of the rainbow thus resides in the very fact of its being; the wonder we experience in the face of those we love lies in the simple fact of their existence and our encounter with them.

The encounter with the extraordinary that often gives rise to wonder—the encounter with the wondrous in its most strikingly immediate forms such as the sublime or the beautiful—brings suddenly to our attention the very fact of encounter. Yet in bringing such encounter to the fore, what is brought forward is not itself something that is extraordinary or unusual, but rather something that is itself "ordinary" and everyday. All of our activity, all of our existence, is constituted in terms of such encounter, although for the most part it is given little notice, and such encounter makes up the very fabric of our lives. In every act we touch something, respond to it, move in relation to it, and our lives are constituted by such encounter and response as if those lives were made up of the reciprocating movements between interconnected threads in a dense and intricate web. Inasmuch as the wonder that arises in the experience of the extraordinary brings such encounter into view, and so brings into view something that may be seen as the most ordinary and ubiquitous of phenomena—such that it may seem trivial and unilluminating to draw attention to it—so it also shows such encounter to be itself extraordinary and even strange.

One might say that although wonder is often immediately evoked by that which is self-evidently remarkable or extraordinary, that which is most remarkable, and which is present in every experience of wonder *as* remarkable, is nothing other than the simple fact of encounter, of intelligibility, of being. But in that case, wonder needs nothing "special" to bring it about. Wonder may often be evoked by the self-evidently extraordinary. It may also arise out of the simple, sudden, immediate awareness of the existence of something—out of the recognition of the questionability, the strangeness of things, and of our encounter with them, as it occurs in the most common and ordinary of ways. Indeed, this is surely wonder at its most basic, the wonder of which Blake seems implicitly to speak in *Auguries of Innocence*: "To see a World in a grain of sand, / And a Heaven in a wild flower, / Hold infinity in the palm of your hand, / And Eternity in an hour."[10] The experience of wonder might thus be understood as encompassing all those modes of encounter in which the ordinary is made remarkable, in which the extraordinary spills over into the mundane, in which the familiar becomes strange.

Often, of course, it is precisely the transformation in experience that comes with wonder (and to which Blake's lines give voice)—whether through the ordinary or the extraordinary—that has been the aim of poetry and art. "In the poetry of the poet," says Heidegger, "and in the thinking of the thinker, there is always so much world-space to spare that each and every thing—a tree, a mountain, a house, the call of a bird—completely loses its indifference and familiarity."[11] Yet if philosophy has its origins in the wonder that art and poetry may be seen as aiming to evoke, it surely does not aim at bringing such a state about. Philosophy

may have its origins in the experience of the transformation of the world—
its lighting up—that comes with wonder, but it is a *response to* that transformation, not its *cause*. Of course, poetry and art can also be seen as
responsive, but they nevertheless have a mimetic quality that philosophy
lacks—a mimetic quality that means that while poetry and art are responsive, they are also themselves "affective." Thus, the artistic or poetic
moment can be seen as "re-presenting" the moment of encounter or
appearance in a way that makes it available to us in a renewed (or sometimes new) form and thereby providing us with something that is itself an
occasion for wonder.[12] Philosophy, for the most part, lacks any such
"mimetic" character, but instead responds to that which appears, and to
the moment of appearance, by way of exploration and articulation of that
appearance and the moment, the region, the world, within which it
occurs.[13] It is easy, nevertheless, to mistake philosophy for poetry, or vice
versa, just because of the way in which each stands in an essential relation
to the event of appearance and encounter, and so to wonder and the wondrous. It is also easy to reject or trivialize the origin of philosophy in
wonder precisely out of a desire to prevent just such a confusion—although
to do so is to commit no less an error.

Inasmuch as wonder arises out of the event of encounter as that event
is brought strikingly to awareness—thereby showing the ordinary as
*extra*ordinary, the familiar as strange—so wonder also constitutes a sudden
awareness of our own existence, not as something separate or apart from
the encounter nor from that which is encountered, but as already given
over to it. The experience of the wondrous is an experience in which we
find ourselves already moved, already affected, already opened up to what
is before us. It requires no effort on our part—no decision or act. The
experience of wonder is an experience of our being already given over to
the world and the things in it. In this sense the experience of wonder is
indeed, as Levinas says of the experience of light, "apparently outside of
any relationship." Just as the experience of opening one's eyes is an experience of the immediate coming to visual presence of things—not the experience of the establishing of some relation, but of things being, simply,
"there"—so the experience of wonder is the experience of ourselves as
already in the sway of wonder, of ourselves as already "there" along with
the wondrous.

In wonder, we encounter things in a way that is prior to encounter as
any sort of *relating* to things; the encounter that wonder brings into view
is just our being already *with* things, already given over to them and them
to us. Thus Levinas talks of the "natural correlation between us and the

world"—although such talk of correlation, no matter how "natural," undoubtedly suggests a sense of correlation that must fail to capture what is really at issue. If there is a "natural correlation" between us and the world, it is a correlation that consists in nothing more than the fact of our already being "in" the world. In the experience of wonder it is our being already "in" that comes to the fore—our being already "there" in the very same place as the things themselves. In our wonder at the rainbow, we find ourselves already in the world and in no need of finding some way to relate to it, to come into coordination with it, to make contact with it. The world is there, and us with it and a part of it, just as we are there with the rainbow, and so with sky and cloud, wind and rain, earth and rock, animal and plant, friend and stranger. In wonder, even in the wondrousness of some single thing, the world is itself brought to appearance and with it our own prior belonging to that world. In this respect, while in wonder things are indeed "made strange," we do not thereby find ourselves "out of place." The "making strange" that occurs in wonder is a making strange of our very belonging inasmuch as that belonging is itself brought to light.

The experience of wonder that I have so far been describing is closely akin to the experience that Gadamer describes as present in the experience of art[14]—and that he also finds elaborated in Heidegger's "The Origin of the Work of Art."[15] Wonder is something that overtakes us, in which we are caught up, and in which we are given over to the wondrous; similarly, the artwork is not some "thing" that stands over against us, but rather something that "happens" to us and into which we are drawn. In the artwork, moreover, we find a form of self-revealing on the part of the work itself that opens up a space in which we encounter something that goes beyond the work—a self-revealing that illuminates the world in which the work stands, as well as our own standing before that work and in that world.[16] The artwork thus always exceeds anything that either the artist or the audience might intend in the work and so always brings with it a certain startlement or surprise:

The work of art that says something confronts us itself. That is, it expresses something in such a way that what is said is like a discovery, a disclosure of something previously concealed. The element of surprise is based on this. "So true, so filled with being" [So wahr, so seiend] is not something one knows in any other way. Everything familiar is eclipsed.[17]

Gadamer takes the working of art, in this respect, to be exemplary of the experience of understanding and so of the very experience of encounter or appearance. Indeed, at the end of Truth and Method, Gadamer uses the concept of the beautiful—understood as "radiance," as that which self-evidently "shines forth"[18]—to explore the character of self-evidence that belongs to that which is intelligible or encounterable. Like beauty, understanding or encounter is an event in which something appears in and of itself, an event in which one finds oneself already caught up, an event that can surprise and surpass.

Gadamer says of beauty that it has the mode of being of *light*, but just as Levinas's use of light in illustrating the character of wonder need not be taken to indicate something that is exclusive to the visual alone, neither should Gadamer's comments be taken to indicate that the beautiful is only to be found within the domain of sight. In both cases, the image or metaphor of light is itself used to reveal something about the wondrous and the beautiful, which we can now see to be themselves closely related, namely, the way in which both are tied to the "self-presencing" of things in appearance or in encounter. The beautiful, then, in the sense Gadamer employs it, is that which is self-evidently apparent; wonder is that in which we find ourselves caught up in our response to such self-evident appearance.

Inasmuch as we find ourselves, in the experience of wonder, already caught up in response, and so, indeed, as already belonging to the world, so we find ourselves already caught up in care for and concern about that world. Wonder is thus a symptom of our prior commitment and involvement, since, although wonder may be possible only when we have the freedom of a certain degree of contemplation (Aristotle emphasizes the way in which philosophy arises only when we have some release from the constant demands of simple survival), it is out of our commitment and involvement that the "desire to know" itself arises. Moreover, as the desire to know drives philosophical activity, so philosophy is itself driven by our being already given over to the world in this way—it is, as I noted in the introduction, because we are already taken up by the issues with which philosophy deals that philosophy is more than a mere game, more than a simple "distraction." Yet inasmuch as the "desire to know," along with philosophy itself, arises out of our prior commitment and involvement in the world, then so we may say that this desire, and philosophical activity as such, has content and significance only insofar as that content and significance is supplied by the concrete circumstances of our involvement, of our being there, of our prior belonging to the world.

Recognition of this point can help to clarify the way in which wonder can be a response to the very fact of encounter or appearance, and so to our prior belonging, and yet it is nevertheless always directed toward some particular appearance, some particular feature or aspect of the world. It is not the world in general that preoccupies us, but the world in its specificity; and, similarly, it is not the world in general that immediately evokes wonder, but some part or aspect of the world. It is, however, through the part—through the particular thing or event—that the whole is brought to light; it is though the particular encounter or appearance that the fact of encounter or appearance as such is brought into view. In wonder, then, we find not merely the doubling up of light with sight, as Levinas puts it, but also the doubling up that is analogous to this, namely, the doubling up of the thing that appears with the appearing itself—what Heidegger refers to as "the twofoldness of what is present and of presence."[19] Properly, then, it is this double "appearance"—of that which appears along with the appearing—that is the stimulus to wonder as well as its focus.

Strangeness and Questionability

In the terms Levinas uses in the passage quoted above, terms that are also echoed in Gadamer's discussion of the beautiful, wonder arises out of a response to the event of "intelligibility"—the event of our encounter with things, the event of experience—in which that event is itself brought to the center of attention. Wonder is a response to existence, to being, that is brought about by the recognition of existence in the sheer fact of something's existing. Yet if the experience of wonder is a response to intelligibility, existence, encounter, and an experience of the very fact of encounter, then it also involves, as Levinas points out, and as Gadamer may also be taken to confirm, a certain surprise, a questioning, in the face of such encounter. Thus wonder halts us, and, like the stars Hamlet describes as brought to a standstill by the grief of Laertes at the death of Ophelia, we are "wonder-wounded."[20] In this respect, the experience of wonder, and the encounter with the wondrous, represents a sudden disabling, an intrusion into our normal activities and a disruption of those activities. The experience of wonder thus takes us out of our ordinary involvement with things and makes what is ordinarily unquestioned, questionable, makes what ordinarily seems familiar, strange.

It is precisely this aspect of wonder, this "making strange," that makes it natural to connect wonder, even if the connection is also misleading, with the experience of puzzlement. But the questionability and strangeness at issue here cannot be dispelled by any solution, since what is at issue—what is rendered strange—is the very fact of appearance and of encounter. Of course, this experience of things "made strange" may also give rise to philosophical (and even scientific) activity: in the face of our prior involvement, and so our prior care and concern, the strangeness and questionability of things constitutes a source of discomfort that we ordinarily seek to resolve or dispel through the search for answers and explanations. Yet although such activity may result in an explanation of that which is the immediate cause and focus for wonder (the rainbow, for instance), and so for the strangeness and questionability that accompanies it, such explanation does not touch the underlying source of wonder, namely, appearance or encounter as such. Indeed, the fact that the surprise and questionability that seem so closely associated with wonder may be present, even though the phenomenon at issue is apparently well understood, can itself be most readily explained by pointing to the distinction between a particular phenomenon (say, the rainbow) and its phenomenal character as such (its appearing or being encountered). To elucidate the former is not to elucidate the latter.

Here, once more, we find the "doubling up" that we saw above, but now the doubling of that which appears with the appearing is matched by a doubling of two modes of strangeness that correspond to these. The strangeness of that which appears leads on to explanation, or may already be satisfied by an existing explanation, but the strangeness of the appearing is amenable to no such resolution. In this respect, wonder may give rise to puzzlement, and puzzlement to explanation, and yet the wonder, and the underlying strangeness, may nevertheless remain. Of course, for just this reason, the strangeness that is present in wonder need not always be doubled: when we encounter what is ordinary and familiar—what is understood and already explicable—as remarkable, strange, and wondrous, then the "doubling" of that which appears with the appearing, of that which is encountered with the encounter, is matched not by two modes of strangeness, but rather by the coupling of the remarkable and the *ordinary*, of the strange and the *familiar*, of that which is outside of any explanation and that which is *explicable*.

There is no way in which one can get behind the simple fact of appearance or encounter, the simple "givenness" of things,[21] to find something more basic from the standpoint of which such encounter, such givenness, might itself be investigated. That is not to say that we do not often try to do just this (indeed, a large part of philosophy is made up of just such attempts), but rather that to try to do so is already to have misunderstood the basic situation in which we find ourselves. In the experience of wonder, what is brought strikingly to awareness is the event of appearing and encounter through a particular instance of such appearing or encounter.

As such, what is also made evident is our own prior belonging to the world, our being "always already" *there*, and yet, in being made evident in this way, our "being-there" is also rendered strange. We may well be able to describe and explain aspects of our concrete situation, both in general and in particular, and yet neither can we describe or explain that situation in its entirety (since there is always more that could be said and more that could be asked), and nor can we even begin to explain the fact of our situatedness as such (since we can never stand outside or apart from such situatedness[22]). Our "being-there," the very fact of our situatedness, cannot properly be made the object of any explanation, and yet it is just such situatedness or belonging—our already "being-there" alongside things, in the encounter with things—that lies at the heart of the experience of wonder and that provides the impetus to explanation with which wonder is also associated.

Both Plato's association of wonder with the rainbow and Levinas's treatment of wonder as like the experience of light suggest a conception of wonder as associated with visibility and *transparency*. Yet inasmuch as wonder is also associated with the inexplicable fact of our situatedness, so it is bound up not merely with transparency, but also with a certain failure of transparency, with a certain *opacity*. In wonder, our "being-there" is suddenly "lit up," and yet in being illuminated, it is also shown as essentially dark—while we can "see into" the intricacies of the world and our situation in it, that there is a world, and that we are already given over to it, is absolutely impenetrable. Our "being-there," our situatedness, on the basis of which the transparency of encounter and of appearance is possible, cannot itself be made transparent, and thus, inasmuch as light is "doubled up" with sight, as that which appears is "doubled up" with the appearing, so also is transparency "doubled up" with opacity.

That there is such opacity here does not indicate, however, some "blindness" on our part, some defect in our intellectual "vision," for there simply is nothing here that can be an object of such vision. The opacity at issue thus represents the proper bound that limits the capacity for explanation and for questioning; inasmuch as it is tied to the situatedness on the basis of which any encounter or appearance, and so any explanation or question, is possible, so it can also be said to limit and to make possible transparency itself. In Gadamer and Heidegger, of course, the interplay between transparency and opacity that appears here as a fundamental element in wonder also appears as a fundamental ontological structure (albeit in somewhat different form), in terms of the interplay of concealing and unconcealing that is the event of truth.[23] For Gadamer and Heidegger, this "event" is constitutive of the openness of the world on the basis of which any particular statement can be true or false or any particular thing can be present or absent. Thus, just as opacity can be said to underlie transparency, so, in the terms Gadamer and Heidegger employ, concealment can be said to underlie openness or unconcealment.

The impossibility of arriving at any complete "transparency" in respect of our situatedness, our "being-there," may be seen as identical with the difficulty that accompanies the attempt to make sense of subjectivity within a pure objective or "naturalistic" framework—a difficulty (though it is not always seen as such) that is associated with various forms of reductionism, materialism, and perhaps also with the so-called problem of consciousness. It would be presumptuous, however, to suppose that this means that it is *subjectivity* that is the problem here—at least so long as one thinks of subjectivity in terms of some inner "mental" realm of "thought," idea, or consciousness. It is not that subjectivity brings a lack of transparency with it, but rather that such subjectivity is itself always situated, already given over to the world, and it is just this situatedness that gives rise to a lack of transparency. To be situated is always to stand in such a way that one is oriented toward some things and not others; it is to find some aspects of the world salient and others not, it is to find oneself literally "there." It is "being-there," in this sense, that is the central element in subjectivity, and subjectivity does not underlie or explain such "being-there."

Just as light illuminates, and yet, in illuminating, is not itself illuminated, so our situatedness, our "being-there," opens up the world and us to it, and yet is itself hidden and closed off. In this respect, we may say that it is our situatedness that enables and yet also restricts our capacity for explanation; and similarly, it is wonder, as a response to the sudden and striking awareness of our situatedness, that stimulates the desire for explanation, and yet also brings explanation to a halt. In wonder, then, explanation finds its origin and its absolute limit, and, consequently, part of the experience of wonder is finding oneself in the somewhat paradoxical situation of being confronted by that which seems both to demand explanation and yet also resists, and indeed stands prior to, such explanation— we are thus led to question while having no capacity to answer. As Levinas says of the question of being (which is one way in which the questionability at issue in the experience of wonder may be expressed): "The questioning of Being is an experience of Being in its strangeness. It is then a way of taking up Being. That is why the question about Being—What is Being?—has never been answered. There is no answer to Being."[24] If there is no answer here, perhaps it is mistaken to suppose that there is really a question. Perhaps what Levinas should be taken to be pointing toward is just the way in which what is at issue is an experience of strangeness—the strangeness of our prior belonging. The strangeness at issue is rather like the strangeness that arises when, as a child, one asks oneself how it is that one is *oneself*, that one belongs just *here*? Such questions are only questions in a somewhat peculiar and perhaps attenuated sense, since not only do they have no possible answers, but it is not clear what form answers could take, nor is it obvious that answers (at least to those questions) are actually what is required.

Focusing not on being, but on the world and reason, Merleau-Ponty writes: "The world and reason are not problematical. We may say, if we wish, that they are mysterious, but their mystery defines them: there can be no question of dispelling it by some 'solution,' it is on the hither side of all solutions."[25] The distinction Merleau-Ponty makes here between the "problematical" and what we may choose to call the "mysterious" (a distinction that echoes Gabriel Marcel's famous contrast between the "problematic" and the "mysterious"[26]) has a particular relevance to the discussion of wonder and the nature of the questioning that may arise in the face of wonder. What wonder reveals, namely, our prior belonging to the world, is something that we may choose to call mysterious and marvelous, and yet, although it may give rise to questioning and surprise, it is not itself something that can ever properly be put into question. The encounter with things and with the world is thus not rendered "uncertain" by the experience of wonder. On the contrary, wonder is the response to the immediacy and reality of encounter, of intelligibility, of existence. It returns us to the world (a world that we never properly leave), rather than taking us away from the world or the world from us. Consequently, although wonder involves a certain experience of strangeness, it does not involve estrangement from the world, but rather constitutes a recognition of our prior belonging to the world—what appears as strange is just that prior belonging. It is just such belonging that leads us on to question and to explain, that makes such questioning and explanation significant, that makes it *matter*.[27]

The Return of Philosophy

If the origin of a thing is what determines it, then the beginning of a thing is both its limit and also its end. The beginning of philosophy in wonder is thus significant, not because it tells us how it is that philosophy happens to come about, but rather because it tells us something about what philosophy is, about what it is not, about that at which it is directed, about that which constitutes its proper concern. Of course, in talking about "philosophy" here, we are not talking about everything that may possibly fall under this label. "Philosophy" names an institutional entity that is, in part, defined simply by a certain set of sociocultural circumstances and may also change with those circumstances; "philosophy" also names a range of problems, activities, and concerns that may vary from one thinker, one time, one place to another. The word "philosophy" is thus used here with all of this in mind, and yet in a way that nevertheless holds to the idea that "philosophy" does name something distinctive that is roughly continuous from the Greeks through to the present and that, whatever the various expressions and incarnations it may go through, remains centrally bound up with the experience of wonder found in Plato and Aristotle. But what more, then, can be said about philosophy, if it does indeed have its origin, and so also its end and limit, in the kind of wonder that has been explored and elaborated upon above?

Inasmuch as it begins in wonder, philosophy has its origin in a response to the original event of encounter in which we find ourselves already given over to the world and to the things in it. In the experience of the wondrous we are brought face to face with that event in a particularly striking way. The experience of wonder, while it is on the one hand an experience of the accessibility and transparency of the world—in wonder we are brought to awareness of the self-evident appearing of things through some particular instance of such self-evident appearance—is also an experience of the strangeness of that accessibility and transparency. The experience of transparency always remains opaque, and the more striking our awareness of it, the more opaque it seems. The experience of wonder is thus an experience of the way in which, to revert to Levinas's metaphor, the lighting up of things, their intelligibility, brings with it an essential and impenetrable darkness. It is not the darkness that arises through lack of light, but the darkness that arises as a consequence of light—like the darkness that stands behind the lit object itself, the darkness that stands behind the source of light.

Yet although philosophy arises out of the experience of this transparency and opacity as they occur together, it seems as if it has often tended to lose sight of this interplay and so of the real nature of the experience of wonder in which it begins. Thus, contemporary philosophy, insofar as it reflects on the matter at all, does indeed tend to interpret its wondrous origin as indicating an origin in puzzlement, questioning, and curiosity, rather than in the wonder that has been at issue in the discussion above. Yet such puzzlement, questioning, and curiosity are not characterized by an experience of transparency as it is also bound to opacity, but rather of an opacity that increasingly gives way to transparency—puzzlement thus gives way to solution, questioning gives rise to answers, curiosity leads on to knowledge. Even if complete transparency is never actually achieved, still it is such complete transparency that is the paradigm. Moreover, when opacity does come to the fore in much contemporary philosophical discussion, it typically does so in a way that rules out the possibility of transparency—in a way that is, indeed, often intended to cast doubt on such transparency. Thus contemporary skepticism and relativism, which might be taken to arise out of a recognition of the inevitability of opacity and the impossibility of complete transparency, do not give recognition to the interplay and reciprocity between opacity and transparency, but instead remain fixated on a contrast between opacity and transparency understood as mutually exclusive alternatives—a contrast that seems only to be resolved on the side of opacity.

To construe matters in this way is to find oneself already cut off from the experience of wonder, and more than just that, it is to find oneself alienated from the world. In this respect, the very desire for transparency seems to lead to a loss in the capacity to see how transparency can ever be possible. Philosophy may thus begin in wonder, but inasmuch as the demand for explanation constitutes a demand for illumination and transparency, so it can also come to constitute a blindness to the interdependence between transparency and opacity, and so also a blindness to the prior belonging to the world that first drives the demand for explanation as such. Philosophy begins in wonder, but it often ends in alienation—alienation from self, from others, and from ordinary things, as well as the extraordinary. Such alienation is not just a matter of the experience of philosophical difficulty in understanding or explaining how there can be knowledge of the external world or of other minds or of one's own "mental states," but also of how philosophical activity can connect up with the fundamental and everyday experiences of human life, with the things that drive us, that affect us, that matter to us.

Historically, it was a desire to return philosophical thinking to the problems of "life"—understood not in terms of some category of *Lebensphilosophie*, but of life as that which takes us up, that makes demands on us, in which we already find ourselves immersed—that drove the work of the young Heidegger and that also led to Gadamer's own engagement with him in the 1920s.[28] It was in this light that Heidegger appropriated the phenomenology of Edmund Husserl, using it not as a means to develop philosophy as a more rigorous "science," but instead as providing a path back to our original, "hermeneutic" situatedness, to our original encounter with things, to our original "being-there." Heidegger's thought was always directed toward such a "turning back" to that situatedness, a turning back to the original happening of being and of truth. In this respect, Heidegger can be viewed as attempting to return to that which is also evident to us in the experience of wonder. Indeed, Heidegger himself says of wonder that it "displaces man into and before beings as such. . . . Wonder is the basic disposition that primordially disposes man into the beginning of thinking, because, before all else, it displaces man into that essence whereby he then finds himself caught up in the midst of beings as such and as a whole and finds himself caught up in them."[29] In returning to recognize the origin of philosophy in wonder, we can see the significance of and motivation behind the sort of philosophical "revolution" that Heidegger attempted. Moreover, in returning to recognize the origin of philosophy in wonder, it also becomes possible to see how the philosophical preoccupation with transparency, and so with opacity as its alternative, first arises, as well as to recognize its deeply problematic character. Transparency is a misguided ideal, and opacity is not so much a barrier to understanding as it is, in part, its enabling condition.

Wonder is not the primary focus of philosophical inquiry or reflection, and yet there can be nothing more fundamental to philosophy than the event of encounter and appearance, and, with it, the interplay of opacity and transparency, that comes to the fore in the experience of wonder. It is this that is properly the "end" of philosophy, understood as that to which philosophy must finally address itself. Inasmuch as this event is not something that can itself be rendered transparent—inasmuch as it remains irreducibly opaque—here philosophy comes up against its own proper bound and limit. Moreover, although the experience of wonder may be unusual, and the event of encounter or appearance may itself be experienced in the throes of wonder as itself extraordinary and remarkable, still in being brought to awareness of such encounter or experience, we are brought to awareness of something that is indeed the most mundane, the most ordinary, the most ubiquitous of "happenings." In this respect, philosophy does not begin in something out of the ordinary, but in the bringing to awareness of the most ordinary; it does not find its limit in something that transcends our everyday experience, but in the very "being-there" of that experience; it does not find its "end" in a space or time beyond, but only in this place—the place in which it already finds itself, which it never properly leaves, and in which there is always something further to explore. Wonder is thus a returning, sometimes with the abruptness of a sudden shock, to the world to which we always already belong—it is in that return that philosophy begins and to which it must always itself go back.

What we call the beginning is often the end / And to make an end is to make a beginning.

—T. S. Eliot, *Four Quartets* ("Little Gidding")

A Note on Eliot's *Four Quartets*

The lines that stand at the beginning and end of this volume are taken from T. S. Eliot's great poetic sequence, *Four Quartets*. The poems that make up this sequence have a particular resonance with many of the themes explored here, not necessarily because of the poems' religiosity (one might argue that they remain within a much more metaphysical frame than is evident here), but because of the way in which they articulate the matter of human relatedness in and to the world in a way that is attentive to the placedness, as well as the fragility, of human and worldly being; because of the way in which their fourfold structure echoes the fourfold dance that appears in Heidegger's late thinking (the figure of the dance itself echoing back into Eliot's lines); and because these are poems that are also tied, at least in their naming, *to places*. In his juxtaposition of end and beginning, Eliot also gives added emphasis to the image of turning and return that is so central to the thinking of *topos*. Perhaps *Four Quartets* can be seen as an example of what Heidegger would call "the poetry that thinks," and so perhaps Eliot can be seen, in a certain way, as moving in the direction of his own topology of being.

Notes

Introduction: The Thinking of Place

1. The inclusion of the Event (*das Ereignis*) here is deliberately provocative. I would argue, however, that it is impossible to think of the Event in a way that does not take seriously its more than temporal—its genuinely topological—character.

2. See chapter 11 below.

3. See Jeff Malpas, "Heidegger's Topology of Being," in *Transcendental Heidegger*, ed. Steven Galt Crowell and Jeff Malpas (Stanford: Stanford University Press, 2007), pp. 119–134.

4. One of the other key figures is surely Immanuel Kant—see Jeff Malpas and Günter Zöller, "Reading Kant Topographically: From Critical Philosophy to Empirical Geography," in *New Essays in Kant Studies*, ed. Adrian W. Moore, Graham Bird, and Roxana Baiasu (London: Palgrave Macmillan, 2011), in press—and another is Walter Benjamin (see chapter 3 below).

5. Jeff Malpas, *Heidegger's Topology: Being, Place, World* (Cambridge, Mass.: MIT Press, 2006)—of which the present book can be viewed as a continuation.

6. Jeff Malpas, *Place and Experience: A Philosophical Topography* (Cambridge: Cambridge University Press, 1999).

7. For a differently oriented discussion of the topology/topography that is at stake in these concepts, see my "Putting Space in Place: Philosophical Topography and Relational Geography," *Environment and Planning D: Society and Space*, forthcoming.

8. In the end, he misconstrues the "inward" aspect of *topos* in a way that severs it from spatiality (which comes to be associated with the outward aspect, with exteriority, but also with the merely "present") and ties it instead to temporality alone.

9. Having said this, it should be noted that there is an underlying critique at work in the very espousal of a topological approach—what is presented is a mode of

philosophy that is quite different from, and some would say, antithetical to, much of what passes for philosophy within contemporary academia.

1   The *Topos* of Thinking

1. See Heidegger, "Seminar in Le Thor 1968," in *Four Seminars*, trans. Andrew Mitchell and François Raffoul (Bloomington: Indiana University Press, 2004), p. 41.

2. One of the few, perhaps the only, thinker to explicitly address the place of thinking is Hannah Arendt, but she does so in a way rather different from that proposed here. Arendt argues that because thinking is always concerned with the universal, and never the particular, so thinking has no proper place—it takes place nowhere. Arendt does focus, however, on thinking as having a mode of temporality that is proper to it, namely, that mode of the present that opens up into the infinite—see Arendt, *The Life of the Mind*, ed. Mary McCarthy (San Diego: Harcourt Brace, 1978), vol. 1, chap. 4 ("Where Are We When We Think?"), pp.197–213 (see also Pierre Hadot's exploration of the philosophical focus on the present moment in *Philosophy as a Way of Life*, trans. Michael Chase [Oxford: Blackwell, 1995, pp. 217–237]). In fact, if one recognizes that *topos* cannot be identified with the spatial alone—a point for which I argue in a number of places (see chapter 6 below, and also *Heidegger's Topology*, p. 103, as well as my discussion in *Place and Experience* [Cambridge, Cambridge University Press, 1999], pp. 159–174)—then what Arendt seems to be intending here, in spite of her comments to the contrary, is precisely a mode of *topos*.

3. These latter two aspects might be said to correspond roughly to the idea of place as it is explored by Aristotle in *Physics* IV (see esp. 212a5–6), where Aristotle uses the term *topos* in a way that does indeed seem to connect with the idea of horizon, and with place as it is explored by Plato in the *Timaeus* (48e–53c), in which the term *chora* is the focus (often translated in English editions of Plato as "receptacle," "womb," or "matrix," but also translated as "place" or "space"), and in which place is understood as sustaining origin or ground (see also my "Putting Space in Place," *Environment and Planning D: Society and Space*, forthcoming). The three aspects distinguished here reappear elsewhere in my discussion throughout the essays collected here—most often in terms of the ideas of origin and ground.

4. In Heidegger, *Off the Beaten Track* (a translation of *Holzwege*), trans. Julian Young and Kenneth Haynes (Cambridge: Cambridge University Press, 2002), pp. 1–56—although even here Heidegger talks of the way in which the original even of "encounter," of presencing, of "truth," occurs in the ordinary in a way that is extraordinary: "In the immediate circle of beings we believe ourselves to be at home. The being is familiar, reliable, ordinary. . . . Fundamentally, the ordinary is not ordinary; it is extra-ordinary, uncanny [*un geheur*]" ("The Origin of the Work of Art," p. 31).

5. This is a point that is thematized more directly in the epilogue below.

6. See Martin Heidegger, *Being and Time*, trans. John Macquarie and Edward Robinson (New York: Harper & Row, 1962), §4, H11–15.

7. See *Being and Time*, H11–14, and H.42—*Dasein* is that being whose own being "is an issue" for it.

8. The theme of questionability that appears here is one that reappears at many points in the discussion below, but see especially chapters 3 and 7, and the epilogue. Note that as I use it questionabililty already implies *listening*.

9. See Heidegger's discussions in *What Is Called Thinking?*, trans. John Glenn Gray (New York: Harper & Row, 1968), esp. pp. 168–170.

10. See chapters 2 and 10 below.

11. See chapter 10, esp. pp. 200–212, below.

12. See especially his comments in the "Appendix" to "The Origin of the Work of Art" (*Off the Beaten Track*, pp. 55), in which Heidegger acknowledges the inadequacy of much of his previous thinking as it addresses the issue of "the relationship of being to human being" and the "distressing" character of the difficulty that it expresses. See also chapter 5 below.

13. See Malpas, *Heidegger's Topology*, pp. 155–175, and also chapters 3 and 6 below.

14. The way this shift in Heidegger's thinking is explicated is complicated, because it is always possible to read back, into what comes earlier, the developments that appear in Heidegger's later thinking—just as one can also, if perhaps less easily, read the earlier into the later. The matter is further complicated by the fact that a term like *Dasein* has an essential ambiguity within it in relation both to place and to the human.

15. See my discussion in *Heidegger's Topology*, pp. 102–104, 126–146.

16. This term first appears in Heidegger's work in the 1935–1936 lectures on Kant published as *What Is a Thing?*, trans. W. B. Barton, Jr., and Vera Deutsch (South Bend, Ind.: Gateway, 1967), pp. 16–17. It is also a key term in Heidegger, *Contributions to Philosophy (from Enowning)*, trans. Parvis Emad and Kenneth Maly (Bloomington: Indiana University Press, 1999); see pp. 259–271, 334–337.

17. See chapters 3 and chapter 6 below.

18. See especially Heidegger, *Being and Time*, §70, H367–369, in which he aims to establish that "Dasein's specific spatiality is grounded in temporality."

19. See Malpas, *Heidegger's Topology*, esp. pp. 104–126.

20. See Malpas, *Heidegger's Topology*, pp. 109–126, 144–145; see also chapter 3 below.

21. See Heidegger, *On Time and Being*, trans. Joan Stambaugh (New York: Harper & Row, 1972), p. 23.

22. See Malpas, *Heidegger's Topology*, pp. 120–126, 219–230.

23. See "Building Dwelling Thinking," in *Poetry, Language, Thought*, trans. Albert Hofstadter (New York: Harper, 1971), pp. 147–149.

24. It is the main focus of the discussion in chapter 5 of *Heidegger's Topology*; see also chapter 3, pp. 56–58, below.

25. See *Heidegger's Topology*, pp. 213–219; see also Heidegger's discussion, already noted above, concerning the belonging together of time and space as *Zeitraum* in *Contributions to Philosophy (from Enowning)*, esp. pp. 259–271.

26. See Malpas, *Heidegger's Topology*, chapter 6; see also Robert Mugerauer, *Heidegger and Homecoming: The Leitmotif in the Later Writings* (Toronto: University of Toronto Press, 2008).

27. See chapter 8 below. Heidegger's understanding of thinking as both remembrance and return home means that he also associates thinking with a form of "homesickness"—the literal meaning of "nostalgia" as given by the Greek from which it is composed.

28. All themes that are also taken up by Albert Camus—appearing in an especially condensed form in "Helen's Exile," in his *Lyrical and Critical Essays*, trans. Philip Thody (London: Hamish Hamilton, 1967), pp. 115–119.

29. The issue of ground (as well as of origin—which is also implicated here), is something to which I return at many points in the discussions included below. It is given particularly direct attention in chapter 4 below.

30. "Transcendental philosophy is the capacity of the self-determining subject to constitute itself *as given* in intuition." Immanuel Kant, *Opus postumum*, trans. Eckart Förster (Cambridge: Cambridge University Press, 1993), p. 254.

31. See my discussion in "The Transcendental Circle," *Australasian Journal of Philosophy* 75 (1997), pp. 1–20, and also chapter 4 below.

32. The change in vocabulary with regard to the notion of the "hermeneutical" is explicitly noted by Heidegger in "A Dialogue on Language," *On the Way to Language*, trans. Peter D. Hertz (New York: Harper & Row, 1971), p. 28.

33. As I note below (see chapter 3), there are two main reasons for Heidegger's move away from the language of the transcendental: its apparent tendency toward subjectivism and its apparent dualism (seen in the separation of conditions from what is conditioned). As I also indicate, though I have been drawn both ways on the question of the convergence or divergence of the transcendental and the

topological, it seems to me, on balance, that Heidegger probably distances himself too much from the idea of the transcendental, and, rather than abandon the concept, it is important to try to retain a reappropriated notion of the transcendental as itself essentially topological. On the general issue of the relation between the transcendental and the topological, see the discussion in chapters 3 and 4 below; see also the brief discussion of this matter in chapter 10.

34. A givenness, it should be noted, that is very different from the givenness identified as "mythical" by Wilfrid Sellars in "Empiricism and the Philosophy of Mind," in *The Foundations of Science and the Concepts of Psychoanalysis*, Minnesota Studies in the Philosophy of Science, vol. I, ed. H. Feigl and M. Scriven (Minneapolis: University of Minnesota Press, 1956), pp. 127–196. Sellars's argument is directed at the idea that one can identify some sensory substrate that is the basis for knowledge, but no such sensory substrate is involved in the givenness of place and world as articulated here. Indeed, as is evident from chapter 10, the topology that is exemplified in Heidegger's thinking is not inconsistent with a thinker such as Davidson who can be seen largely to endorse the Sellarsian rejection of the "myth of the given."

35. This way of putting things calls on both the idea of "end" as itself a mode of place (see Heidegger, "The End of Philosophy and the Task of Thinking," in *On Time and Being*, trans. Joan Stambaugh [New York: Harper and Row, 1972], p. 57) and on the close connection of place with limit or boundary (see, e.g., Heidegger, "Building Dwelling Thinking," p. 154).

2   The Turning to/of Place

1. T. H. White, *The Once and Future King* (London: Collins, 1958). Unfortunately for White's Merlin, this apparently backward temporal trajectory brings no foresight with it, since Merlin is in much the same situation as are we, except that his life runs opposite to ours.

2. The comment is quoted as one of the epigraphs to the epilogue below.

3. Emmanuel Levinas, "Ethics of the Infinite," in *Face to Face with Levinas*, ed. Richard Cohen (Albany: SUNY Press, 1986), p. 18. See also the comment by Edward Relph, quoted in chapter 3 below, p. 66. Gadamer notes that "[Heidegger's] critics are in the habit of saying that after the so-called turn [Kehre] Heidegger's thinking no longer stood on solid ground. *Being and Time* is said to be a magnificent liberation, a work through which . . . the business of philosophical thinking gained a new intensity, and responsibility. But it is also said that after the turn, which is tied up with his topsy-turvy political folly brought on by his own ambition for power and his intrigue with the Third Reich, he no longer spoke of demonstrable things. . . . A mythologist and Gnostic, he speaks as an initiate [*ein Wissender*]— without knowing what he is saying"—Gadamer, "Martin Heidegger—75 Years," in

Heidegger's Ways, trans. John W. Stanley (Albany, NY: SUNY Press, 1994), pp. 20–21.

4. Gadamer, "Martin Heidegger—75 years," pp. 25–26.

5. "Author's Preface to the Seventh German Edition," *Being and Time*, trans. John Macquarie and Edward Robinson (New York: Harper & Row, 1962), p. 17.

6. Whether Heidegger was himself ever in a position to engage properly with the latter is debatable. Not only does his involvement with Nazism in the early 1930s, and especially during the period of the Rectorship, show a tendency to idealize the movement (see Malpas, *Heidegger's Topology* [Cambridge, Mass.: MIT Press, 2006], p. 285) and to overlook its problematic elements, as well as a certain political opportunism combined with some naivety, but as was the case with many Germans of the time, it seems doubtful whether, even after the war, the enormity of what occurred under Hitler was ever something that Heidegger could fully acknowledge. Much of what is written on this topic, however, remains too quick to condemn and too slow (if not unwilling) to understand—and the response that Heidegger's actions do not deserve understanding merely serve to underline the error here. There is no doubt that Heidegger's involvement with Nazism reflects badly on Heidegger the man, but what it tells us about Heidegger's philosophy is much less clear. For one of the few sober assessments of the issue, see the comments by Laurence Paul Hemming in the introduction to *The Movement of Nihilism: Heidegger's Thinking after Nietzsche*, ed. Laurence Paul Hemming, Kostas Amiridis, and Bogdan Costea (London: Continuum, 2011), pp. 2–5. From the point of view of the topological interest at work in the discussion above, it is significant that Heidegger's increasing thematization of place is less a feature of his entanglement with Nazism as of his movement away from and critique of it. This is touched on in chapters 5 and 7 below.

7. This was already briefly addressed in chapter 1, but it will be further explored in the discussion below. Since I take the Turning as it occurs in Heidegger's thought and the turning that belongs essentially to thinking to be bound up together, my use of the uppercase "Turning" will be used to refer to Heidegger's own turning, but in a way that cannot be separated from the turning that belongs to thinking. For the most part, my use of the lowercase form is intended to refer primarily to the turning of thinking, or of place, in its generalized sense.

8. "*Preface* by Martin Heidegger," in William J. Richardson, *Heidegger: Through Phenomenology to Thought* (The Hague: Martinus Nijhof, 1974), esp. pp. xviii–xxi.

9. See Stephan Käufer, "Systematicity and Temporality," *Journal of the British Society for Phenomenology* 33 (2002): 167–187.

10. See Heidegger, *On Time and Being*, trans. Joan Stambaugh (New York: Harper & Row, 1972), p. 23; the failure of any such attempt at derivation seems acknowledged by Heidegger quite early. In *What Is a Thing?* (trans. W. B. Barton, Jr., and Vera

Deutsch [South Bend, Ind.: Gateway, 1967], p. 17), the text of a lecture from 1935, Heidegger comments that "while time plays a special role . . . that should not mean at all that space can be deduced from time or that it is something secondary to it." It remains a question, however, as to what extent Heidegger does arrive at a satisfactory account of time and its relation to space. One might argue that the "temporalism" of the early work is never completely thrown off—although this is complicated by Heidegger's tendency to already think the temporal in topological terms.

11. This is not straightforwardly so, and thus Heidegger emphasizes that *Being and Time* already begins from a position that has abandoned "all subjectivity of the human being as subject." "On the Essence of Truth," in *Pathmarks* (A translation of *Wegmarken*), ed. William McNeill (Cambridge: Cambridge University Press, 1998), p. 153. See also "Preface," Richardson, *Through Phenomenology to Thought*, p. xviii.

12. The point at issue here reflects a more general point about unity as such: properly understood, unity is never something imposed from "without," but always and only arises from "within"—that is, unity must belong to and so arise out of that which is unified. For more on this point see chapter 4, p. 83 below; see also Malpas, *Heidegger's Topology*, pp. 121–122, and Malpas, "The Constitution of the Mind: Kant and Davidson on the Unity of Consciousness," *International Journal of Philosophical Studies* 7 (1999): 12–14. This same point is also important in the understanding of the unity of a life, set out in chapter 9 below.

13. And therefore, on might say, it is not a genuine unity at all—see again chapter 4 below.

14. This work is also a central focus for the discussion in chapter 6 below.

15. Heidegger, *The Fundamental Concepts of Metaphysics: World, Finitude, Solitude*, trans. William McNeill and Nicholas Walker (Bloomington: Indiana University Press, 1995), p. 333.

16. Ibid., p. 177. See also Joseph Fell, "The Familiar and the Strange: On the Limits of Praxis in the early Heidegger," in *Heidegger: A Critical Reader*, ed. Hubert L. Dreyfus and Harrison Hall (Oxford: Blackwell, 1992), p. 66. Fell draws attention to the problem presented by the disclosure of nature in Heidegger's early thinking and the way this is actually distinct from the disclosure that occurs through practical activity. In this respect, Fell can be seen to be advancing an account that is also critical of the tendency toward an oversimplified conception of the supposed priority of practice in Heidegger. See also Heidegger, *The Metaphysical Foundations of Logic*, trans. Michael Heim (Bloomington: Indiana University Press, 1984), p. 181, and Heidegger, "The Essence of Ground," in *Pathmarks* (a translation of *Wegmarken*), p. 370, n. 59.

17. Heidegger, "Seminar in Zähringen 1973," in *Four Seminars*, trans. Andrew Mitchell and François Raffoul (Bloomington: Indiana University Press, 2004), p. 64.

18. Ibid., p. 171.

19. Heidegger, *Zollikon Seminars: Protocols–Conversations–Letters*, trans. Franz Mayr and Richard Askay (Evanston: Northwestern, 2001), p. 119.

20. Heidegger, *What Is a Thing?*, p. 176.

21. See Malpas, *Heidegger's Topology*, chapter 4.

22. See Taminiaux, *Poetics, Speculation, and Judgment: The Shadow of the Work of Art from Kant to Phenomenology* (Albany: SUNY Press, 1993), pp. 153–169.

23. Heidegger, "The Origin of the Work of Art," in *Off the Beaten Track*, trans. Julian Young and Kenneth Hayes (Cambridge: Cambridge University Press, 2002), p. 55. Heidegger's comments here are the subject of a much closer examination in chapter 5 below.

24. Ibid.

25. My discussion in chapter 5 of *Heidegger's Topology* is a partial attempt at working out the structure at issue here, although I would argue that it has to be supplemented by the more explicit analysis of the structure of place that is contained in my *Place and Experience: A Philosophical Topography* (Cambridge: Cambridge University Press, 1999). It is precisely that more explicit analysis of structure to which Casey and Stafanovic object—see note 41 below.

26. See, e.g., Heidegger's discussion in *Basic Questions of Philosophy: Selected Problems of "Logic,"* trans. Richard Rojcewicz and André Schuwer (Bloomington, Indiana: Indiana University Press, 1994), pp. 153–164.

27. Heidegger, "The End of Philosophy and the Task of Thinking," in *On Time and Being*, trans. p. 57.

28. For instance, it sometimes refers to a mode of thinking that seeks always to anchor being and for the world in some univocal foundation (the impulse that underpins metaphysics—and so also ontotheology), and that, as such, is inevitably given over to subjectivism (on this, see chapter 5 below), whereas at other times it seems to refer to that which preserves a genuine possibility for thinking within it. The equivocity that attaches to "philosophy," and to other terms, is not a problematic feature of the thinking that deploys them in this way, but is rather an essential feature of any thinking that does not succumb to forgetfulness.

29. As Casey's philosophical history of place, *The Fate of Place: A Philosophical History* (Berkeley: University of California Press, 1997), surely demonstrates.

30. The tension at issue here is one that I have taken up, in collaboration with Gary Wickham, in a rather different but related fashion in "Governance and Failure: On the Limits of Sociology," *Australian and New Zealand Journal of Sociology* 31 (1995):

37–50, and "Governance and the World: From Joe DiMaggio to Michel Foucault," *UTS Review* 3 (1997): 91–108.

31. Moreover, the way in which it "points" is through retaining within its own position elements of both that which it aims to overcome as well as that toward which it moves. This is why *Being and Time* remains such an ambiguous work—it is also why philosophy and metaphysics must remain similarly ambiguous.

32. Aristotle, *Physics* IV, 212a7–8, quoted by Heidegger as one of two epigraphs to "Art and Space," in *The Heidegger Reader*, ed. Günter Figal, trans. Jerome Veith (Bloomington, Indiana: Indiana University Press, 2009), p. 305. Hussey translates the passage as "Place is thought to be something profound and difficult to grasp," *Aristotle's Physics: Books III and IV*, trans. with notes by Edward Hussey (Oxford: Clarendon Press, 1983), p. 28.

33. See my discussion of this point in Malpas, *Heidegger's Topology*, pp. 10–16.

34. See *What Is Called Thinking?*, trans. John Glenn Gray (New York: Harper & Row, 1968), pp. 138–147, 229, 224.

35. Once again, see my discussion of this matter in Malpas, *Heidegger's Topology*, pp. 219–251.

36. See Aristotle's definition of place or *topos* in *Physics* IV, 212a5–6: "place is . . . the limit of the surrounding body, at which it is in contact with that which is surrounded," *Aristotle's Physics, Books III and IV*, 212a5–6, p. 28. On this account, place can be understood to be identical with the inner containing *surface*.

37. See *Being and Time*, H34–H39.

38. The question of the relation between phenomenology and topology is more fully discussed, and from a slightly different perspective, in chapter 3 below. Clearly, there can be no simple adjudication of this matter. Heidegger's own move away from phenomenology was as much determined by his own intellectual biography and situation as by any purely philosophical considerations, and although it seems that there are some senses of phenomenology that seem inconsistent with topology of the sort pursued here, there are other senses that appear entirely consistent with it. My approach in chapter 3 is to explore certain continuities, while also indicating the way in which a continuing focus on subjectivity in certain forms of phenomenological remain problematic from a topological perspective.

39. On the general issue of the shift away from the transcendental in Heidegger, see Malpas, *Heidegger's Topology*, pp. 155–175.

40. However, as I indicate below (see especially chapter 4, but also chapter 3), there is still the possibility of a revised sense of the transcendental being retained—a sense

of the transcendental as topologically interpreted—just as there may be a revised sense of the phenomenological.

41. See Casey, "J. E. Malpas's Place and Experience: A Philosophical Topography: Converging and Diverging in/on Place," *Philosophy and Geography* 4 (2001): 225–230, and Ingrid Stefanovic, "Speaking of Place: In Dialogue with Malpas," *Environmental and Architectural Phenomenology Newsletter* 15 (2004): 6–8.

42. Suspicion of talk of "structure" may be connected with a similar suspicion that is often directed at the notion of unity. To talk of structure is to talk of a certain sort of unity—a discernible ordering of elements by which those elements are brought into certain relations with one another. The defense and elaboration of a form of philosophical topology that is undertaken here gives a central role to the notion of unity as well as to the idea of a certain form of structural analysis commensurate with the unity at issue. The issue of unity is discussed in more detail in chapter 4 below.

43. Heidegger, "On the Essence of Ground," marginal note, *Pathmarks*, p. 123a.

44. In the sense that it is a move away from the emphasis on *Innerlichkeit* ("inwardness") that characterizes his earlier thinking—a feature of the earlier thinking that is particularly evident in the 1924 article, "Der Begriff der Zeit," that Heidegger wrote for (but had rejected by) the *Deutsche Vierteljahresshrift für Literaturewissenschaft und Geistesgeschichte*, and which is now available in English translation as *The Concept of Time*, trans. Ingo Farin with Alex Skinner (London: Continuum, 2011). *Innerlichkeit* is itself closely tied to the emphasis on temporality, and so can also be discerned in the argument of *Being and Time*. I would argue that *Innerlichkeit* cannot be made sense of in separation from the notion of *topos*, since it is only with respect to a *topos* that there can be any possibility of a distinction between inner and outer— *topos* is the establishing of the very distinction between inner and outer (as can be seen in Aristotle's account in *Physics* IV). The focus on *Innerlichkeit* alone involves a failure to recognize the mutuality that obtains between what is "inner" and what is "outer" that is already implied by the connection to *topos*. One can thus read early Heidegger as unduly preoccupied with the inward-turning character of *topos*, whereas the later Heidegger has recognized that turning as both a turning inward and a turning outward (the idea of *Innerlichkeit* is not abandoned, but transformed). The emphasis on spatiality as coordinate with temporality in his later thinking is one indication of this recognition. I am particularly grateful to Ingo Farin for the opportunity to discuss these issues with him, especially in relation to the 1924 essay, which is often seen as the "first draft" of what was later to become *Being and Time*.

3   The Place of Topology

1. See Joseph P. Fell, *Heidegger and Sartre: An Essay on Being and Place* (New York: Columbia University Press, 1983); Reiner Schürmann, *Heidegger on Being and Acting:*

From Principles to Anarchy, trans. Christine-Marie Gros (Bloomington: Indiana University Press, 1987).

2. See Casey, *The Fate of Place: A Philosophical History* (Berkeley: University of California Press, 1997), chapter 11.

3. See Schatzki, *Martin Heidegger: Theorist of Space* (Stuttgart: Franz Steiner Verlag, 2007), and Elden, *Mapping the Present: Heidegger, Foucault and the Project of a Spatial History* (London: Continuum, 2001). Other works that address the issue more or less directly include Didier Franck, *Heidegger et le problem de l'éspace* (Paris: Minuit, 1986), Emil Kettering—*Nähe: Das Denken Martin Heideggers* (Pfullingen: Neske, 1987), Robert Mugerauer, *Heidegger and Homecoming: The Leitmotif in the Later Writings* (Toronto: University of Toronto Press, 2008), and Alejandro A. Vallega, *Heidegger and the Issue of Space: Thinking on Exilic Grounds* (University Park: Pennsylvania State University Press, 2003).

4. See especially chapter 1, and the epilogue, below.

5. See Steven Galt Crowell, "Is Transcendental Topology Phenomenological?," *International Journal of Philosophical Studies* 19 (2011): 267–276.

6. For more on the ideas of "origin" and "ground" that are at issue here, see especially chapter 4, and also the epilogue, below.

7. See my discussion in Malpas, *Heidegger's Topology*, pp. 213–230.

8. As Günter Figal points out in "Spatial Thinking," *Research in Phenomenology* 39 (2009): 339, Husserl himself emphasizes spatiality (itself closely related to the topological) as essential to appearance—see Husserl, *Thing and Space*, trans. Richard Rojcewicz (Dordrecht: Kluwer, 1997), esp. chap. 5, §§19–24. Figal puts the point thus: "The spatiality of perception lies alone in the fact that it is perspectival. Thus, every view of something has its point of view, and this point of view is bound up to a particular place. This place can only be changed by moving somewhere else, and thus another aspect of what is seen can come into view."

9. Heidegger, *Country Path Conversations*, trans. Bret W. Davis (Bloomington: Indiana University Press, 2010)—originally *Feldweg-Gespräche (1944–45)*.

10. See my discussions of this matter in the following: *Heidegger's Topology*, pp. 156–175; "Heidegger's Topology of Being," in *Transcendental Heidegger*, ed. Steven Galt Crowell and Jeff Malpas (Stanford: Stanford University Press, 2007), pp. 119–134; "The Transcendental Circle," *Australasian Journal of Philosophy* 75 (1997): 1–20 (although in the latter the connection to topology is only briefly addressed). See also chapter 4 below.

11. In this respect, one of the dangers that attends some forms of the contemporary rapprochement between phenomenology and analytic thought, and particularly

between phenomenology and cognitive science, is that the transcendental-topological character of phenomenology is overlooked along with the distinctive character of the transcendental as such. This is a danger exemplified most clearly, it seems to me, in Hubert Dreyfus's work, in which the neglect of a properly transcendental perspective is itself tied to what amounts to a rejection of Kant (and, perhaps, of Husserl).

12. This feature of Kant's treatment of subjectivity, and especially of his treatment of the transcendental, is something to which Jaakko Hintikka draws special attention—see Hintikka, "Transcendental Arguments: Genuine and Spurious," *Noûs* 6 (1972): 274–281.

13. For some further discussion of this matter, see chapter 4 below.

14. See, e.g., Malpas, "The Transcendental Circle," p. 19—although even here a topological orientation is evident, albeit, as I note above, only briefly.

15. In fact, my claim is that any genuine unity is a complex unity—it is always made up of multiple and differentiated elements (see *Heidegger's Topology*, p. 122). If this point appears to be constantly repeated, here as well as in my work elsewhere, it is not only because it is so central to the thinking of *topos*, but also because it is so often overlooked. Genuine unity always involves differentiation in the same way that identity always involves difference.

16. For some preliminary indications as to the directions in which such a reading of Kant might move, see Jeff Malpas and Günter Zöller, "Reading Kant Topologically," in *Kantian Metaphysics Today: New Essays on Space and Time*, ed. Adrian W. Moore, Graham Bird and Roxana Baiasu (London: Palgrave-Macmillan, 2011), in press.

17. Malpas, *Heidegger's Topology*, p. 37.

18. Steven Galt Crowell, "Is Transcendental Topology Phenomenological?," p. 275.

19. I take this to be part of the Davidsonian rejection of the conception of normativity, at least as given terms of rules or conventions, as adequate to ground understanding—see, e.g., Davidson, "A Nice Derangement of Epitaphs," in his *Truth, Language, and History* (Oxford: Clarendon Press, 2005), pp. 89–109. If one takes normativity to be an ongoing *practice*, rather than as equivalent to any codification of such practice, then normativity *may* be given a grounding role here, but this is a much looser sense of normativity than is typically at issue, and it is hard to distinguish such normativity from a generalized notion of intersubjective engagement that also implies engagement within the context of an objective world.

20. For more on the Davidsonian position at issue here, see chapter 10 below; see also my "Philosophy, Topography, Triangulation," in *Triangulation*, ed. Cristina Amoretti and Gerhard Preyer (Frankfurt: Ontos, 2011), pp. 257–279.

21. See Malpas, *Place and Experience*, p. 41.

22. See Malpas, *Heidegger's Topology*, pp. 108–113.

23. Heidegger, *Being and Time*, H329.

24. See Malpas, *Heidegger's Topology*, p. 110.

25. Significantly, on an Aristotelian account, the derivation in both these cases can be understood as each combining at least three of the causes—material, formal, and efficient.

26. It should be noted that derivation may itself be a completely *formal* notion—the derivation of existential spatiality from temporality in *Being and Time* is not a derivation of the *content* of existential spatiality, but rather consists in a claim concerning a relation of formal dependence that looks very close to the sort of asymmetrical dependence advanced by Crowell.

27. On the latter, see chapter 10 below.

28. See chapter 5 below.

29. Miguel de Beistegui, "The Place of Place in Heidegger's Topology," *International Journal of Philosophical Studies* 19 (2011): 277.

30. For instance, in Heidegger, *The Fundamental Concepts of Metaphysics*—see the discussion in chapter 6 below.

31. On the spatial and topological ideas at work in "The Origin," see the discussions in chapters 5 and 12 below.

32. Theodore Schatzki draws directly on the Heideggerian idea of timespace in his own more social scientifically oriented account of the structure of human activity—see Schatzki, *The Timespace of Human Activity: On Performance, Society, and History as Indeterminate Teleological Events* (Lexington, Mass.: Lexington Books, 2010). I have similar hesitations about Schatzki's use of the idea of timespace as I do about Heidegger's. In both cases it seems to me that there remains a problematic prioritization of temporality, and a tendency, therefore, to revert to a reading of what is an essentially topological structure in primarily temporal terms.

33. See Casey, *The Fate of Place*.

34. See Young, "Heidegger's Heimat," *International Journal of Philosophical Studies* 19 (2011): 288.

35. The idea of such a productive rather than merely restrictive limit is one that is addressed in a number of the essays included here, but see especially chapter 4 and chapter 9. The idea of limit is closely tied to the idea of *topos—topos* is itself, one might say, a kind of limit (as Aristotle's account in *Physics* IV can be taken to

show)—and the discussion of place is inevitably bound up with the discussion of limit.

36. See, e.g., Heidegger, "Building Dwelling Thinking," in *Poetry, Language, Thought*, trans. Albert Hofstadter (New York: Harper & Row, 1971), p. 154, and Heidegger, *Parmenides*, trans. André Schuwer and Richard Rojcewicz (Bloomington: Indiana University Press, 1982), p. 82.

37. See chapter 9 below.

38. Heidegger, "Building Dwelling Thinking," p. 152.

39. Schleiermacher, *On Religion: Speeches to Its Cultured Despisers*, ed. Richard Crouter (Cambridge: Cambridge University Press, 1996), p. 52—the idea recurs at a number of other places in the same work. I am grateful to Alex Jensen for drawing this to my attention. For Jensen's own discussion of this and related matters, see Jensen, "Heidegger's Last Passing God and Schleiermacher's Speeches on Religion" (unpublished typescript) and "The Influence of Schleiermacher's Second Speech on Religion on Heidegger's Concept of *Ereignis*," *Review of Metaphysics* 61 (2008): 815–826.

40. Heidegger, *Parmenides*, p.111. The gods are better understood, he says, as "the attuning ones." See also Heidegger's comments on gods in *Contributions to Philosophy (from Enowning)*, trans. Parvis Emad and Kenneth Maly (Bloomington: Indiana University Press, 1999), esp. p. 357: "[Gods] not from within 'religion'; not as something extant, nor as an expedient of man; rather [they come] from out of be-ing, as its decision, [they are] futural in the uniqueness of the last one."

41. See Heidegger, *Contributions*, p. 218, and see my discussion of this structure in *Heidegger's Topology*, pp. 225–227.

42. See, e.g., Malpas, *Place and Experience*, pp. 29–43, and *Heidegger's Topology*, pp. 155–173.

43. On this matter, see the discussion in the epilogue below.

44. Young, "Heidegger's Heimat," p. 290—the embedded quotation is from *Heidegger's Topology*, p. 309.

45. See Malpas, *Place and Experience*, p. 176.

46. That there is indeed a problem here—and one that is configured more or less along the lines that Young sets out—is an issue that has certainly preoccupied me of late, and is the focus for one of my current projects (a book, *Ethos and Topos*, is currently in preparation), but the concern does not underpin my analysis in *Heidegger's Topology* in quite the way Young suggests.

47. Relph, "Disclosing the Ontological Depth of Place: *Heidegger's Topology* by Jeff Malpas," *Environmental & Architectural Phenomenology Newsletter* 19 (2008): 5–8.

48. Ibid., p. 5.

49. See Harvey, *Justice, Nature, and the Geography of Difference* (Oxford: Blackwell, 1996), pp. 293–294.

50. See Massey, *For Space* (London: Sage, 2005), esp. pp. 5–8.

51. See especially Lefebvre, *The Production of Space*, trans. Donald Nicholson Smith (Oxford: Blackwell, 1991).

52. See, e.g., Elden, *Mapping the Present*.

53. Relph, "Disclosing the Ontological Depth of Place," p. 8. In this respect, Relph seems to confirm the widespread prejudice against Heidegger's later thinking and in favor of the earlier discussed in chapter 2 above.

54. See Malpas, *Heidegger's Topology*, pp. 307–308.

55. See Young, "Heidegger's Heimat," p. 286.

56. See Heidegger, *Being and Time*, H54.

57. See Malpas, *Heidegger's Topology*, pp. 74–83.

58. See the development of this idea in Malpas and Wickham, "Governance and Failure: On the Limits of Sociology," *Australian and New Zealand Journal of Sociology* 31 (1995): 37–50, and "Governance and the World: from Joe DiMaggio to Michel Foucault," *UTS Review*, 3 (1997): 91–108.

59. Heidegger, "The Thing," in *Poetry Language Thought*, trans. Albert Hofstadter (New York: Harper & Row, 1971), p. 63; see also Malpas, *Heidegger's Topology*, pp. 278–279.

60. See Malpas, *Heidegger's Topology*, pp. 302–303.

61. Heidegger, "'Only a God Can Save Us': The *Spiegel* Interview (1966)," in *Heidegger: The Man and the Thinker*, ed. Thomas Sheehan (Chicago: Precedent Publishing, 1981), pp. 45–67.

4   Ground, Unity, and Limit

1. Thus, as late as 1955–1956, Heidegger gave a lecture course under the title "Der Satz vom Grund" (published in German in 1957 and appearing in English as *The Principle of Reason*, trans. Reginald Lilly, Bloomington: Indiana University Press, 1991) that focused directly on the issue of ground (the German word "*Grund*" means both reason and ground), taking Leibniz's statement of the principle of sufficient reason as his starting point. In those lectures ground and being are shown as belonging essentially together—as Heidegger puts it through the lectures: "Being and ground/reason: the same"—see *The Principle of Reason*, p. 51.

2. See Heidegger, *The Principle of Reason*, p. 49. And in one of the annotations to the earlier "On The Essence of Ground," he writes, "The question concerning the

essence of ground is therefore the question concerning the *truth of being* [*Seyn*] itself"—"On the Essence of Ground," in *Pathmarks*, ed. William McNeill (Cambridge: Cambridge University Press, 1998), p. 98.

3. Heidegger, *The Principle of Reason*, p. 76.

4. See Heidegger, *Kant and the Problem of Metaphysics*, 5th ed., trans. Richard Taft (Bloomington: Indiana University Press, 1997), p. 1.

5. Heidegger, *The Principle of Reason*, p. 51.

6. It is notable, however, that Heidegger himself refers to freedom as precisely "the ground of ground" in "On the Essence of Ground" (*Pathmarks*, p. 134). Yet he immediately goes on to say that "Freedom's being a ground does not—as we are always tempted to think—have the character of *one* of the ways of grounding, but determines itself as the grounding unity of the transcendental strewal of ground. As *this* ground, however, freedom is the *abyss of ground* [*Ab-grund*] in Dasein."

7. Heidegger, *The Principle of Reason*, p. 51. Notice that here the claim that "being 'is' not" must be taken strictly to mean only that the "is" cannot be applied to being. See *The Metaphysical Foundations of Logic*, p. 153, and "Letter on Humanism," in *Pathmarks*, p. 255.

8. Heidegger, *The Principle of Reason*, p. 111.

9. One might be tempted to say it is characteristic of philosophy *in the West*, except that one finds very similar tendencies in many varieties of non-Western thought also, while Heidegger claims that "Western-European philosophy is, in truth, a tautology . . . because philosophy is Greek in its nature"—Heidegger, *What Is Philosophy?*, trans. William Kluback and Jean T. Wilde, (Plymouth, Mass.: Vision, 1963), pp. 29–33.

10. See "The Question Concerning Technology," in Heidegger, *The Question Concerning Technology and Other Essays*, trans. William Lovitt (New York: Harper & Row, 1977), esp. pp. 14–23.

11. See, e.g., Heidegger's discussion in "Introduction to 'What Is Metaphysics'" (from 1949) in *Pathmarks*, pp. 287–288.

12. These changes can be most readily discerned, perhaps, in the contrast between the two works specifically focused on the problem of ground, "On the Essence of Ground" (1929) and *The Principle of Reason* (1955–1956). Heidegger's annotations to the essay, reprinted in the English translation in *Pathmarks*, indicate some of the changes in his thinking. See also Heidegger's comments on the earlier essay in *The Principle of Reason*, p. 45 (oddly, the reference to "On the Essence of Ground" in the bibliographical notes to *The Principle of Reason*, p. 132, refers to it as being included in *Holzwege*, rather than *Wegmarken*—the latter being the volume of the

Gesamtausgabe translated as *Pathmarks*—an interesting error given Heidegger's own severe criticisms of the essay).

13. Franz Brentano, *On the Several Senses of Being in Aristotle*, trans. Rolf George (Berkeley: University of California Press, 1975, originally 1862).

14. Heidegger, "A Recollection (1957)," in *Heidegger: The Man and the Thinker*, ed. Thomas Sheehan (Chicago: Precedent Publishing, 1981), p. 21. See also his comments in the "Preface" to William J. Richardson, *Heidegger: Through Phenomenology to Thought* (The Hague: Martinus Nijhof, 1974), p. x.

15. Brentano emphasizes the unity of being through its focus on the being of the Categories and so of *ousia*—see *On the Several Senses of Being in Aristotle*, p. 148.

16. Kant, *Critique of Pure Reason* (Cambridge Edition of the Works of Immanuel Kant in Translation), trans. Paul Guyer and Allen W. Wood (Cambridge: Cambridge University Press, 1998), A10.

17. See Kant, *Critique of Pure Reason*, B25.

18. See Heidegger, *The Principle of Reason*, pp. 80–81.

19. Heidegger often characterizes the transcendental as that which concerns *transcendence*—that is, the capacity of thought to move beyond itself to encompass that which is other than itself (see, e.g., "On the Essence of Ground," p. 109). The problem of transcendence is thus a problem that encompasses both objectivity and subjectivity. Inasmuch as transcendence is always transcendence "toward" the object, however, the problem of unity at issue in the Kantian investigation concerns the unity of objectivity (a unity that is articulated through the unifying—the synthesis—of concepts, and of concepts and intuitions)—where that unity is seen as dependent on a structure that does not refer us to anything *beyond* the experience in which the object is given, and yet is *prior to* that experience—as well as the way in which that unity is itself based in the unitary structure of subjectivity, that is, of reason. Heidegger provides a brief discussion of the history of the notion of the transcendental (particularly in its connection with the notion of objectivity) in *The Principle of Reason*, pp. 78–83. There he is especially concerned to mark out the innovative character of the idea of the transcendental in Kant. Heidegger thus elaborates on the difference between Kant's employment of the idea of the transcendental and that which appears in medieval scholasticism, as well as the way in which scholasticism can be seen as taking up the ideas at issue here in ways distinct from Aristotle, even though ultimately derived from Aristotle.

20. In this respect, Heidegger's attempt, in *Kant and the Problem of Metaphysics*, to try to show that sensibility and understanding are really stems from a single root, namely, the imagination, can be seen as mistaken through not recognizing the properly "transcendental" (in the sense suggested here) character of the Kantian

project. Dieter Henrich's criticism of Heidegger on this point is especially interesting. See Henrich, "On the Unity of Subjectivity," in *The Unity of Reason*, ed. Richard Velkley (Cambridge, Mass.: Harvard University Press, 1994), pp. 17–54.

21. Kant, *Critique of Pure Reason*, A65/B90.

22. Ibid., A11–12/B25.

23. Ibid., A783/B811.

24. Ibid., A737/B765.

25. See my discussion of this in Malpas, "The Transcendental Circle," *Australasian Journal of Philosophy*, 1997 (75): 1–20.

26. Heidegger, *What Is a Thing?*, trans. W. B. Barton, Jr., and Vera Deutsch (Chicago: Henry Regnery, 1967), pp. 241–242; see also pp. 223–224.

27. An issue already briefly discussed in chapter 1 above.

28. See Heidegger, *Being and Time*, trans. John Macquarrie and Edward Robinson (New York: Harper & Row, 1962), H315.

29. See Heidegger, "A Dialogue on Language," in *On the Way to Language*, trans. Peter D. Hertz (New York: Harper & Row, 1971), p. 51.

30. This is why skepticism is, on Heidegger's account, philosophically irrelevant, since what it would question is precisely the prior belonging together of thought and world. Hence his comments in *Being and Time*, in regard to the attempt to "prove" the existence of the external world, that "If Dasein is understood correctly, it defies such proofs, because, in its Being, it already is what subsequent proofs deem necessary to demonstrate for it," *Being and Time*, H205. In this respect, and in opposition to the generally accepted view of transcendental argument within, especially, the analytic literature (see, e.g., many of the contributions in Robert Stern [ed.], *Transcendental Arguments: Problems and Prospects* [Oxford: Clarendon Press, 1999], although note the different view presented in that volume by Graham Bird, "Kant and the Problem of Induction: A Reply to Walker," pp. 31–45), the transcendental is mistakenly understood if viewed as having the refutation of skepticism as its aim.

31. See especially Rüdiger Bubner, "Kant, Transcendental Arguments, and the Problem of Deduction," *Review of Metaphysics* 28 (1975): 453–467.

32. Immanuel Kant, *Opus postumum* (Cambridge Edition of the Works of Immanuel Kant in Translation), trans. Eckart Förster (Cambridge: Cambridge University Press, 1993), p. 254.

33. However, see Malpas, "The Constitution of the Mind: Kant and Davidson on the Unity of Consciousness," *International Journal of Philosophical Studies* 7 (1999): 1–30.

34. Kant, *Critique of Pure Reason*, Axii.

35. Aristotle, *Metaphysics, Books I–IX*, Loeb Classical Library, trans. Hugh Tredennick (Cambridge, Mass.: Harvard University Press, 1933), 1022a3–12.

36. It is worth noting that every origin can be construed as a terminus, but not every terminus can be construed as an origin. Thus every positive limit can also be construed as a negative one. To understand limit as origin is also, moreover, to understand it ontologically—that is, as determinative of the being of that which it limits. In contrast, we might say that to understand limit in the merely negative sense as terminus is to understand it ontically—that is, as pertaining only to a feature of beings, rather than as determinative of being. Heidegger tells us that, as he uses it, "ontological" is his word for what Kant meant by "transcendental"—see Heidegger, *Zollikon Seminars: Protocols–Conversations–Letters*, trans. Franz Mayr and Richard Askay (Evanston: Northwestern, 2001), p. 115. In that case, we might make the same distinction between the ontological and ontical here, in Kantian terms, by referring to the transcendental and empirical.

37. Although Kant uses the terms *Grenze* and *Schranke* consistently with the distinction at issue here, translators have not always been so careful. Thus in Kemp Smith, for instance, there is no consistent translation of the terms into English that preserves the clear distinction between them (the more recent Cambridge translation is, on the other hand, generally consistent in translation *Grenze* as boundary and *Schranke* as limit). I am grateful to Eliza Goddard for her work (unfortunately never completed) in investigating Kant's use of the *Grenze/Schranke* distinction and the issues surrounding it.

38. Kant, *Prolegomena to any Future Metaphysics*, ed. Lewis White Beck (Indianapolis: Bobbs-Merrill, 1950), p. 103.

39. See Kant, *Critique of Pure Reason*, A249/B306ff.

40. Kant, *Critique of Pure Reason*, B307. One might say that, in its proper, that is to say, negative, employment, the idea of the *noumenon* must be understood merely in the sense of a positive limit. This is to understand the *noumenon* "transcendentally" or "ontologically" (see note 37 above). When we treat the *noumenon* in a positive sense, however, we treat it as some thing that stands beyond the appearance and marks the point at which the appearance stops and the reality begins. In this way we treat it as a being that stands in relation to other beings and so, in Heideggerian terms, we treat it "ontically" or, in Kantian terms, "empirically" (as that which could be the object of some kind of experience though not ours). The dogmatic metaphysician understands the *noumenon* in just this latter fashion.

41. Kant, *Prolegomena*, p. 103.

42. Ibid., p. 109.

43. Kant, *Opus postumum*, pp. 173–174, 176, 180–181, 184.

44. Kant, *Critique of Pure Reason*, A235/B294.

45. See Jeff Malpas and Karsten Thiel, "Kant's Geography of Reason," in *Reading Kant's Geography*, ed. Stuart Elden and Eduardo Mendieta (New York: SUNY Press, 2011), pp. 195–214.

46. As Kant writes in a note in the *Prolegomena*: "High towers and metaphysically great men resembling them, round both of which there is commonly much wind, are not for me. My place is the fruitful bathos of experience," p. 122.

47. See Heidegger, *The Metaphysical Foundations of Logic*, p. 211: "Temporality temporalizes itself primarily out of the future . . . [which is to say that] the world, which is grounded in nothing other than the ecstatic temporality of the time-horizon, temporalizes itself primarily out of the *for-the-sake-of-which*."

48. See the discussions in chapter 3, "The Place of Topology," above, and chapter 6 below.

49. See Malpas, *Heidegger's Topology*, pp. 12, 249.

50. Heidegger, *Being and Time*, H151.

51. Ibid., H131: "[I]f we inquire about Being-in as our theme, we cannot indeed consent to nullify the primordial character of this phenomenon by deriving it from others—that is to say, by an inappropriate analysis, in the sense of a dissolving or breaking up. But the fact that something primordial is underiveable does not rule out the possibility that a multiplicity of characteristics of Being may be constitutive for it. If these show themselves, then existentially they are equiprimordial. The phenomenon of the equiprimordiality of constitutive items has often been disregarded in ontology, because of a methodological unrestrained tendency to derive everything and anything from some simple primal ground."

52. Kant, *Critique of Pure Reason*, A65/B90.

53. Heidegger, *Zollikon Seminars*, p. 115.

54. See, e.g., "Building Dwelling Thinking," in Heidegger, *Poetry, Language, Thought*, trans. Albert Hofstadter (New York: Harper & Row, 1971), pp. 149–150; see also Henrich, "On the Unity of Subjectivity," pp. 51–53.

55. See "Building Dwelling Thinking," pp. 166–167. See also Julian Young, "The Fourfold," in *The Cambridge Companion to Heidegger*, 2nd ed., ed. Charles Guignon (Cambridge: Cambridge University Press, 2006), pp. 373–392.

56. Heidegger, "Building Dwelling Thinking," p. 154. It is noteworthy that Heidegger uses the term *Grenze* here, translated as *boundary*. It is also worth noting how close is Heidegger's characterization here to that in *Parmenides*: "The limit as thought by the Greeks is not that at which something stops but that in which something originates, precisely by originating therein as being 'formed' in this or that way, i.e.,

allowed to rest in a form and as such to come into presence"—*Parmenides*, trans. André Schuwer and Richard Rojcewicz (Bloomington: Indiana University Press, 1982), p. 82.

57. See chapter 1, pp. 15–17 above; see also chapter 3, p. 61.

58. Heidegger, "The Origin of the Work of Art," in *Off the Beaten Track*, p. 30. The idea of truth as unconcealment here is prefigured in *Being and Time* (see §44) and is also developed in a variety of other discussions—see, e.g., "The Essence of Truth" (1930) and "Plato's Doctrine of Truth" (1930–31 and 1940), in *Pathmarks*, pp. 136–182.

59. Heidegger, "The Origin of the Work of Art," p. 31. Notice that this does not mean that truth is actually falsity, but rather indicates the way in which truth cannot be separated from unconcealment.

60. See Heidegger, *Being and Time*, H33.

61. Heidegger, "The Origin of the Work of Art," p. 30.

62. See, e.g., Husserl, *Ideas Pertaining to a Pure Phenomenology and to a Pheno-menological Philosophy, First Book*, trans. F. Kersten (Dordrecht: Kluwer, 1983), §44. Notice the way in which this also returns us to an almost explicitly topological frame: the character of an aspect is already dependent on orientation or "position in relation to." The idea of aspectuality cannot be elucidated without resort to the idea of the place within which the thing that appears (under some aspect) and the one to whom the thing is presented (under that same aspect) are both located. On the relation between phenomenology and topology see chapter 3 above.

63. See Gadamer, *Truth and Method*, 2nd rev. ed., trans. Joel Weinsheimer and Donald G. Marshall (New York: Continuum, 1992), pp. 269ff. The positive conception of "prejudice" to be found in Gadamer is clearly a development of the idea of the "fore-character" of understanding as set out in *Being and Time*, but Gadamer also emphasizes the way his approach is indebted to the account of truth in "The Origin of the Work of Art"—see Gadamer, "Reflections on My Philosophical Journey," in *The Philosophy of Hans-Georg Gadamer*, ed. Lewis Edwin Hahn, Library of Living Philosophers 24 (Chicago: Open Court, 1997), p. 47. On the topological character of Gadamerian hermeneutics, see Jeff Malpas, "The Beginning of Understanding: Event, Place, Truth," in *Consequences of Hermeneutics*, ed. Jeff Malpas and Santiago Zabala (Chicago: Northwestern University Press, 2010), pp. 261–280.

64. Heidegger, *Parmenides*, p. 82.

65. In talking of "nonbeing" in this way, however, what is meant is not the simple absence of the thing from some part of space, but precisely its hiddenness—its "nonsalience."

66. Thus, in the Le Thor seminar, Heidegger talks of three stages on the path of thought: from the thinking of the meaning of being, to the truth of being, to the place of being. See Heidegger, "Seminar in Le Thor 1969," in *Four Seminars*, trans. Andrew Mitchell and François Raffoul (Bloomington: Indiana University Press, 2004), p. 47.

67. In "On the Essence of Ground," Heidegger writes "[Transcendence] belongs to human Dasein as the fundamental constitution of this being. . . . If one chooses the title of 'subject' for that being that we ourselves in each case are and that we understand as 'Dasein,' then we may say that transcendence designates the essence of the subject, that it is the fundamental structure of subjectivity"—*Pathmarks*, p. 108. It should be noted, however, that this does not imply that *Being and Time* is straightforwardly subjectivist whereas the later work is not (Heidegger himself emphasizes the way in which his early thinking already stands removed from any subjectivism or anthropocentrism—see "On the Essence of Ground, p. 125 incl. n. 66; see also "Preface," in Richardson, *Heidegger: Through Phenomenology to Thought*, p. xviii). Subjectivity may be a necessary element in the structure of being (that is, of presence) and yet this does not mean that being is thereby made "subjective," since subjectivity is not the only nor the most basic element in the structure at issue here (indeed, in "On the Essence of Ground," p. 109, Heidegger claims that "world co-constitutes the unitary structure of transcendence"—see also the discussion of transcendence in "On the Essence of Ground," pp. 125ff). There is no doubt, however, that there are problems with the position Heidegger tries to articulate here, as he himself recognizes, and it may be that part of the problem is an ambiguity in the notion of transcendence itself inasmuch as it seems to refer both to the essential structure of *Dasein* and to that which encompasses both *Dasein and* world. It is notable that the explicit concern with the problem of transcendence, particularly as it relates to the problem of world, is a theme that runs through many of Heidegger's writing from the period 1928–1930—it appears in "On the Essence of Ground" (written 1928), in *The Metaphysical Foundations of Logic* (lectures 1928), and in *The Fundamental Concepts of Metaphysics* (lecture course 1929–30). In these discussions world arises as a problem in relation to the structure of transcendence particularly as that is based in *Dasein*; by the time of "The Origin of the Work of Art" the focus is directly on the structure of world as such—indeed, one might say that the structure of transcendence has there come to be based in the structure of world.

68. In "Letter on Humanism," Heidegger suggests that one of the problems with *Being and Time* is that it has to operate too much within the terms of existing philosophy: "these very terms were bound to lead immediately and inevitably into error. For the terms and conceptual language corresponding to them were not rethought by readers from the matter particularly to be thought" (*Pathmarks*, p. 271).

69. Herman Philipse, *Heidegger's Philosophy of Being: A Critical Interpretation* (Princeton: Princeton University Press, 1998), p. 102.

70. See Heidegger, "On the Essence of Ground," p. 129: "grounding something means *making possible the why-question in general.*" See also Heidegger, *The Metaphysical Foundations of Logic*, p. 213.

5 Nihilism, Place, and "Position"

1. The phrase "a desolate time" is used by Heidegger in "Why Poets?," in *Off the Beaten Track* (a translation of *Holzwege*), trans. Julian Young and Kenneth Haynes (Cambridge: Cambridge University Press, 2002), p. 200. The phrase is taken from Hölderlin's elegy "Bread and Wine," and provides the guiding question for the essay as a whole: "and why poets in a desolate time?"

2. See the discussion of these matters in chapter 7 below.

3. In *Heidegger's Topology* (Cambridge, Mass.: MIT Press, 2006), I argue that Nazism provides a somewhat ambiguous instantiation of modern nihilism—see *Heidegger's Topology*, p. 284 (I should note that this corrects the account of Nazism that I advance in an much earlier discussion in "Retrieving Truth," *Soundings* 75 (1992): 287–306—although I would still hold to many features of that earlier account).

4. What is at issue here is an "economism" that, in the narrowness of its understanding of the world, is also a form of fundamentalism, and like all fundamentalisms, contains within it an essential *irrationalism*—although in the case of contemporary "economism," it is an irrationalism that understands itself precisely in terms of what it is not, namely, rational. The irrationality of modern economism as it is instantiated in modern technology is given an intriguing interpretation, drawing on the work of Jacques Ellul, by Richard Stivers—see his *Technology as Magic: The Triumph of the Irrational* (New York: Continuum, 2001). The way in which modern economism uses the rhetoric of rationality even while the system of its operation denies it can be seen as another indication of its essentially nihilistic character—not even reason remains.

5. See especially chapter 2 above.

6. To some extent this is already suggested in "On the Essence of Truth" from 1930 (in *Pathmarks*, pp. 136–154), as well as in other essays and lectures, but it is only in 1935–36 that the direct focus on the thing and its "placing" first comes properly to the fore.

7. See my discussion of this essay in chapter 12 below.

8. See Gadamer's comments in his autobiographical essay, "Reflections on My Philosophical Journey," in *The Philosophy of Hans-Georg Gadamer*, ed. Lewis Edwin Hahn, Library of Living Philosophers 24 (Chicago: Open Court, 1997), p. 47.

9. Elsewhere Heidegger writes: "According to ordinary usage, the word *Gestell* [frame] means some kind of apparatus, e.g., A bookrack," "The Question Concerning

Technology," in *The Question Concerning Technology and Other Essays*, trans. William Lovitt (New York: Harper & Row, 1977), p. 20.

10. In "Language in the Poem," Heidegger gives particular emphasis to this sense of gathering by reference to the etymology of the German *Ort* (one of the terms by which the English "place" can be translated): "Originally the word '*Ort*' meant the point [*Spitze*] of a spear. In it everything flows together. The *Ort* gathers unto itself into the highest and the most extreme"—"Language in the Poem," in *On the Way to Language*, trans. Peter D. Herz (New York: Harper & Row, 1971), p. 159 (translation modified).

11. Heidegger, "The Origin of the Work of Art," in *Off the Beaten Track*, p. 53. It is worth noting that although the translation takes *Setzen* and *Besetzen* to mean "setting and taking possession," this rendering is not entirely accurate. As Ingo Farin has pointed out to me, *Besetzen* can also mean placing into a setting as one would a jewel (*mit Edelsteinen besetzen*) or the filling of a position (*eine Stelle besetzen*)—senses that seem more directly relevant, given the context, than "taking possession."

12. Ibid.

13. Heidegger, "Building Dwelling Thinking," in *Poetry, Language, Thought*, trans. Albert Hofstadter (New York: Harper & Row, 1975), p. 154.

14. Heidegger, "The Origin of the Work of Art," p. 53. Notice, once again, the way in which the notion of boundary or limit constantly resurfaces in the discussion of place—even place understood in terms of position or *thesis*.

15. Ibid., p. 53; see also Heidegger, *What Is Called Thinking?*, trans. J. Glenn Gray (New York: Harper & Row, 1968). p. 201.

16. See, e.g., Husserl, *Ideas Pertaining to a Pure Phenomenology and to a Phenomenological Philosophy—First Book: General Introduction to a Pure Phenomenology*, trans. F. Kersten (The Hague: Nijhoff, 1982), §117.

17. See Heidegger, *Plato's Sophist*, trans. Richard Rojcewicz and Andre Schuwer (Bloomington: Indiana University Press, 1997), §15, pp. 69–83.

18. See Aristotle, *Physics*, IV, 208b8.

19. As Heidegger emphasizes in his discussion of Aristotle in the *Sophist* lectures, the geometrical is distinct from the arithmetical in that, although both are abstracted from place, position is retained in geometry but not arithmetic—see *Plato's Sophist*, p. 76 (see also p. 72 where Heidegger notes that the full elucidation of this matter requires an inquiry into the question of place and space). The way in which the relation between the geometrical and the arithmetical develops in the history of philosophy, and the way in which *thesis* itself undergoes a transformation through

the transformation of the geometric in relation to the arithmetic and the algebraic, is another part of what might be thought of as the philosophical "history" of topology, although not one that can be dealt with here.

20. The relation between *topos* and *thesis*, and the general relation between place and "position," is both highly significant and yet also often overlooked. There can be no position without place, but much of the history of Western thought can be seen as a move toward the gradual obliteration of place by position, and the rise of a sense of "position" that is itself entirely "positive" or "constructivist." This is so not only in the sense in which the human determination of position is often taken to be determinative of place, but also in the understanding of place as itself a matter of relative spatial position. To some extent, it is this overtaking of place by position that underpins Edward S. Casey's account of the philosophical decline of place in *The Fate of Place* (Berkeley: University of California Press, 1986).

21. In fact, the ambiguity may be thought to be even more problematic than I have allowed here, since what Heidegger does not acknowledge is that even the Greek *thesis* can carry connotations of "positivity" in the sense of the "conventional"—see *Aristotle's Physics, Books III and IV*, trans. with notes by Edward Hussey (Oxford: Clarendon Press, 1983), p. 101—and was sometimes used, admittedly in a way more common among later Greek writers (especially some Hellenistic thinkers), in a way that placed it in direct contrast to *physis*: *thesis* was that mode of *nomos* (the conventional) that was distinct from the *nomos* deriving from *physis*.

22. Heidegger, "The Origin of the Work of Art," p. 55.

23. See especially chapters 6 and 7 below.

24. In the Le Thor seminar from 1969, Heidegger comments that *Being and Time* deploys the concept of "project" in relation to "meaning" in a way that makes it possible "to understand the 'project' as a human performance. Accordingly, project is then only taken to be a structure of subjectivity—which is how Sartre takes it, by basing himself upon Descartes"—"Seminar in Le Thor 1969," in *Four Seminars*, trans. Andrew Mitchell and François Raffoul (Bloomington: Indiana University Press, 2003), pp. 40–41. Heidegger's concern in the Le Thor seminar to preserve a sense of "project" and "projection" that is not subjectivist in this way can be read as an argument for the same "antisubjectivist" reading of *thesis* that is evident in his comments from the 1950s.

25. Heidegger, "Science and Reflection," in *The Question Concerning Technology and Other Essays*, p. 159.

26. Heidegger, "Seminar in Le Thor," p. 41.

27. See the other chapters in this volume, especially those in Part I, as well as *Heidegger's Topology*.

28. See, e.g., Heidegger's comments in *Contributions to Philosophy (from Enowning)*, trans. Parvis Emad and Kenneth Maly (Bloomington: Indiana University Press, 1999), p. 208; see also the comments in "European Nihilism," in *Nietzsche*, trans. David Farrell Krell (San Francisco: Harper & Row, 1979–87), vol. IV (*Nihilism*), p. 141.

29. As James Phillips argues in *Heidegger's Volk* (Stanford: Stanford University Press, 2000), Heidegger's engagement with Nazism is itself partly derived from his attempt to think of *Dasein* as the existence of a historical people, and of his attempt to rethink such existence in the face of the challenge of modernity. This project is continuous with the project of *Being and Time* even though it is also in certain respects divergent from it. The divergence is itself grounded in his attempt to rethink *Dasein* in terms that will address the issues of subjectivism that still seem to trouble the account in the earlier work (in particular, projection is now understood as grounded in the historicality of a people and is understood in terms of the projecting of the history in the form of destining of world). This view can still be discerned in "The Origin of the Work of Art"—something suggested by, for instance, Jacques Taminiaux's reading in *Poetics, Speculation, and Judgment: The Shadow of the Work of Art from Kant to Phenomenology* (Albany, NY: SUNY Press, 1993), pp. 153–169.

30. The *Contributions* should be read as a stage in Heidegger's attempt to work out the difficulty at issue here while nevertheless still enmeshed in that difficulty, rather than offering a definitive solution.

31. I would argue that this problem can only be adequately addressed topologically, and that only as topology can thinking begin adequately to take up the problematic at issue here.

32. Heidegger, *Gesamtausgabe*, vol. 39: *Hölderlins Hymnen "Germanien" und "Der Rhein"* (Frankfurt: Klostermann, 1980), p. 214.

33. See Taminiaux's discussion of this in *Poetics, Speculation, and Judgment*, pp. 153–169, and especially the way Taminiaux sees this as reflected in the differences between the various versions of the essay that were actually delivered.

34. Notice that what occurs here is a movement in which place is first transformed into the positional, which is itself understood in relation to the human, but in which the positional so construed then overtakes not only place, but also the human. Concurrent with this is a tendency to think of the positional in terms of a notion of spatiality as homogeneous extension—as an abstracted mode of space (one that is also essentially determined by *number*—see Stuart Elden, *Speaking against Number: Heidegger, Language, and the Politics of Calculation* [Edinburgh: Edinburgh University Press, 2006]). Place remains only inasmuch as it can be thought of as identical with a simple location within an extended spatial manifold (and so as essentially arbitrary).

35. Even the distinction between subject and object is no longer present in its original form, but is instead radicalized: "The subject-object relation thus reaches, for the first time, its pure 'relational,' i.e., ordering, character in which both the subject and the object are sucked up as standing-reserves [*Bestände*]. This does not mean the subject-object relation vanishes, but rather the opposite: it now attains to its most extreme dominance, which is predetermined from out of Enframing [*Gestell*]. It becomes a standing-reserve to be commanded and set in order." Heidegger, "Science and Reflection," p. 173.

36. See Heidegger, *Being and Time*, H89–101; see also H361–362, where Heidegger notes the way in which, understood in relation to the present-at-hand, the place of a thing "becomes a spatio-temporal position."

37. See, e.g., *What Is Called Thinking?*, p. 200—this passage is also notable in that in it Heidegger makes clear that the Greek thesis "does not mean primarily the act of setting up . . . but that which is set up, that which has set itself up, has settled, and as such lies before us. Θέσις is the situation in which a thing is lying."

38. See, e.g., Heidegger's discussion in the appendix (§9) to "The Age of the World Picture," in *The Question Concerning Technology and Other Essays*, pp. 147–153 (in the preceding section, Heidegger is at pains to explain how it is that subjectivism of the sort to be found in Descartes is not present among the Greeks, not even in the figure of Protagoras). It is no accident that Descartes not only plays a crucial role in the development of "subjectivism," but that he is also pivotal in the development of geometrical thinking, and in the shift toward an increasingly spatialized conception of place as well as a "positive" conception of the spatial itself.

39. Notice that modern subjectivism, although predicated on the bifurcation of epistemology and ontology, can give rise to what might be thought of as a forgetting of ontological issues in the face of the dominance of the epistemological.

40. Heidegger, "Nietzsche's Word: 'God Is Dead,'" in *Off the Beaten Track*, p. 195.

41. In the Le Thor Seminar of 1969, Heidegger tells us that "the concept of place (τόπος) . . . itself disappears before the positing of a body in a geometrically homogenous space, something for which the Greeks did not even have a name"—"Seminar in Le Thor," p. 53.

42. See especially chapter 2 above.

43. Notably in "The Thing" and "Building Dwelling Thinking" (both in *Poetry, Language, Thought*), as well as "Art and Space" (in *The Heidegger Reader*, ed. Günter Figal [Bloomington: Indiana University Press, 2009], pp. 305–309).

44. See Malpas, *Place and Experience: A Philosophical Topography* (Cambridge: Cambridge University Press, 1999) for an exploration of this issue from a somewhat broader perspective.

45. See chapter 6 below.

46. This is a theme that, not surprisingly, recurs throughout many of the essays collected here, but see especially chapter 8 below; see also the conclusion to Malpas, *Heidegger's Topology*, pp. 305–315.

6 Place, Space, and World

1. See Heidegger, *Being and Time*, H53–56. The use of the term "involvement" in this context is taken from Hubert L. Dreyfus, *Being-in-the-World: A Commentary on Heidegger's* Being and Time, *Division I* (Cambridge, Mass.: MIT Press, 1991), pp. 41–44—the contrast term against which Dreyfus sets "involvement" is "inclusion," rather than containment, but the nature of the contrast is the same. Dreyfus comments, in a way that might be thought to preempt some of my own arguments below, that "Heidegger is more radical than those who point out that . . . without metaphors like inside/outside that are based on spatial inclusion, as for example inside and outside our bodies, we could not think about more abstract involvement relations. This still assumes that the spatial relation is the basic one from which we imaginatively project the others" (*Being-in-the-World*, p. 42). As will become evident in the following discussion, although the spatial is more fundamental than Heidegger allows in *Being and Time*, the ideas of space and the spatial cannot be assumed to be identical with their employment in purely physical or "corporeal" contexts. The very nature of space and the spatial is, indeed, part of what is at issue. Moreover, the claim concerning the fundamental role played by spatiality (and ultimately by place) is not based merely on the ubiquity of spatial metaphors nor on any "imaginative projection" of spatial images and figures onto other domains, but instead arises out of close consideration of the concepts and structures at issue here—it is the inevitable conclusion to which any rigorous and consistent analysis of "being-in-the-world" must lead.

2. This is a problem discussed at a number of places in this volume (notably in Part I), but see also Malpas, *Heidegger's Topology* (Cambridge, Mass.: MIT Press, 2006), chapter 3.

3. See chapter 2 above.

4. Naomi Eilan, Rosaleen McCarthy, and Bill Brewer (eds.), *Spatial Representation: Problems in Philosophy and Psychology* (Oxford: Blackwell, 1993), p. 1. See also the successor volume edited by José Luis Bermudez, Anthony Marcel, and Naomi Eilan, *The Body and the Self* (Cambridge, Mass.: MIT Press, 1995), in which the body is the main focus of attention but spatiality also looms large.

5. A reading developed most fully, of course, in Dreyfus's *Being-in-the-World*.

6. "Derivation from," as I use it here, does not imply "reduction to," but instead refers to a relation of "foundation"—see the discussion of the idea of derivation (as

it applies in *Being and Time*) in Malpas, *Heidegger's Topology*, pp. 104–126; see also the various discussions of this issue in Part I above, pp. 26–33 and 52–55.

7. See *Being and Time*, H89–H101.

8. See especially *Being and Time*, §§22–24. I have forgone an account of the details of Heidegger's analysis of existential space here. I address the matter more thoroughly in *Heidegger's Topology*, chapter 3.

9. Heidegger also refers to it in "Time and Being," in *On Time and Being*, trans. Joan Stambaugh (New York: Harper & Row, 1972), p. 23. The "derivation" at issue here does not concern the *content* of spatiality from temporality, but rather its *structural unity*.

10. See Malpas, *Heidegger's Topology*, pp. 104–126.

11. Heidegger comments that: "Dasein's bodily nature hides a whole problematic of its own, though we shall not treat it here," *Being and Time*, H108.

12. Heidegger, *Kant and the Problem of Metaphysics*, 5th ed., trans. Richard Taft (Bloomington: Indiana University Press, 1997), pp. 18–19.

13. As can be seen, for instance, by the essays in Bermudez, Marcel, and Eilan (eds.), *The Body and the Self*, in which Merleau-Ponty appears frequently, but from which Heidegger is almost entirely absent.

14. Heidegger, "Seminar in Le Thor 1968," in *Four Seminars*, trans. Andrew Mitchell and François Raffoul (Bloomington: Indiana University Press, 2004), p. 32; see also the discussion in Heidegger, *Zollikon Seminars*, ed. Medard Boss, trans. Franz Mayr and Richard Askay (Evanston: Northwestern University Press, 2001), pp. 86–87. One might argue that the difficulty in clarifying the notion of the body that appears here is itself a factor in Merleau-Ponty's adoption of the concept of the "flesh" (*le chair*) that appears in his later writing (in, e.g., Merleau-Ponty, *The Visible and the Invisible*, trans. A. Lingis [Evanston: Northwestern University Press, 1969], "flesh" encompasses but is not identical with the body as usually understood, and is perhaps closer to what Heidegger means by "lived body"). It certainly seems to me a mistake to treat the concept of "flesh" as unproblematically continuous with the concept of "body" as it appears in Merleau-Ponty's earlier work. In "On kai khôra: Situating Heidegger between the Sophist and the Timaeus," *Studia Phaenomenologica* 4 (2004): 80, Nadar el Bizri points to Merleau-Ponty's thinking of flesh as providing a critical counter to Heidegger's account of space (in this regard el Bizri also cites Didier Franck, *Heidegger et la problème de l'espace* [Paris: Éditions Minuit, 1986]). In this essay and elsewhere, El Bizri develops a line of argument that has parallels with my own analysis.

15. With an eye to Heidegger's prioritization of temporality, one might be tempted to say that the notion of extended dimensionality that is at issue here already implicates time in that, as Leibniz might have said, it is a dimension of simultaneity.

Consequently one might suppose that the difference between space and time itself depends on a temporal distinction, namely, between simultaneity and succession. This would, however, be to misunderstand the structures at issue. Space and time, as I have emphasized above (see especially chapter 3), and will reiterate below, are indeed intertwined concepts so that each is necessarily implicated in the other. The distinction between space and time can thus be captured in temporal terms, by means of the distinction between simultaneity and succession, but it can also be captured spatially in the distinction between juxtaposition and superposition. Indeed, the very idea of succession, which seems to lie at the heart of temporality, requires the notion of superposition—we can say, in fact, that the temporal dimensionality involved in succession (or even duration) presupposes a sameness of space (or literally of position) that enables difference in time just as does the idea of difference in space also presuppose sameness in time. It is curious that whereas the importance of time to the understanding of space is frequently noted, it is very seldom that similar note is given to the importance of space in the understanding of time—Kant is a remarkable exception in this regard.

16. The emphasis on the idea of "ordering" here is significant, since what is at issue, and the source for much of the difficulty in Heidegger's discussion of spatiality, concerns the unity that properly belongs to spatiality—a unity expressed in the very idea of a spatial ordering.

17. See the discussion in Malpas, *Heidegger's Topology*, §3.3. The complexity of the space that is required here is also something that becomes evident in Dreyfus, *Being-in-the-World*, chap. 7.

18. One might say that a large part of the problem is simply a tendency already to assume that spatiality cannot be a source of unity. Spatiality is thus already taken to be such as to isolate and disperse, and it is temporality, reaching back into and encompassing spatiality, that unifies and orders it. The question is: what justifies the assumption that takes spatiality to isolate and disperse, and temporality to unify?

19. Heidegger, *Being and Time*, H369.

20. In the absence of some preliminary characterization of spatiality, the distinction between a notion of spatial containment or inclusion and of existential involvement, even as developed by Dreyfus, does nothing to dispel the obscurity that is already present in Heidegger's treatment of space—a treatment that Dreyfus himself notes is "fundamentally confused" (*Being-in-the-World*, p. 129).

21. See Heidegger, *Being and Time*, H55.

22. See Aristotle, *Physics* IV. Heidegger's criticisms of the idea of containment in *Being and Time* can be construed as partly directed at the Aristotelian analysis. In fact, those criticisms seem to beg the question at issue (as does much of Heidegger's

treatment of space and spatiality), by opposing involvement and containment right from the start.

23. The point is one made by Kant, in (among other places) "What Is Orientation in Thinking?" (1786) in *Political Writings*, 2nd ed., ed. Hans Reiss, trans. H. B. Nisbet (Cambridge: Cambridge University Press, 1991), pp. 238–239. In *Being and Time*, H109, Heidegger advances what seems intended to be a counterexample to the Kantian position. If one enters a darkened, but familiar room in which the usual positions of things have been altered or reversed, then one will be disconcerted and disoriented. One might conclude, therefore, that our grasp of space is not based in a grasp we have in our own person, but on our equipmental engagement. In fact, what Heidegger's example shows is that our grasp of space depends on being able to connect the sense of space in our own person with the larger space that surrounds us, and the capacity to make that connection does indeed depend on being able to relate ourselves to that space by means of things within that space and the regions in which they are located—which is precisely Kant's point.

24. See, e.g., Kant, "What Is Orientation in Thinking?," but also "Concerning the Ulitmate Ground of the Differentiation of Directions in Space" (1768), in *Theoretical Philosophy, 1755–1770* (Cambridge Edition of the Works of Immanuel Kant in Translation), ed. David Walford (Cambridge: Cambridge University Press, 1992), pp. 361–372.

25. See Heidegger, *Being and Time*, H109–110.

26. See the brief discussion of this matter as it arises in Kant's work in Jeff Malpas and Günter Zöller, "Reading Kant Topographically: From Critical Philosophy to Empirical Geography," in *Kantian Metaphysics Today: New Essays on Space and Time*, ed. Adrian W. Moore, Graham Bird, and Roxana Baiasu (London: Palgrave-Macmillan, 2011), in press.

27. The way "objective" is used here is thus not in the sense of what is constituted as an object for a subject (which is the sense in which it is almost always used by Heidegger), but rather the sense that involves a certain sort of independence from the subject. "Objective space," as I use the term (and as it is used in much of the existing literature on spatiality) thus refers to a space that is the space *of things* and we might say of *regions*, rather than the space of the subject or of the subject's body. It is also important to reaffirm once again that the concept of space as objective does not imply that space so understood is therefore entirely to be understood within the framework of natural science. Objectivity is used in a related sense (also distinguished from that employed by Heidegger) in chapter 12 below.

28. Kant endorses neither a Newtonian nor a Leibnizian view of space, although he certainly argues against Leibniz and for Newton on the issue of the relationality of space. One might argue that he does, in fact, combine Newtonian with

Leibnizian elements, treating space itself as unitary and nonrelational, whereas our sense of orientation and location is dependent on a grasp of certain forms of relationality.

29. The practical here appears as not prior to, but as already entangled with, the spatial, and the same is true of the relation between the practical and the *theoretical*. Rather than construe the practical and theoretical as modes of engagement and detachment, we should rather understand them as different modes of engagement in their own right, though typically also implicating one another (as the subjective is implicated with the objective). Heidegger's well-known critique of the idea that we can understand our "being-in-the-world" on the model of formalized, "theoretical" modes of comportment should be viewed not as an argument for prioritizing the practical over the theoretical, but for reconceptualizing the theoretical as itself a mode of practice.

30. Much depends, of course, on exactly how the subjective is understood here (and this is so independently of Heidegger's more general treatment of "subjectivism" in terms of foundationalism as discussed earlier in chapter 5). There is a possibility that the subjective might be taken to be a central structure and yet not be construed "subjectively" (that it might itself be understood as, for instance, a form of *topos*—a possibility I allowed in the discussion of Crowell's approach earlier in chapter 3). This is an especially important question in relation to Kant (as well as Heidegger). So far as Kant in particular is concerned, though he does takes the structure of subjectivity to determine the structure of experience, he also seems to treat subjectivity as encompassing more than just the subject.

31. See chapter 2 above.

32. *Critique of Pure Reason*, A25/B39. The unity of space also means that there cannot be multiple spaces—every putative space has to be able to be positioned in respect of every other such space. This is often thought to be a claim easily refuted—see Anthony Quinton, "Spaces and Times," *Philosophy* 37 (1962): 130–147—but it is only so if one treats the unity of space in a way that fails to attend to the manner in which this unity is itself tied to the unitary and interconnected nature of experience, and also action, as such. The idea of properly multiple spaces, even if understood in terms of multiple experiential spaces, makes for serious difficulties in relation to the unity that it seems must belong to experience as such.

33. Certainly this is true for any *finite* subject, that is, for any subject reliant on the deliverances of sensibility—see *Critique of Pure Reason*, A26/B42–A30/B45. I have not made this qualification explicit in my discussion above, but have assumed that it is indeed finite subjects or agents with whom we are concerned.

34. See Eugene T. Gendlin's discussion of this point as it relates to Heidegger's own discussion of Kant—Eugene T. Gendlin, "Time's Dependence on Space: Kant's Statements and Their Misconstrual by Heidegger," in *Kant and Phenomenology*, ed. Thomas

M. Seebohm and Joseph J. Kockelmans (Washington: University Press of America, 1985), pp. 147–160. It is one of the curious features of Heidegger's interpretation of Kant that he never seems to recognize the mutual dependence that obtains between time and space in Kant's work, but remains narrowly focused on the supposed prioritization of time.

35. See especially the papers that make up Dreyfus's debate with John McDowell, beginning with "Overcoming the Myth of the Mental: How Philosophers Can Profit From the Phenomenology of Everyday Expertise," *Proceedings and Addresses of the American Philosophical Association* 79 (2005): 47–65; "The Return of the Myth of the Mental," *Inquiry* 50 (2007): 352–365; and "Response to McDowell," *Inquiry*, 50 (2007):, 371–377. The exchange with McDowell often seems to operate at cross-purposes, and there is clearly much that unites Dreyfus with McDowell. However, what this exchange does suggest, and it is an suggestion reinforced by many of Dreyfus's other writings, is that Dreyfus's reading of Heidegger is more indebted to early Merleau-Ponty than to Heidegger himself, and, in some respects (particularly Dreyfus's rejection of the very idea of "mindedness"), Dreyfus's position even comes to sound rather like a more sophisticated form of Rylean behaviorism (a Ryleanism inflected by Merleau-Ponty together with elements from contemporary neurophysiology). Thus, while Dreyfus has been enormously and rightly influential in opening up Heidegger to an English-speaking audience, his work has also tended to skew the reading of Heidegger in a direction that is not altogether sympathetic to the character of Heidegger's own thinking.

36. Even apart from other considerations, there is something odd in the idea of content that cannot be given any conceptual or propositional characterization, and this alone should give us pause. This is not, however, the only problem to which the idea of nonconceptual content gives rise—see Jeff Speaks, "Is There a Problem about Nonconceptual Content?," *Philosophical Review* 114 (2005): 359–398, for an examination of some of these difficulties; see also my own earlier discussion in "Acção, Intencionalidade e Conteúdo [Action, intentionality, and content]," in *A Explicação da Interpretação Humana*, ed. João Sàágua (Lisbon: Edições Colibri, 2005), pp. 345–258.

37. Much of the difficulty in relation to nonconceptual content seems to arise from a failure to recognize the nature of the conceptual or the representational as it stands in relation to that of which it is a representation or conceptualization—a failure that is not well recognized in the existing literature. That spatiality, for instance, does not have a "content" that is nonconceptual should be evident from the fact that we have no difficulty in providing conceptual or representational characterizations of space—this is precisely what we do with maps, with written and spoken directions, and so on. Of course, those concepts and representations never exhaust the character of the spatiality at issue, but this is not because some content exists here that cannot be captured. Rather, the very nature of representation is always to be distinct from that which it represents and, as such, representation is never able

to capture all of the content of that which is represented (representation is not duplication). We might put this difference in terms of a difference between the conceptual and the nonconceptual, where the nonconceptual refers to that which is distinct from the concept (as the thing is distinct from the name), but such a contrast is misleading, since what is really at issue is the difference between the conceptual or the representational, and that to which the concept or representation refers. That the point at issue is not about two different sorts of content should be evident from the fact that, in the case of maps, for instance, any map can itself be made the subject of representation (most obviously in the form of a written or spoken description), and the resulting representation will stand in the same relation to the map represented as the map does to the space it maps—in both cases, there will always be the possibility of other representations, and in no case will the "content" of that which is represented be fully captured by any specific representation.

38. In chapter 2, part 2, of *The Fundamental Concepts of Metaphysics* (trans. William McNeill and Nicholas Walker [Bloomington: Indiana University Press, 1996]), Heidegger introduces three theses: "the stone is *worldless*, the animal is *poor in world*, man is *world-forming*" (p. 176).

39. Ibid., p. 269. The fact that the animal must have some access to world, although it is somehow also in certain key respects an impoverished access, leads Heidegger to say at one point that "With the *animal* we find a *having of world* and a *not-having of world*"—ibid., p. 268.

40. Ibid., §42, pp. 176–178.

41. Ibid., p. 243.

42. Ibid., p. 247.

43. Giorgio Agamben draws just such a parallel in *The Open: Man and Animal*, trans. Kevin Attell (Stanford: Stanford University Press, 2004); see my discussion of Agamben and related issues (some of which overlaps with the discussion here) in chapter 7 below.

44. Notably in von Uexküll, *Umwelt und Innenwelt der Tiere* [The Environment and Inner World of Animals], 2nd ed. (Berlin: Verlag von Julius Springer, 1921)—one reason for using the more popular work in my discussion is that not only does it provide a useful summary of von Uexküll's thinking, but it is more readily accessible to contemporary English-speaking readers than is the earlier work. It is, however, to von Uexküll's 1921 work that Heidegger refers in *The Fundamental Concepts of Metaphysics* along with von Uexküll's papers in the *Zeitschrift für Biologie*.

45. Von Uexküll, "A Stroll through the Worlds of Animals and Men" (1934), in *Instinctive Behavior: The Development of a Modern Concept*, ed. Claire H. Schiller (New York: International Universities Press, 1957), p. 5.

46. Ibid., p. 14. Von Uexküll's separation of these three spaces is significant, running counter to the emphasis on the unity of space that I discussed above (one indication of how different von Uexküll's neo-Kantian phenomenalism is from Kant's own position). In this respect, von Uexküll seems to make exactly the mistake of confusing different modes of spatial access or articulation with different modes of space. Von Uexküll's prioritization, in the case of the human, of the visual and the tactile is also noteworthy—he gives no significance to any notion of human auditory space.

47. Ibid., p. 48. The racialized character of von Uexküll's example presents a somewhat unsettling element given von Uexküll's own racist and anti-Semitic views, as well as his close involvement with the Nazi party (an involvement that seems to have run much deeper than Heidegger's). On von Uexküll's racial and political views see Anne Harrington, *Reenchanted Science: Holism in German Culture from Wilhelm II to Hitler* (Princeton: Princeton University Press, 1999), pp. 56–71. It is notable that in spite of his anti-Semitism, von Uexküll argued against an excessive focus on the issue of race, and, in 1933 in particular, made very clear his opposition to the anti-Jewish measures imposed by the Nazis (see Harrington, *Reenchanted Science*, pp. 70–71).

48. Von Uexküll, "A Stroll through the Worlds of Animals and Men," p. 48.

49. Heidegger is nevertheless surprisingly generous to von Uexküll in *The Fundamental Concepts of Metaphysics*. Thus Heidegger writes in that "It would be foolish if we attempted to impute or ascribe philosophical inadequacy to von Uexküll's interpretations, instead of recognizing that the engagement with concrete investigations like this is one of the most fruitful things that philosophy can learn from contemporary biology" (*Fundamental Concepts*, p. 263). On the other hand, while Heidegger notes the convergence of his analysis of the captivation of the animal with von Uexküll's approach, Heidegger is also quite clear in pointing out that "the whole [of von Uexküll's] approach does become philosophically problematic if we proceed to talk about the human world in the same manner" (*Fundamental Concepts*, p. 265). Heidegger's comments on the concept of *Umwelt* in *Being and Time* are somewhat more dismissive. Talk of *Umwelt*, he says, is "ontically trivial, but ontologically it presents a problem" (*Being and Time*, H58). Significantly, Heidegger does not mention von Uexküll in this connection, although he does refer to the biologist Karl Ernst von Bauer (1792–1876), who was acknowledged by von Uexküll as a major influence on his own work. In his 1925 Kassel Lectures on Dilthey—"Wilhelm Dilthey's Research and the Struggle for a Historical Worldview," in *Supplements: From the Earliest Essays to* Being and Time *and Beyond*, ed. John van Buren (Albany: SUNY Press, 2002), pp. 163–164, Heidegger also refers to the idea of the *Umwelt*, again without any reference to von Uexküll, but in direct connection with a discussion of spatiality (a discussion that in outline foreshadows that of *Being and Time*). Significantly, in this 1925 discussion, Heidegger appears to treat human "being-in-the-world" in a way that draws explicitly on the idea of the *Umwelt* (writing, for instance, that "The

environing world [*Umwelt*] is initially given in practical circumspection [*Umsicht*] ("Wilhelm Dilthey's Research," p. 164), but without expressing any hesitation or qualification about this usage.

50. The difference at issue here is frequently asserted to be nothing more than a result of anthropocentric bias, and to have been shown to be so by the work of thinkers such as Nietzsche as well as Darwin. Darwin's own claim, in *The Descent of Man*, is that the difference of human intelligence from that of animals "great as it is, certainly is one of degree and not of kind" (although Darwin's claim was based on the same anecdotal evidence that had for centuries been cited in discussions of this issue—see Darwin, *The Descent of Man and Selection in Relation to Sex* [New York: D. Appleton, 1871], pp. 65–113). Yet although many researchers in the area of comparative cognition repeat this claim, the actual empirical evidence seems not to bear it out (at least not in the manner in which it is usually understood), but rather to show that, while animals do indeed exhibit very highly developed forms of intelligence in specific areas, none exhibit the same general capacity for "intelligence" that is, for the most part, centered on the cognitive and behavioral differences associated with the singular linguistic capacities of humans (for an exploration of some of the issues relating to human uniqueness that are relevant here, see Louise Röska-Hardy and Eva M. Neumann-Held, eds., *Learning from Animals? Examining the Nature of Human Uniqueness* [Hove, East Sussex: Psychology Press, 2009]). It is significant that Heidegger also focuses on language as crucial in this regard, and that he emphasizes the importance of the grasp of world as such *and as a whole*. This characterization may appear opaque, but it nevertheless points to the capacity for human "intelligence" (if that is the right word in this context—and from a Heideggerian perspective one would suggest that it is misleading to say the least) to be such as to enable a capacity to recognize and articulate a unity that goes beyond that of any particular feature or aspect of things. It is this, of course, that Heidegger often refers to in terms of the "ontological difference," but which we can also understand in terms of the more fundamental idea of the play of identity and difference that is given in the play of time-space, in the unity of *topos* or "place." Whether and how such a notion could enter into the contemporary discussion of comparative cognition are interesting questions, and yet what is at issue here is nothing other the essential question of the nature, and so also the uniqueness, of the mode of being that is properly associated with the human.

51. See Heidegger, *Fundamental Concepts*, pp. 281–282.

52. See especially Heidegger, *Fundamental Concepts*, pp. 274–275. Gadamer is quite explicit in making a distinction between the animal's *Umwelt* and the human's *Welt* (see Gadamer, *Truth and Method*, trans. Joel Weinsheimer and Donald G. Marshall [New York: Continuum, 1995], p. 443). John McDowell cites Gadamer approvingly on just this point in *Mind and World* (Cambridge, Mass.: Harvard University Press, 1994), pp. 116–117. In the light of the issues being explored here, it is interesting

to reflect on the possible role and significance of "space" in McDowell's own concept of the "space of reasons."

53. Heidegger, *Fundamental Concepts*, p. 274. Elsewhere Heidegger talks about world as "the accessibility of beings" (ibid., p. 198).

54. Ibid., p. 284.

55. In fact, as Heidegger clarifies matters (and here he is concerned to distance his position from any subjectivist reading): "world-formation is something that occurs, and only on this ground can a human being exist in the first place. Man as man is world-forming. This does not mean that the human being running around in the street as it were is world-forming, but that the *Da-sein* in man is world-forming" (ibid., p. 285).

56. Ibid., p. 274.

57. Ibid., p. 301.

58. In the Le Thor Seminar of 1968 Heidegger writes that "There is only 'world' where there is language, that is, understanding of being" ("Seminar in Le Thor 1968," in *Four Seminars*, p. 32).

59. It is an argument already presaged in *Being and Time*, H218–219, and developed elsewhere—see, e.g., Heidegger, "On the Essence of Truth," in *Pathmarks*, ed. William McNeill (Cambridge: Cambridge University Press, 1998), pp. 136–154.

60. Heidegger, *Fundamental Concepts*, p. 339.

61. See the extended discussion in of *Zeit-Spiel-Raum* (as well as *Zeitraum*) in Heidegger, *Contributions to Philosophy (from Enowning)*, trans. Parvis Emad and Kenneth Maly (Bloomington: Indiana University Press, 1999), pp. 259–271 and also pp. 334–337. The idea of *Spielraum* appears in the discussion of the supposedly derivative character of spatiality in *Being and Time*, §70, where Heidegger talks of the "here" of *Dasein*'s factical situation as "never signifying a position in space, but . . . rather the leeway [*Spielraum*] of the range of that equipmental totality with which it is most closely concerned" (H369).

62. Heidegger, *Fundamental Concepts*, p. 369.

63. Ibid., p. 362.

64. Heidegger, *Introduction to Metaphysics*, trans. Gregory Fried and Richard Polt (New Haven: Yale University Press, 2000), p. 174.

65. "*In projection there occurs the letting-prevail of the being of beings in the whole of their possible binding character in each case,*" Heidegger, *Fundamental Concepts*, p. 365 (italics in original).

66. Ibid., p. 363.

67. It is notable that, in his talk of "turning toward" in *Fundamental Concepts*, Heidegger employs the German *Zukehren*. The way in which the idea of "turning" emerges in Heidegger's thinking in *Fundamental Concepts* (and is repeated in similar fashion elsewhere) suggests the intriguing possibility of a connection between the "turning toward" (*die Zukehr*) that is at issue in this originary event of world-formation and the "turning" (*die Kehre*) that comes to prominence in Heidegger's thought from the 1930s onward (referring, as noted above, to the Turning in Heidegger's own thought and the turning that is supposed to occur in the transition from "being and time" to "time and being"). One could well ask to what extent might the turning/Turning already be such as to depend essentially on the spatial, and to what extent might it be understood as the turning of and into the play of time-space—see chapter 2 above.

68. Heidegger, "Letter on Humanism," in *Pathmarks*, p. 272.

69. All of the aforementioned concepts are already evident in Heidegger's thinking by the mid- to late-1930s, with spatial ideas and images especially prominent in the *Contributions to Philosophy*.

70. Kant, *Critique of Pure Reason*, B293.

71. Ibid., A240/B 299.

72. Although the notion of the transcendental presents some difficulties for Heidegger as he attempts to shift away from what he takes to be the problematic character of the framework of his earlier thinking, that does not mean that the notion is not significant or that it is irretrievable—see, e.g., chapter 4 above.

73. Marcel Proust, *In Search of Lost Time*, 6 vols., trans. C. K. Scott Moncrieff and Terence Kilmartin, rev. D. J. Enright (New York: Vintage, 1996 [1913–1927]).

74. See Malpas, *Place and Experience* (Cambridge: Cambridge University Press, 1999), pp. 157–158; see also Georges Poulet, *Proustian Space* (Baltimore: Johns Hopkins University Press, 1977). The discussion in *Place and Experience* treats space alongside time as necessary elements in the structure of place as such—the focus in the present discussion, however, has been more directly on space alone.

75. In "Différance," Derrida writes that *différance* "(is) (simultaneously) spacing (and) temporization" (Jacques Derrida, "Différance," in *Margins of Philosophy*, trans. Alan Bass [Chicago, University of Chicago Press, 1982], p. 13).

76. Ibid., pp. 22–27.

77. See Malpas, *Heidegger's Topology*, pp. 311–314. On the concept of timespace, see also chapter 3, "The Place of Topology," above.

78. See Heidegger, "Seminar in Le Thor 1969," in *Four Seminars*, p. 41. The line of development that is indicated here is the main focus of the explorations in *Heidegger's Topology*.

7 Geography, Biology, and Politics

1. See especially Emmanuel Levinas, "Heidegger, Gagarin, and Us," in *Difficult Freedom: Essays on Judaism*, trans. Seán Hand (Baltimore: Johns Hopkins University Press, 1990), pp. 231–234. Levinas can be seen as something of an exemplary proponent of this position—the basic ideas Levinas advances here, and even something of his style, can be found in by many other writers. It should be noted right from the start, and the point is reiterated in the main body of my discussion, that the fact of Heidegger's personal implication with Nazism is not what is at issue here, but the nature and extent to which the holistic and "topological" elements in his thinking are themselves so implicated. This is an issue that I address in more detail, taking Levinas's arguments as an important starting point, in *Ethos and Topos: Toward a Topographic Ethics*, currently in preparation.

2. Just as Heidegger's personal involvement with Nazism is often seen as itself sufficient to demonstrate the politically reactionary character of key elements in Heidegger's philosophy, so the fact that many environmentalists in interwar Germany allied themselves with the Nazi movement, while the Nazis also gave support to various environmental initiatives, is often taken to demonstrate the politically dangerous and reactionary character of environmental thinking as such. The real picture is, not surprisingly, rather more complicated. Environmental thinking is not the primary focus of my discussion here, but much of what I have to say can also be applied, *mutatis mutandis*, to such thinking. For more specific discussions of the history of environmentalism in the Nazi period, see *How Green Were the Nazis?*, ed. Franz-Josef Brüggemeir, Mark Cioc, and Thomas Zeller (Ohio: Ohio University Press, 2005) and also Frank Uekoetter, *The Green and the Brown: A History of Conservation in Nazi Germany* (Cambridge: Cambridge University Press, 2006).

3. See especially chapter 2 above, "The Turning to/of Place," above; see also Malpas, *Heidegger's Topology* (Cambridge, Mass.: MIT Press, 2006), pp. 126–146, 155–175.

4. In *Heidegger's Topology*, p. 256 (see also chapter 2 above), I suggest that the Fourfold can be understood as made up of two axes, one spatial and one temporal (thought these axes also implicate one another). The temporal axis is that of the Mortals and Gods, and the spatial axis is that of Earth and Sky. As the Fourfold is realized in the happening of a specific place, so the temporal axis takes on the character of a specific history, and the spatial that of a specific geography.

5. This is a theme throughout much of this volume—it is central to the very idea of topology; see also Malpas, *Heidegger's Topology*, pp. 33–35, and Malpas, *Place and Experience: A Philosophical Topography* (Cambridge: Cambridge University Press, 1999), p. 40.

6. Heidegger's thinking on this point is, of course, indebted to that of Edmund Husserl—"being-in-the-world" is a development of the Husserlian analysis of intentionality. That analysis involves an understanding of consciousness as always already

involved with its objects, while the structure of intentionality is also such that the intentional object is always embedded within a larger horizon—see Husserl, *Cartesian Meditations*, trans. Dorion Cairns (Dordrecht: Kluwer, 1977—originally 1931). In this respect, I would argue (as I also argue in chapter 3 above) that Husserlian phenomenology already constitutes itself "topologically," even though such a way of speaking does not appear explicitly in Husserl. It is thus not surprising that much contemporary thinking that is explicitly oriented toward issues of place and space, and that typically adopts a relational or holistic approach to those issues, operates within a phenomenological framework.

7. Lucien Febvre, *A Geographical Introduction to History*, trans. E. G. Mountford and J. H. Paxton (New York: Alfred Knopf, 1925), p. 20.

8. Key works here include, among others, Anne Buttimer and David Seamon (eds.), *The Human Experience of Space and Place* (London: Croom Helm, 1980); Edward Relph, *Place and Placelessness* (London: Routledge & Kegan Paul, 1976); Yi-Fu Tuan, *Place and Space: The Perspective of Experience* (Minneapolis: University of Minnesota Press, 1977). For an excellent survey of recent articles on humanistic geography see Paul Adams, Steven Hoelscher, and Karen E Till (eds.), *Textures of Place: Exploring Humanist Geographies* (Minneapolis: University of Minnesota Press, 2001).

9. See Anne Harrington, *Reenchanted Science: Holism in German Culture from Wilhelm II to Hitler* (Princeton: Princeton University Press, 1999).

10. Giorgio Agamben, *The Open: Man and Animal*, trans. Kevin Attell (Stanford: Stanford University Press, 2004), pp. 42–43.

11. Troy Paddock, "*Gedachtes Wohnen*: Heidegger and Cultural Geography," *Philosophy and Geography* 7 (2004): 237–238.

12. In this respect, the comments in Paddock's reply seem to be rather weaker, and certainly less clear, in the connection they assert between Heidegger, Ratzel, and Nazism, than those to be found in his original article—see Paddock, "In Defense of Homology and History: A Response to Allen," *Philosophy and Geography* 7 (2004): 257–258.

13. Paddock, "*Gedachtes Wohnen*," p. 248.

14. Although he does not treat of the geographical tradition that includes Ratzel and Vidal de la Blache, in *Mapping the Present: Heidegger, Foucault, and the Project of a Spatial History* (London: Continuum, 2001), Stuart Elden does explore the way in which Foucault's thought can be seen as continuing a mode of spatialized or place-oriented thinking already present in Heidegger.

15. See, e.g., Julian Young, *Heidegger, Philosophy, Nazism* (Cambridge: Cambridge University Press, 1997), in which Young dissects the details of Heidegger's Nazi entanglements, and yet also argues that "neither the early philosophy of *Being and*

Time, nor the later, post-war philosophy, nor even the philosophy of the mid-1930s . . . stand in any essential connection to Nazism" (p. 5).

16. See, e.g., Charles Bambach's discussion of the role of the idea of "rootedness" (*Bodenständigkeit*), and associated notions, in Heidegger's writings and speeches from the 1930s, in *Heidegger's Roots: Nietzsche, National Socialism, and the Greeks* (Ithaca: Cornell University Press, 2003), pp. 12–68. Bambach argues that the preoccupation with rootedness and autochthony is present throughout Heidegger's thinking, not only in the 1930s, and that these notions are always marked by the logic of exclusion. Bambach's position seems to depend, however, more on the *assumption* of such an association than on any *demonstration* of it.

17. For more on the development in Heidegger's thinking that is at issue here, see Malpas, *Heidegger's Topology*, especially chapters 4 and 5.

18. See chapter 2, "The Turning to/of Place," above; see also Malpas, *Heidegger's Topology*, pp. 213–230.

19. See Malpas, *Heidegger's Topology*, chapter 4. See also Stuart Elden, "Heidegger's Hölderlin and the Importance of Place," *Journal of the British Society for Phenomenology* 30 (1999): 258–274.

20. One might argue that such a reading can be drawn, in part, from James Phillips's argument in *Heidegger's Volk: Between National Socialism and Poetry* (Stanford: Stanford University Press, 2005), although Phillips focuses more on the idea of "the people" and the role of poetry in Heidegger's thinking in this period, than on place as such (see, however, Phillips's discussion of the "uncanny homeland"—"*unheimliche Heimat*"—on pp. 169–217).

21. See Harrington, *Reenchanted Science*, pp. 53–54; Harrington refers to von Uexküll, "Die neue Umweltlehre. Ein Bindeglied zwischen Natur- und Kultur-Wissenschaft," *Die Erziehung: Monatschrift für den Zussamenhang von Kultur und Erziehung im Wissenschaft und Leben* 13 (1937): 199.

22. My own view is that the influence is likely, if it exists at all, to be at a fairly general level simply because of the neo-Kantian subjectivism (discussed further below) that is such a central element in Uexküll's thinking, and which Heidegger clearly attempts to avoid, if not entirely successfully, even in *Being and Time*. Heidegger and von Uexküll may have both accepted a holistic construal of the relation between the human, or animal, and the world, but they differ significantly in the way that holistic relation is understood (the analogy between "being-in-the-world" and the idea of the animal in its *Umwelt* is thus somewhat superficial, even though both can be seen as exemplifying a similar holistic tendency).

23. Thus Harrington quotes from a letter from von Uexküll to Chamberlain in which von Uexküll writes: "The cohesive power of the Jewish state is admirable. For

that, the Jews are completely incapable of building a state. All they produce is just a parasitic net that everywhere corrodes national structures and transforms the Volk into fermenting piles of pulp," Letter to Chamberlain, April 10, 1921; quoted in Harrington, *Reenchanted Science*, p. 60.

24. In *The Basic Problems of Phenomenology*, trans. Albert Hofstadter (Bloomington: Indiana University Press, 1989), p. 165, Heidegger writes that "The elucidation of the concept of world is one of the most central tasks of philosophy. The concept of world and the phenomenon it designates that has never yet been recognized in philosophy at all."

25. Heidegger, *The Fundamental Concepts of Metaphysics*, p. 264. See chapter 6, "Place, Space, and World," for a fuller discussion of some of the issues at stake here.

26. Heidegger, "The Origin of the Work of Art," in *Off the Beaten Track* (English translation of *Holzwege*), trans. Julian Young and Kenneth Barnes (Cambridge: Cambridge University Press, 2002), p. 55.

27. Heidegger, *Contributions to Philosophy (from Enowning)*, trans. Parvis Emad and Kenneth Maly (Bloomington: Indiana University Press, 1999), p. 208; see also his comments in "European Nihilism," in *Nietzsche*, trans. David Farrell Krell (San Francisco: Harper & Row, 1979–1987), vol. 4 (*Nihilism*), p. 141. See the discussion in chapter 5, "Nihilism, Place, and 'Position,'" above.

28. See Malpas, *Heidegger's Topology*, chapter 3; see also William Blattner, *Heidegger's Temporal Idealism* (Cambridge: Cambridge University Press, 1999), esp. pp. 277–310.

29. Quoted by Harrington, from von Uexküll's unpublished autobiographical notes, in *Reenchanted Science*, p. 41.

30. See Joachim Wolschke-Bulmahn, "Violence as the Basis of National Socialist Landscape Planning," in Brüggemeir, Cioc, and Zeller (eds.), *How Green Were the Nazis?*, pp. 243–256, and also Gert Gröning and Joachim Wolschke-Bulmahn, "Politics, Planning, and the Protection of Nature: Political Abuse of Early Ecological Ideas in Germany, 1933–45," *Planning Perspectives* 2 (1987): 127–148.

31. For instance, in his *Die Landschaftsfibel* (Landscape Primer) (Berlin: Deutsch Landbuchhandlung, 1942), Heinrich Friedrich Wiepking-Jürgensmann writes that "The landscape is always a form, an expression, and a characteristic of the people [Volk] living within it. . . . it is the infallible, distinctive mark of what a people feels, thinks, creates, and does." Similarly, Ludwig Clauss writes that "The manner in which the soul reaches out into its world fashions the geographical area of this world into a 'landscape.' A landscape is not something that the soul alights upon, as it were, something ready-made. Rather it is something that it fashions by virtue of its species-determined way of viewing its environment," Clauss, *Die nordische Seele: Eine Einführung in die Rassenseelenkunde* (The Nordic Soul: An Introduction to Racial

Psychology) (Munich: J. F. Lehmanns Verlag, 1932), p. 19 (this passage is also discussed in Malpas, *Heidegger's Topology*, p. 24). Although this passage neatly exemplifies the prioritization of soul and race over place, Clauss actually seems to have been personally opposed to the racial policies of Nazism (something not acknowledged in the discussion in *Heidegger's Topology*)—see Peter Weingart, *Doppel-Leben: Ludwig Ferdinand Clauss zwischen Rassenforschung und Widerstand* (Frankfurt: Campus, 1995). I am grateful for the reference to Weingart's work in Thomas Zeller, "Molding the Landscape of Nazi Environmentalism," in Brüggemeir, Cioc, and Zeller (eds.), *How Green Were the Nazis?*, pp. 164–165, n.15, who also refers to this passage from Clauss. The fact that Clauss's own politics diverged from the racial politics of Nazism indicates just how difficult (and dangerous) it can be to infer political from philosophical commitments.

32. Ratzel, *History of Mankind*, trans. A. J. Butler from 2nd German ed., 3 vols. (London: Macmillan, 1896–1898), p. 4.

33. Robert E. Dickinson, *The Makers of Modern Geography* (London: Routledge & Kegan Paul, 1969), p. 71.

34. See Mark Bassin, "Blood or Soil?," in Brüggemeir, Cioc, and Zeller (eds.), *How Green Were the Nazis?*, pp. 204–242, for a detailed exploration of the way Ratzel's ideas were appropriated and modified within the history of German geopolitical theory in the interwar period, and, more particularly, of the problems in reconciling Ratzelian ideas with Nazi race-theory.

35. Deleuze and Guattari, *A Thousand Plateaus: Capitalism and Schizophrenia*, trans. and foreword by Brian Massumi (Minneapolis: University of Minnesota Press, 1987).

36. See, e.g., Paul Vidal de la Blache, *Tableau de la géographie de la France* (Paris: Hachette, 1911).

37. See J. Nicholas Entrikin and Vincent Berdoulay, "The Pyrenees as Place: Lefebvre as guide," *Progress in Geography* 29 (2002): 143.

38. F. Ratzel, *Deutschland: Einführung in die Heimatkunde* (Leipzig: Grunow, 1898).

39. As Frank Uekoetter notes, in *The Green and the Brown: A History of Conservation in Nazi Germany* (Cambridge: Cambridge University Press, 2006), pp. 37–38; see also Celia Applegate, *A Nation of Provincials: The German Idea of Heimat* (Berkeley: University of California Press, 1990), p. 212.

40. See Thomas Rohkrämer, "Martin Heidegger, National Socialism, and Environmentalism," in Brüggemeir, Cioc, and Zeller (eds.), *How Green Were the Nazis?*, p. 181. Rohkrämer emphasizes the way in which Heidegger viewed this modern tendency toward nihilism and subjectivism as also tied to "humanism." The four volumes of Heidegger's Nietzsche lectures appear in English in two bound volumes as *Nietzsche*, trans. David Farrell Krell (San Francisco: Harper & Row, 1979–1987); elements of Heidegger's critique of Nietzsche also occur in a number of other works

from the same period. Heidegger's reading of Nietzsche was largely based on an acceptance of the volume *The Will to Power* as a legitimate part of the Nietzschean canon. In fact, as is now recognized, the work that appeared with this title was produced by Nietzsche's sister, Elisabeth Förster-Nietzsche, on the basis of her own selections and arrangements from her brother's unpublished writings. The volume reflected Elisabeth Förster-Nietzsche own pro-Nazi sympathies—sympathies her brother would almost certainly not have shared.

41. Bassin, "Blood or Soil?," p. 230—the embedded quotations are from Otto Maull, *Das Wesen der Geopolitik*, 3rd. ed. (Leipzig: B. G. Teubner, 1941), pp. 60–62.

42. In "Heidegger, Gagarin, and Us," p. 232, Levinas writes that "One's implementation in a landscape, one's attachment to Place, without which the universe would become insignificant and would scarcely exist, is the very splitting of humanity into natives and strangers. And in this light technology is less dangerous than the spirits [*génies*] of the *Place*."

43. See Malpas, *Heidegger's Topology*, chapter 3.

44. See Heidegger, "Seminar in Le Thor 1969," in *Four Seminars*, trans. Andrew Mitchell and François Raffoul (Bloomington: Indiana University Press, 2004), pp. 41, 47.

45. Heidegger, "Art and Space," in *The Heidegger Reader*, ed. Gunter Figal (Bloomington: Indiana University Press, 2009), p. 307.

46. See Plato, *Timaeus*, 48E–52D.

47. For a more detailed account, see Malpas, *Heidegger's Topology*, chapter 6.

48. See my brief comment on Tuan's work in Malpas, *Place and Experience*, p. 30, n.33.

49. See Entrikin, *The Betweenness of Place: Toward a Geography of Modernity* (London: Palgrave Macmillan, 1990).

50. See Doreen Massey, "Power-Geometry and a Progressive Sense of Place," in *Mapping the Futures*, ed. Jon Bird et al. (London: Routledge, 1993), pp. 64–67.

51. See Massey, *Space, Place, and Gender* (Minneapolis: University of Minnesota Press, 1994), esp. pp. 117–172. It should be noted, however, that the extent to which it is really *place* that takes center-stage in Massey's account, is debatable (a point also made in chapter 3, "The Place of Topology," above). What seems to concern Massey is actually the *imagination* of place, along with its sociopolitical formation, and not *place* as such (which she barely addresses).

52. Heidegger, *Parmenides*, trans. André Schuwer and Richard Rojcewicz (Bloomington: Indiana University Press, 1992), p. 117.

53. Heidegger, "Letter on 'Humanism,'" in *Pathmarks*, ed. William McNeill (Cambridge: Cambridge University Press, 1998), pp. 257–58. See, once again, James Phillips's discussion of this idea of the "uncanny homeland" (*"unheimliche Heimat"*) in *Heidegger's Volk*, pp. 169–217. The passage is briefly discussed in Malpas, *Heidegger's Topology*, p. 308.

54. Of course, within Nazi ideology, this prioritization of the human is always subject to the understanding of the human as determined by its racial-biological nature—as a consequence, the human is also subject to the competitive struggle for supremacy between racial groups.

55. Jules Michelet, quoted by Lucien Febvre, *A Geographical Introduction to History*, pp. 9–10.

8 Philosophy's Nostalgia

1. Naumann Naqvi provides a useful survey and discussion of the rise of nostalgia as a critical term in *The Nostalgic Subject: Genealogy of the "Critique of Nostalgia,"* C.I.R.S.D.I.G Working Paper n.23 (Messina: Centro Interuniversitario per le ricerche sulla Sociologia del Diritto e delle Istituzioni Giuridiche, no date), http://www.cirsdig.it (accessed November 2010).

2. Johannes Hofer first used the term in 1688 in his *Dissertatio Medica de nostalgia* (Basel)—see Johannes Hofer, "Medical Dissertation on Nostalgia," trans. Carolyn Kiser Anspach, *Bulletin of the History of Medicine* 2 (1934): 376–391.

3. This point is almost always overlooked in the existing literature—and especially when it comes to the discussion of nostalgia. The treatment of place as opposed to time, and as more or less identical with space, underpins the view that nostalgia, in its contemporary form at least, is fundamentally temporal in character. On the nature and importance of the distinction, as well as the relation, between time, space, and place that is at issue here, see Malpas, *Place and Experience* (Cambridge: Cambridge University Press, 1999), pp. 19–30.

4. However, in *The Aesthetics of Decay* (New York: Peter Lang, 2006), pp. 54–55, Dylan Trigg argues that nostalgia and homesickness are *essentially* temporal in character. The apparent shift here is presumably, on this account, a shift only in how nostalgia and homesickness are viewed, and not a shift in the character of nostalgia as such. Trigg cites Kant as having already recognized the temporal character of nostalgia when he writes that: "The homesickness of the Swiss . . . is the result of a longing that is aroused by the recollection of a carefree life and neighborly company in their youth, a longing for places where they enjoyed the very simple pleasures of life," Kant, *Anthropology from a Pragmatic Point of View* (Carbondale: Southern Illinois University Press, 1978), p. 69, quoted in Trigg, *The Aesthetics of Decay*, p. 54. In fact, what Kant's comments as well as the

position advanced by Trigg seem to indicate is the way space and time are both bound up with nostalgia through nostalgia's very relation to home and so also to place.

5. See, e.g., Janelle L. Wilson, *Nostalgia: Sanctuary of Meaning* (Lewisburg: Bucknell University Press, 2005), pp. 22–23.

6. In her discussion of the early history of "nostalgia," Svetlana Boym reports that "Swiss scientists found that rustic mothers' soups, thick village milk and the folk melodies of Alpine valleys were particularly conducive to triggering a nostalgic reaction in Swiss soldiers. Supposedly the sounds of 'a certain rustic cantilena' that accompanied shepherds in their driving of the herds to pasture immediately provoked an epidemic of nostalgia among Swiss soldiers serving in France. Similarly, Scots, particularly Highlanders, were known to succumb to incapacitating nostalgia when hearing the sound of bagpipes—so much so, in fact, that their military superiors had to prohibit them from playing, singing or even whistling native tunes in a suggestive manner," Boym, *The Future of Nostalgia* (New York: Basic Books, 2001), p. 4.

7. See Wilson, *Nostalgia: Sanctuary of Meaning*, p. 23.

8. From a Freudian psychoanalytic viewpoint, according to Trigg, nostalgia is "synonymous with regression," and the desire for home is "tantamount to a desire for parental supervision." See Trigg, *The Aesthetics of Decay*, pp. 53–54.

9. Peter Fritzsche, "Specters of History: On Nostalgia, Exile, and Modernity," *American Historical Review* 106 (2001): 5, 9. Fritzsche draws on a number of analyses of historical modernity, especially the work of Reinhart Koselleck, *Futures Past: On the Semantics of Historical Time* (Cambridge, Mass.: MIT Press, 1985).

10. It is just such a more encompassing sense of time that is the object of Proust's search in *A la recherche du temps perdu* ("In search of lost time")—a work whose final book, *Le temps retrouvé* ("Time regained") ends with the reclamation of time understood as a form of encompassing place—see *Le temps retrouvé, A la recherche du temps perdu*, vol. 3 (Paris: Gallimard, 1954), p. 1048; see also my discussion in *Place and Experience*, pp. 161–163.

11. Theodore Ziolkowski, "Review of *Five Portraits: Modernity and the Imagination in Twentieth-Century German Writing*, Michael André Bernstein," *Modernism/Modernity* 8 (2001): 360.

12. See the discussion in chapter 11, "Heidegger in Benjamin's City," below.

13. Allan Megill, *Prophets of Extremity* (Berkeley: University of California Press, 1985), p. 125.

14. Albert Borgman, *Technology and the Character of Contemporary Life* (Chicago: University of Chicago Press, 1984), p. 196.

15. See, e.g., Heidegger, *Basic Concepts*, trans. Gary E. Aylesworth (Bloomington: Indiana University Press, 1993), p. 75, and also, once again, "Letter on 'Humanism,'" pp. 257–258.

16. Heidegger, *The Fundamental Concepts of Metaphysics*, trans. William McNeill and Nicholas Walker (Bloomington: Indiana University Press, 1995), p. 5—the citation from Novalis is given in Heidegger's text as Novalis, *Schriften*, ed. J. Minor, vol. II (Jena, 1923), p. 179, fr. 21.

17. Heidegger, "Who Is Nietzsche's Zarathustra?," trans B. Magnus, *Review of Metaphysics* 20 (1967): 412.

18. Trigg is critical of what he terms "Heidegger's spatial-centrism" (*The Aesthetics of Decay*, p. xvi), claiming that "Heidegger's musings on homelessness persistently reference the geometrical-spatial field, and so revert to the pre-reflective diagnosis of nostalgia as geographical displacement, and that alone. His failure to grasp homesickness in temporal terms is especially striking given the attention time receives in *Being and Time*. The omission is further heightened, since temporality is at the structural core of nostalgia" (*The Aesthetics of Decay*, p. 54). Trigg's criticisms sit rather oddly, however, with some of his discussion of Heidegger elsewhere in the book, especially in chapter 15, pp. 199–207, where the issue of "spatial-centrism" seems to have disappeared, and there appears to be a stronger appreciation of the centrality of place in Heidegger's account. Moreover, Trigg seems to give little or no attention to the shifts in Heidegger's thinking of space, nor to the problematic character of Heidegger's treatment of space (and place) in his magnum opus.

19. Poulet, *Proustian Space* (Baltimore: Johns Hopkins University Press, 1977).

20. See my discussion of Proust in *Place and Experience*, pp. 157–174. When I say there that Proust's work is "not primarily a work of nostalgic recollection, but is instead a project of recovery and reclamation" (p. 159), I am employing a rather narrower sense of the nostalgic than I have used here, the main point being that Proust's work is not oriented toward passive reminiscence, but is directed instead at a more active task of retrieval.

21. Fred Davis thus distinguishes between collective and individual nostalgia—see Davis, *Yearning for Yesterday: A Sociology of Nostalgia* (New York: The Free Press, 1979), p. 222.

22. Boym, *The Future of Nostalgia*, pp. 12, 17.

23. Davis, *Yearning for Yesterday*.

24. Wilson, *Nostalgia: Sanctuary of Meaning*.

25. *Stimmung* can mean "mood," "temper," or "disposition," as well as "tuning" or "tonality," and comes from the verb *stimmen* (meaning "to tune"—as in the tuning of an instrument—and "to vote"), as well as to *Stimme* (meaning "voice"

and "vote"—the latter in the sense of that which one gives to a candidate); it is also related to *bestimmen*, which means "to will," "to determine," or "to decide."

26. Otto Bollnow, *Das Wesen der Stimmungen* (Klostermann: Frankfurt am Main, 1941), pp. 40–41 (translation by the author).

27. Casey, "The World of Nostalgia," *Man and World* 20 (1987): 368. Casey adds that "on the other hand, it is not the simple summation of these memories."

28. On the connection between memory and place, see my discussion in *Place and Experience*, pp. 100–107; see also Edward S. Casey, *Remembering: A Phenomenological Study* (Bloomington: Indiana University Press, 1987), chapter 9, pp. 181–215.

29. Heidegger, "Introduction to 'What Is Metaphysics,'" in *Pathmarks*, p. 283.

30. See Malpas, *Heidegger's Topology* (Cambridge, Mass.: MIT Press, 2006), chapters 2 and 3.

31. Boym, *The Future of Nostalgia*, p. xviii, see also p. 49.

32. Fritzsche, "Specters of History," p. 11.

33. Wilson, *Nostalgia: Sanctuary of Meaning*, p. 157.

34. The discontinuity present here is thus an essential feature of our mode of being-in-the-world, and so of our mode of being-in-place, even though it is in the experience of nostalgia that it becomes most clearly evident. On the estrangement that is an inevitable part of our sense of self as well as our sense of place, see my "Philosophising Place in *The Joshua Tree*," in *U2 and Philosophy*, ed. Mark Wrathall (Chicago: Open Court, 2006), pp. 45–59.

35. Maurice Merleau-Ponty, *The Phenomenology of Perception*, trans. Colin Smith (London: Routledge & Kegan Paul, 1962), p. 407.

36. Crowell, "Spectral History: Narrative, Nostalgia, and the Time of the I," *Research in Phenomenology* 29 (1999): 96. Crowell acknowledges that his approach follows that of Frank Ankersmit's "Historiography and Postmodernism: A Phenomenology of Historical Experience," in *History and Tropology: The Rise and Fall of Metaphor* (Berkeley: University of California Press, 1994), quoting Ankersmit's claim that nostalgia represents "an authentic experience of the past in which the past can still assert its independence from historical writing" (Ankersmit, "Historiography and Postmodernism," p. 94, quoted by Crowell in "Spectral History," p. 86).

37. Crowell, "Spectral History," p. 97.

38. The strangeness at issue here is directly connected with the strangeness that is also encountered in the attempt to grasp our own mortality—see my "The Discomfit of Strangeness," *Philosopher's Magazine* 27 (2004): 34–36.

39. Casey, "The World of Nostalgia," p. 361.

40. Heidegger, *Basic Concepts*, p. 78; see also Heidegger's comments in *Kant and the Problem of Metaphysics*, 5th ed., trans. Richard Taft (Bloomington: Indiana University Press, 1997), p. 164, in which he talks of metaphysics as a "remembering again"; see also his brief comment on the character of thinking as remembrance and also as thanksgiving in *Sojourns*, trans. John Panteleimon Manoussakis (Albany: SUNY Press, 2005), p. 35.

41. Heidegger, "Who Is Nietzsche's Zarathustra?," p. 412.

9   Death and the End of Life

1. Tom Stoppard, *Rosencrantz and Guildenstern Are Dead*, act 2 (New York: Grove Weidenfeld, 1967), pp. 71–72.

2. See Bernard Williams, "The Makropulos Case: Reflections on the Tedium of Immortality," in his *Problems of the Self: Philosophical Papers 1956–1972* (Cambridge: Cambridge University Press, 1973), pp. 82–100.

3. Williams also argues against the Lucretian and Epicurean position that death is never an evil, concluding that "death is at any time an evil, and it is always better to live than to die," ibid., p. 81. Notwithstanding the contemporary attention this question has received (mostly from within an analytic framework), it is not a question to which I will attend here; but see my brief comments in "The Discomfit of Strangeness," *Philosopher's Magazine* 27 (2004): 35.

4. Whereas Williams's account is perhaps one that does not go quite far enough, Jorge Luis Borges advances a view of the connection between mortality and the having of life that is much closer to the Heideggerian account that I advance here. In his short story "The Immortal" (in *Collected Fictions*, trans. Andrew Hurley [New York: Penguin, 1998], pp.183-195) he describes those who have drunk from the river of immortality as having lost not merely their appetite, but their very capacity for properly human life (I refer to Borges's treatment in the discussion below). Although focusing much more directly on the ethical character of a life, some of Martha Nussbaum's work is also suggestive of a strong connection between the possibility of human life and the mortality and contingency of that life—see her "Aristotle on Human Nature and the Foundations of Ethics," in *World, Mind, and Ethics*, ed. J. E. J. Altham and Ross Harrison (Cambridge: Cambridge University Press, 1995), pp. 86–131, and *The Fragility of Goodness* (Cambridge: Cambridge University Press, 1986). The idea that human life is necessarily a mortal life, and that its value and significance is inseparable from its finitude, is, of course, a widespread theme in much art and literature.

5. Heidegger, "The End of Philosophy and the Task of Thinking," in *On Time and Being*, trans. Joan Stambaugh (New York: Harper & Row, 1972), p. 57. Does this mean that death is therefore to be viewed, to paraphrase Heidegger, as "that in which the whole of a life is gathered in its most extreme possibility"? Perhaps not in quite the

sense that Heidegger uses in this essay, in which the emphasis is on the way in which the end of philosophy is the attaining of a set of extreme possibilities, prefigured in philosophy's beginning, that are now evident in the dominance of technological-bureaucratic rationality. Yet if this gathering of possibility is to be understood in terms of the way in which, at the ending of a life, the character of that life becomes evident (in something like the sense at issue in Solon's injunction "call no man happy until he is dead" repeated by Aristotle in *Nicomachean Ethics* 1.10, but also in the sense in which, in the language of *Being and Time*, death is *Dasein*'s "ownmost possibility," *Being and Time*, H250), then death may indeed be understood in just this fashion. Although some care still needs to be exercised—see the note immediately below.

6. It is striking that in *Being and Time*, H244–245, Heidegger includes a brief discussion of "end," emphasizing that "end," as it applies to death, cannot mean "stopping," "fulfilling" (as a mode of being finished), or "disappearing" (being used up or run out of). Neither the end of philosophy nor the end of life can thus be thought of in terms of a stopping, a fulfilling (or finishing), or a disappearing—at least not if we are to think of these in a sense that is ontologically significant.

7. Some of the issues at stake here were briefly dealt with in the discussion of Julian Young's criticism of the idea of death as a "dark limit" in chapter 3, "The Place of Topology," above.

8. The argument is also one that draws on ideas present in Davidson's work, and so the discussion can be seen to adumbrate some of what is developed further in the following chapter, chapter 10, "Topology, Triangulation, and Truth."

9. Getting clear on the nature of this difference is one of the most difficult tasks in philosophy. One of Heidegger's most sustained attempts to explore this difference (as it arises specifically in the comparison between our own relation to the world and that of other entities, especially animals), is undertaken by Heidegger in *The Fundamental Concepts of Metaphysics: World, Finitude, Solitude*, trans. William McNeill and Nicholas Walker (Bloomington: Indiana University Press, 1996). See the discussion above in chapter 6, "Place, Space, and World." Getting clear as to the nature of this difference is also impossible, I would argue, without getting clear as to the nature and significance of place.

10. One might say that there is a reciprocal placing at work here in which our own placedness both draws on, but also contributes to, the placedness of the world and of what is given in the world. As we have already seen throughout many of the discussions above, such reciprocity is characteristic of the topological; see also Malpas, *Place and Experience* (Cambridge: Cambridge University Press, 1999), pp. 157–158.

11. A more detailed argument for this claim is set out in the core chapters of Malpas, *Place and Experience*—especially chapters 3–5.

12. Insofar as I locate the sight of the bird within such a worldly frame, then my experience of the bird, though it is an experience of the same bird as that in which my cat shows such keen interest, is also a very different experience. And in this latter sense I may be said to have a different "grasp" of the bird from that of my cat.

13. A lack or deficit can only arise in relation to a lack or deficit in the very mode of being proper to the creature or entity—in its contingent inability to realize some capacity proper to it.

14. The point at issue here reflects a more general point about unity (one already dealt with at a number of points in the discussion above—see, e.g., chapter 4): properly understood, unity is never something imposed from "without," but always and only arises from "within"—that is, unity must belong to and so arise out of that which is unified.

15. The distinction between time and space, and the focus on the temporal in the understanding of a life, and of the activity that makes up a life, derives not so much from the underlying structure of the world (in which time and space are inseparable elements of place), but rather from the structure that enables our engagement in the world as the kinds of agents that we are. In this respect, one might see Heidegger's analysis in *Being and Time* as inevitably skewed precisely by the fact that it begins with the analysis of *Dasein's* own structure as given in its activity. It can provide important insight into that structure (which is why there are analogues to it here), but the account is also both incomplete and (in the absence of any recognition of its limitation) misleading—even, one might say, mistaken.

16. Here the apparent focus on temporality conceals the spatiality that is also invoked, and thereby leaves implicit the larger topological frame at issue here.

17. I do not deal with the matter here, but there is no doubt that not only death, but also birth, plays a role in the structure at issue here. I have discussed this further in "Fragility and Responsibility," in *Vivir para pensar*, ed. Fina Birulés (Barcelona: Paidos, 2011), in press. The emphasis on what Hannah Arendt calls "natality" should not be taken to run counter to the emphasis on mortality, but rather to supplement it. Nevertheless, bringing natality into the picture does enable a more properly topological account—not only does it move us away from the overly simple structure that takes death to be solely determinative of the structure of a life, but it also draws us back to attend to the concrete, factical character of human being, and so to the way in which human being, and the possibilities it consists in, is given in its own prior placedness.

18. In *Being and Time*, as I have noted elsewhere, Heidegger gives priority to "projection" (*Entwerfen*) over the "facticity" involved in one's relation to the past. The reasons for this are not reasons that apply in the same way here, and thus I make no claims for any such priority. Moreover, the fact that a certain fundamental

orientation is necessary for any project (and this is so even though such orientation is a product, in part, of previous projects) should make us suspicious of according priority to projection alone. That the idea of projection is not one that should be abandoned, in spite of the problems attaching to its treatment in *Being and Time*, is evident from Heidegger's use of the term in his later thinking in a way that also shifts the understanding of projection away from the idea of some sort of human "performance." The human itself is thus seen, not as projecting, but a itself "projected": see, e.g., Heidegger, *Introduction to Metaphysics*, trans. Gregory Fried and Richard Polt (New Haven: Yale University Press, 2000), p. 174, and also, though much later, "Seminar in Le Thor 1969," in *Four Seminars*, trans. Andrew Mitchell and François Raffoul (Bloomington: Indiana University Press, 2003), pp. 40–41. See also the brief discussion of this issue in chapter 6 above. The account of projection deployed immediately above leaves open the question as to exactly how projection should be conceived—is it simply a performance or act of the agent or is it rather to be understood as arising only on the basis of the complex of agent and world (on the basis of a certain *topos*)?—although the latter conception is one that comes more directly to the fore as the discussion proceeds. Such a conception is itself bound up with the understanding of human being as, in a sense, a "function" of place. The latter is a key idea in my *Place and Experience*, and is also an issue to which I return below.

19. Since the account offered here does, of course, tie the having of complex attitudes such as belief and desire, and the capacity for a certain sort of complex, purposive behavior, together with the having of a sense of one's existence as a temporally extended creature located within a larger world, so this account must be committed to the denial not only that my cat (and creatures like her) can be said to have a life, but also that my cat can be said to possess beliefs, desires, and the rest. On the face of it this might seem counterintuitive, as my cat certainly seems to behave in a way that is indicative of purpose, intelligence, and awareness, and the vocabulary of belief, desire, and so forth can be used very effectively to predict and to explain her behavior. Yet just as I resisted, at the outset, the idea that my cat can be said to have a life in quite the same way that I can be said to have a life, so I would resist the idea that belief (or any of the other crucial terms here) can be applied univocally both to myself and my feline companion. Indeed, although "belief" may be applied analogously to myself and my cat in a way that is consistent with the equivocal nature of the term, still *my* belief that there is a wattlebird outside the window is a different state from *my cat's* belief that there is a wattlebird outside the window, and this difference is exemplified in the fact that there is no clear sense in which my cat believes that the bird outside the window is a wattlebird, or that it is outside *my* window, or that, insofar as it is outside the window, it is outside the house, that it is therefore in the garden, and so on. It is precisely the way in which, as we can see here, my belief is implicated in a vast mass of beliefs and other attitudes that implicate in turn a notion both of myself and of the world in which I stand that marks my belief as a state different from the state my cat might be said

to be in when she also sees the very same bird. I also address this issue, from a slightly different perspective, in *Place and Experience*, pp. 45–48.

20. See Heidegger, *Being and Time*, H42.

21. See Davidson, "Thought and Talk," in his *Inquiries into Truth and Interpretation*, 2nd ed. (Oxford: Clarendon Press, 2001), p. 170.

22. It is, however, a somewhat idiosyncratic externalism, and one that also owes much to the work of Donald Davidson. On this, see chapter 10, "Topology, Triangulation, and Truth," below. For more on the holistic externalism at issue here, see (particularly in relation to Davidson), Malpas, *Donald Davidson and the Mirror of Meaning* (Cambridge: Cambridge University Press, 1992), as well as *Place and Experience* (especially chapter 3).

23. Notice the equivocal sense of the preposition—they are orderings "of" in the sense that they *belong to* the world, that they are orderings *directed toward* the world, and that they are themselves orderings *given by* the world.

24. For further discussion of this issue see Malpas, "The Constitution of the Mind: Kant and Davidson on the Unity of Consciousness," *International Journal of Philosophical Studies* 7 (1999): 1–30.

25. As Durrell puts it, "as functions of a landscape," "Landscape and Character," in *Spirit of Place: Mediterranean Writings* (London: Faber & Faber, 1969), p. 156.

26. This issue arises in a related fashion in the discussion of the unity of content as explored in Malpas, "The Constitution of the Mind" (see also n.14 above); see also Malpas, *Place and Experience*, pp. 35–36, 107–108.

27. Although not taken up in any direct way here, this way of thinking about the character of a life, and the character of the person, also implies a thoroughly relational conception according to which lives and persons are not to be construed as independent of other lives and other persons. See, e.g., Malpas, *Place and Experience*, chapter 6.

28. See Parfit, *Reasons and Persons* (Oxford: Oxford University Press, 1984).

29. The emphasis on narrative here parallels aspects of the discussion in chapter 8 above, as well as in Malpas, *Place and Experience*, esp. pp. 79–82, 179–188.

30. One might argue that the focus on narrative is something largely absent from Heidegger—although the emphasis on historicality does open up in precisely this direction. An explicit concern with narrative, however, is certainly present in the larger hermeneutic tradition, as the work of Paul Ricoeur demonstrates—see Ricoeur, *Time and Narrative*, trans. Kathleen McLaughlin and David Pellauer (Chicago: University of Chicago Press, 1984–1988) and *Oneself as Another*, trans. Kathleen Blamey (Chicago: Chicago University Press, 1992); see also Ricoeur, "Life in Quest of a Narrative," in *On Paul Ricoeur*, ed. David Wood (London: Routledge, 1991), pp. 20–33.

31. See Bruno Bettelheim, *The Uses of Enchantment* (New York: Alfred A. Knopf, 1976).

32. See MacIntyre, *After Virtue* (Notre Dame, Ind.: University of Notre Dame Press, 1981); see also MacIntyre, "Crises, Narrative, and Science," *Monist* 60 (1977): 453–472.

33. See Louis O. Mink, "History and Fiction as Modes of Comprehension," *New Literary History* 1 (1969–70): 557, and Hayden White, "The Historical Text as Literary Artifact," in *Tropics of Discourse: Essays in Cultural Criticism* (Baltimore: Johns Hopkins University Press, 1978), p. 90.

34. Notice that it is not death as some *physical event* that is at issue here—nor is it at issue elsewhere in this discussion—but rather death as what might be called an *ontological structure*. Put in condensed form, one can say that death is thus the ending that is required by the possibility of the unity of a life. Since death understood ontologically is distinct from death as physical event, this also means that one might fear the physical event (and especially the pain, suffering, and perhaps even the loss that may accompany it), and yet not the ontological structure (indeed the very idea of the latter as an object of fear is rather odd). Understanding the intimate connection of life with its ending may nevertheless also make death as physical event somewhat more bearable than it may be otherwise. The distinction between death as physical event and ontological structure is important for the discussion of Sartre below.

35. Sartre, *Being and Nothingness*, trans. Hazel E. Barnes (New York: Washington Square Press, 1966), p. 700. One might be tempted to read Sartre, although against the grain of his text, as arguing in a way not too far removed from my own position here. On my account, a life that was lived unendingly would still be mortal, since if it was constituted as a life at all, it would be constituted as a series of lives—there could not be a single life that was also an unending life; analogously, one might argue, Sartre's final comment in the passage quoted indicates that, for him, a life lived unendingly would still be finite. The question, however, is whether Sartre would regard an unending life as constituting a single life. Taking the broader context of his discussion into account, it seems clear that he would. This is, perhaps, the real difference between my account (and Heidegger's) and that of Sartre.

36. Ibid., p. 698.

37. This is essentially the same distinction between death as physical event and death as ontological structure set out in n. 34 above.

38. This way of putting things is not wholly satisfactory, since it may be taken to suggest that a life is something apart from the body. Yet lives are always and only lived as embodied lives (see, e.g., Malpas, *Place and Experience*, pp. 132–136, for an argument in support of this claim—it can be seen to follow directly from the conception of the essentially placed character of a life). We might say that lives

supervene on bodies, just as minds do, although neither lives nor minds supervene only on bodies understood as distinct from the wider contexts in which those bodies are situated.

39. Borges, "The Immortal," p. 191. Borges also claims that "There is nothing very remarkable about being immortal; with the exception of mankind, all creatures are immortal, for they know nothing of death" (ibid.).

40. See Parfit, *Reasons and Persons*, pp. 281–282.

41. Ricoeur, *Oneself as Another*, p. 137.

42. It is notable that even the stories told by Scheherazade come to an end, as they are framed within the story of Scheherazade's own life; moreover, it is only the story of Scheherazade, and her royal husband, that provides the unifying link that makes the stories of the *Thousand and One Nights* part of a single story at all.

43. See, once again, Malpas, *Place and Experience*, for a more detailed account of the structure at issue here.

44. The complication here is, as is so often the case, partly a consequence of the equivocity that attaches to talk of "body." We often use the term as if its meaning were clear, but the dead body is not the same as the living body, and the extent of the body is itself uncertain, sometimes being coextensive with that which is enclosed by the skin, and sometimes with that which extends well beyond. In one sense, one might take the body to be identical with the full extent of one's *activity*, and so to extend itself outward to encompass parts of the wider world. See the brief comments on the issue of the body as it arises in Heidegger in chapter 6, "Place, Space, and World", above.

45. In *Place and Experience*, pp. 190–193, I develop this line of argument in direct opposition to the Wordsworthian conception of place as arising precisely out of a desire for the secure and permanent; see also the discussion in my "Fragility and Responsibility."

46. See Heidegger, *Being and Time*, H390.

47. Although I have not made much of the point in the discussion here, the considerations relating to the necessary interconnection of time with space that have been noted in previous chapters (see esp. chaps. 3 and 6) mean that the idea of unity, even when thought in primarily temporal terms, must always be topological, and so encompass both the temporal and the spatial. Thus, a spatially unified region, for example, is so unified only through the possibility of movement within and through it, and such movement presupposes temporal unity or connectedness; equally, a unified span of time is so unified only through the persistence of entities and events within that time whose own identity, and so capacity to persist, itself depends on spatial localization (only thus can there be differentiation between entities and events either at a time or over time).

48. Heidegger, "The Thing," in *Poetry, Language, Thought*, trans. Albert Hofstadter (New York: Harper & Row, 1971), pp. 178–179.

49. Only if what is given *in the world* is already meaningful in its own worldly relatedness, can there be any possibility of a meaning (should that even be looked for) that lies *outside or beyond the world*. The mistake of metaphysics (in all its guises) is to look for a meaning that is only to be found outside or beyond, as if that would somehow overcome any lack of meaning in the world. In fact, the move outside or beyond is already a denial of worldly meaning; no movement outside or beyond can ever supply a meaning that is not already given within.

10   Topology, Triangulation, and Truth

1. In this respect the shift, as Heidegger characterizes it, from meaning to place (see "Seminar in Le Thor 1969," in *Four Seminars*, trans. Andrew Mitchell and François Raffoul [Bloomington: Indiana University Press, 2004], p. 47), is not a shift in which each term is successively abandoned, but rather one in which each is taken up more primordially through that which succeeds it—thus we might say that the question of understanding is not abandoned, but rather taken up in a more original way through the question of place.

2. In *Donald Davidson and the Mirror of Meaning* (Cambridge: Cambridge University Press, 1992), I advance a reading of Davidson that draws explicitly on hermeneutic and phenomenological ideas, arguing for important parallels between aspects of Davidson's thought and that of Heidegger as well as Gadamer. From the other direction, in *Heidegger's Pragmatism* (Ithaca: Cornell University Press, 1988), Mark Okrent advances a reading of Heidegger that brings him close to Davidson as well as Quine, and Richard Rorty's work, notably *Philosophy and the Mirror of Nature* (Princeton: Princeton University Press, 1980), has also been extremely important in drawing together figures such as Heidegger and Gadamer with Quine, Sellars, and Davidson. A number of essays contained in *Dialogues with Davidson: Acting, Interpreting, Understanding*, ed. Jeff Malpas (Cambridge, Mass.: MIT Press, 2011), also engage Davidson with Heidegger, and a substantial body of additional material has now grown up around the topic.

3. Heidegger, "Seminar in Le Thor 1968," in *Four Seminars*, , p. 41.

4. It is reconfigured, it should be added, in a way that allows for a nonsubjectivist understanding. Understanding is thus itself seen as not merely a function of an individual knower, but as arising as a mode of placedness.

5. Thus, in spite of his more general hostility toward a Davidsonian account, Hubert Dreyfus writes that "for Heidegger different understandings of being reveal different sorts of entities, and since no one way of revealing is exclusively true, accepting one does not commit us to rejecting the others. There is a deep similarity between

Heidegger and Donald Davidson on this point. Both would agree that we can make reality intelligible using various descriptions and that what our claims are true of under a given description has whatever properties it has even if those descriptions are not reducible to a single description, and whether we describers and our ways of describing things exist or not"—Dreyfus, *Being-in-the-World* (Cambridge, Mass.: MIT Press, 1991), p. 63.

6. For this reason, in *Donald Davidson and the Mirror of Meaning*, pp. 274–275, I characterize Heidegger and Davidson as both espousing a certain form of "realism" according to which they begin with our being already given over to a world that is understood as meaningful and humanly significant. Like Davidson, however (and also as a result of Rorty's urgings), I now tend to think that the term "realism" shares much the same drawbacks as does "correspondence": both terms stand too much within a problematic metaphysical framework that presupposes a separation of language from world. Rorty is sternly critical of my use of "realism" in his *Philosophy and Social Hope* (London: Penguin, 2000), p. 43, n.24; on the related issue of "correspondence" see note 65 below.

7. There is a sense in which Husserlian "bracketing" itself functions to set aside the possibility of our estrangement from the world, and so provides a way of ensuring that we begin "in" the world, but it does so in a way that also introduces complications of its own.

8. Heidegger, "The Origin of the Work of Art," in *Off the Beaten Track* (English translation of *Holzwege*), trans. Julian Young and Kenneth Barnes (Cambridge: Cambridge University Press, 2002), pp. 1–56.

9. See especially the discussion in chapter 12 below.

10. Heidegger, "Building Dwelling Thinking" and "The Thing," both in *Poetry, Language, Thought*, trans. Albert Hofstadter (New York: Harper & Row, 1971), pp. 141–160 and 161–184, respectively.

11. See chapter 4 above.

12. Heidegger, "Introduction to 'What Is Metaphysics?,'" trans. Walter Kaufmann, in *Pathmarks* (translation of *Wegmarken*), ed. William McNeill (Cambridge: Cambridge University Press, 1998), p. 283. The terms translated as "place" and "locality" arc, respectively, *Stelle* and *Ortschaft*. See also the similar comments in Heidegger, *Introduction to Metaphysics*, Trans. R. Manheim (New Haven: Yale University Press, 1959), p. 205—in the latter passage Heidegger uses the term *Stätte*, which Manheim translates as "site," but which could equally be translated as "place."

13. An issue already discussed at some length in previous chapters—see especially chapter 6 above.

14. See chapters 1 and 2 above.

15. See Malpas, "The Beginning of Understanding: Event, Place, Truth," in *Consequences of Hermeneutics*, ed. Jeff Malpas and Santiago Zabala (Chicago: Northwestern University Press, 2010), pp. 261–280.

16. See also chapters 1 and 2 above.

17. Disclosedness is no mere static presentation, but rather a dynamic interplay of concealing and unconcealing. For it to be otherwise would be to reduce disclosedness to merely "being present." See also the discussion of this matter in chapter 4 above.

18. See Donald Davidson, *Plato's Philebus* (New York: Garland Publishing, 1990).

19. Donald Davidson and Patrick Suppes, *Decision Making: An Experimental Approach* (Stanford: Stanford University Press, 1957).

20. As is indicated by Davidson's comments in "Philosophy as Psychology," in *Essays on Actions and Events*, 2nd ed. (Oxford: Clarendon Press, 2001), pp. 237–238.

21. I leave "rational" in scare quotes here since what the term might mean in this context cannot be simply assumed. Indeed, the Davidsonian project should itself be viewed as providing an explication of the idea of "rationality" just as much as it provides an explication of, for instance, "meaning."

22. See Quine, *Word and Object* (Cambridge, Mass.: MIT Press, 1960), chapter 2.

23. Ibid., p. 29.

24. Such a theory is one that is capable of recursively generating, for every sentence of the object language (the language for which the theory of meaning is a theory of), a "T-sentence" of the form "s is true if and only if p" that matches up a named sentence ("s") in the object language with a sentence ("p") in the interpreter's own language and which thereby specifies the meaning of each sentence in the sense of specifying the conditions under which it is true. See Davidson, "Truth and Meaning," in *Inquiries into Truth and Interpretation*, 2nd ed. (Oxford: Clarendon Press, 2001), pp. 17–36.

25. See especially Davidson, "A Nice Derangement of Epitaphs," in *Truth, Language, and History* (Oxford: Clarendon Press, 2005), pp. 89–108.

26. Ibid., p.107. Gadamer also comments, "I regard learning to speak and the acquiring of an orientation to the world as inseparably woven together in the fabric making up the history of the cultural development of man. . . . the playing of the language-game. . . is also the playing of the world-game," Gadamer, "Reflections on my Philosophical Journey," in *The Philosophy of Hans-Georg Gadamer*, ed. Lewis Edwin Hahn (Chicago: Open Court, 1997), pp. 42–43.

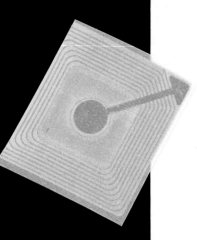

27. For a fuller account of the holism at issue in Davidson's thinking, see especially Malpas, *Donald Davidson and the Mirror of Meaning*.

28. We understand our own and others' engagement with things always under some description or other. Thus, understood as action, a particular movement of parts of my body in relation to a certain object or objects in the world is identical with my typing of this sentence. Yet although every object or event is always encountered under some particular description, it is the objects or events that are encountered rather than the descriptions. This is particularly important since objects and events are publicly available in a way that descriptions are not. In a similar fashion, it is our interaction with things (always understood, once again, under some description) that underlies interpretation, rather than interaction under any particular description. In this light, interpretation can be viewed as a process by which an interpreter, on the basis of the descriptions she already employs to order her own interactions with her surroundings, seeks to find a set of descriptions that best order the interaction of another speaker in relation to those same surroundings. On this see also Malpas, "What Is Common to All: Davidson on Agreement and Understanding," in Malpas (ed.), *Dialogues with Davidson*, pp. 259–280.

29. See Malpas, "Self-knowledge and Scepticism," *Erkenntnis* 40 (1994): 165–184, and "Truth, Narrative, and the Materiality of Memory: An Externalist Approach in the Philosophy of History," *Journal of the Philosophy of History* 4 (2010): 328–353; see also *Place and Experience: A Philosophical Topography* (Cambridge: Cambridge University Press, 1999), pp. 95–102.

30. The idea of triangulation first appeared in Davidson's 1981 essay "Rational Animals," reprinted in *Subjective, Intersubjective, Objective* (Oxford: Clarendon Press, 2001), pp. 95–106.

31. For more on the role of spatiality and agency here, see Malpas, *Place and Experience: A Philosophical Topography*, chapters 4 and 5.

32. Although in "The Third Man," in *Truth, Language, and History*, pp. 159–166, Davidson does suggest a more literally spatialized and embodied reading of triangulation.

33. This is an objection advanced early on by Jerry Fodor, in *Psychosemantics* (Cambridge, Mass.: MIT Press, 1987), pp. 56–57; a related objection—one that focuses on the way in which holism supposedly makes linguistic understanding impossible—is advanced by Michael Dummett in "What Is a Theory of Meaning?," in *Mind and Language*, ed. Samuel Guttenplan (Oxford: Oxford University Press, 1975), p. 133. Together with Ernest Lepore, Fodor develops a more general and sustained attack on holism, including Davidsonian holism, in *Holism: A Shopper's Guide* (Oxford: Blackwell, 1992), and Lepore has continued in a similar vein in his work with Kirk Ludwig—see, e.g., *Donald Davidson: Meaning, Truth, Language, and Reality* (Oxford: Oxford University Press, 2005).

34. See Malpas, "Holism and Indeterminacy," *Dialectica* 45 (1991): 47–58, and also *Donald Davidson and the Mirror of Meaning*, chapter 4.

35. Akeel Bilgrami claims that "The deliverances of a holistic meaning-theory do not . . . have anything directly to do with contents as we attribute them is explanations of behavior. Meaning-theories merely provide a pool of resources and no more. Content as it enters into the explanation of behavior, content as it is attributed in response to the specific questions such as what does so-and-so believe about . . .?, is always local"—Bilgrami, *Belief and Meaning* (Oxford: Blackwell, 1992), pp. 11–12. It is significant that Bilgrami emphasizes the role of action explanation in this context, since it is specifically in relation to action—that is, in relation to the active engagement of speakers with things in the world—that interpretation, and intentional content, is possible. See Malpas, *Place and Experience*, chapter 4.

36. See Taylor, *Philosophical Arguments* (Cambridge, Mass.: Harvard University Press, 1995), pp. 81–82.

37. And, as I note again below, that understanding can indeed be taken to be primarily based in rules or conventions is something Davidson explicitly denies. On this point see not only Davidson, "A Nice Derangement of Epitaphs," but also "Communication and Convention," in *Inquiries into Truth and Interpretation*, pp. 265–280, and "The Social Aspect of Language," in *Truth, Language, and History*, pp. 109–126.

38. Of course, it need not always mean going on in this way (and there is no reason to suppose that it means this in Davidson); "being able to go on" is fundamentally a matter of achieving a certain coordination or accommodation of response, and this can be achieved simply through what one does and without recourse to any particular act of saying, writing, or thinking (though this is not to say that such action is therefore independent of what one might say, write, or think).

39. See chapter 6 above.

40. Mark Wrathall, "The Conditions of Truth in Heidegger and Davidson," *Monist* 82 (1999): 318. The position Wrathall enunciates here echoes that of Hubert Dreyfus—see the brief discussion in chapter 6.

41. Davidson's own account of linguistic understanding in his later thinking tends increasingly to blur the boundary between linguistic and nonlinguistic capacities and behavior. Thus Davidson's attack on convention in "A Nice Derangement of Epitaphs" also undermines the idea of any sharp distinction between linguistic and other capacities, whereas in essays such as "What Metaphors Mean' (*Inquiries into Truth and Interpretation*, pp. 245–264) and "James Joyce and Humpty Dumpty" (*Truth, Language, and History*, pp. 143–158), he also emphasizes the complex nature of our relation to language. "Seeing through Language" (in *Truth, Language, and History*, pp. 127–142) reiterates a point evident throughout much of Davidson's thought: language is not identical with the world and yet neither can it be prised

off from it nor set off against it—a theme also present in "On the Very Idea of a Conceptual Scheme" (*Inquiries into Truth and Interpretation*, pp. 183–198). See, once again, my "What Is Common to All."

42. See also the discussion in chapter 6 above, as well as in Malpas, "Sprache ist Gespräch: On Gadamer, Language and Philosophy," in *Between Description and Interpretation: The Hermeneutic Turn in Phenomenology*, ed. Andrzej Wiercinski (Toronto: The Hermeneutic Press, 2005), pp. 413–416.

43. Davidson, "Rational Animals," in *Subjective, Objective, Intersubjective* (Oxford: Clarendon Press, 2001), p. 105.

44. See the brief comment in chapter 3, n. 19, above—Davidson rejects the idea of normativity inasmuch as it is seen to consist in the application of prior rules or conventions.

45. *Spiel* is sometimes translated as "game" rather than "play" (usually because of the prevalence within English philosophy of the idea of "language game"—the translation of Wittgenstein's *Sprachspiel*). Such a translation would be especially misleading in the present context, however, since it is precisely the playfulness of play rather than the rule-governed character of the game that is at issue. See Gadamer, *Truth and Method*, 2nd rev. ed., trans. Joel Weinsheimer and Donald G. Marshall (New York: Continuum, 1992), pp. 101–102. Moreover, one of the problems that the Wittgensteinian notion of a language-game has engendered is the idea that the rule-governed character of games might provide a model for the rule-governed character of language and other "normative" practices—the way rules operate in games, however, is very different from the way rules operate in language or elsewhere. In language, and in other similar practices, rules can be broken in a way that is not possible in a game—thus a failure to abide by a linguistic rule need not undermine the capacity for successful communication, whereas the failure to abide by a rule, whether of chess or football, is no longer to play the game.

46. On this issue, see Malpas, "What Is Common to All," pp. 259–280.

47. Stephen Mulhall, *On Being in the World: Wittgenstein and Heidegger on Seeing Aspects* (London: Routledge, 1990), pp. 104–105.

48. Davidson, "On the Very Idea of a Conceptual Scheme," in *Inquiries into Truth and Interpretation*, pp. 183–198. One might also say that it is a version of the Sellarsian "myth of the given," to which Davidson no more subscribes than does Sellars himself.

49. See, e.g., Davidson, "A Coherence Theory of Truth and Knowledge," in *Subjective, Intersubjective, Objective*, pp. 142–152.

50. For instance, in relation to hearing, see Heidegger, *Being and Time*, H164.

51. This is not to say that we are always, even among our family and friends, faced with what is alien to us; nor is it to deny that much of the time we rely on familiar patterns of understanding. It does mean, however, that we cannot take familiarity as indicative of some underlying determinacy or self-evidence to the meanings we encounter. There is, of course, a difference between encountering someone who speaks the same language as we do and encountering someone who speaks another tongue (or has a usage that deviates significantly from our own). And this is because speaking "the same" language means being able to rely, to a great extent, on a certain established coordination in our patterns of interaction. But such prior coordination is not *essential* to understanding (just as rules or conventions are not essential) and it can easily (and often does—though most often in not especially disruptive ways) break down. The alien can emerge even in the midst of what seems most familiar.

52. David C. Hoy, "Post-Cartesian Interpretation: Hans-Georg Gadamer and Donald Davidson," in *The Philosophy of Hans-Georg Gadamer*, ed. Lewis Edwin Hahn (Chicago: Open Court, 1997), p. 116–117.

53. On the larger question of the "commonality"—what we may think of as the "commonplace"—that underpins Davidsonian interpretation (and that also appears in Gadamer and Heidegger), see Malpas, "What Is Common to All."

54. In this respect, it is important to note the special place in his thinking that Gadamer gives to Heidegger's "The Origin of the Work of Art"—an essay that, as I noted above, is clearly directed toward a thoroughly topographical mode of inquiry. Gadamer writes that "My philosophical hermeneutics seeks precisely to adhere to the line of questioning of this essay *and the later Heidegger* and to make it accessible in a new way," Gadamer, "Reflections on My Philosophical Journey," p. 47 (italics in the original).

55. Davidson, "Three Varieties of Knowledge," in *Subjective, Intersubjective, Objective*, pp. 205–220.

56. See Heidegger, *Being and Time*, H202 and H228–H229. The Davidsonian rejection of skepticism (and both Heidegger and Davidson are reluctant to talk of a refutation here) appears at many places in his writings, including "Three Varieties of Knowledge" and "A Coherence Theory of Truth and Knowledge." See also my discussion of the Davidsonian position in "Self-knowledge and Scepticism," *Erkenntnis* 40 (1994): 165–184.

57. Heidegger takes "truth" to refer both to the concept of disclosedness or unhiddenness (*aletheia*) and to the ordinary notion of "correctness" that is dependent on it. Heidegger retained this twofold sense of truth until 1966, when, perhaps under the influence of Tugendhat's critique (see the discussion below), he modified his position, identifying *aletheia* with that which "first grants the possibility of truth," and as distinct from truth understood as "the correspondence of knowledge with beings

demonstrated in being . . . and as the certainty of the knowledge of being"—"The End of Philosophy and the Task of Thinking," in *On Time and Being*, trans. Joan Stambaugh (New York: Harper & Row, 1972), p. 69.

58. See especially Daniel Dahlstrom, *Heidegger's Concept of Truth* (New York: Cambridge University Press, 2001), chapter 5, pp. 407–422.

59. This is a mode of understanding that can give rise, at least as Heidegger sees it, to a problematic separation of elements within what is an essentially unitary structure—see chapter 4 above.

60. See, e.g., "The Folly of Trying to Define Truth," in *Truth, Language, and History*, pp. 19–38; "The Centrality of Truth," in *Truth and Its Nature (If Any)*, ed. Jaroslav Peregrin (Dordrecht: Kluwer, 1999), pp. 105–115; and *Truth and Predication* (Cambridge, Mass.: Harvard University Press, 2008), especially pp. 29–48. The relation between Heidegger and Davidson on truth is also a theme in Malpas, *Donald Davidson and the Mirror of Meaning*, chapter 7.

61. See Davidson, *Truth and Predication* (Cambridge, Mass.: Harvard University Press, 2008), p. 75.

62. Davidson, "The Centrality of Truth," p. 14.

63. See Davidson, "Reality without Reference," in *Inquiries into Truth and Interpretation*, pp. 215–225.

64. The idea of the proposition is, one might say, a remnant of a pre-Wittgensteinian conception of meaning as something that stands apart from and independently of language in its use. Davidson can find no role for such a reified conception of either "meaning" or "proposition"; consequently his approach was always one that focused on sentences, rather than propositions, as the primary truth bearers, and, indeed, as the primary focus for any inquiry into truth or meaning. This is perhaps particularly clear, as Okrent argues (following Jeff Speaks in his review of *Truth and Predication* in *Notre Dame Philosophical Reviews*, August 2006, http://ndpr.nd.edu/review.cfm?id=7224 [accessed November 2010]), in *Truth and Predication*, but is also evident throughout much of the rest of Davidson's work.

65. This might be taken to mean that truth as it belongs to sentences will always involve some form of correspondence—and for a long time I took this view myself. Davidson certainly adopts such a view in "A Coherence Theory of Truth and Knowledge" (see p. 139), as well as several earlier essays—see especially "True to the Facts," *Inquiries into Truth and Interpretation*, pp. 37–54. The form of correspondence at issue here cannot, however, be construed as ontologically fundamental, and Davidson eventually comes to have serious misgivings about any talk of correspondence at all precisely because of the ontological baggage the notion seems to carry. Thus, in his later comments on the position set out in "A Coherence Theory of Truth and Knowledge," he gives up on the idea that correspondence can be usefully employed to

elucidate the concept of truth—see "Afterthoughts (1987)," in *Subjective, Intersubjective, Objective*, pp.154–155 (see also *Truth and Predication*, pp. 40–42). The problem presented by the notion of correspondence is, as indicated in note 6 above, a problem for talk of "realism" also.

66. Davidson, *Truth and Predication*, p. 7. Compare this with Heidegger's claims that "'There is' truth only in so far as Dasein is and so long as Dasein is" (Heidegger, *Being and Time*, H226). The comparison is noted and discussed by Mark Okrent in "Heidegger, Davidson, and Truth," in Malpas (ed.), *Dialogues with Davidson*, pp. 87–111.

67. See Davidson, *Truth and Predication*, pp. 8–14.

68. This also means that truth is not to be taken to be identical with some body of truths—"the facts"—that are somehow identical with the world. Moreover, just as truth is not to be identified with some single monolithic "Truth," so truth is always multiple—if there is one truth then there is a plurality of truths—even while it remains objective, since such plurality is still constrained by requirements of consistency and implication. See Malpas, "The Two-fold Character of Truth: Heidegger, Davidson, Tugendhat," in *The Multidimensionality of Hermeneutic Phenomenology*, ed. Babette Babich and Dimitri Ginev (Dordrecht: Springer, forthcoming, 2012).

69. Davidson, "A Coherence Theory of Truth and Knowledge," p. 153.

70. Davidson, "Three Varieties of Knowledge," p. 213.

71. See Tugendhat, "Heidegger's Idea of Truth," in *Critical Heidegger*, ed. Christopher Macann (New York: Routledge, 1996), pp. 227–240. For a more detailed discussion of Tugendhat's critique see Malpas, "The Two-fold Character of Truth: Heidegger, Davidson, Tugendhat."

72. See Heidegger, "The End of Philosophy and the Task of Thinking," in *On Time and Being*, trans. Joan Stambaugh (New York: Harper & Row, 1972).

73. This is part of the point of Wittgenstein's *On Certainty* (ed. G. E. M. Anscombe and G. H. von Wright, trans. Denis Paul and G. E. M. Anscombe [Oxford: Blackwell, 1975]), and its insistence that questioning and doubt can only make sense within specific contexts, and against a larger background in which questioning and doubt are held in abeyance. The failure to recognize this point, or its Davidsonian–Heideggerian relatives, is not only a feature of much contemporary critique, whether political or philosophical, which misidentifies the proper nature and direction of genuinely critical inquiry, but also of a wide range of contemporary management and organizational practices that look to constantly reiterated practices of audit and accountability.

74. See Davidson, "A Nice Derangement of Epitaphs," but also "Communication and Convention," in *Inquiries into Truth and Interpretation*, pp. 265–280, and "The Social Aspect of Language," in *Truth, Language, and History*, pp. 109–126.

75. This should not be taken to suggest that their miscommunication constitutes some sort of "practical refutation" of either the Davidsonian or Gadamerian accounts of the possibility of interpretation and communication. What it does show is the way in which such dialogue is always complicated by the personal situations of those involved—and one cannot assume that communication is ever assured or that it will always proceed in a way that is completely successful (especially when it is so constrained as was the engagement between Davidson and Gadamer).

76. Perhaps so much so that it is even a little misleading to talk of "externalism" at all here, inasmuch as the topographical-topological approach would seem to undermine the very idea of there being a clear contrast between the "internality" of the intentional and the "externality" of things—both stand within the same overarching structure, the same topological-topographic frame, the same "place." See my comments on this matter in "Truth, Narrative, and the Materiality of Memory."

11 Heidegger in Benjamin's City

1. See Adam Scharr, *Heidegger's Hut* (Cambridge, Mass.: MIT Press, 2006).

2. Heidegger, "Why Do I Stay in the Provinces?," in *Heidegger: The Man and The Thinker*, ed. Thomas Sheehan (Chicago: Precedent, 1981), p. 27.

3. Ibid., p. 28.

4. Ibid., p. 29.

5. Ibid., p. 28.

6. Simmel, "The Metropolis and Mental Life," in *The Sociology of Georg Simmel*, ed. Kurt Wolff (New York: Free Press, 1950), p. 410.

7. Benjamin, *The Arcades Project*, trans. Howard Eiland and Kevin McLaughlin (Harvard: Harvard University Press, 1999), p. 83.

8. Walter Benjamin, "The Work of Art in the Age of Mechanical Reproduction," in *Illuminations*, ed. Hannah Arendt (New York: Harcourt, Brace & World, 1968), pp. 219–253.

9. Benjamin, *The Arcades Project*, p. 447.

10. See esp. Arendt, *The Human Condition* (Chicago: Chicago University Press, 1958), pp. 57–58.

11. Heidegger, *Parmenides*, trans. André Schuwer and Richard Rojcewicz (Bloomington: Indiana University Press, 1992), pp. 89–90.

12. See James Phillips, *Heidegger's Volk: Between National Socialism and Poetry* (Stanford: Stanford University Press, 2003), esp. chapter 4, pp. 169–170.

13. See Arendt, "Walter Benjamin: 1892–1940," in *Men in Dark Times* (New York: Harcourt Brace Jovanovich, 1968), esp. pp.194–200. As already indicated in n. 2 to chapter 1 above, Arendt herself has a discussion of the place of thinking in *The Life of the Mind*, ed. Mary McCarthy (San Diego: Harcourt Brace, 1978), vol. 1, chap. 4 ("Where Are We When We Think?"), pp. 197–213. Arendt's discussion raises a somewhat different (though not unconnected) set of issues to those discussed here.

14. One may argue, of course, that Heidegger does not deny the possibility of thought within the space of the city, but is instead concerned to criticize a certain deadening of thought that takes place within modernity—something that is also the focus of the famous discussion of *Das Man* in *Being and Time*, §27, H126ff, and that is also briefly taken up by Hannah Arendt in the preface to *Men in Dark Times*, p. ix. So far as Heidegger's comments in the "Provinces" essay are concerned, it is important that the particular context of that essay should not be overlooked—it is written just after Heidegger's resignation from the position of Rector at Freiburg.

15. Benjamin, *The Arcades Project*, pp. 457–458.

16. Sebald, *Austerlitz* (Harmondsworth: Penguin, 2001), pp. 363–365.

12   The Working of Art

1. "Objectivity" is being used here in a deliberately idiosyncratic fashion that is not intended to imply any notion of factual correctness; it is "ontological" rather than "epistemological" in its orientation. "Objectivity" refers to the way in which an object is an object—to its being (or becoming) as object—in a way that is intended to direct attention away from a concern with identity or individuation conditions and toward the question of the object (or more properly the thing) in its active or process-character. It is also a use that, as I note later, is not to be construed (as it normally would) as implying an essential opposition to "subjectivity."

2. As materially presented, artworks may be said to take many forms: paint on canvas, shaped stone or wood, combinations of sounds, assemblages of things found. Yet what we take to be the material presentation of a work, in any particular case, depends on that from which the material presentation is to be distinguished. In the case of our viewing of some painting, we may say that the object presented is simply stretched canvas to which paint has been applied. Yet it might well be said that even such an apparently minimal description goes beyond what is materially presented, since one might argue that what is presented is not canvas, paint, and frame at all, but rather certain arrangements of color, texture, and shape. In fact, it seems that there is no unique or uncontroversial way of specifying the "objective" component in any presentation. Instead, what we take to be an objective description, capturing just what is materially presented, is most often a description of what

is presented at a level immediately below the level at which our attention is primarily directed. Thus, if what we are looking at is one of Cézanne's late paintings of Mont-Sainte-Victoire (a particularly apt example since there the very appearance of the object is itself deconstructed into phenomenologically simple elements), we will take the arrangement of paints of various colors and textures on canvas to be what is materially present; if it is the appearance of certain textures or colors of paint that is of interest, we may take the material presentation to consist just in certain combinations of reflected light differing in hue, brightness, and saturation. Similarly, if metaphor is the focus of attention, we will look to words or sentences; if the words or sentences themselves are of interest, we will look to the marks or sounds (or perhaps to arrangements of letters or of phonemes) as the material presentation on which the words or sentences supervene. Of course, in each case, these presentations occur within a particular context or horizon—they are determined within a lager framework of significance—although it is not the context of horizon of presentation that is thematized.

3. This brief gesture in the direction of place should already indicate the way in which what is at issue here is not merely the nature of the artwork, but also the relation between place and appearance as such.

4. The role of the "text" here is significant, since the more the work is constituted by its performative element, the more the work may be thought to be constituted by its particular material realization—for example, in some improvisational musical or poetic works.

5. Strawson, *Individuals* (London: Methuen, 1959), p. 231. As I note below, this general line of argument is also taken up by, among others, Richard Wollheim—see Wollheim, *Art and Its Objects* (New York: Harper & Row, 1968).

6. See, e.g., R. G. Collingwood, *The Principles of Art* (Oxford: Clarendon Press, 1938).

7. Andrew Benjamin, *Disclosing Spaces: On Painting* (Manchester: Clinamen Press, 2004), p. 11, n.2; see also Benjamin, *Object Painting: Philosophical Essays* (London: Academy Group, 1990).

8. See Maitland, "Identity, Ontology, and the Work of Art," *Southwestern Journal of Philosophy* 6 (1975): 181–196.

9. Ibid., p. 189.

10. What characterizes Benjamin's work is a close engagement with individual artists and works that operates within a particular theoretical frame and yet refuses the tendency to approach the works in a way that would reduce them to mere exemplifications of the general theoretical approach that is at issue. The attention is thus given to the works as such rather than as they indicate or show something else (although this does not mean that Benjamin rejects any larger theoretical engagement, only that he sees that engagement as necessarily worked out in close

relation to the engagement with the works themselves). This is a point on which Benjamin himself draws a distinction, which is also a point of disagreement, between his approach and that of Heidegger. See Benjamin, *Disclosing Spaces*, p. 36, n.3.

11. The artwork should not, for instance, be construed (though it may be easy to do so) in terms of the "object" that stands always "against" a subject—see Heidegger's comments in the appendix to "The Origin of the Work of Art," in *Off the Beaten Track*, ed. and trans. Julian Young and Kenneth Haynes (Cambridge: Cambridge University Press, 2002), p. 53; "Der Ursprung des Kunstwerkes," in *Holzwege* (Frankfurt: Klostermann, 1994), pp. 70–71. It is the possibility of just such a construal that partly underlies my caution regarding the way in which my own use of "objectivity" here is to be understood.

12. Heidegger, "The Origin of the Work of Art," p. 18. (The German term translated by "thingly reality" is *dinghaften Wirklichkeit*—see "Der Ursprung des Kunstwerkes," p. 25.)

13. Indeed, on the basis of the considerations set out in n. 2 above, what we take to be a specification of the material objectivity of a thing could never function as a starting point here, since what we take the thing to be in its material objectivity is dependent on how we understand the thing in the first place—on that to which we are attentive in the thing.

14. The work by Cozens reproduced here shows the two Paestum temples as desolate ruins with three figures apparently fleeing before them. Piranesi's drawings of Paestum, almost gothic in character, also focus on the temples' ruinous condition. It is, indeed, its quality as a ruin, and so as evoking not merely a picturesque beauty but also mortality and monumental decline (presented with especially dramatic power in Cozen's work), that makes the temple such a point of focus for these eighteenth-century interpretations. In contrast, Heidegger's account depends on envisioning the temple in its original state as a functioning center of civic and religious life. Although Heidegger is often taken to have the Paestum temple in mind, Babette Babich discusses Heidegger's essay using the temple of Apollo at Bassae as her example (see Babich, "From Van Gogh's Museum to the Temple at Bassae: Heidegger's Truth of Art and Schapiro's Art History," *Culture, Theory & Critique* 44 [2003]: 151–169). Vassilis Ganiatsas of the School of Architecture at the National Polytechnic University in Athens has suggested to me that there are reasons for thinking that, if Heidegger does have a specific temple in mind, it is Bassae rather than Paestum: the Bassae temple stands alone; it is a much more significant and unusual temple than that at Paestum (incorporating both Doric and Ionic elements—that at Paestum is purely Doric); and Heidegger himself visited Bassae a number of times during his visits to Greece in the 1960s (which suggests that he had a special interest in the place). In favor of the Paestum identification, however, is the fact that the temple at Paestum (which was well known when that at Bassae was still being discovered) was an important focus for European engagement with

ancient Greek art and culture, as is evident not only in the work of Cozens and Piranesi, but also in Goethe (who visited Paestum in 1787), and Winckelmann, among others. For a recent discussion of the influence of the Paestum temple on aspects of European architectural and aesthetic thought, see Christiane Kunst, "Paestum Imagery in European Architecture," in *Imagines: La Antigüedad en las artes escénicas y visuales*, ed. Pepa Castillo, Silke Knippschild, Marta García Morcillo, and Carmen Herreros (Logroño: Servicio de Publicaciones, Universidad de La Rioja, 2008), pp. 321–332.

15. Heidegger, "The Origin of the Work of Art," pp. 20–21 ("Der Ursprung des Kunstwerkes," pp. 27–29).

16. Heidegger, "The Origin of the Work of Art," p. 23.

17. They relate directly, for instance, to the Apollonian and Dionysian elements in art distinguished by Nietzsche—see the discussion of this in Julian Young, *Heidegger's Philosophy of Art* (Cambridge: Cambridge University Press, 2001), p. 40.

18. See Heidegger, "The Origin of the Work of Art," p. 24.

19. Ibid., p. 26;

20. Ibid.

21. Benjamin, *Disclosing Spaces*, p. 36, n.3. Benjamin goes on to say that, for this reason, specific works are, in Heidegger, "located in what could be described as a logic of exemplarity. It is not surprising in this regard then, when Heidegger introduces Van Gogh's painting, he does so with the preparatory words: 'we take as an example.'"

22. Thus, an artwork that is thought to be well understood may take on a new character when set alongside other works or into a new locale. The actualization of such new modes of understanding—the lighting up of works in new ways—is a major concern of curatorial practice (or, at least, it ought to be). The fact that a work may appear different when placed in contiguity with other works or surroundings should not, it must be emphasized, detract from the centrality of the objectivity of the work in its being as a work—when a work is seen differently, then the difference seen must be a difference evident in the work itself, even though it may be a difference that was not previously evident. As Jonathan Holmes has pointed out to me, a striking example of the way in which the character of a work may change significantly according to its setting is provided by Courbet's *The Painter's Studio, Real Allegory Determining a Phase of Seven Years in My Artistic Life* (1854–55). When this work was moved from the Louvre to the newly opened Musée d'Orsay in 1986, the perception of the painting changed considerably. Whereas it had appeared in the Louvre as an endpoint in the great clash between classicism, Romanticism, and realism, when placed among the impressionist works brought from the Jeu de Paume, it seemed (along with *A Burial at Ornans*) instead to be the first great and

emphatic statement of early modernism, opening up the world to impressionism and symbolism.

23. See Vincent Scully's account of the way the Greek temple can be seen to contradict the landscape in which it is set—Scully, *The Earth, the Temple, and the Gods: Greek Sacred Architecture* (New Haven: Yale University Press, 1962), pp. 2–3.

24. Quoted in Barbara Rose, "An Interview with Robert Rauschenberg," in *Rauschenberg*, Vintage Contemporary Masters Series (New York: Random House, 1987), p. 58.

25. An interesting parallel arises here with Donald Davidson's account of the basis of intentionality—Davidson argues that a difference in causal histories between two speakers can make for a difference not only in the content, but in the very intentional character of their behavior. See Davidson, "Knowing One's Own Mind," in *Subjective, Intersubjective, Objective* (Oxford: Clarendon Press, 2001), pp. 15–38, esp. pp. 32–33.

26. From an interview by Calvin Tomkins, in Tomkins, *Off the Wall: Robert Rauschenberg and the Art World of Our Time* (New York: Penguin, 1981), p. 137.

27. See the discussion of *Bed* in James Leggio, "Robert Rauschenberg's *Bed* and the Symbolism of the Body," in *Essays on Assemblage: Studies in Modern Art 2*, ed. John Elderfield (New York: Museum of Modern Art, 1992), pp. 79–117.

28. See Davidson, "First Person Authority," in *Subjective, Intersubjective, Objective*, pp. 3–14, esp. pp. 10–14.

29. As Janet Wolff writes from a somewhat different perspective: "The author as fixed, uniform and unconstituted creative source has indeed died. The concept of authorial dominance in the text has also been thrown open to question. But the author, now understood as constituted in language, ideology and social relations, retains a central relevance, both in relation to the meaning of the text (the author being the first person to fix meaning, which will of course subsequently be subject to re-definition and fixing by future readers), and in the context of the sociological understanding of literature." Wolff, *The Social Production of Art* (London: Macmillan, 1981), p. 136.

30. See Heidegger, "The Origin of the Work of Art," pp. 13–15; "Der Ursprung des Kunstwerkes," pp. 18–21.

31. See Meyer Schapiro, "The Still Life as Personal Object—A Note on Heidegger and van Gogh," and "Further Notes on Heidegger and Van Gogh," in *Theory and Philosophy of Art: Style, Artist, and Society* (New York: Braziller, 1994), pp. 135–142, pp. 143–151. Interestingly, the real issue that Schapiro unintentionally raises here concerns the nature of still life as such, and the way in which the still life often involves the depiction of objects that have a dual significance both as the objects

or things that they are and as things that are owned by, and so stand in a certain relation of intimacy with, the artist (even if the relation of intimacy consists purely in the objects' use as still-life models). I have in mind here not only Van Gogh's shoes, but also, for instance, the skulls that appear in some of Cézanne's works, and that were part of the collection of objects found in his studio.

32. One might construe this as an alternative way of putting the essential Heideggerian point concerning being: being is being-present, but it is not merely that; more adequately thought, being is the constant coming to presence of the present (and here "present" encompasses both a sense of the temporal present as well as spatial "presentness"). See Malpas, *Heidegger's Topology* (Cambridge, Mass.: MIT Press, 2006), pp. 10–13.

33. This way of thinking about the artwork, and about the presencing of things in the material, might thus be understood as a form of "Romantic materialism" inasmuch as that which supposedly goes beyond the material (the "Romantic") nevertheless always comes to presence in and through the material. It might equally be understood, with some qualifications, as a form of "transcendent immanentism."

Epilogue: Beginning in Wonder

1. Aristotle, *Metaphysics, Bks. I–IX*, Loeb Classical Library, trans. Hugh Tredennick (Cambridge, Mass.: Harvard University Press, 1933), 82b11–12.

2. Plato, *Theatatus*, in *The Dialogues of Plato*, trans. Benjamin Jowett, vol. III, 4th ed. (Oxford: Clarendon Press, 1953), 155d.

3. R. W. Hepburn provides some indication of the extent to which the importance of wonder has been acknowledged throughout the Western philosophical tradition in his "Wonder," in *"Wonder" and Other Essays* (Edinburgh: University of Edinburgh Press, 1984), pp. 131–154.

4. Plato, *Theatatus*, 155d.

5. Aristotle, *Metaphysics* A, 982b19–20.

6. Ibid., 1013a20.

7. "Iris" can refer to the goddess or to the rainbow or to both. Whereas the other messenger of the gods, Hermes, had winged helmet and sandals so as to move between heaven and earth, the rainbow is Iris's bridge between the two realms. Within Greek tradition, in contrast to the Judeo-Christian story of the rainbow that appears in Genesis, Iris had the dubious distinction of being the messenger who brought discord, whereas it was Hermes who brought peace.

8. Emmanuel Levinas, *Existence and Existents*, trans. A. Lingis (The Hague: Martinus Nijhof, 1978), p. 22.

9. See Gadamer's discussion of light and radiance in connection with beauty and intelligibility in *Truth and Method*, 2nd rev. ed., trans. Joel Weinsheimer and Donald G. Marshall (New York: Continuum, 1992), pp. 480–487. Gadamer's treatment of this issue will be mentioned briefly below.

10. William Blake, "Poems from the Pickering MS," in *Blake: Complete Writings*, ed. Geoffrey Keynes (London: Oxford University Press, 1966), p. 431. The ideas of eternity and infinity invoked by Blake suggest a notion of transcendence that is sometimes taken to be an element of the experience of wonder, as well as of other phenomena, and that is itself worthy of investigation in its own right. See especially R. W. Hepburn, "Time Transcendence and Some Related Phenomena in the Arts," in Hepburn, *"Wonder" and Other Essays*, pp. 108–130. Gadamer takes a certain "time-transcendence" or, or better, the transcendence of "ordinary" time and the emergence of, as he puts it, "fulfilled" or "autonomous" time, particularly as it is associated with the festival, as an important element in the experience of art. See Gadamer, "The Relevance of the Beautiful," in *The Relevance of the Beautiful and Other Essays*, trans. Robert Bernasconi (Cambridge: Cambridge University Press, 1986), pp. 41–45.

11. Martin Heidegger, *An Introduction to Metaphysics*, trans. Gregory Fried and Richard Polt (New Haven: Yale University Press, 2000), p. 28.

12. Notice that this form of "mimesis" is not mere "imitation," but *realization*. See Gadamer's discussion of mimesis in *Truth and Method*, pp. 110–121.

13. David Rothenberg writes of the difference between philosophy and poetry that "It is not that one seeks to explain, while the other evokes. It is that the former must ask and ask, and keep on asking, until our very sense of perplexity becomes exact, complete, not solvable, but a place to contemplate and inhabit through *wonder*, a positive word, a state of grace, an excited way of loving the world." David Rothenberg, "Melt the Snowflake at Once! Toward a History of Wonder," in *Wilderness and the Heart*, ed. Edward F. Mooney (Athens: University of Georgia Press, 1999), p. 20.

14. Gadamer, *Truth and Method*, pp. 101–169.

15. See Gadamer, "The Truth of the Work of Art," in *Philosophical Hermeneutics*, trans. and ed. David E. Linge (Berkeley: University of California Press, 1976), pp. 213–228, and Heidegger, "The Origin of the Work of Art," in *Off the Beaten Track*, trans. Julian Young and Kenneth Baynes (Cambridge: Cambridge University Press, 2002), pp. 1–56.

16. See chapter 12 above, "The Working of Art."

17. Gadamer, "Aesthetics and Hermeneutics," in *Philosophical Hermeneutics*, p. 101.

18. In German, the word *scheinen*, meaning "to shine" as well as "to appear," is itself related to the word *schön*, meaning "beautiful."

19. Martin Heidegger, "Cézanne," in *Denkerfahrungen 1910–1976* (Frankfurt: Klostermann, 1983), p. 163.

20. See *Hamlet*, act 5, scene 1:

What is he, whose grief
Bears such an emphasis, whose phrase of sorrow
Conjures the wand'ring stars, and makes them stand
Like wonder-wounded hearers?

Shakespeare's conjoining of "wonder" and "wound" may be taken to reflect a deeper etymological connection. As Howard Parsons speculates: "Wonder, from the old English *wundor*, might be cognate with the German *Wunde* or *wound*. It would thus suggest a breach in the membrane of awareness, a sudden opening in a man's system of established and expected meanings, a blow as if one were struck or stunned. To be wonderstruck is to be wounded by the sword of the strange event, to be stabbed awake by the striking." Howard L. Parsons, "A Philosophy of Wonder," *Philosophy and Phenomenological Research* 30 (1969–70): 85.

21. Note that the "givenness" at issue here, namely, our prior belonging to the world, is not the same "givenness" at issue in Sellars's famous "myth of the given"— see Sellars, *Empiricism and the Philosophy of Mind* (Cambridge, Mass.: Harvard University Press, 1997). The latter consists in the idea that there must be some level of immediacy (sense data, "experiences," facts, etc.) that provides the noninferential basis for knowledge, and as such the "myth of the given" remains a response within an essentially epistemological framework according to which our prior belonging is already, in some sense or other, in question.

22. It is important to note that our inability to escape from our situatedness does not imply an inability to escape from the particular details of our situation (whether we can so escape is a contingent matter), but only an inability to escape from, and so to make an object of explanation, the fact of situatedness as such. A failure to appreciate this point often leads to the acceptance of relativist or historicist positions. Similarly, the fact that our being in the world always takes on a *particular* character and orientation does not make it any less a mode of situatedness or any less a mode of involvement in the world as such. Our being situated and involved is always something singular, and yet this does not mean that it cannot be reflected upon or thought about in more general, "abstract" terms. To suppose that there is something problematic about this is to misunderstand the nature of thought and conceptuality.

23. See, e.g., Gadamer, "The Truth of the Work of Art," esp. pp. 225–228. On the understanding of truth in Gadamer and Heidegger, see the discussion in chapter 10 above.

24. Emmanuel Levinas, *Existence and Existents*, p. 22.

25. Merleau-Ponty, *Phenomenology of Perception*, trans. Colin Smith (London: Routledge & Kegan Paul, 1962), p. xx.

26. See Gabriel Marcel, *Being and Having*, trans. Katherine Farrer (Boston: Beacon Press, 1951), p. 100: "A problem is something met with which bars my passage. It is before me in its entirety. A mystery, on the other hand, is something in which I find myself caught up, and whose essence is therefore not to be met before me in its entirety."

27. The apparently problematic status of questioning as it relates to wonder may be taken to cast doubt on the idea that there is indeed a fundamental questionability that lies at the heart of any properly topological mode of thinking. This might seem confirmed by a comment Heidegger makes in *On the Way to Language*, trans. Peter D. Herz (New York: Harper & Row, 1971), p. 72: "The true stance of thinking cannot be to put questions, but must be to listen to that which our questioning vouchsafes." Heidegger makes this comment (which has drawn the attention of a number of commentators) in direct reference to his claim, in "The Question Concerning Technology," that "questioning is the piety of thought"—see *The Question Concerning Technology*, trans. William Lovitt (New York: Harper & Row, 1977), p. 35. Yet although there is indeed a sense in which listening takes priority over *questioning*, there is another sense in which listening already incorporates a fundamental *questionability* within it. To listen is to hold oneself open to that which comes forth into the space in which it sounds, and such "holding open" is the essence of questionability as it is tied to place. Questionability is thus not a matter simply of the putting of questions, but rather concerns a responsive attentiveness to the place in which our questions first arise. It is also no accident that Heidegger uses listening to elucidate what is at issue here, for the possibility of listening is tied, in an exemplary way, to the opening of a space of presence that is essentially undetermined in its very opening—as sound appears in the midst of silence, and as silence can itself be a form of sounding, of presencing, of placing.

28. See, e.g., Gadamer, "Reflections on My Philosophical Journey," in *The Philosophy of Hans-Georg Gadamer*, ed. Lewis Edwin Hahn (Chicago: Open Court, 1997), pp. 8–9.

29. Heidegger, *Basic Questions of Philosophy: Selected Problems of "Logic,"* trans. Richard Rojcewicz and André Schwer (Bloomington: Indiana University Press, 1994), p. 147.

Bibliography

Adams, Paul, Steven Hoelscher, and Karen E. Till, eds. *Textures of Place: Exploring Humanist Geographies*. Minneapolis: University of Minnesota Press, 2001.

Agamben, Giorgio. *The Open: Man and Animal*. Trans. Kevin Attell. Stanford: Stanford University Press, 2004.

Ankersmit, Frank. Historiography and postmodernism: A phenomenology of historical experience. In Frank Ankersmit, *History and Tropology: The Rise and Fall of Metaphor*, 182–238. Berkeley: University of California Press, 1994.

Applegate, Celia. *A Nation of Provincials: The German Idea of Heimat*. Berkeley: University of California Press, 1990.

Arendt, Hannah. In *The Life of the Mind*. Ed. Mary McCarthy. San Diego: Harcourt Brace, 1978.

Arendt, Hannah. *Men in Dark Times*. New York: Harcourt Brace Jovanovich, 1968.

Aristotle. *Aristotle's Physics: A Revised Text with Introduction and Commentary*. Trans. and ed. Sir David Ross. Oxford: Clarendon Press, 1936.

Aristotle. *Aristotle's Physics, Books III and IV*. Trans. with notes by Edward Hussey. Oxford: Clarendon Press, 1983.

Aristotle. *Metaphysics, Books I–IX*. Loeb Classical Library. Trans. Hugh Tredennick. Cambridge, Mass.: Harvard University Press, 1933.

Aristotle. *Nicomachean Ethics*. Loeb Classical Library. Trans. H. Rackham. Rev. ed. Cambridge, Mass.: Harvard University Press, 1934.

Aristotle. *Physics, Books I–IV*. Loeb Classical Library. Trans. P. H. Wicksteed and F. M. Cornford. Rev. ed. Cambridge, Mass.: Harvard University Press, 1957.

Babich, Babette. From Van Gogh's museum to the Temple at Bassae: Heidegger's truth of art and Schapiro's art history. *Culture, Theory & Critique* 44 (2003): 151–169.

Bambach, Charles. *Heidegger's Roots: Nietzsche, National Socialism, and the Greeks.* Ithaca: Cornell University Press, 2003.

Bassin, Mark. Blood or soil? In *How Green Were the Nazis?* ed. Franz-Josef Brügge-meir, Mark Cioc, and Thomas Zeller, 204–242. Athens, Ohio: Ohio University Press, 2005.

Beistegui, Miguel de. The place of place in Heidegger's topology. *International Journal of Philosophical Studies* 19 (2011): 277–283.

Benjamin, Andrew. *Disclosing Spaces: On Painting.* Manchester: Clinamen Press, 2004.

Benjamin, Andrew. *Object Painting: Philosophical Essays.* London: Academy Group, 1990.

Benjamin, Walter. *The Arcades Project.* Trans. Howard Eiland and Kevin McLaughlin. Cambridge, Mass.: Harvard University Press, 1999.

Benjamin, Walter. The work of art in the age of mechanical reproduction. In *Illuminations,* ed. Hannah Arendt, 219–253. New York: Harcourt, Brace & World, 1968.

Bermudez, José Luis, Anthony Marcel, and Naomi Eilan, eds. *The Body and the Self.* Cambridge, Mass.: MIT Press, 1995.

Bettelheim, Bruno. *The Uses of Enchantment.* New York: Alfred A. Knopf, 1976.

Bilgrami, Akeel. *Belief and Meaning.* Oxford: Blackwell, 1992.

Bird, Graham. Kant and the problem of induction: A Reply to Walker. In *Transcendental Arguments: Problems and Prospects,* ed. Robert Stern, 31–45. Oxford: Clarendon Press, 1999.

Blake, William. *Blake: Complete Writings.* Ed. Geoffrey Keynes. London: Oxford University Press, 1966.

Blattner, William. *Heidegger's Temporal Idealism.* Cambridge: Cambridge University Press, 1999.

Bollnow, Otto. *Das Wesen der Stimmungen.* Frankfurt: Klostermann, 1988.

Boym, Svetlana. *The Future of Nostalgia.* New York: Basic Books, 2001.

Borges, Jorge Luis. The Immortal. In *Collected Fictions,* 183–195. Trans. Andrew Hurley. New York: Penguin, 1998.

Borgman, Albert. *Technology and the Character of Contemporary Life.* Chicago: University of Chicago Press, 1984.

Brentano, Franz. *On the Several Senses of Being in Aristotle.* Trans. Rolf George. Berkeley: University of California Press, 1975. Originally published 1862.

Brüggemeir, Franz-Josef, Mark Cioc, and Thomas Zeller, eds. *How Green Were the Nazis?* Athens, Ohio: Ohio University Press, 2005.

Bubner, Rüdiger. On the ground of understanding. In *Hermeneutics and Truth*, ed. Brice Wachterhauser, 68–82. Evanston, Ill.: Northwestern University Press, 1994.

Bubner, Rüdiger. Kant, transcendental arguments, and the problem of deduction. *Review of Metaphysics* 28 (1975): 453–467.

Buttimer, Anne, and David Seamon, eds. *The Human Experience of Space and Place*. London: Croom Helm, 1980.

Campbell, John. *Past, Space, and Self*. Cambridge, Mass.: MIT Press, 1994.

Camus, Albert. *Lyrical and Critical Essays*. Trans. Philip Thody. London: Hamish Hamilton, 1967.

Casey, Edward S. J. E. Malpas's *Place and Experience: A Philosophical Topography*: Converging and diverging in/on place. *Philosophy and Geography* 4 (2001): 225–230.

Casey, Edward S. *Remembering: A Phenomenological Study*. Bloomington: Indiana University Press, 1987.

Casey, Edward S. *The Fate of Place*. Berkeley: University of California Press, 1997.

Casey, Edward S. The world of nostalgia. *Man and World* 20 (1987): 361–384.

Clauss, Ludwig. *Die nordische Seele: Eine Einführung in die Rassenseelenkunde*. Munich: J. F. Lehmanns Verlag, 1932.

Collingwood, R. G. *The Principles of Art*. Oxford: Clarendon Press, 1938.

Cordford, Francis Macdonald. *Plato's Cosmology: The Timaeus of Plato, translated with a running commentary*. London: Routledge & Kegan Paul, 1937.

Crowell, Steven Galt. Is transcendental topology phenomenological? *International Journal of Philosophical Studies* 19 (2011): 267–276.

Crowell, Steven Galt. Spectral history: Narrative, nostalgia, and the time of the I. *Research in Phenomenology* 29 (1999): 83–104.

Dahlstrom, Daniel O. *Heidegger's Concept of Truth*. New York: Cambridge University Press, 2001.

Darwin, Charles. *The Descent of Man and Selection in Relation to Sex*. New York: D. Appleton, 1871.

Davidson, Donald. *Essays on Actions and Events*, 2nd ed. Oxford: Claredon Press, 2001.

Davidson, Donald. *Inquiries into Truth and Interpretation*, 2nd ed. Oxford: Clarendon Press, 2001.

Davidson, Donald. *Plato's* Philebus. New York: Garland Publishing, 1990.

Davidson, Donald. *Subjective, Intersubjective, Objective*. Oxford: Clarendon Press, 2001.

Davidson, Donald. The centrality of truth. In *Truth and Its Nature (If Any)*, ed. Jaroslav Peregrin, 105–115. Dordrecht: Kluwer, 1999.

Davidson, Donald. *Truth and Predication*. Cambridge, Mass.: Harvard University Press, 2008.

Davidson, Donald. *Truth, Language, and History*. Oxford: Clarendon Press, 2005.

Davidson, Donald, and Patrick Suppes. *Decision Making: An Experimental Approach*. Stanford: Stanford University Press, 1957.

Davis, Fred. *Yearning for Yesterday: A Sociology of Nostalgia*. New York: The Free Press, 1979.

Deleuze, Gilles, and Felix Guattari. *A Thousand Plateaus: Capitalism and Schizophrenia*. Trans. and foreword Brian Massumi. Minneapolis: University of Minnesota Press, 1987.

Derrida, Jacques. Différance. In *Margins of Philosophy*, 1–27. Trans. Alan Bass. Chicago: University of Chicago Press, 1982.

Dickinson, Robert E. *The Makers of Modern Geography*. London: Routledge & Kegan Paul, 1969.

Dreyfus, Hubert L. *Being-in-the-World: A Commentary on Heidegger's* Being and Time, *Division I*. Cambridge, Mass.: MIT Press, 1991.

Dreyfus, Hubert L. Overcoming the myth of the mental: How philosophers can profit from the phenomenology of everyday expertise. *Proceedings and Addresses of the American Philosophical Association* 79 (2005): 47–65.

Dreyfus, Hubert L. Response to McDowell. *Inquiry* 50 (2007): 371–377.

Dreyfus, Hubert L. The return of the myth of the mental. *Inquiry* 50 (2007): 352–365.

Dummett, Michael. What is a theory of meaning? In *Mind and Language*, ed. Samuel Guttenplan, 97–138. Oxford: Oxford University Press, 1975.

Durrell, Lawrence. Landscape and character. In Lawrence Durrell, *Spirit of Place: Mediterranean Writings*. London: Faber & Faber, 1969.

Eilan, Naomi, Rosaleen McCarthy, and Bill Brewer, eds. *Spatial Representation: Problems in Philosophy and Psychology*. Oxford: Blackwell, 1993.

El Bizri, Nadar. On kai khôra: Situating Heidegger between the sophist and the Timaeus. *Studia Phaenomenologica* 4 (2004): 73–98.

Elden, Stuart. Heidegger's *Hölderlin* and the importance of place. *Journal of the British Society for Phenomenology* 30 (1999): 258–274.

Elden, Stuart. *Mapping the Present: Heidegger, Foucault, and the Project of a Spatial History.* London: Continuum, 2001.

Elden, Stuart. *Speaking against Number: Heidegger, Language, and the Politics of Calculation.* Edinburgh: Edinburgh University Press, 2006.

Eliot, T. S. *Collected Poems 1909–1962.* London: Faber & Faber, 1963.

Entrikin, J. Nicholas. *The Betweeness of Place: Towards a Geography of Modernity.* London: Palgrave Macmillan, 1990.

Entrikin, J. Nicholas, and Vincent Berdoulay. The Pyrenees as place: Lefebvre as guide. *Progress in Geography* 29 (2002): 129–147.

Febvre, Lucien. *A Geographical Introduction to History.* Trans. E. G. Mountford and J. H. Paxton. New York: Alfred Knopf, 1925.

Fell, Joseph. The familiar and the strange: On the limits of praxis in the early Heidegger. In *Heidegger: A Critical Reader*, ed. Hubert L. Dreyfus and Harrison Hall, 65–80. Oxford: Blackwell, 1992.

Fell, Joseph P. *Heidegger and Sartre: An Essay on Being and Place.* New York: Columbia University Press, 1983.

Fell, Joseph P. Heidegger's mortals and gods. *Research in Phenomenology* 15 (1985): 29–41.

Figal, Günter. Spatial thinking. *Research in Phenomenology* 39 (2009): 333–343.

Fodor, Jerry. *Psychosemantics.* Cambridge, Mass.: MIT Press, 1987.

Fodor, Jerry, and Ernest Lepore. *Holism: A Shopper's Guide.* Oxford: Blackwell, 1992.

Franck, Didier. *Heidegger et la la problème de l'espace.* Paris: Éditions Minuit, 1986.

Fritzsche, Peter. Specters of history: On nostalgia, exile, and modernity. *American Historical Review* 106 (2001): 1587–1618.

Gadamer, Hans-Georg. *Heidegger's Ways.* Trans. John W. Stanley. Albany, N.Y.: SUNY Press, 1994.

Gadamer, Hans-Georg. *Philosophical Hermeneutics.* Trans. and ed. David E. Linge. Berkeley: University of California Press, 1976.

Gadamer, Hans-Georg. Reflections on my philosophical journey. In *The Philosophy of Hans-Georg Gadamer*, ed. Lewis Edwin Hahn, 3–63. Library of Living Philosophers, vol. 24. Chicago: Open Court, 1997.

Gadamer, Hans-Georg. *The Relevance of the Beautiful and Other Essays*. Trans. Robert Bernasconi. Cambridge: Cambridge University Press, 1986.

Gadamer, Hans-Georg. *Truth and Method*, 2nd rev. ed. Trans. Joel Weinsheimer and Donald G. Marshall. New York: Continuum, 1992.

Gendlin, Eugene T. Time's dependence on space: Kant's statements and their misconstrual by Heidegger. In *Kant and Phenomenology*, ed. Thomas M. Seebohm and Joseph J. Kockelmans, 147–160. Washington: University Press of America, 1985.

Gröning, Geet, and Joachim Wolschke-Bulmahn. Politics, planning, and the protection of nature: Political abuse of early ecological ideas in Germany, 1933–45. *Planning Perspectives* 2 (1987): 127–148.

Hadot, Pierre. *Philosophy as a Way of Life*. Trans. Michael Chase. Oxford: Blackwell, 1995.

Harrington, Anne. *Reenchanted Science: Holism in German Culture from Wilhelm II to Hitler*. Princeton: Princeton University Press, 1999.

Harvey, David. *Justice, Nature, and the Geography of Difference*. Oxford: Blackwell, 1996.

Heidegger, Martin. A recollection (1957). In *Heidegger: The Man and the Thinker*, ed. Thomas Sheehan, 21–22. Chicago: Precedent Publishing, 1981.

Heidegger, Martin. Art and space. In *The Heidegger Reader*, ed. Günter Figal, 305–309. Bloomington: Indiana University Press, 2009.

Heidegger, Martin. *Basic Concepts*. Trans. Gary E. Aylesworth. Bloomington: Indiana University Press, 1993.

Heidegger, Martin. *Basic Questions of Philosophy: Selected Problems of "Logic."* Trans. Richard Rojcewicz and André Schwer. Bloomington: Indiana University Press, 1994.

Heidegger, Martin. *Being and Time*. Trans. John Macquarie and Edward Robinson. New York: Harper & Row, 1962.

Heidegger, Martin. *Contributions to Philosophy (from Enowning)*. Trans. Parvis Emad and Kenneth Maly. Bloomington: Indiana University Press, 1999.

Heidegger, Martin. *Country Path Conversations*. Trans. Bret W. Davis. Bloomington: Indiana University Press, 2010.

Heidegger, Martin. *Denkerfahrungen 1910–1976*. Frankfurt: Klostermann, 1983.

Heidegger, Martin. *Elucidations of Hölderlin's Poetry.* Trans. Keith Hoeller. New York: Humanity Books, 2000.

Heidegger, Martin. *Four Seminars.* Trans. Andrew Mitchell and François Raffoul. Bloomington: Indiana University Press, 2004.

Heidegger, Martin. *Gesamtausgabe,* vol. 39: *Hölderlins Hymnen "Germanien" und "Der Rhein."* Frankfurt: Klostermann, 1980.

Heidegger, Martin. *Holzwege.* Frankfurt: Klostermann, 1994.

Heidegger, Martin. *Introduction to Metaphysics.* Trans. Gregory Fried and Richard Polt. New Haven: Yale University Press, 2000.

Heidegger, Martin. *Kant and the Problem of Metaphysics,* 5th ed. Trans. Richard Taft. Bloomington: Indiana University Press, 1997.

Heidegger, Martin. *Nietzsche.* Trans. David Farrell Krell. San Francisco: Harper & Row, 1979–1987.

Heidegger, Martin. *Off the Beaten Track.* [A translation of Holzwege.] Trans. Julian Young and Kenneth Haynes. Cambridge: Cambridge University Press, 2002.

Heidegger, Martin. *On the Way to Language.* Trans. Peter D. Hertz. New York: Harper & Row, 1971.

Heidegger, Martin. *On Time and Being.* Trans. Joan Stambaugh. New York: Harper & Row, 1972.

Heidegger, Martin. "Only a God Can Save Us": The *Spiegel* Interview (1966). In *Heidegger: The Man and the Thinker,* ed. Thomas Sheehan, 45–67. Chicago: Precedent Publishing, 1981.

Heidegger, Martin. *Parmenides.* Trans. André Schuwer and Richard Rojcewicz. Bloomington: Indiana University Press, 1992.

Heidegger, Martin. *Pathmarks.* [A translation of Wegmarken.] Ed. William McNeill. Cambridge: Cambridge University Press, 1998.

Heidegger, Martin. *Plato's Sophist.* Trans. Richard Rojcewicz and Andre Schuwer. Bloomington: Indiana University Press, 1997.

Heidegger, Martin. *Poetry, Language, Thought.* Trans. Albert Hofstadter. New York: Harper & Row, 1971.

Heidegger, Martin. *Seminare, Gesamtausgabe 15.* Frankfurt: Klostermann, 1986.

Heidegger, Martin. *Sojourns.* Trans. John Panteleimon Manoussakis. Albany, N.Y.: SUNY Press, 2005.

Heidegger, Martin. *Supplements: From the Earliest Essays to* Being and Time *and Beyond.* Ed. John van Buren. Albany, N.Y.: SUNY Press, 2002.

Heidegger, Martin. *The Basic Problems of Phenomenology*. Trans. Albert Hofstadter. Bloomington: Indiana University Press, 1989.

Heidegegr, Martin. *The Concept of Time*. Trans. Ingo Farin with Alex Skinner. London: Contuinuum, 2011.

Heidegger, Martin. *The Fundamental Concepts of Metaphysics: World, Finitude, Solitude*. Trans. William McNeill and Nicholas Walker. Bloomington: Indiana University Press, 1996.

Heidegger, Martin. *The Metaphysical Foundations of Logic*. Trans. Michael Heim. Bloomington: Indiana University Press, 1984.

Heidegger, Martin. *The Principle of Reason*. Trans. Reginald Lilly. Bloomington: Indiana University Press, 1991.

Heidegger, Martin. *The Question Concerning Technology and Other Essays*. Trans. William Lovitt. New York: Harper & Row, 1977.

Heidegger, Martin. *What Is Called Thinking?* Trans. J. Glenn Gray. New York: Harper & Row, 1968.

Heidegger, Martin. *What Is Philosophy?* Trans. William Kluback and Jean T. Wilde. Plymouth: Vision, 1963.

Heidegger, Martin. *What Is a Thing?* Trans. W. B. Barton, Jr., and Vera Deutsch. South Bend: Gateway, 1967.

Heidegger, Martin. Who is Nietszche's Zarathustra? Trans B. Magnus. *Review of Metaphysics* 20 (1967).

Heidegger, Martin. Why do I stay in the Provinces? In *Heidegger: The Man and the Thinker*, ed. Thomas Sheehan, 27–30. Chicago: Precedent, 1981.

Heidegger, Martin. *Zollikon Seminars: Protocols–Conversations–Letters*. Trans. Franz Mayr and Richard Askay. Evanston: Northwestern University Press, 2001.

Heidegger, Martin, with Eugen Fink. *Heraclitus Seminar*. Trans. Charles H. Seibert. Tuscaloosa: University of Alabama Press, 1979.

Hemming, Laurence Paul, Kostas Amiridis, and Bogdan Costea (eds.). *The Movement of Nihilism: Heidegger's Thinking after Nietzsche*. London: Continuum, 2011.

Henrich, Dieter. On the unity of subjectivity. In *The Unity of Reason*, ed. Richard Velkley, 17–54. Cambridge, Mass.: Harvard University Press, 1994.

Hepburn, R. W. *"Wonder" and Other Essays*. Edinburgh: University of Edinburgh Press, 1984.

Hintikka, Jaakko. Transcendental arguments: Genuine and spurious. *Noûs* 6 (1972): 274–281.

Hofer, Johannes. Medical dissertation on nostalgia [Hofer, Dissertatio Medica de nostalgia—Basel]. Trans. Carolyn Kiser Anspach. *Bulletin of the History of Medicine* 2 (1934): 376–391.

Homer. *The Odyssey*. Trans. Robert Fagles. New York: Penguin, 1997.

Hoy, David C. Post-Cartesian interpretation: Hans-Georg Gadamer and Donald Davidson. In *The Philosophy of Hans-Georg Gadamer*, ed. Lewis Edwin Hahn, 111–130. Library of Living Philosophers, vol. 24. Chicago: Open Court, 1997.

Husserl, Edmund. *Cartesian Meditations*. Trans. Dorion Cairns. Dordrecht: Kluwer, 1977.

Husserl, Edmund. *Ideas Pertaining to a Pure Phenomenology and to a Phenomenological Philosophy, First Book: General Introduction to a Pure Phenomenology*. Trans. F. Kersten. Dordrecht: Kluwer, 1983.

Husserl, Edmund. *Thing and Space*. Trans. Richard Rojcewicz. Dordrecht: Kluwer, 1997.

Jensen, Alex. Heidegger's last passing god and Schleiermacher's speeches on religion. Unpublished ms.

Jensen, Alex. The influence of Schleiermacher's second speech on religion on Heidegger's concept of *Ereignis*. *Review of Metaphysics* 61 (2008): 815–826.

Kant, Immanuel. *Anthropology from a Pragmatic Point of View*. Carbondale: Southern Illinois University Press, 1978.

Kant, Immanuel. Concerning the ultimate ground of the differentiation of directions in space. In *Theoretical Philosophy, 1755–1770*, ed. David Walford, 361–372. Cambridge Edition of the Works of Immanuel Kant in Translation. Cambridge: Cambridge University Press, 1992.

Kant, Immanuel. *Critique of Pure Reason*. Trans. Paul Guyer and Allen W. Wood. Cambridge Edition of the Works of Immanuel Kant in Translation. Cambridge: Cambridge University Press, 1998.

Kant, Immanuel. *Opus postumum*. Trans. Eckart Förster. Cambridge Edition of the Works of Immanuel Kant in Translation. Cambridge: Cambridge University Press, 1993.

Kant, Immanuel. *Prolegomena to Any Future Metaphysics*. Ed. Lewis White Beck. Indianapolis: Bobbs-Merrill, 1950.

Kant, Immanuel. What is orientation in thinking? In *Political Writings*, 2nd ed., ed. Hans Reiss, trans. H. B. Nisbet, 238–239. Cambridge: Cambridge University Press, 1991.

Käufer, Stephan. Systematicity and temporality. *Journal of the British Society for Phenomenology* 33 (2002): 167–187.

Kettering, Emil. *Nähe: Das Denken Martin Heideggers*. Pfullingen: Neske, 1987.

Koselleck, Reinhart. *Futures Past: On the Semantics of Historical Time*. Cambridge, Mass.: MIT Press, 1985.

Kunst, Christiane. Paestum imagery in European architecture. In *Imagines: La Antigüedad en las artes escénicas y visuales*, ed. Pepa Castillo, Silke Knippschild, Marta García Morcillo, and Carmen Herreros, 321–332. Logroño: Servicio de Publicaciones, Universidad de La Rioja, 2008.

Lefebvre, Henri. *The Production of Space*. Trans. Donald Nicholson Smith. Oxford: Blackwell, 1991.

Leggio, James. Robert Rauschenberg's *Bed* and the symbolism of the body. In *Essays on Assemblage: Studies in Modern Art 2*, ed. John Elderfield, 79–117. New York: Museum of Modern Art, 1992.

Levinas, Emmanuel. *Existence and Existents*. Trans A. Lingis. The Hague: Martinus Nijhof, 1978.

Levinas, Emmanuel. Ethics of the infinite. In *Face to Face with Levinas*, ed. Richard Cohen, 13–33. Albany, N.Y.: SUNY Press, 1986.

Levinas, Emmanuel. Heidegger, Gagarin, and us. In *Difficult Freedom: Essays on Judaism*, 231–234. Trans. Seán Hand. Baltimore: Johns Hopkins University Press, 1990.

MacIntyre, Alasdair. *After Virtue*. Notre Dame: University of Notre Dame Press, 1981.

MacIntyre, Alasdair. Crises, narrative, and science. *Monist* 60 (1977): 453–472.

Maitland, Jeffrey. Identity, ontology, and the work of art. *Southwestern Journal of Philosophy* 6 (1975): 181–196.

Malpas, Jeff. Acção, Intencionalidade e Conteúdo. In *A Explicação da Interpretação Humana*, ed. João Sàágua, 345–358. Lisbon: Edições Colibri, 2005.

Malpas, Jeff. *Donald Davidson and the Mirror of Meaning*. Cambridge: Cambridge University Press, 1992.

Malpas, Jeff. *Ethos and Topos: Toward a Topographic Ethics*. In preparation.

Malpas, Jeff. Fragility and responsibility. In *Vivir para pensar*, ed. Fina Birulés. Barcelona: Paidos, 2011.

Malpas, Jeff. *Heidegger's Topology*. Cambridge, Mass.: MIT Press, 2006.

Malpas, Jeff. Heidegger's topology of being. In *Transcendental Heidegger*, ed. Steven Galt Crowell and Jeff Malpas, ed., 119–134. Stanford: Stanford University Press, 2006.

Malpas, Jeff. Holism and indeterminacy. *Dialectica* 45 (1991): 47–58.

Malpas, Jeff. Philosophy, topography, triangulation. In *Triangulation*, ed. Cristina Amoretti and Gerhard Preyer, 257–259. Frankfurt: Ontos, 2011.

Malpas, Jeff. *Place and Experience: A Philosophical Topography*. Cambridge: Cambridge University Press, 1999.

Malpas, Jeff. Philosophising place in *The Joshua Tree*. In *U2 and Philosophy*, ed. Mark Wrathall, 45–59. Chicago: Open Court, 2006.

Malpas, Jeff. Putting space in place: Philosophical topography and relational geography. *Environment and Planning D: Society and Space*, forthcoming.

Malpas, Jeff. Retrieving truth. *Soundings* 75 (1992): 287–306.

Malpas, Jeff. Self-knowledge and scepticism. *Erkenntnis* 40 (1994): 165–184.

Malpas, Jeff. Sprache ist Gespräch: On Gadamer, language, and philosophy. In *Between Description and Interpretation: The Hermeneutic Turn in Phenomenology*, ed. Andrzej Wiercinski, 408–417. Toronto: Hermeneutic Press, 2005.

Malpas, Jeff. The beginning of understanding: Event, place, truth. In *Consequences of Hermeneutics*, ed. Jeff Malpas and Santiago Zabala, 261–280. Chicago: Northwestern University Press, 2010.

Malpas, Jeff. The centrality of truth. In *The Nature of Truth (If Any)*, ed. Jaroslav Peregrin, 3–14. Prague: Kluwer, 1997.

Malpas, Jeff. The constitution of the mind: Kant and Davidson on the unity of consciousness. *International Journal of Philosophical Studies* 7 (1999): 1–30.

Malpas, Jeff. The discomfit of strangeness. *Philosopher's Magazine* 27 (2004): 34–36.

Malpas, Jeff. The transcendental circle. *Australasian Journal of Philosophy* 75 (1997): 1–20.

Malpas, Jeff. The two-fold character of truth: Heidegger, Davidson, Tugendhat. In *The Multidimensionality of Hermeneutic Phenomenology*, ed. Babette Babich and Dimitri Ginev. Dordrecht: Springer, forthcoming, 2012.

Malpas, Jeff. Truth, narrative, and the materiality of memory: An externalist approach in the philosophy of history. *Journal of the Philosophy of History* 4 (2010): 328–353.

Malpas, Jeff. Uncovering the space of disclosedness: Heidegger, technology, and the problem of spatiality in *Being and Time*. In *Heidegger, Authenticity and Modernity: Essays in Honour of Hubert L. Dreyfus*, vol. 1, ed. Mark Wrathall and Jeff Malpas, 205–228. Cambridge, Mass.: MIT Press, 2001.

Malpas, Jeff, and Karsten Thiel. Kant's geography of reason. In *Reading Kant's Geography*, ed. Stuart Elden and Eduardo Mendieta, 195–214. Albany, N.Y.: SUNY Press, 2011.

Malpas, Jeff, and Gary Wickham. Governance and failure: On the limits of Sociology. *Australian and New Zealand Journal of Sociology* 31 (1995): 37–50.

Malpas, Jeff, and Gary Wickham. Governance and the world: From Joe DiMaggio to Michel Foucault. *UTS Review* 3 (1997): 91–108.

Malpas, Jeff, and Günter Zöller. Reading Kant topographically: From critical philosophy to empirical geography. In *Kantian Metaphysics Today: New Essays on Space and Time*, ed. Adrian W. Moore, Graham Bird, and Roxana Baiasu. London: Palgrave-Macmillan, 2011.

Marcel, Gabriel. *Being and Having*. Trans. Katherine Farrer. Boston: Beacon Press, 1951.

Massey, Doreen. *For Space*. London: Sage, 2005.

Massey, Doreen. Power-geometry and a progressive sense of place. In *Mapping the Futures*, ed. Jon Bird, Barry Curtis, Tim Putnam, George Robertson, and Lisa Tickner, 64–67. London: Routledge, 1993.

Massey, Doreen. *Space, Place, and Gender*. Minneapolis: University of Minnesota Press, 1994.

Maull, Otto. *Das Wesen der Geopolitik*, 3rd ed. Leipzig: B. G.Teubner, 1941.

McDowell, John. *Mind and World*. Cambridge, Mass.: Harvard University Press, 1994.

Megill, Allan. *Prophets of Extremity*. Berkeley: University of California Press, 1985.

Merleau-Ponty, Maurice. *The Phenomenology of Perception*. Trans. Colin Smith. London: Routledge & Kegan Paul, 1962.

Merleau-Ponty, Maurice. *The Visible and the Invisible*. Trans. A. Lingis. Evanston: Northwestern University Press, 1969.

Mink, Louis O. History and fiction as modes of comprehension. *New Literary History* 1 (1969–70): 541–558.

Mugerauer, Robert. *Heidegger and Homecoming: The Leitmotif in the Later Writings*. Toronto: University of Toronto Press, 2008.

Mulhall, Stephen. *On Being in the World: Wittgenstein and Heidegger on Seeing Aspects*. London: Routledge, 1990.

Naqvi, Naumann. The nostalgic subject: Genealogy of the "Critique of Nostalgia." C.I.R.S.D.I.G Working Paper n. 23. Messina: Centro Interuniversitario per le ricerche sulla Sociologia del Diritto e delle Istituzioni Giuridiche, no date. http://www.cirsdig .it.

Novalis, Schriften, ed. *J. Minor*. Jena: E. Diederich, 1923.

Nussbaum, Martha. Aristotle on human nature and the foundations of ethics. In *World, Mind, and Ethics*, ed. J. E. J. Altham and Ross Harrison, 86–131. Cambridge: Cambridge University Press, 1995.

Nussbaum, Martha. *The Fragility of Goodness*. Cambridge: Cambridge University Press, 1986.

Okrent, Mark. Davidson, Heidegger, and Truth. In *Dialogues with Davidson: Acting, Interpreting, Understanding*, ed. Jeff Malpas, 87–111. Cambridge, Mass.: MIT Press, 2011.

Okrent, Mark. *Heidegger's Pragmatism*. Ithaca: Cornell University Press, 1988.

Okrent, Mark. Intending the intender, Or, Why Heidegger isn't Davidson. In *Heidegger, Authenticity and Modernity: Essays in Honour of Hubert L. Dreyfus*, vol. 1, ed. Mark Wrathall and Jeff Malpas, 279–304. Cambridge, Mass.: MIT Press, 2001.

Paddock, Troy. *Gedachtes Wohnen*: Heidegger and cultural geography. *Philosophy and Geography* 7 (2004): 239–253.

Paddock, Troy. In defense of homology and history: A response to Allen. *Philosophy and Geography* 7 (2004): 239–253.

Parfit, Derek. *Reasons and Persons*. Oxford: Oxford University Press, 1984.

Parsons, Howard L. A philosophy of wonder. *Philosophy and Phenomenological Research* 30 (1969–70): 84–101.

Philipse, Herman. *Heidegger's Philosophy of Being: A Critical Interpretation*. Princeton: Princeton University Press, 1998.

Phillips, James. *Heidegger's Volk: Between National Socialism and Poetry*. Stanford: Stanford University Press, 2005.

Plato. *The Dialogues of Plato*, 4 vols., 4th ed. Trans. Benjamin Jowett. Oxford: Oxford University Press, 1953.

Pögeller, Otto. *Martin Heidegger's Path of Thinking*. Trans. Daniel Magurshak and Sigmund Barber. Atlantic Highlands, N.J.: Humanities Press, 1987.

Poulet, Georges. *Proustian Space*. Baltimore: Johns Hopkins University Press, 1977.

Proust, Marcel. *In Search of Lost Time*, 6 vols. Trans C. K. Scott Moncrieff and Terence Kilmartin, rev. D. J. Enright. New York: Vintage, 1996.

Proust, Marcel. *Le temps retrouvé, A la recherche du temps perdu*. Paris: Gallimard, 1954.

Quine, W. V. O. *Word and Object*. Cambridge, Mass.: MIT Press, 1960.

Quinton, Anthony. Spaces and times. *Philosophy* 37 (1962): 130–147.

Ramberg, Bjørn. *Donald Davidson's Philosophy of Language: An Introduction*. Oxford: Blackwell, 1989.

Ratzel, Friedrich. *Deutschland: Einführung in die Heimatkunde*. Leipzig: Grunow, 1898.

Ratzel, Friedrich. *History of Mankind*, 3 vols. Trans. A. J. Butler, from 2nd German ed. London: Macmillan, 1896–1898.

Relph, Edward. Disclosing the ontological depth of place: *Heidegger's Topology* by Jeff Malpas. *Environmental & Architectural Phenomenology Newsletter* 19 (2008): 5–8.

Relph, Edward. *Place and Placelessness*. London: Routledge & Kegan Paul, 1976.

Richardson, William J. *Through Phenomenology to Thought*. The Hague: Martinus Nijhof, 1974.

Ricoeur, Paul. Life in quest of a narrative. In *On Paul Ricoeur*, ed. David Wood, 20–33. London: Routledge, 1991.

Ricoeur, Paul. *Oneself as Another*. Trans. Kathleen Blamey. Chicago: Chicago University Press, 1992.

Ricoeur, Paul. *Time and Narrative*. Trans. Kathleen McLaughlin and David Pellauer. Chicago: University of Chicago Press, 1984–1988.

Relph, Edward. *Place and Placelessness*. London: Routledge & Kegan Paul, 1976.

Rohkrämer, Thomas. Martin Heidegger, National Socialism, and environmentalism. In *How Green Were the Nazis?* ed. Franz-Josef Brüggemeir, Mark Cioc, and Thomas Zeller, 171–203. Athens, Ohio: Ohio University Press, 2005.

Rorty, Richard. *Philosophy and the Mirror of Nature*. Princeton: Princeton University Press, 1980.

Rorty, Richard. *Philosophy and Social Hope*. London: Penguin, 2000.

Rose, Barbara (ed.). *Rauschenberg*. Vintage Contemporary Masters Series. New York: Random House, 1987.

Röska-Hardy, Louise, and Eva M. Neumann-Held, eds. *Learning from Animals? Examining the Nature of Human Uniqueness*. Hove, East Sussex: Psychology Press, 2009.

Rothenberg, David. Melt the snowflake at once! Toward a history of wonder. In *Wilderness and the Heart*, ed. Edward F. Mooney, 18–31. Athens: University of Georgia Press, 1999.

Sartre, Jean-Paul. *Being and Nothingness*. Trans. Hazel E. Barnes. New York: Washington Square Press, 1966.

Schapiro, Meyer. *Theory and Philosophy of Art: Style, Artist, and Society*. New York: Braziller, 1994.

Scharr, Adam. *Heidegger's Hut*. Cambridge, Mass.: MIT Press, 2006.

Schatzki, Theodore R. *Martin Heidegger: Theorist of Space*. Stuttgart: Franz Steiner Verlag, 2007.

Schatzki, Theodore. *The Timespace of Human Activity: On Performance, Society, and History as Indeterminate Teleological Events*. Lexington, Mass.: Lexington Books, 2010.

Schleiermacher, Friedrich. In *On Religion: Speeches to Its Cultured Despisers*. Ed. Richard Crouter. Cambridge: Cambridge University Press, 1996.

Schürmann, Reiner. *Heidegger on Being and Acting: From Principles to Anarchy*. Trans. Christine-Marie Gros. Bloomington: Indiana University Press, 1987.

Scully, Vincent. *The Earth, the Temple, and the Gods: Greek Sacred Architecture*. New Haven: Yale University Press, 1962.

Sebald, W. G. *Austerlitz*. Harmondsworth: Penguin, 2001.

Sellars, Wilfrid. Empiricism and the philosophy of mind. In *The Foundations of Science and the Concepts of Psychoanalysis*, Minnesota Studies in the Philosophy of Science, vol. I, ed. H. Feigl and M. Scriven, 127–196. Minneapolis: University of Minnesota Press, 1956.

Simmel, Georg. The metropolis and mental life. In *The Sociology of Georg Simmel*, ed. Kurt Wolff, 409–424. New York: Free Press, 1950.

Speaks, Jeff. Is there a problem about nonconceptual content? *Philosophical Review* 114 (2005): 359–398.

Speaks, Jeff. Review of Donald Davidson, *Truth and Predication*. *Notre Dame Philosophical Reviews*, August 2006, http://ndpr.nd.edu/review.cfm?id=7224 (accessed November 2010).

Stefanovic, Ingrid. Speaking of place: In dialogue with Malpas. *Environmental and Architectural Phenomenology Newsletter* 15 (2004): 6–8.

Stern, Robert (ed.). *Transcendental Arguments: Problems and Prospects*. Oxford: Clarendon Press, 1999.

Stivers, Richard. *Technology as Magic: The Triumph of the Irrational*. New York: Continuum, 2001.

Stoppard, Tom. *Rosencrantz and Guildenstern Are Dead*. New York: Grove Weidenfeld, 1967.

Strawson, P. F. *Individuals*. London: Methuen, 1959.

Stueber, Karsten R. Understanding truth and objectivity: A dialogue between Donald Davidson and Hans-Georg Gadamer. In *Hermeneutics and Truth*, ed. Brice Wachterhauser, 172–189. Evanston, Ill.: Northwestern University Press, 1994.

Taminiaux, Jacques. *Poetics, Speculation, and Judgement: The Shadow of the Work of Art from Kant to Phenomenology*. Albany: SUNY Press, 1993.

Taylor, Charles. *Philosophical Arguments*. Cambridge, Mass.: Harvard University Press, 1995.

Tomkins, Calvin. *Off the Wall: Robert Rauschenberg and the Art World of Our Time*. New York: Penguin, 1981.

Trigg, Dylan. *The Aesthetics of Decay*. New York: Peter Lang, 2006.

Tuan, Yi-Fu. *Place and Space: The Perspective of Experience*. Minneapolis: University of Minnesota Press, 1977.

Tugendhat, Ernst. Heidegger's idea of truth. In *Critical Heidegger*, ed. Christopher Macann, 227–240. New York: Routledge, 1996.

Uekoetter, Frank. *The Green and the Brown: A History of Conservation in Nazi Germany*. Cambridge: Cambridge University Press, 2006.

Vallega, Alejandro A. *Heidegger and the Issue of Space: Thinking on Exilic Grounds*. University Park: Pennsylvania State University Press, 2003.

Vidal de la Blache, Paul. *Tableau de la géographie de la France*. Paris: Hachette, 1911.

von Uexküll, Jakob. A stroll through the worlds of animals and men. In *Instinctive Behavior: The Development of a Modern Concept*, ed. Claire H. Schiller, 5–80. New York: International Universities Press, 1957.

von Uexküll, Jakob. Die neue Umweltlehre: Ein Bindeglied zwischen Natur- und Kultur-Wissenschaft. *Die Erziehung: Monatsschrift für den Zussamenhang von Kultur und Erziehung im Wissenschaft und Leben* 13 (1937): 185–201.

von Uexküll, Jakob. *Umwelt und Innenwelt der Tiere* [The Environment and Inner World of Animals], 2nd ed. Berlin: Verlag von Julius Springer, 1921.

Weingart, Peter. *Doppel-Leben: Ludwig Ferdinand Clauss zwischen Rassenforschung und Widerstand*. Frankfurt: Campus, 1995.

White, Hayden. The historical text as literary artifact. In Hayden White, *Tropics of Discourse: Essays in Cultural Criticism*, 81–100. Baltimore: Johns Hopkins University Press, 1978.

White, Kenneth. *Open World: The Collected Poems 1960–2000*. Edinburgh: Polygon, 2003.

White, T. H. *The Once and Future King*. London: Collins, 1958.

Wiepking-Jürgensmann, Heinrich Friedrich. *Die Landschaftsfibel*. Berlin: Deutsch Landbuchhandlung, 1942.

Williams, Bernard. The Makropulos case: Reflections on the tedium of immortality. In Bernard Williams, *Problems of the Self: Philosophical Papers 1956–1972*, 82–100. Cambridge: Cambridge University Press, 1973.

Wilson, Janelle L. *Nostalgia: Sanctuary of Meaning*. Lewisburg: Bucknell University Press, 2005.

Wolff, Janet. *The Social Production of Art*. London: Macmillan, 1981.

Wollheim, Richard. *Art and Its Objects*. New York: Harper & Row, 1968.

Wolschke-Bulmahn, Joachim. Violence as the basis of National Socialist landscape planning. In *How Green Were the Nazis?* ed. Franz-Josef Brüggemeir, Mark Cioc, and Thomas Zeller, 243–256. Ohio: Ohio University Press, 2005.

Wrathall, Mark. The conditions of truth in Heidegger and Davidson. *Monist* 82 (1999): 304–323.

Wrathall, Mark. Heidegger and truth as correspondence. *International Journal of Philosophical Studies* 7 (1999): 69–88.

Young, Julian. The fourfold. In *The Cambridge Companion to Heidegger*, 2nd ed., ed. Charles Guignon, 373–392. Cambridge: Cambridge University Press, 2006.

Young, Julian. *Heidegger, Philosophy, Nazism*. Cambridge: Cambridge University Press, 1997.

Young, Julian. Heidegger's Heimat. *International Journal of Philosophical Studies* 19 (2011): 285–293.

Young, Julian. *Heidegger's Later Philosophy*. Cambridge: Cambridge University Press, 2001.

Young, Julian. *Heidegger's Philosophy of Art*. Cambridge: Cambridge University Press, 2001.

Zeller, Thomas. Moulding the landscape of Nazi environmentalism. In *How Green Were the Nazis?* ed. Franz-Josef Brüggemeir, Mark Cioc, and Thomas Zeller, 164–165. Ohio: Ohio University Press, 2005.

Ziolkowski, Theodore. Review of *Five Portraits: Modernity and the Imagination in Twentieth-Century German Writing*, Michael André Bernstein. *Modernism/Modernity* 8 (2001): 359–360.

Index